Mediterranean Spain

Costas del Azahar, Dorada & Brava

ROYAL CRUISING CLUB PILOTAGE FOUNDATION

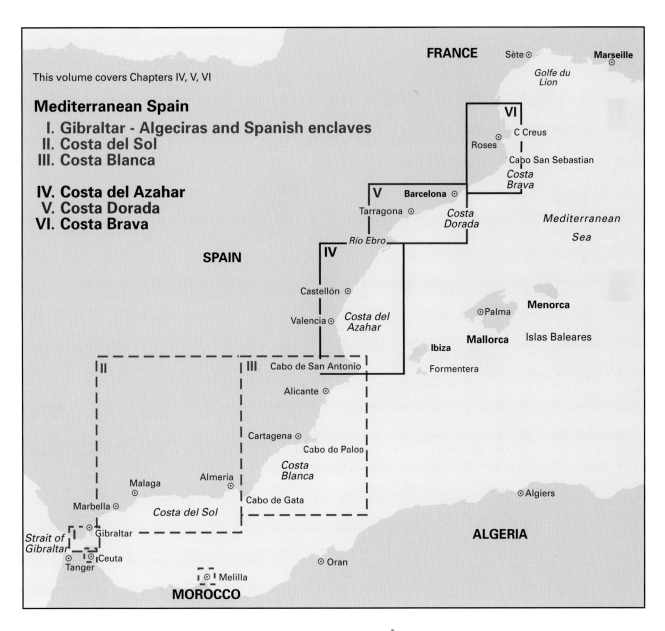

This volume covers Chapters IV, V, VI

Mediterranean Spain
  I. **Gibraltar - Algeciras and Spanish enclaves**
  II. **Costa del Sol**
  III. **Costa Blanca**

  IV. **Costa del Azahar**
  V. **Costa Dorada**
  VI. **Costa Brava**

FRANCE   Sète ⊙   Marseille ⊙

Golfe du Lion

VI

C Creus

Roses ⊙

Cabo San Sebastian

Costa Brava

V   Barcelona ⊙

Tarragona ⊙   *Costa Dorada*

Mediterranean Sea

Río Ebro

SPAIN   IV

Castellón ⊙

Valencia ⊙   *Costa del Azahar*

Menorca

⊙ Palma

Mallorca   Islas Baleares

Ibiza

Formentera

III   Cabo de San Antonio

Alicante ⊙

Cartagena ⊙

Cabo do Paloo

Costa Blanca

II

Malaga ⊙   Almeria ⊙

⊙ Algiers

Marbella ⊙

Cabo de Gata

Costa del Sol

ALGERIA

Strait of Gibraltar   I   Gibraltar

Tanger ⊙   ⊙ Ceuta

⊙ Oran

⊙ Melilla

MOROCCO

Imray Laurie Norie & Wilson

Published by
Imray Laurie Norie & Wilson Ltd
Wych House St Ives Huntingdon
Cambridgeshire PE27 5BT, England 2002
☎ +44 (0)1480 462114 *Fax* +44 (0)1480 496109
Email ilnw@imray.com
www.imray.com
2008

1st edition 1989
2nd edition 1995
3rd edition 1999
4th edition 2002
5th edition 2008

ISBN 978 184623 080 6

British Library Cataloguing in Publication Data.
A catalogue record for this book is available from
the British Library.

This work, based on surveys over a period of many years,
has been corrected to December 2007 from land-based visits
to the ports and harbours of the coast, from contributions
by visiting yachtsmen and from official notices. The air
photographs were taken by Anne Hammick in September
1997, and Patrick Roach in 2004.

Printed in Singapore by Craft Print

CORRECTIONAL SUPPLEMENTS

This pilot book may be amended at intervals by the issue of
correctional supplements. These are published on the internet
at our web site www.imray.com (and also via www.rccpf.org.uk)
and may be downloaded free of charge. Printed copies are also
available on request from the publishers at the above address.
Like this pilot, supplements are selective. Navigators requiring
the latest definitive information are advised to refer to official
hydrographic office data.

ADDITIONAL INFORMATION

Additional information may be found under the Publications
page at www.rccpf.org.uk. This includes a downloadable
waypoint list, links to Google maps, additional photographs and
mid season updates when appropriate. Passage planning
information may also be found on that website.

CAUTION

Whilst every care has been taken to ensure that the information
contained in this book is accurate, the RCC Pilotage Foundation, the
authors and the publishers hereby formally disclaim any and all
liability for any personal injury, loss and/or damage howsoever
caused, whether by reason of any error, inaccuracy, omission or
ambiguity in relation to the contents and/or information contained
within this book. The book contains selected information and thus is
not definitive. It does not contain all known information on the
subject in hand and should not be relied on alone for navigational
use: it should only be used in conjunction with official hydrographic
data. This is particularly relevant to the plans which should not be
used for navigation.

The RCC Pilotage Foundation, the authors and publishers believe
that the information which they have included is a useful aid to
prudent navigation, but the safety of a vessel depends ultimately on
the judgment of the skipper, who should assess all information,
published or unpublished.

POSITIONS

All positions in the text have been derived from C-Map electronic
charts at WGS 84 datum.
Positions given in the text and on plans are intended purely as an aid
to locating the place in question on the chart. A WGS 84 position
check was carried out at each harbour in 2007.

Over the past few years the Spanish Authorities have been updating
their charts/documents to WGS 84 datum although many charts in
current use will be to European 1950 datum or other. The differences
are usually only ±0´.1 (that is 200 yards or 180 metres) but, as
always, care must be exercised to work to the datum of the chart in
use.

WAYPOINTS

This edition of the Mediterranean Spain pilot includes the
introduction of waypoints. The RCC Pilotage Foundation consider a
waypoint to be a position likely to be helpful for navigation if entered
into some form of electronic navigation system for use in conjunction

with GPS. In this pilot they have been derived from electronic
charts. They must be used with caution. All waypoints are given
to datum WGS 84 and every effort has been made to ensure their
accuracy. Nevertheless, for each individual vessel, the standard of
onboard equipment, aerial position, datum setting, correct entry
of data and operator skill all play a part in their effectiveness. In
particular it is vital for the navigator to note the datum of the
chart in use and apply the necessary correction if plotting a GPS
position on the chart.

Our use of the term 'waypoint' does not imply that all vessels can
safely sail directly over those positions at all times. Some – as in
this pilot – may be linked to form recommended routes under
appropriate conditions. However, skippers should be aware of the
risk of collision with another vessel, which is plying the exact
reciprocal course. Verification by observation, or use of radar to
check the accuracy of a waypoint, may sometimes be advisable
and reassuring.

We emphasise that we regard waypoints as an aid to navigation
for use as the navigator or skipper decides. We hope that the
waypoints in this pilot will help ease that navigational load.

PLANS

The plans in this guide are not to be used for navigation – they are
designed to support the text and should always be used together
with navigational charts.

It should be borne in mind that the characteristics of lights may be
changed during the life of the book, and that in any case
notification of such changes is unlikely to be reported
immediately. Each light is identified in both the text and where
possible on the plans (where it appears in magenta) by its
international index number, as used in the *Admiralty List of
Lights*, from which the book may be updated.

All bearings are given from seaward and refer to true north.
Symbols are based on those used by the British Admiralty – users
are referred to *Symbols and Abbreviations (NP 5011)*.

Contents

THE RCC PILOTAGE FOUNDATION

In 1976 an American member of the Royal Cruising Club, Dr Fred Ellis, indicated that he wished to make a gift to the Club in memory of his father, the late Robert E Ellis, of his friends Peter Pye and John Ives and as a mark of esteem for Roger Pinckney. An independent charity known as the RCC Pilotage Foundation was formed and Dr Ellis added his house to his already generous gift of money to form the Foundation's permanent endowment. The Foundation's charitable objective is 'to advance the education of the public in the science and practice of navigation', which is at present achieved through the writing and updating of pilot books covering many diffent parts of the world.

The Foundation is extremely grateful and privileged to have been given the copyrights to books written by a number of distinguished authors and yachtsmen including the late Adlard Coles, Robin Brandon and Malcolm Robson. In return the Foundation has willingly accepted the task of keeping the original books up to date and many yachtsmen and women have helped (and are helping) the Foundation fulfil this commitment. In addition to the titles donated to the Foundation,

several new books have been created and developed under the auspices of the Foundation. The Foundation works in close collaboration with three publishers – Imray Laurie Norie and Wilson, Adlard Coles Nautical and On Board Publications – and in addition publishes in its own name short run guides and pilot books for areas where limited demand does not justify large print runs. Several of the Foundation's books have been translated into French, German and Italian.

The Foundation runs its own website at www.rccpf.org.uk which not only lists all the publications, and provides additional information to support the Pilot books, but also contains free downloadable web pilots and Passage Planning Guides.

The overall management of the Foundation is entrusted to trustees appointed by the Royal Cruising Club, with day-to-day operations being controlled by the Director. These appointments are unpaid. In line with its charitable status, the Foundation distributes no profits; any surpluses are used to finance new books and developments and to subsidise those covering areas of low demand.

PUBLICATIONS OF THE RCC PILOTAGE FOUNDATION

Imray
Norway
Faroe, Iceland and
 Greenland
Norway
The Baltic Sea
Channel Islands
North Brittany and
 the Channel Islands
Isles of Scilly
North Biscay
South Biscay
Atlantic Islands
Atlantic Spain & Portugal
Mediterranean Spain
 Costas del Sol and Blanca
 Costas del Azahar,
 Dorada & Brava
 Islas Baleares
Corsica and North
 Sardinia

Adlard Coles Nautical
Atlantic Crossing Guide
Pacific Crossing Guide

On Board Publications
South Atlantic Circuit
Havens and Anchorages
for the South American
Coast

The RCC Pilotage Foundation
Supplement to Falkland
Island Shores
Guide to West Africa

RCCPF Website
www.rccpf.org.uk
Supplements
Support files for books
Passage Planning Guides
Web Pilots

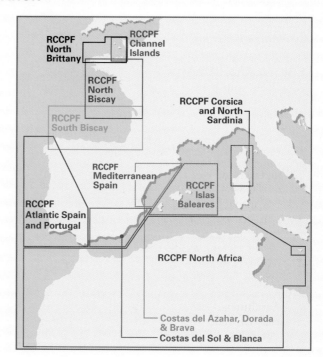

Preface

Foreword to the fifth edition

The origins of this book go back to the late Robin Brandon's *East Spain Pilot*, first produced in 1975. It is one of a family of three – the others being *Mediterranean Spain Costas del Sol and Blanca*, and *Islas Baleares*. The RCCPF titles in the Eastern Mediterranean also include *North Africa*, and *Corsica and North Sardinia*.

This coast has become increasingly popular with yachtsmen whether they be passing through or cruising in slow time; or as a good place to keep a yacht in the sun or to overwinter with easy access by land and air. It has become particularly busy in high season, but is still worth visiting.

Since 1975 regular updates and revisions have been made to keep up with the constant development along this Spanish Mediterranean coast. The major work of the 1990s, by Oz Robinson, Claire James and Anne Hammick, has been continued by John Marchment. He followed an extensive revision in 2001 with yearly supplements and a visit to all the harbours in 2004. In the same year, Patrick Roach flew the full length of the coast and photographed all the harbours that he could gain access to – air traffic control limitations proving insurmountable near Barcelona. In September 2007 Peter Taylor and Robin Rundle carried out very detailed recces and identified many changes which had not been apparent from *Notices to Mariners*, press releases or reports from yachtsmen. This work, with contributions by other yachtsmen, has led to this edition.

In addition to factual updating we have restructured the fifth Edition to enable more rapid use of information. We have reworked all positions to datum WGS 84 and have included Coastal and Harbour Approach Waypoints. Navigators please note comments on the use of Waypoints under Cautions, the Introduction and Appendix; also note that a book of this nature cannot keep pace with the rapid spread of fish farming activity.

This pilot is prepared by yachtsmen for yachtsmen. The Pilotage Foundation warmly thanks John Marchment and all those who have contributed to this edition, and again to John Marchment who will continue to maintain future supplements.

Recent changes have been both rapid and substantial. More are expected within the life of this book. Therefore, in addition to the supplements, which may be obtained from the Publisher, the Pilotage Foundation web site – www.rccpf.org.uk –

will maintain support files which may include: waypoint lists, mid-season updates, additional photos and access to Google Maps.

We welcome feedback and contributions from those currently sailing the coast so that we may continue to update this book, and our supporting website, when practicable.

Martin Walker
Director
RCC Pilotage Foundation
March 2008

ACKNOWLEDGEMENTS

I am most grateful to John Hunt who, in 2005, alerted us to major silting problems along parts of the coast and to Graham Hutt for advising of recent significant changes to some harbours. The fourth edition of this book, and John Marchment's subsequent five supplements, provided the starting point but it would not have been possible to update and restructure this book without Patrick Roach's air photographs and, in particular, the excellent detailed work, on the ground, by Peter Taylor and Robin Rundle. They bought back many details which were not available from official sources or by long range discussion. These was added to the continuing work by John Marchment who subsequently identified facts which had not otherwise been apparent. As always, the team at Imray have gone the extra mile to update all the plans and prepare this revised book at a time of rapid change. My thanks go to all those who had a hand in this work.

Martin Walker

Note about current developments

Because of the continuing very major investment in many harbours and marinas along these coasts, this book includes early, and sometimes scant information, on works in progress. Also included are photographs of harbour models or advertising boards showing future plans. Far from being mere pipedreams, we believe that many will be constructed during the life of this book; despite some unavoidably poor photographs, the proposals have therefore been included to alert yachtsmen to the possibility of major changes to some harbours.

Key to symbols used on plans

English	Spanish
harbourmaster/ port office	capitán de puerto
fuel	gasoil, gasolina
yacht chandler	efectos navales
crane	grua
travel-lift	grua giratoria
yacht club	club náutico
showers	ducha
information	información
post office	correos
slipway	grada
anchorage	fondeadero
anchoring prohibited	fondeaderoprohibido
waypoint	
yachts	yates

Introduction

Overview of the region

This pilot, with its companion, covers from the western entrance to the Mediterranean and along the six hundred miles Spanish coastline to the French border. Millions of tourists are drawn regularly to the area and the effect is clear to see – high rise and densely packed resorts, strip development along the coast line, packed beaches and the noise of bars, restaurants and discos. However, there are still areas that the developers have yet to reach and much more to Spain than this popular image. The yachtsman has plenty to choose from – both afloat and ashore. The area offers a clear climate, good food, great scenery, modern marinas and many anchorages as well as the cultural heritage of the Moors and Christians.

Mediterranean Spain Costas del Sol and Blanca covers Chapters l to lll. This book covers Chapters IV to Vl.

Chapter 1 includes the Straits, Algeciras Bay and Gibraltar and also the two Spanish enclaves of Ceuta and Melilla. Yachtsmen heading along the North African coast should consult Imray/RCCPF pilot book *North Africa* by Graham Hutt.

Chapter II Costa del Sol. This sun coast stretches for east of Gibraltar to Cabo de Gata. West lie the sherry bodegas of Jerez. North is the dramatic ravine town of Rhonda and the white rural villages of Andalucia. Further east is Grenada and the wonders of the Alambra Palace – and easy access to the skiing mountains of the Sierra Nevada. Coastal villages offer the chance to anchor for a swim or a paella lunch ashore.

Chapter III Costa Blanca. The white coast provides anchorages to the north of Cabo de Gata before giving way to the sports grounds of La Manga and the tourist resorts stretching up to Cabo de la Nau.

Chapter IV Costa Azahar. The high cliffs in the south rapidly give way to long sandy beaches running up to the Ebro Delta. Azahar means blossom and reflects the huge groves of orange and lemon trees. The Amerca's Cup of 2007 has led to much recent development around Valencia.

Chapter V Costa del Dorada. This area runs between the rivers Ebro and Tordera. The major ports of Tarrogona and Barcelona break the run of golden beaches which give this coast its name.

Chapter VI Costa Brava. The rocky savage coast, with few marinas but many deep calas, heads towards the Pyrénées and the border with France.

In the Mediterranean, yachts are usually in commission from May to October, the north European holiday season. Whilst there is little chance of a gale in summer, there are few days when there is a good sailing breeze. In winter, whilst it is true that off-shore the Mediterranean can be horrid, there are many days with a good sailing breeze and the weather is warmer and sunnier than the usual summer in the English Channel. Storms and heavy rain do occur but it is feasible to dodge bad weather and slip along shore from harbour to harbour as they are not far apart. In general the climate is mild and, particularly from January to March, very pleasant. A great advantage is that there are no crowds and the local shops and services are freer to serve the winter visitor. Many Clubs Náutico, which have to turn people away in summer, welcome visitors. Local inhabitants can be met, places of interest enjoyed and the empty beaches and coves used in privacy.

History

There are many traces of prehistoric inhabitants but recorded history starts with a group of unknown origin, the Ligurians, who came from N Africa and established themselves in southern Spain in about the 6th century BC; with the Carthaginians at Málaga and the Phoenicians who had been trading in the area since the 12th century BC and living in various small colonies dotted along the coast.

In 242 BC a force of Carthaginians under Hamilcar Barca, who had previously been driven from Sicily by the Romans, captured and held the south of Spain until 219 BC when the Romans took over occupation, which lasted until the Barbarian invasion in the 5th century AD. This period was one of development and construction when many of the towns were first established. The Barbarians – the Suevi, Vandals and Alans – were, in turn, overrun by the Visigoths who held the area from the 5th to the 8th century AD.

In 711 AD a huge force of Moors and Berbers under Tarik-ibn-Zeyab crossed the Strait of Gibraltar and captured the whole of Spain except for a small enclave in the N. The Moors took over the S and the Berbers the N. By the 10th century AD huge strides had been made in education and development and Cordoba which had become independent was renowned throughout Europe as a seat of learning.

By the 13th century, the Moors and Berbers had been driven out of the country by a long series of

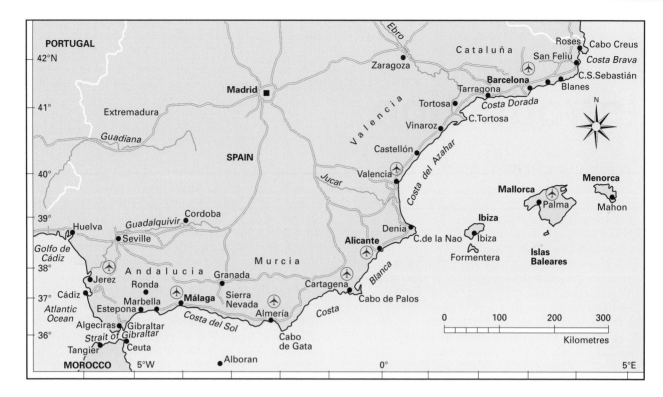

wars undertaken by numerous Spanish forces who were supported by the armies of the nobles of France. Granada alone remained under the Moors until 1491 when they were finally driven out by Isabella of Castile and Ferdinand of Aragon who united Spain under one crown.

Then followed a period of world-wide expansion and, when the crown went to the house of Hapsburg in the 16th century, of interference in the affairs of Europe which continued when the house of Bourbon took over in the 18th century.

Over the years the country has been in constant turmoil. Wars and rebellions, victories and defeats, sieges and conquests were common occurrences but none were quite as terrible as the Civil War which started in 1936 and lasted for two-and-a-half years, leaving nearly a million dead. Since then the country has moved away from a dictatorship into the different turmoils of democracy and the European Union, but the Civil War has not been forgotten. Though the country is governed centrally from Madrid, provinces have considerable local autonomy.

Local economy

Along all the coasts tourism is of course a significant factor in the economy but this coastal development is, in a manner of speaking, skin-deep. Inland, agricultural patterns remain though some of them have been drastically developed, for instance by the introduction of hydroponics supported by kilometres of plastic greenhouses. Fishing fleets, inshore and mid-range, work out of many ports and they, together with a supporting boat building industry, help provide the skills on which marinas depend.

Language

The Castilian spoken in Andalucía sounds different to that spoken further north, principally in that the cedilla is not lisped. In Catalunya, Catalan is actively promoted. Though close to Spanish, there are Catalan alternatives for Castilian Spanish, some of which have French overtones, such as: *bondia* – good morning (rather than *buenos días*), *bon tarde* – good afternoon (*buenos tardes*), *s'es plau* – please (*por favor*).

Many local people speak English or German, often learnt from tourists, and French is taught as a second language at school.

Place names appear in the Spanish (i.e. Castilian) form where possible – the spelling normally used on British Admiralty charts – with local alternatives, including Catalan, in brackets.

Currency

The unit of currency is the Euro. Major credit cards are widely accepted, as are Eurocheques. Bank hours are normally 0830 to 1400, Monday to Friday, with a few also open 0830 to 1300 on Saturday. Most banks have automatic telling machines (ATM).

Time zone

Spain keeps Standard European Time (UT+1), advanced one hour in summer to UT+2 hours. Changeover dates are now standardised with the rest of the EU as the last weekends in March and October respectively.

Unless stated otherwise, times quoted are UT.

National holidays and fiestas

There are numerous official and local holidays, the latter often celebrating the local saint's day or some historical event. They usually comprise a religious procession, sometimes by boat, followed by a fiesta in the evening. The Fiesta del Virgen de la Carmen is celebrated in many harbours during mid-July. Official holidays include:

1 January	*Año Nuevo* (New Year's Day)
6 January	*Reyes Magos* (Epiphany)
19 March	*San José* (St Joseph's Day)
	Viernes Santo (Good Friday)
	Easter Monday
1 May	*Día del Trabajo* (Labour Day)
early/mid-June	*Corpus Christi*
24 June	*Día de San Juan* (St John's Day, the King's name-day)
29 June	*San Pedro y San Pablo* (Sts Peter and Paul)
25 July	*Día de Santiago* (St James' Day)
15 August	*Día del Asunción* (Feast of the Assumption)
11 September	Catalan National Day
12 October	*Día de la Hispanidad* (Day of the Spanish Nation)
1 November	*Todos los Santos* (All Saints)
6 December	*Día de la Constitución* (Constitution Day)
8 December	*Inmaculada Concepción* (Immaculate Conception)
25 December	*Navidad* (Christmas Day)

When a national holiday falls on a Sunday it may be celebrated the following day.

Practicalities

OFFICIAL ADDRESSES

See Appendix VIII

USEFUL WEB PAGES

Spanish Tourist Office www.tourspain.co.uk
British Airways www.britishairways.com
Iberia Airlines www.iberia.com
Andalucía www.andalucia.org
Murcia www.murciaturistica.es
Valencia www.comunidadvalenciana.com
Port websites at each port

VAT

Note Value Added Tax (VAT) is called *Impuesto de Valor Agregado* (IVA) and the standard rate is 16%.

Documentation

Spain is a member of the European Union. Other EU nationals may visit the country for up to 90 days with a passport but no visa, as may US citizens. EU citizens wishing to remain in Spain may apply for a *permiso de residencia* once in the country; non-EU nationals can apply for a single 90-day extension, or otherwise obtain a long-term visa from a Spanish embassy or consulate before leaving home.

In practice the requirement to apply for a *permiso de residencia* does not appear to be enforced in the case of cruising yachtsmen, living aboard rather than ashore and frequently on the move. Many yachtsmen have cruised Spanish waters for extended periods with no documentation beyond that normally carried in the UK. If in doubt, check with the authorities before departure.

Under EU regulations, EU registered boats are not required to fly the Q flag on first arrival unless they have non-EU nationals or dutiable goods aboard. Nevertheless, clearance should be sought either through a visit to or from officials or through the offices of the larger marinas or yacht clubs. Passports and the ship's registration papers will be required. A Certificate of Competence (or equivalent) and evidence of VAT status may also be requested. Other documents sometimes requested are a crew list with passport details, the radio licence and evidence of insurance. Subsequently, at other ports, clearance need not be sought but the *Guarda Civil* may wish to see papers, particularly passports. Marina officials often ask to see yacht registration documents, the skipper's passport, and sometimes evidence of insurance.

Marine insurance is compulsory in most countries around the Mediterranean and it is essential that territorial cruising limits are extended to cover the planned voyage. The minimum third party insurance required in Spain is €1,000,000 and the insurers should provide a letter to this effect written in Spanish. This is usually provided free of cost and should be requested from the insurers if not sent out with the policy.

Temporary import and laying up

A VAT paid or exempt yacht should apply for a *permiso aduanero* on arrival in Spanish waters. This is valid for twelve months and renewable annually, allowing for an almost indefinite stay. Possession of a *permiso aduanero* establishes the status of a vessel and is helpful when importing equipment and spares from other EU countries.

A boat registered outside the EU fiscal area on which VAT has not been paid may be temporarily imported into the EU for a period not exceeding six months in any twelve before VAT is payable. This period may sometimes be extended by prior agreement with the local customs authorities (for instance, some do not count time laid up as part of the six months). While in EU waters the vessel may only be used by its owner, and may not be chartered or even lent to another person, on pain of paying VAT (*see Appendix VI for further details*). If kept in the EU longer than six months the vessel normally becomes liable for VAT. There are marked differences in the way the rules are applied from one harbour to the next, let alone in different countries – check the local situation on arrival.

Chartering

There is a blanket restriction on foreign-owned and/or skippered vessels based in Spain engaging in charter work. See Appendix VII for details.

Light dues

A charge known as *Tarifa G5* is supposedly levied on all vessels. Locally-based pleasure craft (the status of a charter yacht is not clear) pay at the rate of €5 per square metre per year, area being calculated as LOA x beam. Visiting pleasure craft pay at one tenth of that sum and are not charged again for ten days. Boats of less than 7m LOA and with engines of less than 25hp make a single payment of €30 per year. In practice this levy appears to be added to the marina or mooring charges on a daily basis.

Charts

See Appendix II. Current British Admiralty information is largely obtained from Spanish sources. The Spanish Hydrographic Office re-issues and corrects its charts periodically, and issues weekly Notices to Mariners. Corrections are repeated by the British Admiralty, generally some months later.

Pilot books

Details of principal harbours and some interesting background information appear in the British Admiralty Hydrographic Office's *Mediterranean Pilot Vol 1 (NP 45)*. NP 291, *Maritime Communications* will be found useful.

For French speakers, *Votre Livre de Bord – Méditerranée* (Bloc Marine) may be helpful. In German there are *Spanische Gewässer, Lissabon bis Golfe du Lion* (Delius Klasing). See also Appendix III.

Positions and Waypoints

All positions in this pilot are to WGS 84 and have been derived from C-Map electronic charts. If plotting onto paper charts then the navigator is reminded that some source charts of this area remain at European 1950 datum (ED50) and appropriate use of offsets may be necessary.

This pilot includes waypoints: note the caution on page ii. A full list is given in Appendix I and may be downloaded from rccpf.org.uk.

Coastal waypoints are indicated there in bold and are shown on the plans at the beginning of each chapter. They form a series with which one is able to steer from off Cap de la Nao to the French border. However, it is essential to keep a good look out at all times while making a coastal passage in this area.

Waypoints which are not listed in bold, have been selected as close approach waypoints for all but the most minor harbours. The detail is shown in the data section at the beginning of each port and on the associated harbour plan. They have not been proven at sea and should be used with caution. Where scale permits they have been plotted on the harbour plan. The track line from waypoint to harbour mouth may be given on these plans to help orientation. Where the waypoint has been positioned more than 0·1M from the harbour the bearing and distance from waypoint to harbour is given with the port data.

The numerical sequence of the waypoint list does not indicate that port waypoints may be grouped together to form a route from one harbour to another. The navigator will need to plot them on a chart in order to plan a hazard-free route.

Magnetic variation

Magnetic variation is noted in the introduction to the coastal sections.

Traffic zones

There are traffic separation zones in the Straits of Gibraltar, off Cabo de Gata, Cabo de Palos and Cabo de la Nao.

Navigation aids

Lights

The four-figure international numbering system has been used to identify lights in the text and on plans – the Mediterranean falls in Group E. As each light has its own four figure number, correcting from *Notices to Mariners* or the annual *List of Lights and Fog Signals*, whether in Spanish or English, is straightforward. Certain minor lights and all buoys with a five figure number are listed in the Spanish *Faros y Señales de Niebla Part II* but are not included in the international system.

Harbour lights follow the IALA A system and are normally listed in the order in which they become relevant upon approach and entry, working from Gibraltar towards France.

It should be noted that, whilst every effort has been taken to check the lights agree with the documents mentioned above, the responsibility for maintaining the lights appears to rest with the local *capitanía* and, depending on their efficiency, this can mean some lights may be defective or different from the stated characteristics at times.

Buoyage

Buoys follow the IALA A system, based on the direction of the main flood tide. Yellow topped black or red rusty buoys 500m offshore mark raw sewage outlets. Many minor harbours, however, maintain their own buoys to their own systems. Generally, yellow buoys in line mark the seaward side of areas reserved for swimming. Narrow lanes for water-skiing and sailboarding lead out from the shore and are also buoyed.

Hazards

Restricted areas
Restricted areas are outlined in the coastal sections.

Night approaches
Approaches in darkness are often made difficult by the plethora of background lights – fixed, flashing, occulting, interrupted – of all colours. Though there may be exceptions, this applies to nearly all harbours backed by a town of any size. Powerful shore lights make weaker navigation lights difficult to identify and mask unlit features such as exposed rocks or the line of a jetty. If at all possible, avoid closing an unknown harbour in darkness.

Skylines
Individual buildings on the coast – particularly prominent hotel blocks – are built, demolished, duplicated, change colour, change shape, all with amazing rapidity. They are not nearly as reliable as landmarks as might be thought. If a particular building on a chart or in a photograph can be positively identified on the ground, well and good. If not, take care.

Tunny nets and fish farms
During summer and autumn these nets, anchored to the sea bed and up to 6 miles long, are normally laid inshore across the current in depths of 15–40m but may be placed as far as 10 miles offshore. They may be laid in parallel lines. The outer end of a line should be marked by a float or a boat carrying a white flag with an 'A' (in black) by day, and two red or red and white lights by night. There should also be markers along the line of the net.

These nets are capable of stopping a small freighter but should you by accident, and successfully, sail over one, look out for a second within a few hundred metres. If seen, the best action may be to sail parallel to the nets until one end is reached.

The Pilotage Foundation is not aware of nets being laid off the Costas Azahar, Dorada and Brava.

However, many *calas* and bays had fish farms proliferating. These latter are often lit with flashing yellow lights but great care should be taken when entering small *calas* at night.

The positions of some fish farms are indicated on the latest charts but be aware these farms change position frequently. Fish farming is developing along this coast and navigators must be prepared to encounter ones not shown on plans and charts.

Commercial fishing boats
Commercial fishing boats should be given a wide berth. They may be:
- Trawling singly or in pairs with a net between the boats.
- Laying a long net, the top of which is supported by floats.
- Picking up or laying pots either singly or in groups or lines.
- Trolling with one or more lines out astern.
- Drifting, trailing nets to windward.

Do not assume they know, or will observe, the law of the sea – keep well clear on principle.

Small fishing boats
Small fishing boats, including the traditional double-ended *llauds*, either use nets or troll with lines astern and should be avoided as far as possible. At night many *lámparas* put to sea and, using powerful electric or gas lights, attract fish to the surface. When seen from a distance these lights appear to flash as the boat moves up and down in the waves and can at first be mistaken for a lighthouse.

Speed boats etc
Para-gliding, water-skiing, speedboats and jet-skis are all popular, and are sometimes operated by unskilled and thoughtless drivers with small regard to collision risks. In theory they are not allowed to exceed 5 knots within 100m of the coast or within 250m of bathing beaches. Water-skiing is restricted to buoyed areas.

Scuba divers and swimmers
A good watch should be kept for scuba divers and swimmers, with or without snorkel equipment, particularly around harbour entrances. If accompanied by a boat, the presence of divers may be indicated either by International Code Flag A or by a square red flag with a single yellow diagonal, as commonly seen in north America and the Caribbean.

Preparation

THE CREW

Clothing
Summer sunburn is an even more serious hazard at sea, where light is reflected, than on land. Lightweight, patterned cotton clothing is handy in this context – it washes and dries easily and the pattern camouflages the creases! Non-absorbent, heat retaining synthetic materials are best avoided. When swimming wear a T-shirt against the sun and shoes if there are sea-urchins around.

Some kind of headgear, preferably with a wide brim, is essential. A genuine Panama Hat, a *Montecristi*, can be rolled up, shoved in a pocket and doesn't mind getting wet (they come from Ecuador, not Panama, which has hi-jacked the name). A retaining string for the hat, tied either to clothing or around the neck, is a wise precaution whilst on the water.

Footwear at sea is a contentious subject. Many experienced cruisers habitually sail barefoot but while this may be acceptable on a familiar vessel, it would be courting injury on a less intimately known deck and around mid-day bare soles may get burnt. Proper sailing shoes should always be worn for harbour work and anchor handling. Ashore, if wearing sandals the upper part of the foot is the first area to get sunburn.

At the other end of the year, winter weather may be wet and cold. Foul weather gear as well as warm sweaters etc. will be needed.

Shoregoing clothes should be on a par with what one might wear in the UK – beachwear is not often acceptable in restaurants and certainly not on more formal occasions in yacht clubs.

Medical

No inoculations are required. Minor ailments may best be treated by consulting a *farmacia* (often able to dispense drugs which in most other countries would be on prescription), or by contact with an English-speaking doctor (recommended by the *farmacia*, marina staff, a tourist office, the police or possibly a hotel). Specifically prescribed or branded drugs should be bought before setting out in sufficient quantity to cover the duration of the cruise. Medicines are expensive in Spain and often have different brand names from those used abroad.

Apart from precautions against the well recognised hazards of sunburn (high factor sun cream is recommended) and stomach upsets, heat exhaustion (or heat stroke) is most likely to affect newly joined crew not yet acclimatised to Mediterranean temperatures. Carry something such as *Dioralyte* to counteract dehydration. Insect repellents, including mosquito coils, can be obtained locally.

UK citizens should carry a European Health Insurance Card (EHIC) application for which can be obtained at a Post Office or online at www.ehic.org.uk. This provides for free medical treatment under a reciprocal agreement with the National Health Service. Private medical treatment is likely to be expensive and it may be worth taking out medical insurance (which should also provide for an attended flight home should the need arise).

THE YACHT

A yacht properly equipped for cruising in northern waters should need little extra gear, but the following items are worth considering if not already on board.

Radio equipment

In order to receive weather forecasts and navigational warnings from Coast Radio Stations, a radio capable of receiving short and medium wave Single Sideband (SSB) transmissions will be needed. Do not make the mistake of buying a radio capable only of receiving the AM transmissions broadcast by national radio stations, or assume that SSB is only applicable to transmitting radios (transceivers).

Most SSB receivers are capable of receiving either Upper Side Band (USB) or Lower Side Band (LSB) at the flick of a switch. The UK Maritime Mobile Net covering the Eastern Atlantic and Mediterranean uses USB, and again it is not necessary to have either a transceiver or a transmitting licence to listen in, just a receiver. All Coast Radio Stations broadcast on SSB – whether on USB or LSB should be easy to determine by trial and error.

Digital tuning is very desirable, and the radio should be capable of tuning to a minimum of 1kHz and preferably to 0·1kHz.

Ventilation

Modern yachts are, as a rule, better ventilated than their older sisters though seldom better insulated. Consider adding an opening hatch in the main cabin, if not already fitted, and ideally another over the galley. Wind scoops over hatches can be a major benefit.

Awnings

An awning covering at least the cockpit provides much relief for the crew, while an even better combination is a bimini which can be kept rigged whilst sailing, plus a larger 'harbour' awning, preferably at boom height or above and extending forward to the mast.

Fans

Harbours can be hot and windless. The use of 12v fans for all cabins can have a dramatic effect on comfort.

Cockpit tables

It is pleasant to eat civilised meals in the cockpit, particularly while at anchor. If nothing else can be arranged, a small folding table might do.

Refrigerator/ice-box/freezer

If a refrigerator or freezer is not fitted it may be possible to build in an ice-box (a plastic picnic coolbox is a poor substitute), but this will be useless without adequate insulation. An ice-box designed for northern climes will almost certainly benefit from extra insulation, if this can be fitted – 100mm (4in) is a desirable minimum, 150mm (6in) even better. A drain is also essential.

If a refrigerator/freezer is fitted but electricity precious, placing ice inside will help minimise battery drain.

Hose

Carry at least 25 metres. Standpipes tend to have bayonet couplings of a type unavailable in the UK – purchase them on arrival. Plenty of 5 or 10 litre plastic carriers will also be useful.

Deck shower

If no shower is fitted below, a black-backed plastic bag plus rose heats very quickly when hung in the rigging. (At least one proprietary model is available widely).

Mosquito nets

Some advocate fitting screens to all openings leading below. Others find this inconvenient, relying instead on mosquito coils and other insecticides and repellents. For some reason mosquitoes generally seem to bother new arrivals more than old hands, while anchoring well out will often decrease the problem.

Harbours, marinas and anchorages

In spite of the growth in both the number and size of marinas and yacht harbours there is still a chronic shortage of berths. A recent expansion of many marinas has eased the situation. One must check in advance whether a berth is available and note that mobile phones are replacing VHF for this function.

Harbour organisation

At local level, the ultimate authority for the workings of a harbour is the *capitán de puerto* whose office is the *capitanía*. In fishing ports there may also be a *guarda de puerto*; in this case the *capitán* looks after the waters of the harbour and delegates berthing arrangements to the *guarda*.

At ports where there is an organised yachting presence, there is almost always a *club náutico*, a marina or both, and arrangements for handling yachts are delegated to them. For the visiting yacht, the first point of reference is the marina if there is one; and if not, the *club náutico*.

Harbour charges

All harbours and marinas charge, at a scale which varies from season to season and usually increases from year to year. May to September are normally 'high season' with charges that are normally nearly double that of the 'low season'. Longer term contracts may work out up to a third cheaper than the daily rate. Some marinas include water, electricity, harbour and light dues, while others charge separately. Published rates rarely include the IVA (at 16%) and sometimes the published information does not always specify all the charges. One should take great care in checking what exactly one is paying for if one is to avoid problems when finally settling up.

With the shortage of berths, mentioned above, costs have risen drastically and, with a few exceptions, are now fairly similar along the entire stretch of coast covered by this volume. Charges for a 12 metre craft average around €30 a night (€25 with water and electricity etc. charged separately) in high season and around €20 a night (€15 with water and electricity charged separately) in low season. Departures from these average figures are sometimes great. A further complication is that the newer marinas are beginning to charge by beam times length (or sometimes beam alone). It is not practical either to generalize further on harbour dues or to give detailed charges, let alone give an opinion on value for money but the foregoing may provide some guidance for financial planning. Where a relatively expensive or cheap rate has been found this is noted in the text. *El Mercado Náutico* – the Boat Market, which generally appears every other month during the summer, carries tariffs and is probably the most up-to-date guide to be found.

Berthing

Due to the vast numbers of yachts and limited space available, berthing stern-to the quays and pontoons is normal.

For greater privacy berth bows-to. This has the added advantages of keeping the rudder away from possible underwater obstructions near the quay and making the approach a much easier manoeuvre. An anchor may occasionally be needed, but more often a bow (or stern) line will be provided, usually via a lazyline to the pontoon though sometimes buoyed. This line may be both heavy and dirty and gloves will be useful. Either way, have plenty of fenders out and lines ready.

Most cruising skippers will have acquired some expertise at this manoeuvre but if taking over a chartered or otherwise unfamiliar yacht it would be wise both to check handling characteristics and talk the sequence through with the crew before attempting to enter a narrow berth.

Detailed instructions regarding Mediterranean mooring techniques will be found in *Mediterranean Cruising Handbook* by Rod Heikell.

Mooring lines – surge in harbours is common and mooring lines must be both long and strong. It is useful to have an eye made up at the shore end with a loop of chain plus shackles to slip over bollards or through rings. Carry plenty of mooring lines, especially if the boat is to be left unattended for any length of time.

Gangplanks – if a gangplank is not already part of the boat's equipment, a builder's scaffolding plank, with holes drilled at either end to take lines, serves well. As it is cheap and easily replaced it can also be used outside fenders to deal with an awkward lie or ward off an oily quay. A short ladder, possibly the bathing ladder if it can be adapted, is useful if berthing bows-to.

Moorings

Virtually all moorings are privately owned and if one is used it will have to be vacated should the owner return. There are generally no markings to give any indication as to the weight and strength of moorings so they should be used with caution. Lobster pot toggles have been mistaken for moorings.

Laying up

Laying up either afloat or ashore is possible at most marinas, though a few have no hardstanding. Facilities and services provided vary considerably, as does the cost, and it is worth seeking local advice as to the quality of the services and the security of the berth or hardstanding concerned.

In the north of the area, the northwesterly *tramontana* (*maestral*) can be frequent and severe in winter and early spring, and this should be borne in mind when selecting the area and site to lay up. Yachts with wooden decks and varnished brightwork will benefit with protection from the winter sun.

The paperwork associated with temporary import and laying up is detailed on page 3.

Yacht clubs

Most harbours of any size support at least one *club náutico*. However the grander ones in particular are basically social clubs – often with tennis courts, swimming pools and other facilities – and may not welcome the crews of visiting yachts. Often there is both a marina and a club, and unless there are special circumstances the normal first option for a visitor is the marina. That said, many *club náuticos* have pleasant bars and excellent restaurants which appear to be open to all, while a few are notably helpful and friendly to visitors. The standard of dress and behaviour often appears to be somewhat more formal than that expected in a similar club in Britain.

General regulations

Harbour restrictions

All harbours have a speed limit, usually 3 knots. The limits are not noted in the text and none are known which is less than 3 knots. There is a 5 knot speed limit within 100m of coast, extending to 250m off bathing beaches.

In most harbours anchoring is forbidden except in emergency or for a short period while sorting out a berth.

Harbour traffic signals

Traffic signals are rare, and in any case are designed for commercial traffic and seldom apply to yachts.

Storm signals

The signal stations at major ports and harbours may show storm signals, but equally they may not. With minor exceptions they are similar to the International System of Visual Storm Warnings.

Flag etiquette

A yacht in commission in foreign waters is legally required to fly her national maritime flag; for a British registered yacht, this is commonly the Red Ensign. If a special club ensign is worn it must be accompanied by the correct burgee. The courtesy flag of the country visited, which normally is the national maritime flag, should be flown from the starboard signal halliard. The flag for Spain is similar to the Spanish national flag but without the crest in the centre.

Insurance

Many marinas require evidence of insurance cover, though third party only may be sufficient. Many UK companies are willing to extend home waters cover for the Mediterranean, excluding certain areas.

Garbage

It is an international offence to dump garbage at sea and, while the arrangements of local authorities may not be perfect, garbage on land should be dumped in the proper containers. Marinas require the use of their onshore toilet facilities or holding tanks.

Large yachts

Many harbours are too small, or too shallow, for a large yacht, which must anchor outside whilst its crew visit the harbour by tender. It is essential that the skipper of such a yacht wishing to enter a small harbour telephones or radios the harbour authorities well in advance to reserve a berth (if available) and receive necessary instructions.

Scuba diving

Inshore scuba diving is strictly controlled and a licence is required from the *Militar de Marina*. This involves a certificate of competence, a medical certificate, two passport photographs, the passport itself (for inspection), knowledge of the relevant laws and a declaration that they will be obeyed. The simplest approach is to enquire through marina staff. Any attempt to remove archaeological material from the seabed will result in serious trouble.

Spearfishing

Spearfishing while scuba diving or using a snorkel is controlled and, in some places, prohibited.

Water-skiing

There has been a big increase in the use of high powered outboards for water-skiing over the past decade, accompanied by a significant increase in accidents. In most of the main ports and at some beaches it is now controlled and enquiries should be made before skiing. It is essential to have third party insurance and, if possible, a bail bond. If bathing and water-skiing areas are buoyed, yachts are excluded.

Security

Crime afloat is not a major problem in most areas and regrettably much of the theft which does occur can be laid at the door of other yachtsmen. Take sensible precautions – lock up before leaving the yacht, padlock the outboard to the dinghy, and secure the dinghy (particularly if an inflatable) with chain or wire rather than line. Folding bicycles are particularly vulnerable to theft, and should be chained up if left on deck.

Ashore, the situation in the big towns is no worse than in the UK and providing common sense is applied to such matters as how handbags are carried, where not to go after the bars close etc., there should be no problem.

The officials most likely to be seen are the *guardia civil*, who wear grey uniforms and deal with immigration as well as more ordinary police work, the *Aduana* (customs) in navy blue uniforms, and the *Policía*, also in blue uniforms, who deal with traffic rather than criminal matters.

Anchorages

There are a large number of attractive anchorages in *calas* and off beaches, even though many have massive buildings in the background and crowds in the foreground. Where known, particular hazards are mentioned but an absence of comment in the text or on the sketch charts does not mean there are no hazards. There are always hazards approaching and anchoring off the shoreline. The plans are derived from limited observation and not from a professional survey; depths, shapes, distances etc. are approximate. Any approach must be made with due care. Skippers are advised that anchorages near hotels and towns may be cordoned off, by small floating buoys, to protect swimmers and therefore not be suitable. It cannot be assumed that anchorages listed in this book are always available for use by cruising yachtsmen.

The weather can change and deteriorate at short notice. During the day the sea breeze can be strong, especially if there is a valley at the head of an anchorage. Similarly a strong land breeze can flow down a valley in the early hours of the morning. If anchored near the head of a *cala* backed by a river valley, should there be a thunderstorm or heavy downpour in the hills above take precautions against the flood of water and debris which will descend into the *cala*.

Many *cala* anchorages suffer from swell even when not open to its off-shore direction. Swell tends to curl round all but the most prominent headlands. Wash from boats entering and leaving, as well as from larger vessels passing outside, may add to the discomfort. If considering a second anchor or a line ashore in order to hold the yacht into the swell, take into account the swinging room required by yachts on single anchors should the wind change.

In a high-sided *cala* winds are often fluky and a sudden blow, even from the land, may make departure difficult. This type of anchorage should only be used in settled calm weather and left in good time if swell or wind rise.

Whatever the type of *cala*, have ready a plan for clearing out quickly, possibly in darkness. It is unwise to leave an anchored yacht unattended for any length of time.

Choice of anchor

Many popular anchorages are thoroughly ploughed up each year by the hundreds of anchors dropped and weighed. At others the bottom is weed-covered compacted sand. Not without good reason is the four-pronged grab the favourite anchor of local fishermen, though difficult to stow. A conventional fisherman-type anchor is easier to stow and a useful ally. If using a patent anchor – Danforth, CQR, Bruce, Fortress etc. – an anchor weight (or chum) is a worthwhile investment and will encourage the pull to remain horizontal.

Anchoring

Once in a suitable depth of water, if clarity permits look for a weed-free patch to drop the anchor. In rocky or otherwise suspect areas – including those likely to contain wrecks, old chains etc. – use a sinking trip line with a float (an inviting buoy may be picked up by another yacht). Chain scope should be at least four times the maximum depth of water and nylon scope double that. It is always worth setting the anchor by reversing slowly until it holds, but on a hard or compacted bottom this must be done very gently in order to give the anchor a chance to bite – over enthusiasm with the throttle will cause it to skip without digging in.

Supplies and services

Fresh water

In many places drinking water (*agua potable*) is scarce. Expect to pay for it, particularly if supplied by hose, and do not wash sails and decks before checking that it is acceptable to do so. In those harbours where a piped supply is not available for yachts, a public tap can often be found – a good supply of 5 or 10 litre plastic cans will be useful.

Water quality is generally good. However it varies from place to place and year to year. Always check verbally and taste for salinity or over-chlorinating before topping up tanks. If caught out, bottled water is readily available in bars and supermarkets.

Ice

Block ice for an ice-box is widely obtainable – use the largest blocks that will fit; chemical ice is sometimes available in blocks measuring 100 x 20 x 20cms. The latter must not be used in drinks, the former only after inquiring of those who have tried the product. Cube or 'small' ice is obtainable and generally of drinks quality, particularly if bought in a sealed bag.

Fuel

Diesel (*gasoleo*, *gasoil* or simply *diesel*) is sold in two forms throughout Spain, *Gasoleo B* which attracts a lower tax and is only available to fishing craft, and *Gasoleo A* which is available to yachts. Not all harbours sell *Gasoleo A*, particularly the smaller fishing harbours. A more limited number also have a pump for petrol (*gasolina*). *Petróleo* is paraffin (kerosene). Credit cards are widely, but not universally, accepted – if in doubt, check first.

Bottled gas

Camping Gaz is widely available from marinas, supermarkets or *ferreterias* (ironmongers), in the 1.9kg bottles identical to those in the UK.

As of 2002 REPSOL/CAMPSOL depots will no longer fill any UK (or any other countries') Calor Gas bottles even with a current test certificate. It is therefore essential to carry the appropriate regulator and fittings to permit the use of Camping Gas bottles. Yachts fitted with propane systems should consult the Calor Gas Customer service agent (☎ 0800 626 626).

Electricity

The marina standard is 220 volt, 50 Hz, generally via a two-pin socket for which an adapter will be needed, though some marinas provide 380 volt supplies to berths for yachts over 20–25m. If using 110 volt 60 Hz equipment seek advice – frequency may be a greater problem than voltage. Even if the yacht is not wired for mains, a 25m length of cable and a trickle charger may be useful.

Food and drink

There are many well stocked stores, supermarkets and hypermarkets in the larger towns and cities and it may be worth doing the occasional major stock-up by taxi. As a rule, availability and choice varies with the size of the town. Most older settlements (though not all tourist resorts) have a market with local produce at reasonable prices. Alcohol is cheap by UK standards with, unsurprisingly, good value Spanish wines. Spanish gin and vodka are also good value; Scotch whisky can only come from Scotland but the genuine article is often lower in price than in the U.K. Shop prices generally are noticeably lower away from tourist resorts.

Most shops, other than the largest supermarkets, close for *siesta* between 1400 and 1700 and remain closed on Sunday though some smaller food shops do open on Sunday mornings. In larger towns the produce market may operate from 0800 to 1400, Monday to Saturday; in smaller towns it is more often a weekly affair. An excellent way to sample unfamiliar delicacies in small portions is in the form of bar snacks, *tapas* or the larger *raciónes*. Tapas once came on the house but are now almost invariably charged – sometimes heavily.

Repairs and chandlery

There are many marinas equipped to handle all aspects of yacht maintenance from laying up to changing a washer. Nearly all have travel-hoists and the larger have specialist facilities – GRP work, electronics, sailmaking, stainless welding and so forth. Charges may differ – widely so – if practicable, shop around.

The best equipped chandleries will be found near the larger marinas. Smaller harbours or marinas are often without a chandlery, though something may be found in the associated town. Basic items can sometimes be found in *ferreterias* (ironmongers).

Telephones and Fax

Telephone kiosks are common, both local and *teléfono internacional*, and most carry instructions in English. Both coins and phonecards, available from tobacconists (*estancos*), are used. If no kiosk is available marina offices have telephones and many have faxes. Most bars and hotels have metered telephones and the latter usually have faxes, though these are seldom metered. Wi-Fi is widely available.

- When calling from within Spain, dial the whole code (beginning with the figure 9) whether or not the number you are calling has the same code. In some areas the number of digits to be dialled is nine, in others eight. To make an international call, dial 00 followed by the relevant country code (44 for the UK). If calling the UK do not dial the first figure of the number if it is 0.

- To reach the international operator dial 025. A telephone number beginning with the figure 6 indicates a mobile telephone which will have no area code and its own code for calling its international operator. The number for information is 1003 and the land based emergency services can be contacted by this route.

- To call Spain from abroad, dial the international access code (00 in the UK) followed by the code for Spain (34), then the area code (which begins with 9 except for mobile phones) followed by the individual number.

Warning Apart from a major re-organisation of area codes, individual numbers in Spain change surprisingly often.

Mail

Letters may be sent *poste restante* to any post office (*oficina de corréos*). They should be addressed with the surname (only) of the recipient followed by *Lista de Corréos* and the town. Do not enter the addressee's initials or title: that is likely to cause misfiling. Collection is a fairly cumbersome procedure and a passport is likely to be needed. Alternatively, most marinas and some *club náuticos* will hold mail for yachts, but it is always wise to check in advance if possible. Uncollected letters are seldom returned.

Mail to and from the UK should be marked 'air mail' (*por avión*) but even so may take up to ten days, so if speed is important communicate by fax or Email. Post boxes are yellow; stamps are available from tobacconists (*estancos*), not from post offices though the latter will accept and frank mail. Almost every town has a post office; ask – *donde esta el Correo?*

Tourist offices

There is at least one tourist office in every major town or resort. Their locations vary from year to year – ask at the port or marina office.

Transport and travel

Every community has some form of public transport, if only one *autobús* a day and many of the coastal towns are served by rail as well.

Taxis are easily found in the tourist resorts though less common outside them, but can always be ordered by telephone. Car hire is simple, but either a full national or international driving licence must be shown and many companies will not lease a car to a driver over 70 years old.

Air – Alicante, Barcelona and Valencia have year round international flights and seasonal charter flights; Gibraltar has year round connections with the U.K. Other airports, Málaga, Murcia, Alicante and Tarragona, have international scheduled and charter flights in summer and year round connections within Spain.

Western Mediterranean weather

The weather pattern in the basin of the western Mediterranean is affected by many different systems. It is largely unpredictable, quick to change and often very different at places only a short distance apart. See Appendix III for Spanish meteorological terms.

WINDS

Winds most frequently blow from the west, northwest, north and east but are considerably altered by the effects of local topography. The Mediterranean is an area of calms and gales and the old saying that in summer there are nine days of light winds followed by a gale is very close to reality. Close to the coast, normal sea and land breezes are experienced on calm days. Along the Costa Brava, northwest, north and northeast winds are most common, especially in winter, though winds from other directions frequently occur. This area is particularly influenced by the weather in the Golfo de León and is in the direct path of the northwesterly *tramontana* (see below), making it particularly important to listen to regular weather forecasts.

The winds in the Mediterranean have been given special names dependent on their direction and characteristics. Those that affect this coast are detailed below.

Northwest – *tramontana*

This wind, also known as the *maestral* near Río Ebro and the *mistral* in France, is a strong, dry wind, cold in winter, which can be dangerous. It is caused by a secondary depression forming in the Golfo de León or the Golfo de Génova on the cold front of a major depression crossing France. The northwesterly airflow generated is compressed between the Alps and the Pyrenees and flows into the Mediterranean basin. In Spain it chiefly affects the coast to the north of Barcelona, the Islas Baleares, and is strongest at the northern end of the Costa Brava.

The *tramontana* can be dangerous in that it can arrive and reach gale force in as little as fifteen minutes on a calm sunny day with virtually no warning. Signs to watch for are brilliant visibility, clear sky – sometimes with cigar-shaped clouds – very dry air and a steady or slightly rising barometer. On rare occasions the sky may be cloudy when the wind first arrives although it clears later. Sometimes the barometer will plunge in normal fashion, rising quickly after the gale has passed. If at sea and some way from land, a line of white on the horizon and a developing swell give a few minutes' warning. The only effective warning that can be obtained is by radio – Marseille (in French) and Monaco (in French and English) are probably the best bet. *See page 13 for transmission details.*

The *tramontana* normally blows for at least three days but may last for a week or longer. It is frequent in the winter months, blowing for a third of the time and can reach F10 (50 knots) or more. In summer it is neither as strong nor as frequent.

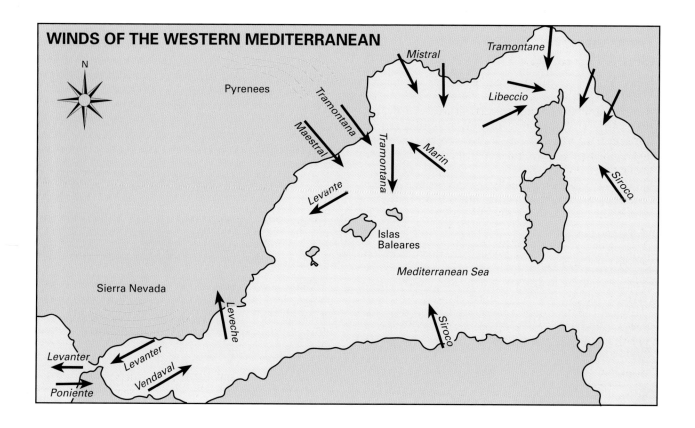

WINDS OF THE WESTERN MEDITERRANEAN

West – *vendaval*

A depression crossing Spain or southern France creates a strong southwest to west wind, the *vendaval* or *poniente*, which funnels through the Strait of Gibraltar and along the south coast of Spain. Though normally confined to the south and southeast coasts, it occasionally blows in the northeast of the area. It is usually short-lived and at its strongest from late autumn to early spring.

East – *levante*

Encountered from Gibraltar to Valencia and beyond, the *levante*, sometimes called the *llevantade* when it blows at gale force, is caused by a depression located between the Islas Baleares and the North African coast. It is preceded by a heavy swell (*las tascas*), cold damp air, poor visibility and low cloud which forms first around the higher hills. Heavy and prolonged rainfall is more likely in spring and autumn than summer. A *levante* may last for three or four days.

South – *siroco*

The hot wind from the south is created by a depression moving east along or just south of the North African coast. By the time this dry wind reaches Spain it can be very humid, with haze and cloud. If strong it carries dust, and should it rain when the cold front comes through, the water may be red or brown and the dust will set like cement. This wind is sometimes called the *leveche* in southeast Spain. It occurs most frequently in summer, seldom lasting more than one or two days.

Clouds

Cloud cover of between ⅛ and ⅝ in the winter months is about double the summer average of ⅜. Barcelona, however, seems to manage a year round average of ⅜ to ⅝. The cloud is normally cumulus and high level. In strong winds with a southerly component, complete cloud cover can be expected.

Precipitation

Annual rainfall is moderate and decreases towards the north from about 760mm at Gibraltar to 560mm at Barcelona. The rainy seasons predominantly in autumn and winter and in most areas the summer months are virtually dry. The Costa Brava however usually manages about 25mm of rain during each summer month. Most of the rain falls in very heavy showers of 1–2 hours.

Thunderstorms

Thunderstorms are most frequent in the autumn at up to four or five each month, and can be accompanied by hail.

Water spouts

Water spouts occur in the Strait of Gibraltar in winter and spring, usually associated with thunderstorms.

Snow

Snow at sea level is very rare but it falls and remains on the higher mountain ranges inland. Snow on the Sierra Nevada is particularly noticeable from the sea.

Visibility

Fog occurs about four days a month in summer along the Costa de Sol but elsewhere is very rare. Occasionally dust carried by the southerly *siroco* reduces visibility and industrial areas such as Valencia and Barcelona produce haze.

Temperature

Winter temperatures at Gibraltar average 10–15°C, rising steadily after March to average 20–29°C in July and August. Afternoon (maximum) temperatures may reach 30–33°C in these months. At Barcelona, summer temperatures are much the same as at Gibraltar but winter temperatures are lower, 6–13°C.

Humidity

The relative humidity is moderate at around 60% to 80%. With winds from the west, northwest or north, low humidity can be expected; with winds off the sea, high humidity is normal. The relative humidity increases throughout the night and falls by day.

Local variations

In the northeastern area, the common winds blow between northwest and northeast. Gales may be experienced for 10% of the time during the winter, dropping to 2% in July and August, sometimes arriving with little warning and rapidly building to gale force.

The sea

Currents

There is a constant E-going surface current of 1 to 2 knots, passing in to the Mediterranean through the Strait of Gibraltar between the Costa del Sol and the African coast to replace water lost by evaporation. Northeast of Cabo de Gata up to the border with France, a significant inshore counter-eddy runs roughly SSW at 1 to 1½ knots. The shape of the coast produces variations in both direction and strength, especially around promontories.

Tides

Tides should be taken into account at the west end of the Costa del Sol and are noted in the introduction to that section. From Alicante to the border with France, the tide is hardly appreciable.

Swell

Winds between NE and SE can produce a dangerous swell on the E coast. Swell has a nasty capability of going round corners and getting into *calas*.

Scouring and silting

Many harbours and anchorages are located in sandy areas where depths can change dramatically in the course of a storm or a season. Dredging is a common feature but there is no certainty that depths will be maintained. Charts and drawings give no sure guide. When approaching or entering such areas, it is of great importance to sound carefully and to act on the information received.

Sea temperature

Sea temperatures in February are around 14°C on the Costa del Sol and 12°C on the Costa Brava. In summer, along the Costa Blanca it can rise to 20°C. Winds from the south and east tend to raise the temperature and those from the west and north to lower them.

Radio and weather forecasts

Details of coast radio stations, weather forecasts, weatherfax (radio facsimile) Navtex and Inmarsat-C coverage follow. See individual harbour details for port and marina radio information. All times quoted are in UT (universal time) unless otherwise specified. France Inter on LW, 163kHz, France Info on MW and Monaco 3AC on 4363kHx all use local time. Details of frequencies, channel and times are to be found in ALRS Vol 3 (1), RYA Booklet G5 and on the Internet.

Coast radio stations

VHF/MF

Coast radio stations are controlled from Malaga or Valencia – see diagram p 14. Full details will be found in the Admiralty *List of Radio Signals Vol 1 Part 1 (NP281/1)*.

On receipt of traffic, Spanish coast radio stations will call vessels once on Ch 16; after that the vessel's call sign will be included in scheduled MF traffic lists.

Weather forecasts

Marine VHF and MF

Inshore waters and Sea area forecasts are broadcast in Spanish and English on marine VHF all round Mediterranean Spain and the Balearic Islands. There are also broadcasts of Inshore waters forecasts and actual weather in Spanish only. *For details see the tables on page 14.*

Sea area forecasts can also be heard in English and Spanish on MF radio (*Table page 14*).

Non-radio weather forecasts

A recorded marine forecast in Spanish is available by telephoning (906) 36 53 71. The 'High Seas' bulletin includes the Islas Baleares.

Spanish television shows a useful synoptic chart with its land weather forecast every evening after the news at approximately 2120 weekdays, 1520 Saturday and 2020 Sunday. Most national and local newspapers also carry some form of forecast.

Nearly all marinas and yacht harbours display a synoptic chart and forecast, generally updated daily (though often posted rather late to be of use).

Rescue and emergency services

In addition to VHF Ch 16 (MAYDAY or PAN PAN as appropriate) the marine emergency services can be contacted by telephone at all times on 900 202 202.

The National Centre for Sea Rescue is based in Madrid but has a string of communications towers. On the spot responsibility for co-ordinating rescues lies with the Capitanías Marítimas with support from the Spanish Navy, customs, guardia civil etc. Lifeboats are stationed at some of the larger harbours but the majority do not appear to be all-weather boats.

The other emergency services can be contacted by dialling 003 for the operator and asking for policía (police), bomberos (fire service) or Cruz Roja (Red Cross). Alternatively the police can be contacted direct on 091.

Radio fax and teleprinter

Northwood (RN) broadcasts a full set of UK Met Office charts out to 5 days ahead on 2618.5, 4610, 8040 and 11086.5kHz. (Schedule at 0236, surface analysis at 3 hourly intervals from 0300 to 2100 and 2300.) Deutscher Wetterdienst broadcasts German weather charts on 3855, 7880 and 13882.5kHz. (Schedule at 1111, surface analysis at 0430, 1050, 1600, 2200.)

DWD broadcasts forecasts using RTTY on 4583, 7646 and 10001.8kHz (in English at 0415 and 1610), 11039 and 14467.3kHz (in German at 0535). Note that the 4583 and 14467.3kHz may not be useable in the Mediterranean. The most useful products are forecasts up to 5 days ahead at 12 hourly intervals and up to 2 days ahead at 6 hour intervals. Alternatively, a dedicated receiver 'Weatherman' will record automatically: see www.nasamarine.com.

UK Maritime Mobile Net

The Net covering the Eastern Atlantic and the Mediterranean, can be heard daily on 14303kHz USB at 0800 and 1800 UT. On Saturday morning the broadcast sometimes contains a longer period outlook. Forecasts will be a rehash of what the Net leader has gleaned from various sources. No licence is required if a receive-only HF radio is used.

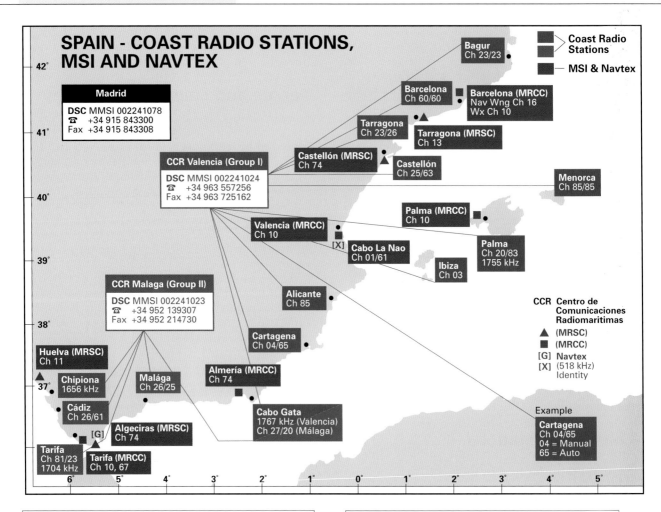

SPAIN - COAST RADIO STATIONS, MSI AND NAVTEX

Coast Radio Stations

MSI & Navtex

Madrid
DSC MMSI 002241078
☎ +34 915 843300
Fax +34 915 843308

Bagur
Ch 23/23

Barcelona
Ch 60/60

Barcelona (MRCC)
Nav Wng Ch 16
Wx Ch 10

Tarragona
Ch 23/26

Tarragona (MRSC)
Ch 13

Castellón (MRSC)
Ch 74

Castellón
Ch 25/63

Menorca
Ch 85/85

CCR Valencia (Group I)
DSC MMSI 002241024
☎ +34 963 557256
Fax +34 963 725162

Palma (MRCC)
Ch 10

Valencia (MRCC)
Ch 10

[X]

Cabo La Nao
Ch 01/61

Palma
Ch 20/83
1755 kHz

Ibiza
Ch 03

CCR Malaga (Group II)
DSC MMSI 002241023
☎ +34 952 139307
Fax +34 952 214730

Alicante
Ch 85

CCR Centro de
Comunicaciones
Radiomaritimas
▲ (MRSC)
■ (MRCC)
[G] Navtex
[X] (518 kHz)
Identity

Cartagena
Ch 04/65

Huelva (MRSC)
Ch 11

Chipiona
1656 kHz

Malága
Ch 26/25

Almería (MRCC)
Ch 74

Cádiz
Ch 26/61

[G]

Algeciras (MRSC)
Ch 74

Cabo Gata
1767 kHz (Valencia)
Ch 27/20 (Málaga)

Example

Cartagena
Ch 04/65
04 = Manual
65 = Auto

Tarifa
Ch 81/23
1704 kHz

Tarifa (MRCC)
Ch 10, 67

Inshore waters forecasts and reports of actual weather are broadcast in English and Spanish as follows.

MRCC	VHF Ch	Time UT
CZCS Tarifa	10, 67, 73	H2+15
CLCS Algeciras	74	0315, 0515, 0715, 1115, 1515, 1915, 2315
CRCS Almería	10, 67, 73	H1+15
CRCS Barcelona	10	0600, 0900, 1500, 2000
CRCS Valencia	10, 67	H2+15
CLCS Tarragona	13	0533, 0933, 1533, 2033
CRCS Palma	10	0735, 1035, 1535, 2035

H1 = odd hours. H2 = even hours

Sea area and inshore waters forecasts are broadcast in Spanish as follows

MRCC Málaga	VHF Ch	Times UT
Cádiz	26	
Tarifa	81	0833, 1133, 2003
Málaga	26	
Cabo Gata	27	
MRCC Valencia	**VHF Ch**	**Times UT**
Cartagena	4	
Alicante	85	
Cabo La Nao	2	
Castellón	25	
Tarragona	23	0910, 1410, 2110
Barcelona	60	
Bagur	23	
Menorca	85	
Palma	20	
Ibiza	3	

Sea area forecasts are broadcast in English and Spanish as follows

Station	kHz	Time UT
Chipiona	1656kHz	0733, 1233, 1933
Tarifa	1704kHz	0733, 1233, 1933
Cabo de Gata	1767kHz	0750, 1303, 1950
Palma	1755kHz	0750, 1303, 1950

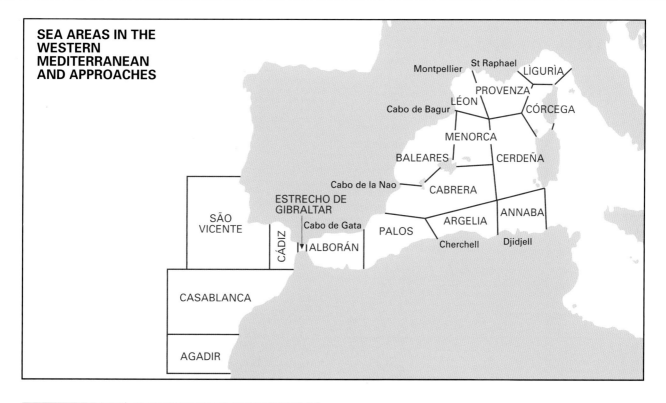

SEA AREAS IN THE
WESTERN
MEDITERRANEAN
AND APPROACHES

The Spanish and French use a common set of sea areas and use the same names although spelling and pronunciation differ at times. The French names for the Mediterranean Sea areas are Alboran, Palos, Alger, Cabrera, Baléares, Minorque, Lion, Provence, Ligure, Corse, Sardaigne, and Annaba. In the approaches to the Mediterranean the French names are identical to the Spanish.

Monaco 3AC

Monaco 3AC broadcasts on 8728 and 8806kHz USB at 0715 and 1830 in French and English. The texts are those broadcast by INMARSAT-C for the western part of METAREA III. Monaco also broadcasts on 4363kHz at 0903 and 1915 LT in French and English and at 1403 in French only. Texts are as the latest Toulon NAVTEX broadcast.

NAVTEX AND INMARSAT-C

NAVTEX and INMARSAT-C are the primary GMDSS modes for transmission of all Marine Safety Information. Broadcast times for weather are as follows

Transmitter	Times (UTC)
Tarifa – G (518kHz)	0900 and 2100
Cabo la Nao – X (Valencia) (518kHz)	0750 and 1950
La Garde – W (Toulon) (518kHz)	1140 and 2340
La Garde – S (Toulon) (490kHz)	0700 and 1900
INMARSAT-C METAREA III	1000 and 2200

Internet

Many sites provide weather information and most, even the official sites, do change from time to time. For a good starting point, the RCCPF recommends Frank Singleton's site www.franksingleton.clara.net Also see www.rccpf.org.uk under technical matters. Skippers are urged to use the Internet as a supplementary source of information and to ensure that CMDSS forecasts can be obtained on board.

GRIB coded forecasts (Salidocs)

This service enables arrow diagram forecasts for up to 5 days ahead, and other information to be obtained in email form (or by marine HF and HAM radio). The data is highly compressed so that a great deal of information can be acquired quickly, even using a mobile phone connected to a laptop. For details of one popular service, *Email* query@saildoc.com, subject field 'any'. There is no charge for this service.

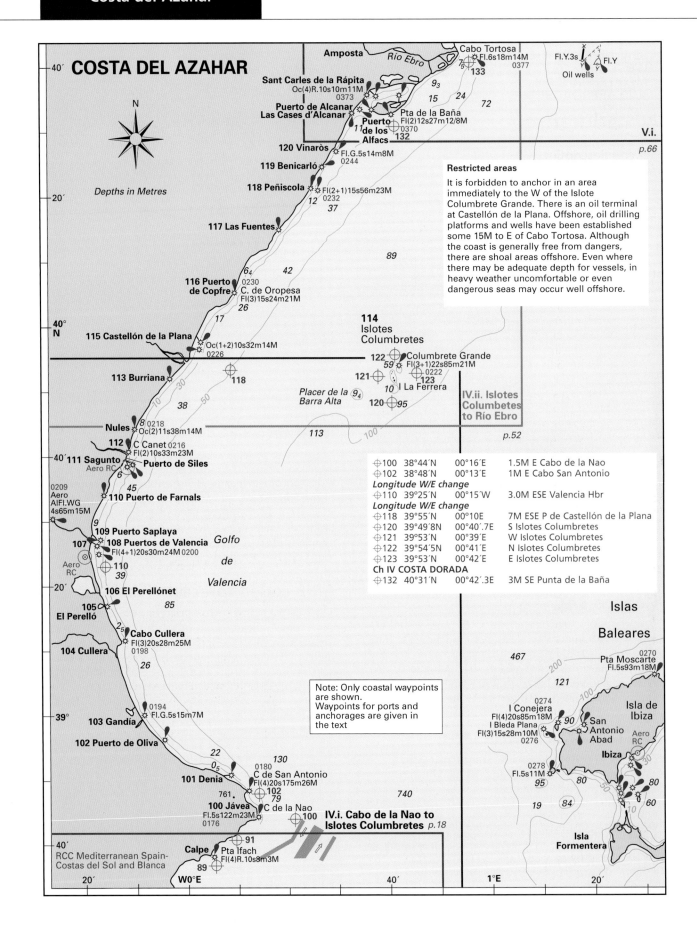

COSTA DEL AZAHAR

N

Depths in Metres

40′

20′

**40°
N**

40′

20′

39°

40′

20′ **W0°E** **40′**

Amposta — Río Ebro — Cabo Tortosa
Fl.6s18m14M
0377
7₅ **133**
Fl.Y.3s Fl.Y
Oil wells

9₃
15 24 72

V.i.
p.66

Sant Carles de la Rápita
Oc(4)R.10s10m11M
0373

**Puerto de Alcanar
Las Cases d'Alcanar**

Pta de la Baña
Puerto Fl(2)12s27m12/8M
de los 0370
Alfacs 11 **132**

120 Vinaròs
Fl.G.5s14m8M
0244

119 Benicarló

118 Peñiscola Fl(2+1)15s56m23M
12 0232
37

117 Las Fuentes

89

6₄ 42

116 Puerto
de Copfre 0230
C. de Oropesa
Fl(3)15s24m21M
26

17

114
Islotes
Columbretes

115 Castellón de la Plana
Oc(1+2)10s32m14M
0226

122 Columbrete Grande
59 Fl(3+1)22s85m21M
121 0222
123
113 Burriana
30 **118**

10 I La Ferrera

Placer de la 9₄
Barra Alta **120** **95**

IV.ii. Islotes
Columbetes
to Río Ebro
p.52

38 50

Nules 8 0218
Oc(2)11s38m14M
113 100

112 C Canet 0216
Fl(2)10s33m23M
111 Sagunto
Aero RC **Puerto de Siles**
6

0209
Aero
AlFl.WG
4s65m15M 45

110 Puerto de Farnals
9

109 Puerto Saplaya
107 **108 Puertos de Valencia** *Golfo*
Fl(4+1)20s30m24M 0200 *de*
Aero **110**
RC 39 *Valencia*

106 El Perellónet
105 85
El Perelló

2₅ **Cabo Cullera**
Fl(3)20s28m25M
0198

104 Cullera

26

0194
Fl.G.5s15m7M
103 Gandía

102 Puerto de Oliva

22
0₅ 130
0180
C de San Antonio
Fl(4)20s175m26M
101 Denia

761 **102**
79
100 Jávea C de la Nao 740
Fl.5s122m23M
0176 **100** IV.i. Cabo de la Nao to
Islotes Columbretes p.18

91
Calpe Pta Ifach
Fl(4)R.10s8m3M
89
RCC Mediterranean Spain-
Costas del Sol and Blanca

Restricted areas

It is forbidden to anchor in an area immediately to the W of the Islote Columbrete Grande. There is an oil terminal at Castellón de la Plana. Offshore, oil drilling platforms and wells have been established some 15M to E of Cabo Tortosa. Although the coast is generally free from dangers, there are shoal areas offshore. Even where there may be adequate depth for vessels, in heavy weather uncomfortable or even dangerous seas may occur well offshore.

⊕100	38°44′N	00°16′E	1.5M E Cabo de la Nao
⊕102	38°48′N	00°13′E	1M E Cabo San Antonio
Longitude W/E change			
⊕110	39°25′N	00°15′W	3.0M ESE Valencia Hbr
Longitude W/E change			
⊕118	39°55′N	00°10E	7M ESE P de Castellón de la Plana
⊕120	39°49′8N	00°40′.7E	S Islotes Columbretes
⊕121	39°53′N	00°39′E	W Islotes Columbretes
⊕122	39°54′5N	00°41′E	N Islotes Columbretes
⊕123	39°53′N	00°42′E	E Islotes Columbretes
Ch IV COSTA DORADA			
⊕132	40°31′N	00°42′.3E	3M SE Punta de la Baña

Note: Only coastal waypoints are shown.
Waypoints for ports and anchorages are given in the text

Islas

Baleares

467 0270
Pta Moscarte
Fl.5s93m18M
200
121

0274
I Conejera 90 San
Fl(4)20s85m18M Antonio
I Bleda Plana Abad Aero
Fl(3)15s28m10M RC
0276 Isla de
Ibiza

0278 **Ibiza**
Fl.5s11M
95 80 80
19 84 60

*Isla
Formentera*

1°E 20′

IV. Costa del Azahar

Introduction

General description

This 115M section of coast, which stretches from a point just to the N of Cabo de San Antonio to a few miles to the S of the Río Ebro, is called the Costa del Azahar (Orange Blossom Coast) because of the huge areas of orange groves which stretched along the coast of Valencia. Sections of this coast have since been industrialised and both sea and air pollution are such that it might easily be called the Costa Negra (Black Coast) in places! Where industry does not exist the coast is pleasant and to a large extent unspoilt even by tourist development though construction of large apartment blocks continues apace.

From the high cliffs and mountains immediately to the N of Cabo San Antonio, of which Montaña Mongó is a conspicuous feature, the coast becomes low and flat. This whole section of coast has, in general, straight sandy beaches, sometimes with low cliffs or sand dunes behind them and with mountain ranges some distance inland. The only exceptions are near Cabos Cullera, Oropesa and Irta where there are mountainous features on the coast. A number of rivers flow into the sea, most of which do not dry out in summer. The Arabs brought prosperity to the area by building and organising the irrigation system and introducing the orange and lemon trees which they planted in huge orchards but it is perhaps due to the lack of natural harbours the larger towns are of comparatively recent origin.

Visits

Details of interesting places to visit are given in the section dealing with the harbour concerned. There are large numbers of caves, some of which were occupied by prehistoric man, located in the hills which lie inland of the S section of this coast.

The old town of Sagunto is an exceptional place and it should be visited even if not going to the harbour itself; it can easily be reached from Valencia. Onda, where the famous blue *azulejas* tiles are made, also has a ruined castle which can be visited. It lies inland from Castellón de la Plana. For those who like walking, the Monasterio del Desierto de las Palmas which lies behind Benicasim should be visited. Inland from Vinaroz lies the exceptional town of Morella which has remains of Iberian, Celtic, Greek, Carthaginian, Roman and Arab civilisations.

Many other places of interest lie further inland and can be visited by taxi, bus and some by train. Details are best obtained from the local tourist office.

Gales – harbours of refuge

Gales are rare and hardly ever occur in summer. The *levante* from the E, preceded by heavy swell and rain, is possibly the worst. In the event of onshore winds and heavy seas, Valencia, Sagunto and Castellón de la Plana are the safest to enter.

Planning guide

Distance (Miles)

Magnetic variation

1°10'W (2008) decreasing 6' annually.

IV. COSTA DEL AZAHAR
i. Cabo de la Nao to Islotes Columbretes

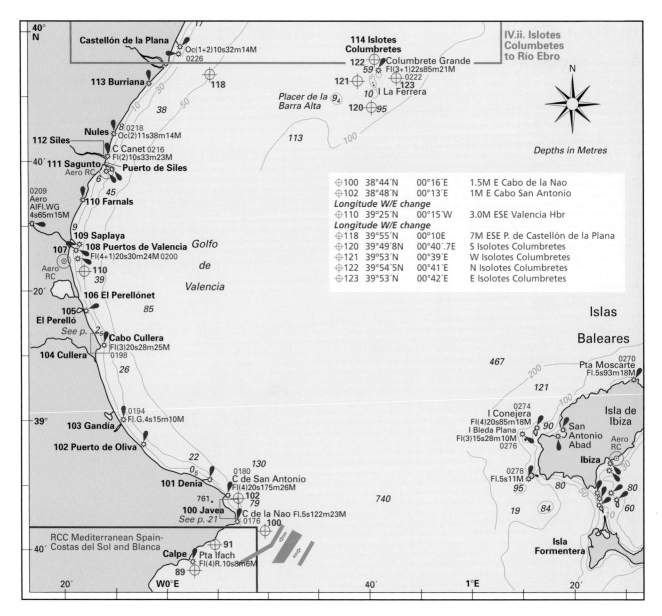

⊕100	38°44′N	00°16′E	1.5M E Cabo de la Nao
⊕102	38°48′N	00°13′E	1M E Cabo San Antonio
Longitude W/E change			
⊕110	39°25′N	00°15′W	3.0M ESE Valencia Hbr
Longitude W/E change			
⊕118	39°55′N	00°10E	7M ESE P. de Castellón de la Plana
⊕120	39°49′8N	00°40′.7E	S Islotes Columbretes
⊕121	39°53′N	00°39′E	W Isolotes Columbretes
⊕122	39°54′5N	00°41′E	N Isolotes Columbretes
⊕123	39°53′N	00°42′E	E Isolotes Columbretes

PORTS OF COSTA AZAHAR BETWEEN CAP DE LA NAO AND ISLOTES COLUMBRETES

100 Puerto de Jávea
101 Puerto de Denia
102 Puerto de Oliva
103 Puerto de Gandía
104 Cullera
105 Puerto El Perelló
106 Puerto El Perellónet
107 Valencia Yacht harbour
108 Valencia Darsena interior and Admirals Cup marina

109 Puerto Saplaya (Puerto de Alboraya)
110 Pobla Marina (Puerto de Farnals)
111 Puerto de Sagunto
112 Puerto de Siles (Canet de Berenguer)
113 Puerto de Burriana
114 Islotes Columbretes

IV. i. COSTA DEL AZAHAR

Cabo de la Nao looking W

Isla Columbretes looking SW

Anchorages between Cap de la Nao and Jávea

⚓ **PUNTA NEGRA** 38°45'·2N 00°13'·6E

The anchorage is to the south of the point off Playa de Portichol.

⚓ **ISLA DEL PORTICHOL** 38°45'·4N 00°13'·9E

⚓ **CABO DE SAN MARTIN** 38°45'·8N 00°13'·5E

⚓ **CALA SARDINERA** 38°45'·7N 00°13'E

⚓ **CALA CALCE** 38°46'N 00°12'·5E

A very small cove offering anchorage for small craft in stone 1·5m. Open between N and NE.

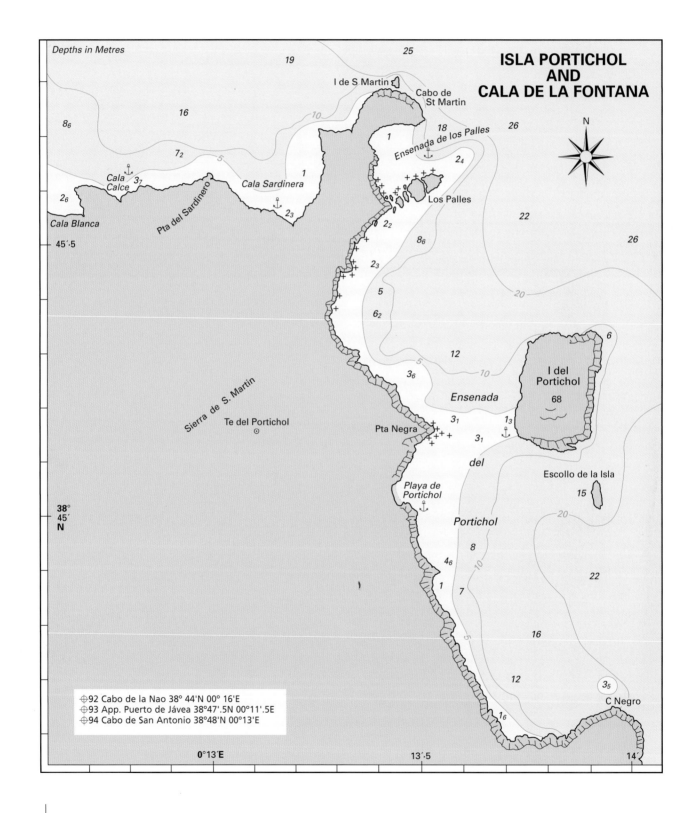

Cabo Negro from the NE

Isla del Portichol from the SE

Cabo de San Martin and Cala Sardinera from NE

⚓ **CALA DE LA FONTANA** 38°46´·4N 00°11´·5W

A suburb of Jávea. Open between NE and E. The bay is silting up.

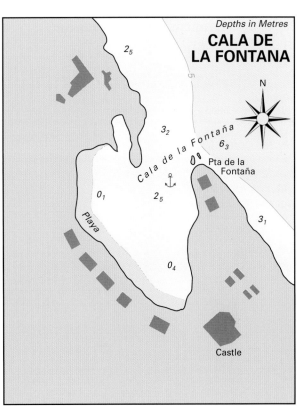

Cala de la Fontaña

IV. i. COSTA DEL AZAHAR

100. Puerto de Jávea

38°48´.9N 00°11´.2E

Charts

British Admiralty *1700, 1701.* Imray *M12*
French *7296, 4719.* Spanish *474, 4741*

⊕101 38°47´.5N 00°11´.5E 300°/0·3M to harbour

Lights

To the southeast
0176 **Cabo de la Nao** Fl.5s122m23M White octagonal
    tower and house 20m 049°-vis-190°
Harbour
0179 **Dique head** Fl.G.3s11m5M Green octagonal tower
    6m
0179.4 Contradique head Fl(2)R.6s9m4M Red tower 6m
To the northeast
0180 **Cabo de San Antonio** Fl(4)20s175m26M White
    tower and building 17m

Port communications

Club Nautico de Javea VHF Ch9 ☎ 96579 10 25
Fax 965 79 60 08 *Email* info@cnjavea.net
www.cnjavea.net

Warning

A traffic Control Zone lies 5M off Cabo de la Nao to the
S and is relevant to yachts heading to/from the Baleares.

Pleasant but crowded harbour

A pleasant yachting and fishing harbour, in
attractive surroundings and very full in summer.
Approach and entrance are easy, and there is
protection from all winds except SE to S.

There are many caves in the area, some of which
can only be visited by boat. The Gothic church at
Jávea and the modern boat-shaped church near the
harbour are both worth visiting. The view from the
top of Cabo de San Antonio is good. There is a fine
sandy beach about a mile south of the marina and a
small pebbly one at the root of the Muelle de
Levante.

Approach

From the SE Round Cabo de San Martin which has
several off-lying islets and, sometimes, tunny nets.
The wide Ensenada de Jávea then opens up. The
town stretches south and harbour is in the NW
corner under the steep-sided mountain with
abandoned windmills on the skyline.

From the NW Round Cabo de San Antonio which is
a high, steep-sided, flat-topped promontory with a
conspicuous lighthouse and signal station; follow
round onto a SW course and the harbour wall will
be seen in the closer approach.

From all directions the high pyramid-shaped
Montaña Mongo, which stands to the W of the
harbour, is very conspicuous.

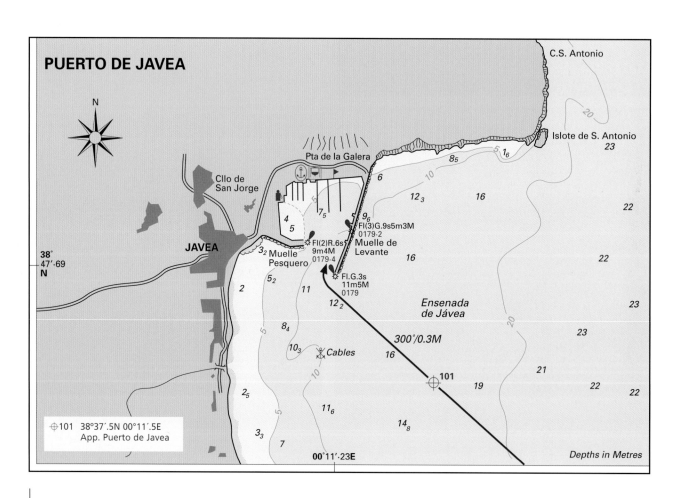

Puerto de Jávea

Anchorage in the approach

Anchoring is prohibited S of the harbour; *see plan*.

Entrance

The breakwaters have stone feet and should be given a good 10m berth.

Berths

Berth stern-to the yacht club quay on the N side of harbour with anchor and trip-line from the bow or in a similar manner to a pontoon using the pick-up buoys. An alternative berth is sometimes available on the inner side of the *dique*, secured stern-to. There are underwater projecting rocky foundations to the *dique*: the three short spurs are in constant use.

Charges

High.

Facilities

Maximum length overall: 22m.
Limited hull and engine repairs.
Slipway to the W side of the yacht club.
65-tonne travel-lift and 6-tonne crane.
Water from a hose at the yacht club.
220v AC points at the yacht club.
Ice from the yacht club.
Gasoleo B only.
Club Náutico de Jávea with bar, restaurant, cabins, showers, swimming pool, etc.

Small shops and supermarket near the harbour, large supermarket, most shops, launderette and the market itself are in the town, about a mile away.

Communications

Buses and railway in town. ☎ Area code 96.
Taxis ☎ 579 32 24.

Cabo de San Antonio to the E of Jávea – from the S

101. Puerto de Dénia

38°50'·88N 00°07'·53E

Charts

British Admiralty *1515, 1700, 1701*. Imray *M12*
French *7296, 4719*. Spanish *474, 4741*

⊕103 38°50'·95N 00°07'·68E 228°/0·75M to harbour

Lights

To the southeast
0180 **Cabo de San Antonio** Fl(4)20s175m26M White
   tower and building 17m
Harbour
0184 **Dique Norte head** Fl(3)G.11s13m5M Green tower
   7m
0185 **Dique Sur head** Fl(4)R.11s9m3M Red tower 7m
0186 Dir. Light 229° DFl.RWG.2·5s10m6/7/6M White
   column, black bands 9m 227°-G-228·5°-W-229·5°-
   R-231°
To the northwest
0198 **Cabo Cullera** Fl(3)20s28m25M White tower on
   house 16m
Note that between 0188 and 0188·5 there is a line of
   small red cylindrical buoys which must be left to port
   on entry.

Port communications

VHF Ch 9. Club náutico ☎ 965 78 09 89 *Fax* 965 78 08 50
Email info@cndenia.es www.cndenia.es
VHF Ch 9. Marina de Dénia ☎ 966 42 43 07
Fax 966 42 43 87
Email mar@marinadedenia.com
www.marinadedenia.com

Commercial harbour with good marina facilities

A fishing, ferry and commercial harbour occupied
by all invaders from the Greeks (600 BC) onwards;
the latest are the tourists. Repair and other facilities
are good. The old town, castle and the surrounding
area are attractive. Sandy beaches on either side of
the harbour, those to the N being best.

The port can still be crowded in high season and
a major expansion is currently being considered for
a massive project to make Dénia one of the largest
pleasure harbours in Europe. The marina is now
fully operational with bars, restaurants, shops etc.
which reduces the need to go on the long walk into
the town.

Approach

From the SE Round the high, steep-sided, flat-
topped promontory of Cabo de San Antonio and
follow the coast keeping a mile offshore to avoid
shoals. In the closer approach, Castillo de Dénia will
be seen on a small hill behind the harbour and the
Dique del Norte. Do not cut the corner but make for
a position 200m to NE of the head of this *dique*.

From the NW The low sandy coast is backed by high
ranges of mountains. Montaña Mongo which lies
behind this harbour, and the vertically faced Cabo de
San Antonio which lies beyond it can be seen from
afar. In the closer approach the Castillo de Dénia on
its small hill and the long Dique del Norte will be
seen. Keep at least 1M off the coast owing to shoals
and make for a position 200m to NE of the head of
Dique del Norte.

The head of the Dique del Norte has been washed
away and underwater obstructions may still remain
up to 100m to NE of the present visible head.

Anchorage in the approach

Anchor 300m to the E of the head of Dique del
Norte in 7m sand.

Entrance

From at least 200m to NE, approach the entrance on
a SW course, give the head of Dique del Norte 30m
and follow it in at this distance off.

Note the leading lines have been replaced with a
single directional tri-colour light on the front
platform if entering at night.

Berths

There are three marinas in the harbour. The
Municipal Marina, at the NW end, is for small craft
(<7m) only and it is for private berth holders only.
The yacht club is still available for visiting yachts
(call *Real Club Náutico* on Ch 9) but is expensive.
There is a fairly new, and welcoming, marina
immediately to port on entering (call *Marina de
Dénia* on Ch 9 or phone) which has 400 berths and
although further away from the town most stores
are now available on site.

Charges

Medium; at the *club náutico*, high.

Facilities

All ship work bar radar.
Two slipways, maximum 100 tonnes.
Cranes up to 12 tonnes. 70-tonne travel lift.
Chandler's shop behind the shipyard.
Water from taps around the yacht harbour and on the
   Muelle de Atraque.
Gasoleo A and petrol in the port and, for members only,
   the *club náutico*.
Ice factory to the E of the Castillo de Dénia. Ice is also
   available from the yacht club.
The Real Club Náutico de Dénia has a large modern
   clubhouse with bar, lounge, restaurant, showers and so
   on. It is responsible for the S corner of the harbour. An
   introduction may be required.
A good range of shops in the town and an excellent
   market.
Launderettes in the town.

Communications

Bus service. Dénia is one terminus of the coastal narrow
gauge rail system. Ferries to Islas Baleares (new terminal
2008).
☎ Area code 96. Taxi ☎ 578 34 98.

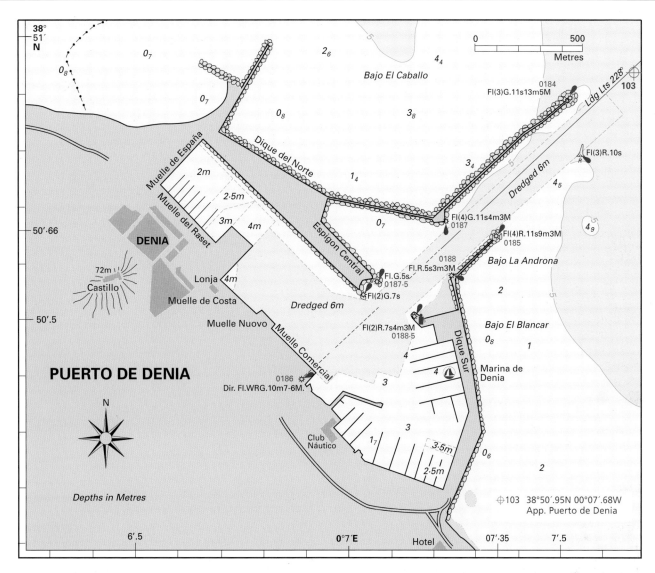

Puerto de Dénia looking N

⚓ **CALA DEL ALMADRABA** 35°52′N 00°02′E

Cala del Almadraba. Anchor off the beach in 3m. Open between NW and E - use only when the wind is off shore

102. Puerto de Oliva

38°55′·98N 0°05′·54W

Charts

British Admiralty *1701*. Imray *M13*
French *4719*
Spanish *834*

⊕104 38°55′·97N 00°05′·4W. Then 280°/0·09M to harbour

Lights

0190 **Dique de Abrigo** 38°56′·1N 0°05′·4W Fl(2)G.5s7m4M
   White tower, green top 4m
0190·2 **Contradique** Fl(3)R.12s7m4M White tower, red
   top 4m

Port communications

Capitanía VHF Ch 9 ☎ 962 850 596 *Fax* 962 839 000.
Club náutico ☎ 962 853 423 for bookings.
Fax 962 85 8612 *Email* info@clubnauticoliva.com
www.clubnauticoliva.com

Warning

Harbour is subject to silting; small buoys may be placed
   in the entrance channel to assist pilotage.

Modern yacht harbour. Beware shoals

This is a modern artificial yacht harbour that has been built out from the coast between Denia (12M) and Gandia (5M) and is not overlooked by high-rise buildings. The harbour and entrance have to be dredged of silt dumped in flash floods from the small river which flows at the head of the harbour. Undredged, the natural level seems to be about 1m only. Long sandy beaches on each side of the harbour.

Approach

It is most important to sound carefully and go slowly when entering, leaving or manoeuvring inside this harbour. In bad weather the area of the Algar de la Almadraba 7M to SE should be avoided because of heavy seas.

From the south Round the high, steep-to Cabo San Antonio which is backed by Montaña Mongó (753m). Pass the breakwaters of the Puerto de Denia and keep 4M off the coast to avoid rough seas over the shallow area, Algar de la Almadraba. The breakwaters and conspicuous *club náutico* of this harbour will be seen in the close approach.

From the north Round Cabo Cullera which is conspicuous and looks like an island in the distance. Follow the coast at 2M passing the breakwaters of the Puerto de Gandia which, with its cranes, and harbour-works, will easily be recognised. The breakwaters and *club náutico* of this harbour are also conspicuous in the close approach from this direction.

Anchorage in the approach
Anchor 200m to NE of the entrance in 10m, sand.

Entrance
Approach the entrance on a SW course. Round the head of the Dique de Abrigo leaving it 15m to starboard.

Berths
Secure to a vacant berth beside the *club náutico* and ask at the office for a visitor's berth.

Charges
High.

Facilities
Maximum length overall 12m.
Small slipway to SE of the *club náutico* and another at NW corner of the harbour.
5-tonne crane at NW end of the harbour. 30-tonne travel lift.
Water taps on pontoons and quays.
220v AC sockets on pontoons and quays.
Gasoleo A.
Small ice from *club náutico* bar.
Club Náutico de Oliva has bars, lounges, terrace, swimming pool, showers/WC etc.
Basic provisions from shops nearby; more shops in the town of Oliva 1½M inland.

Communications
Bus and rail service from Oliva.

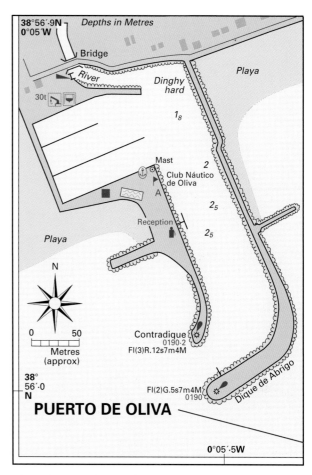

⊕104 38°55′97N 00°05′4W App. Puerto de Oliva

Puerto de Oliva

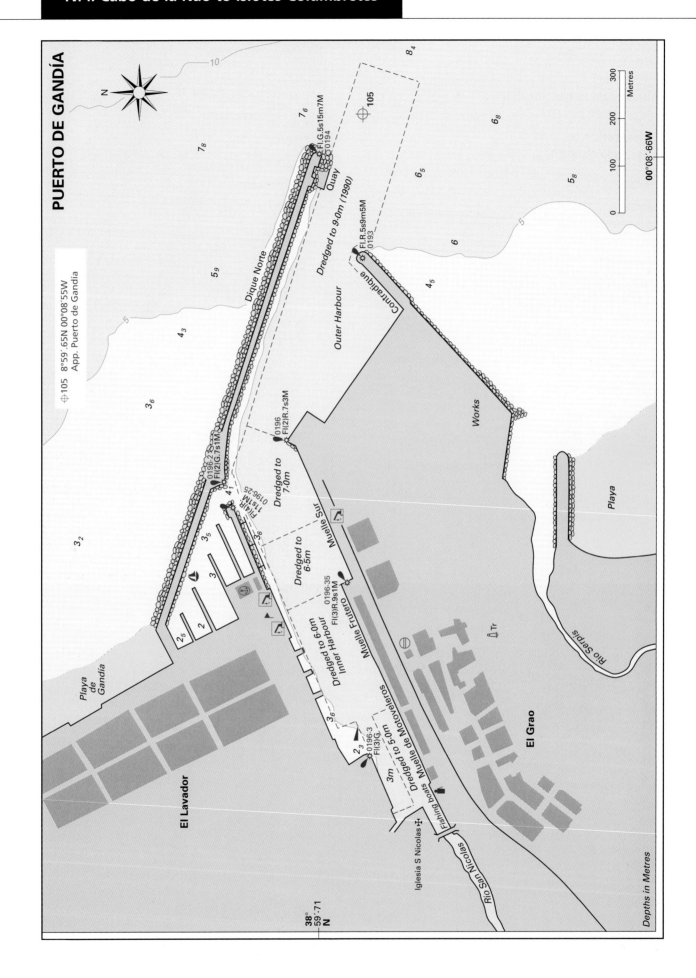

PUERTO DE GANDÍA

⊕105   8°59'·65N 00°08'55W
App. Puerto de Gandia

N

38°
59'·71
N

10

7·8

7·6

8·4

⊕ 105

6·8

6·5

5·8

300

200

100

0

Metres

00°·08'·66W

Dredged to 9·0m (1990)

Quay

Fl.G.5s15m7M
0194

Fl.R.5s9m5M
0193

Outer Harbour

Contradique

Dique Norte

5·9

5

4·3

4·5

6

5

3·6

0196·2
Fl(2)G.7s1M

0196
Fl(2)R.7s3M

Dredged to
7·0m

Works

Playa

Río Serpis

3·2

4·1

Fl(4)R.
11s1M
0196·25

3·5

3·6

3

Dredged to
6·5m

Muelle Sur

2·5   2

3·6

Dredged to 6·0m
Inner Harbour

0196·35
Fl(3)R.9s1M

Tr

Muelle Frutero

3·6

0196·3
Fl(3)G.

2·3

Dredged to 5·0m
Muelle de Motoveleros

3m

Fishing boats

Iglesia S Nicolas ⌖

Río San Nicolas

El Lavador

Playa
de
Gandía

El Grao

Depths in Metres

103. Puerto de Gandía

39°00'N 0°09'W

Charts

British Admiralty *1515, 1701*. Imray *M13*
French *7296, 4719*
Spanish 475, *4752*

⊕105 8°59'·65N 00°08'·55W

Lights

0194 **Dique Norte head** Fl.G.5s15m7M Green triangular
   tower 12m
0193 **Contradique head** Fl.R.5s9m3M Red triangular
   tower 7m
0196 **Muelle Sur head** Fl(2)R.7s5m3M Red column 3m

Port communications

VHF Ch 9. Real Club Náutico de Gandía
☎/*Fax* 962 841 050 *Email* rcgn@rcgandia.com
www.rcgandia.com

A mainly commercial port

A commercial and fishing port with a large ship-breaking yard. It is easy to approach and enter and offers good protection except in gales from SE. The self-contained, and welcoming, yacht harbour is on the N side of the harbour.

In 1485 the Dukedom of the Borgia was founded nearby by the ancestors of the famous Italian family. The harbour is known for the large amount of oranges it exports.

The Palace of the Dukes of Gandía, the Collegiate Church, the Castillo de Bayrén, Cova de Parpalló and, a little distance away the monastery of San Jerónimo de Cotalba, are all worth visiting. There is a long sandy beach to N of the harbour. Local holidays are: St Francis Borgia, 9–10 October and St Joseph, 19 March.

Approach

From the south The coast from Cabo San Antonio (167m, which has a vertical cliff-face and is backed by Montaña Mongó, 753m) becomes low and sandy with ranges of hills in the hinterland. Pass the long breakwater of Puerto de Denia and keep an eye on depths and the chart if you close the shore. A high peak, Montaña Monduber (841m), will be seen to the W of this port, which will be recognised by the houses, cranes and the *diques*.

From the north Having rounded the conspicuous Cabo Cullera, which has the appearance of an offshore island when viewed from afar, the coast becomes low, flat and sandy. Gandia may be seen standing isolated in a flat plain at the foot of a valley, the blocks of flats being conspicuous from this direction. Keep clear of a fish farm some 2 miles north of the breakwater which has 4 buoys Fl(3)Y.9s3M with cross topmarks.

Anchorage in the approach

Anchor 500m to SW of the head of Dique Norte in 7m sand. Sound carefully in the approach due to silting.

Entrance

To the S of the entrance the Río Serpis deposits silt and depths decrease steadily. The harbour is periodically dredged but sound carefully when entering.

Approach Dique Norte on a W course, leaving the Dique Norte 50m to starboard. The narrow entrance is reduced by rod-fishermen operating from the *dique*. Follow Dique Norte at this distance and pass Dique Sur. The yacht harbour entrance lies ahead between two lit pier heads just beyond a building on the Dique Norte. Entering involves an S-bend, first to starboard then to port.

Puerto de Gandía

IV. i. COSTA DEL AZAHAR

Berths

Ask at the *club náutico*.

Anchorages

Anchoring in the outer harbour is forbidden.

Charges

High.

Facilities

Maximum length overall 25m.
70-tonne travel-lift.
10-tonne crane at the *club náutico*. More powerful cranes are available at the Muelle Comercial. Contact *capitán de puerto*.
A small slipway on the N side of the harbour.
Engine repairs, GRP, painting, joinery in the port.
Two small chandlers near the harbour and two others in the town of Gandia.
Water from taps on the quay and pontoons by the *club náutico* and on the Muelle Comercial and pontoons. Check with notices to see if it is considered to be drinkable.
220v AC on pontoons.
Gasoleo A by the yacht club.
Ice from a factory at the N end of the bridge over the Río San Nicolás.
Club Náutico de Gandia has several bars, lounges, terraces, a restaurant, snack bar, showers, swimming pool, etc.
A few shops near the *club náutico*, some more to the W and S of the harbour and very many in the town of Gandia where there is a daily market.
Laundry and launderettes in the town of Gandia.

Communications

Rail and bus services. Taxi ☎ 284 30 30.

⚓ **EL BROQUIL** 39°07'.5N 00°13'.7W

El Broquil. A river accessible by small boats in calm weather without swell. 1-1·5m in the canal which silts. No facilities.

104. Puerto de Cullera

39°09'·07N 0°14'·0W

Charts

British Admiralty *1701*. Imray *M13*
French *4719*
Spanish *834*

⊕107 39°09'·05N 00°13'·9W. 280°/0·8M to harbour

Lights

0197·2 **Malecón Sur near head** Fl(2)R.5s10m3M Red round tower on square base 7m
0197 **Malecón Norte head** Fl.G.3s10m5M Green round tower on square base 7m
Note 0197 light is about 20m from head of breakwater and 0197.2 is 40m from the south head.
To the north
0198 **Cabo Cullera** 39°11'·1N 0°13'·0W Fl(3)20s28m25M White conical tower 16m
Beacon
A black post with a black ▲ topmark (5·5m) on the rock Escollo del Moro (0·7m) marks a shallow patch of rocks which is located ¼M to NNE of the entrance.

Port communications

VHF Ch 9. Club Náutico de Cullera ☎ 961 721 154
Fax 961 721 778 *Email* cncullera@cncullera.com
www.cncullera.com

A river harbour

This harbour lies about 1M up the Río Júcar. The approach is easy but the entrance into the river mouth can only be undertaken in good conditions and is not possible with winds between NE and SE. It is reported that depth in the river is maintained at a minimum of 2·0m. There is very good shelter once inside, alongside an attractive old town which has many shops and good communications. A huge development consisting of high apartment blocks has been built around the hills to NE of the town to cater for the thousands of holiday-makers. The remains of an old castle and the Ermita de la Virgen del Castillo on the hill nearby, with a fine view, should be visited. The fine sandy beaches on either side of the Sierra de Cullera are very crowded in the high season. The Saturday following Easter is a holiday in honour of Nuestra Señora del Castillo. In July and August there is a regatta.

The site has been occupied since the fourth century BC and there are ruins of a city wall dating from this period. Like several places with an isolated mountain and marshy land around, it claims to be the site of Hemeroskopeion, the first Phoenician town in Spain.

Approach

From the south The low, flat, sandy coast is backed by mountain ranges which recede from the coast as one proceeds to the N. The isolated feature, the Sierra de Cullera (222m) which is surrounded by flat lands, appears as an offshore island in the distance.

In the closer approach the town of Cullera will be seen at the SW foot of this feature. The entrance to the river has two low rocky training walls with some coastal buildings and apartment blocks nearby and

IV. i. COSTA DEL AZAHAR

Río Júcar

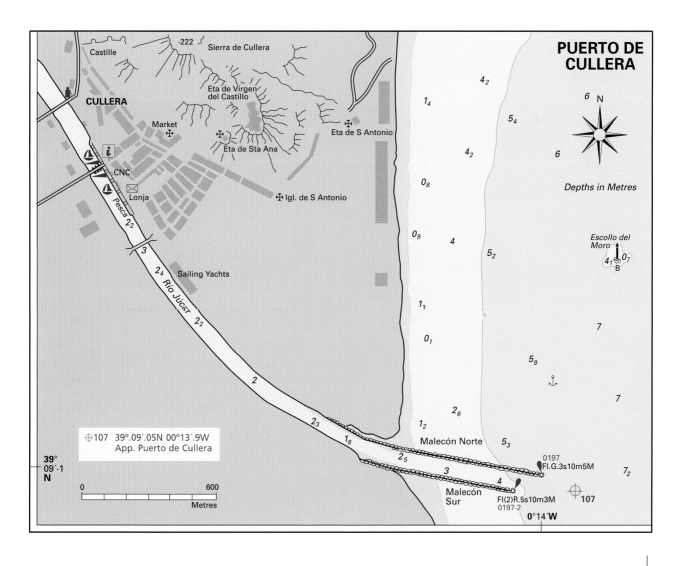

Castille

.222

Sierra de Cullera

CULLERA

Eta de Virgen del Castillo

Market

Eta de Sta Ana

Eta de S Antonio

CNC

Lonja

Igl. de S Antonio

Pesca

2_2

3

2_4 Sailing Yachts

Río Júcar

2_2

2

2_3

1_8

2_5

3

4

Malecón Sur

4_2

1_4

5_4

4_2

0_8

0_9 4

5_2

1_3

0_1

5_9

2_6

1_2

Malecón Norte 5_3

PUERTO DE CULLERA

6 N

6

Depths in Metres

Escollo del Moro

4_1 0_7
B

7

7

7

0197
Fl.G.3s10m5M

7_2

Fl(2)R.5s10m3M
0197-2

107

⊕107 39°.09′.05N 00°13′.9W
App. Puerto de Cullera

**39°
09′·1
N**

0   600

Metres

0°14′W

an isolated factory chimney which should be approached on a bearing of 280°.

From the north Having passed the very conspicuous harbour walls of Valencia the countryside is low and flat and the coast sandy. There are a number of high-rise buildings in groups along the coast and more under construction. Again the Sierra de Cullera appears as an offshore island in the distance. Round the steep-cliffed Cabo Cullera which has a conspicuous lighthouse and is steep-to, keeping on a S course and changing to SW after 1½M to avoid the Escollo del Moro (0·7m) marked by a black beacon with a ▲ topmark (5·5m). In the closer approach the rocky training walls should be seen.

Anchorage in the approach

Anchor 400m to NE of the entrance in 7m, sand and mud.

Entrance

Line up the two rocky training walls, approach on 280° and enter between. The depths in the river vary with the amount of water flowing and the silt deposited. Anchorage in the river is forbidden.

Berths

Note A new road bridge has been built downstream of the Lonja with a marked air draft of 10m.

Berth alongside the quay on the starboard hand with bow upriver just inside the entrance or just short of the lower road bridge and check with the Club Náutico de Cullera. Yachts without masts may prefer to secure further up channel. If all berths are taken secure outside a suitable yacht.

Charges

Low.

Facilities

A small shipyard above the road bridge can carry out simple repairs. There are several engine mechanics.

15-tonne crane below the lower bridge.

A small slipway by the lower road bridge and another above it, both on the NE bank.

Limited chandlery from the shipyard and from a shop near the *club náutico*.

Taps on pontoons and quays also a water point above the lower road bridge and also near the mouth of the river. Water on quay by the *club náutico* is not drinkable.

220v AC points below the lower road bridge.

Gasoleo A and petrol from garage 300m beyond the upper road bridge on the way to Valencia.

The Club Náutico de Cullera is on the NE bank below the lower road bridge.

A number of shops nearby and a large market.

Launderette in the town.

Puerto de Cullera

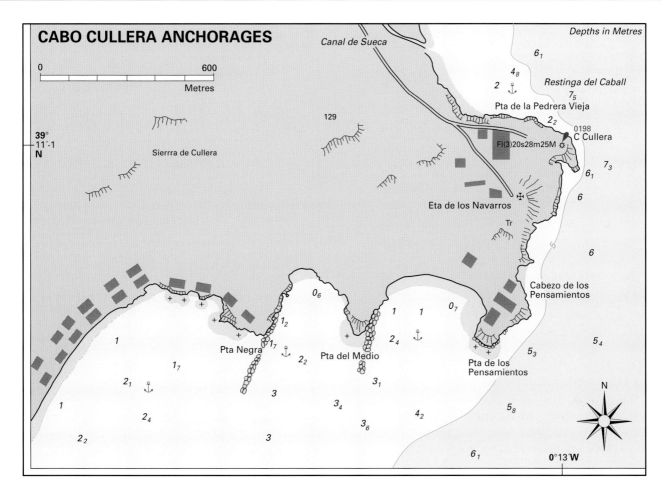

CABO CULLERA ANCHORAGES

Depths in Metres

0   600

Metres

Canal de Sueca

6_1

4_8

2 ⚓

Restinga del Caball

7_5

Pta de la Pedrera Vieja

129

2_2

0198

C Cullera

39°
11'·1
N

Sierrra de Cullera

Fl(3)20s28m25M ☀

7_3

6_1

6

Eta de los Navarros

Tr

6

Cabezo de los Pensamientos

0_6

1   1

0_7

1_2

Pta Negra 1_7 ⚓ 2_2

Pta del Medio

2_4 ⚓

Pta de los Pensamientos

5_4

5_3

1_7

2_1 ⚓

3

3_4

3_1

4_2

5_8

N

2_4

3_6

1

2_2

3

6_1

0°13'W

⚓ **S OF CABO CULLERA** 39°10'·7N 0°13'·3W

⚓ **N OF CABO CULLERA** 39°11'·3N 0°13'·1W

A rather exposed anchorage open to NE with swell from NW and SE. Anchor close inshore under the protection of Punta la Pedrera Vieja in 4m sand but sound carefully because the depths can change after strong winds. The road to the conspicuous lighthouse also leads to Cullera (2½M) There are a few shops in the area to S of Cabo Cullera (½M). Good sandy beaches nearby.

⚓ **CABO CULLERA**

Looking NW. The rather exposed anchorages on one or other side are usually in a lee but swell from both NE and SE can reach round to the other side of the point.

South of Cabo Cullera. A spacious anchorage in sand S of the range of hills which culminates at Cabo Cullera. It is open to SE with swell from NE but is otherwise well protected

IV. i. COSTA DEL AZAHAR

105. Puerto El Perelló

39°17'N 0°16'W

Charts

British Admiralty *1701*. Imray *M13*
French 4719
Spanish 476, 834

⊕108 39°16'·65N 00°16'W. Steer 275°/0·27M to harbour entrance

Lights

To the south
0198 **Cabo Cullera** 39°11'·1N 0°13'·0W Fl(3)20s28m25M
    White conical tower 16m
Harbour
0199 **Dique de Levante head** Fl(3)G.15s8m4M Green tower 3m
0199·2 **Dique de Poniente head** Fl(3)R.11s7m4M Red tower 5m

Port communications

VHF Ch 9. Club Náutico El Perelló ☎ 961 770 386
    Fax 961 770 412 *Email* info@cnelperello.com
    www.cnelperello.com

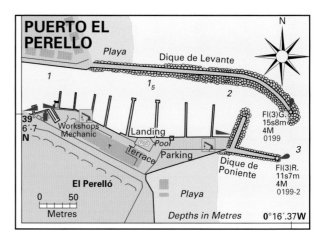

⊕108 39°16'.65N 00°16'W
    App. Puerto El Perelló

A large artificial harbour

This artificial harbour has been built in the mouth of the largest river which drains the huge inland lagoon, swamp and rice fields of La Albufera. Approach and entrance is not difficult with offshore winds but it is not advisable with Easterly winds. Space is limited and facilities are confined to everyday requirements.

There are large areas of rice fields inland, frequented by aquatic birds, and sandy beaches on either side of the harbour.

Approach

From the south Cabo Cullera with its lighthouse is unmistakable. The coast N of it is low and flat and has sandy beaches. High-rise apartment blocks are visible either side of this harbour and its breakwaters can be seen when close-to.

From the north Between the massive breakwaters of Puerto de Valencia and Perelló the coast is low and flat with sandy beaches. The houses at El Saler, the large Parador of Luis Vives, the Torre Nueva and some high-rise buildings near the Puerto El Perellónet may be identified. In the close approach the apartment blocks and breakwaters of El Perelló will be seen.

Anchorage in the approach

Anchor ½M to E of the harbour entrance in 10m, mud and sand.

Entrance

The entrance is narrow and shallow and silts easily. After rain the river may be in spate and a strong current will flow through the harbour. With onshore winds seas may break in the entrance. Sound carefully because depths may change with the flow of water and silting.

Approach the entrance on a SW course and leave the head of the Dique Norte 15m to starboard. Follow this *dique* round into the harbour leaving the two heads of the *contradique* 20–30m to port.

Puerto El Perelló

Berths

Secure to the first pontoon on the port-hand side in a vacant berth and ask to the *club náutico* for a berth.

Charges

Low.

Facilities

Maximum length overall 12m.
A 12·5-tonne crane near the second pontoon and a 3-tonne crane near the slipway.
10-tonne slipway to NW of the *club náutico*.
Engine repairs.
Water taps on quays and pontoons.
220v AC point on quays and pontoons.
Gasoleo A and petrol.
Small ice from the bar at the *club náutico*.
Club Náutico El Perelló has a restaurant, bar, terrace, lounge, swimming pool, shower/WC and sports room.
Shops in the village can supply everyday requirements.

Communications

Bus service along the coast and rail service from Sollana 7M inland.

Note There are plans to extend this harbour by extending the Dique de Levante and excavating around the southern jetty.

106. Puerto El Perellónet

39°19′N 0°17′W

⊕109 39°18′·6N 00°17′·2W. Steer 250°/0·24M to harbour entrance

A small craft harbour with a nasty shallow entrance

A smaller version of Puerto El Perelló and situated 2M to NW of it. Only suitable for small boats and dinghies. The entrance is dangerous with onshore winds and/or swell. Facilities are very limited.

Puerto El Perellónet

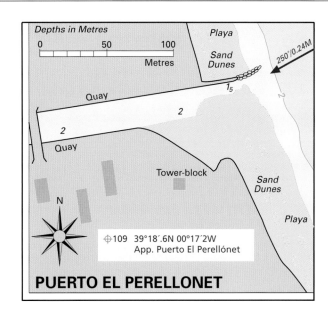

PUERTO EL PERELLONET

Approach

From the south Cabo Cullera with its lighthouse on top and surrounded by apartment blocks is easily identified. Northwards the low, flat sandy coast is broken by the Puerto El Perelló which has two breakwaters with light towers; Puerto El Perellónet is 2M N.

From the north Puerto de Valencia is easily recognised by its high, long breakwater. A group of apartment blocks and houses at El Salar may be seen as well as a large hotel, the Parador Luis Vives. The lone Torre Nueva lies 2M to NW of this harbour which can be recognised by some apartment blocks and a lone tower-block.

Anchorage in the approach

Anchor in 10m sand ½M to E of the harbour entrance.

Entrance

The mouth of this harbour is difficult to locate but the apartment blocks and a tower block indicate the area. The sandbanks at the entrance shift from time to time. Approach the entrance on a SW course. There will be a strong current in the river after heavy rain and depths may be changed by this or by strong onshore winds. Sound carefully in the approach and entrance.

Berths

Secure to port-hand side (SW) bows-to quay with anchor from stern, a trip-line is advised. If the current is strong find a vacant place to lie alongside.

Facilities

Water from café/bars.
A limited range of shops 2M to SE at El Perelló.

Puertos de Valencia

107. Yacht Harbour - RCN
108. America's Cup Marina and Darsena Interior

⊕110 39°25'N 00°15'W 3M ESE Valencia harbour

Commercial harbour 39°27'N 0°18'W
Yacht Harbour 39°25'·5N 0°19'4W
Admirals Cup Marina 39°65'N 0°18'·5W

Charts
British Admiralty *562, 518, 1701.* Imray *M13*
French *7276, 4719, 4720*
Spanish *4811, 481A, 476, 481*

⊕111 39°25'·3N 00°19'·4W. 296°/0·5M to harbour

⊕112 39°25'·82N 00°18'·2W

Lights
0200 **Lighthouse Nuevo Dique del Este North End**
  39°27'·0N 0°18'·1W Fl(4+1)20s30m24M Pyramid stone
  tower on 8-sided base 22m
0200·4 **Nuevo Dique del Este head** Fl.G.5s21m5M Green
  column 4m
0201·1 **Contradique** S Q(6)+LFl.15s17m3M S card s
0201.11 **Contradique** E elbow Fl(2)R.7s21m3M Red
  column 9m
0209 **Aeropuerto de Manises** 39°29'·6N 0°28'·2W Aero
  AlFl.WG.4s65m15M On control tower 15m Occasional
Northern Entrance
0199.9 **Dique de Abrigo head** Q.R.9m5M Red tower 3m
0199.95 **Dique de Abrigo** S elbow Q(3)10s9m3M Cardinal
  E post 3m
0199.91 **Contradique head** Q.G.6m3M Green post 3m

Port communications
Commercial: Pilots VHF call Ch 16,
  work Ch 11, 12, 14 and 20.
Real Club Náutico: VHF Ch 9 ☎ 963 679 011
  Fax 963 677 737 *Email* info@valenciayachtport.com
  www.rcnauticovalencia.com
Port America's Cup VHF 67, ☎ 963 542 162 *Fax* 963 542
  169 *Email* marina@americascup.com
  www.portamericascup.com

A large port with two yacht marinas

Valencia is the third largest city in Spain with a commercial port complex handling cargoes and ship building and breaking sections. Yachts should not enter the main harbour except in emergency. There are separate entrances for pleasure craft to the south (Real Club Náutico) of the main harbour and to the north (Americas Cup Marina).

The Real Club Náutico is clear of the noise, dirt and heavy wash experienced in the commercial harbour. A very major extension to the RCN mooring area will be completed in 2008. This harbour is a long way from the city. The northern America's Cup marina is closer to the city.

The city has had a long, complicated and turbulent history commencing with a Greek settlement followed in 139 BC by the Romans. In 75 BC it was sacked by Pompey and subsequently rebuilt as Valentía Edetanorum, a Roman colony. It fell to the Barbarian Goths in 413 AD and then to the Moors in 714. In 1012 Valencia became an independent kingdom under several kings including the famous El Cid (Rodrigo Diaz de Rivar) whose widow Ximena was driven out by the Moors; they in turn were driven out by Jaime I in 1238. It remained under the house of Arigón for the next 400 years and prospered. However, in 1808 its people rose up against the French and it suffered much damage in the ensuring wars and in the subsequent rebellions against the Spanish crown. During the Spanish Civil War it was the seat of the Republican Government of Spain. Recently developments, and the arrival of the Americas Cup races, have revitalised the city and environs.

Local holidays The Fallas de San José from 17–19 March are world famous fiestas which include masses of flowers and huge satirical statues which are burnt. There are fairs and religious processions throughout the year.

Approach
From the south The conspicuous isolated mountainous feature Sierra de Cullera is easily identified. From here the coast is straight, low, flat and sandy and is backed by the inland lake La Albufera and associated marshes. There are several groups of high-rise buildings under construction along this coast but the mass of buildings of Valencia and its industrial fog and smoke can be seen several miles off as can the high Nuevo Dique del Este.

From the north The 1700m pier extending from beside Puerto de Sagunto is conspicuous. The low sandy coast is lined with houses and inland the valleys slope to the ranges of hills further away. The high Nuevo Dique del Este is conspicuous.

Facilities at RCN
Maximum length overall 120m.
Major repairs can be undertaken in the commercial

RCN Valencia. Looking N   *Peter Taylor*

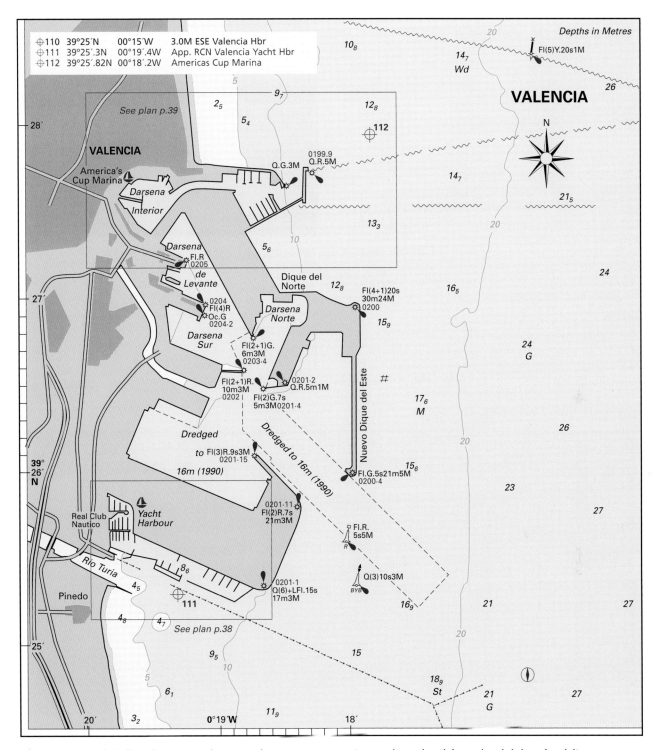

⊕110	39°25′N	00°15′W	3.0M ESE Valencia Hbr
⊕111	39°25′.3N	00°19′.4W	App. RCN Valencia Yacht Hbr
⊕112	39°25′.82N	00°18′.2W	Americas Cup Marina

harbour to both hull and engines. There are also workshops attached to the club.

Hard-standing and a small slipway beside the club náutico.

50-tonne travel-lift.

10-tonne and 3-tonne cranes near the club náutico. Cranes up to 80 tonnes in the commercial harbour.

Some chandlery at the yacht harbour; otherwise a number of shops in Avda de Puerto on the way to the city from the commercial harbour.

Water points on the quays and pontoons.

Electricity 220v AC from supply points on all yacht pontoons and quays.

Gasoleo A and petrol.

Ice can be ordered from the club bar, for delivery next day, or from the bar at SW of yacht harbour.

The Real Club Náutico de Valencia is well appointed and has a restaurant and a swimming pool. Ask at the office for use of its facilities.

A number of small provision shops just to W of the commercial port on the way to the city.

Communications

Rail and bus services. International airport some 5M away. Services by sea to the Islas Baleares and other Mediterranean ports. Taxi ☎ 963 571 313/963 479 862 or via the yacht club.

107. RCN de Valencia Yacht Harbour

⊕ 111 39°25′·3N 00°19′·4W

Yacht Harbour control VHF Ch 69
☎ 00 34 629 60 19 79 or 96 367 90 11
Email directives@rcnauticovalencia.com
www.rcnauticovalencia.com

Puerto de Valencia (yacht harbour) showing west of entrance only

Entrance to the Yacht Harbour

The Real Club Náutico yacht harbour is on the southwest side of the *contradique*; it was greatly extended in 2007. If coming from the north, give the harbour walls and main harbour entrance a good berth (commercial vessels have right of way). Follow the quay and breakwater round (towards ⊕111) and make a 90° turn north when level with the yacht harbour entrance.

Berths

The control tower is at the mole end on the east side of the entrance; visitors' reception pontoon is immediately inside the entrance to starboard. After registration visitors will normally be allocated berthing in the section immediately west of the helipad. Shops, restaurants and showers will be developed to the east of the helipad during 2008. Visitors are still welcome at the RCN and may use the facilities as usual.

Charges

High.

Facilities

See page 37.

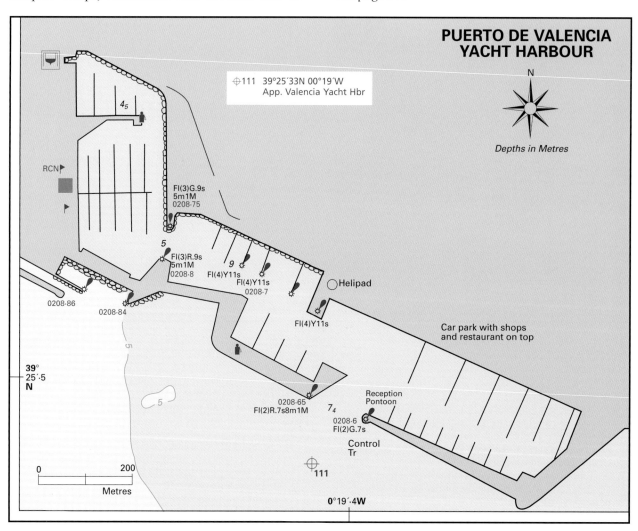

108. America's Cup marinas

⊕112   39°25'·82N 00°18'·2W

Marina Control VHF 67 – Port Americas Cup
☎ 963 542 160 *Fax* 963 542 169
Email marina@americascup.com
 www.portamericascup.com

Entrance and berthing

Approach from the NE (⊕112) and beware of large vessels exiting. The arrivals pontoon is just inside the northern quay beyond the fuel dock. Berthing will normally be in the North Marina with its shoreside facilities. Superyachts go to the main jetty in Darsena interior.

Looking down canal towards North Marina and entrance
Peter Taylor

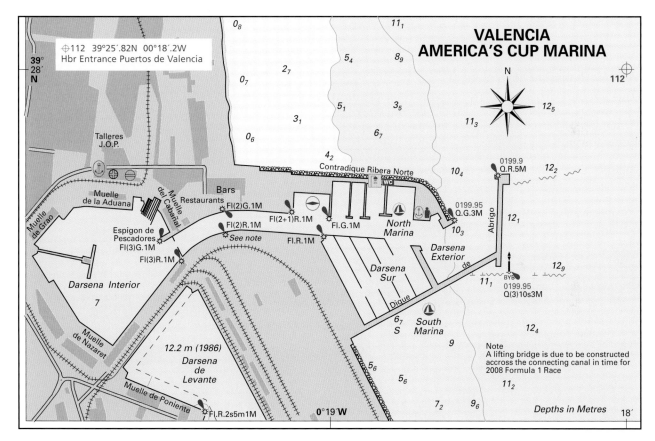

Valencia. America's Cup Harbour, inner basin *Peter Taylor*

109. Puerto Saplaya
(Puerto de Alboraya)

39°31'N 0°19'W

Charts
British Admiralty *518, 1701*. Imray *M13*
French *7276, 4719, 4720*
Spanish *4811, 481A, 476, 481, 835*

⊕113 39°30'·5N 00°18'·85W. Steer 300°/0·2M to harbour

Lights
0209·6 **Dique Sur head** Fl(4)R.12s8m4M White tower, red bands 5m
0209·7 **Dique Nordeste head** 39°30'·7N 0°19'·0W
Fl.G.4s9m4MGreen tower 5m
26190(S) **Buoy** 39°32'·8N 0°16'·9W Fl(2)10s3m3M – isolated danger

Port communications
VHF Ch 9. Club náutico ☎ 963 724848
Email cnps@xpress.es

A modern marina development

This is an artificial marina with blocks of apartments and houses lining a series of waterways. A number of berths are reserved for visitors and is probably more convenient for Valencia than the yacht harbour there. It has good protection and the usual facilities. The harbour mouth tends to silt up and has to be dredged frequently. With strong winds and swell from N through SE entry could be dangerous. Vast sandy beaches on both sides of the harbour.

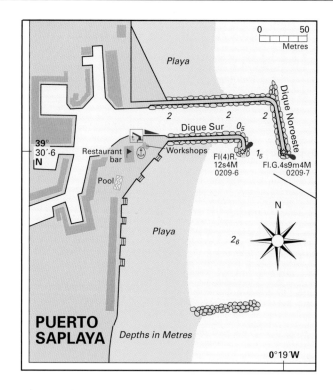

⊕113 39°30'.5N   00°18'.85W App. Puerto de Saplaya

Puerto Saplaya

Puerto Saplaya from the E

Approach

From the south Puerto Saplaya is three miles north of the huge harbour breakwaters protecting Valencia. The group of high blocks of flats located behind Puerto Saplaya will be seen from just past Valencia and, nearer in, two rocky groynes will be seen. The breakwaters at the entrance to Puerto Saplaya are low and their heads have light towers. Do not mistake the light tower of Espigón No. 1 for the entrance.

From the north Puerto de Sagunto is unmistakable due to the 1700m-long jetty extending from beside the harbour. The breakwaters and high-rise buildings of Puerto de Farnals are also very conspicuous. In the closer approach the high block of flats and the breakwaters of Puerto Saplaya are easily recognised.

Anchorage in the approach

Anchor in 7m, sand, ½M to SE of the entrance to the harbour, paying attention to the foul ground, Algar de Albuixech, lying N of the anchorage.

Entrance

Approach the harbour entrance at slow speed heading NW. Sound continuously as the entrance can silt up. Keep clear of the head of Dique Sur where there are shallows and enter leaving Dique Nordeste 15m to starboard. Follow this *dique* at 15–20m around and into the harbour.

Berths

Secure alongside quay on the port-hand side near the crane and ask at the *club náutico*. Visitors to 12m welcome.

Facilities

Maximum length overall 12m.
Two slipways near root of Dique Nordeste.
6-tonne crane near *club naútico* workshop area.
A mechanic at the workshop near the *club náutico*.
Water taps and 220v AC on the quays.
No fuel.
Small ice from the bar of the *club náutico*.
Club Náutico de Saplaya is at the root of the Dique Nordeste. It has a lounge, restaurant, bar, terrace, swimming pool etc.
Several shops and a small supermarket

Communications

Buses and rail services to Valencia and elsewhere.

Port Sapalaya. Capitania   *Peter Taylor*

110. Pobla Marina (Puerto de Farnals)

39°34'N 0°17'W

Charts

British Admiralty *518, 1701.* Imray *M13*
French *7276, 4720*
Spanish *481A, 481, 835*

⊕114 39°33'·3N 00°16'·8W. Steer 315°/0·25M to harbour

Lights

0210 **Escollera de Levante head** 39°33'·5N 0°16'·7W
Fl(3)G.12·5s9m5M Green tower 5m
0210·5 **Contradique S head** Fl.R.3·5s8m3M Red tower 5m
0210·7 **Dique Sur head** Fl(2)R.9s5m2M Red post 2m

Port communications

VHF Ch 9, 04, 27. Marina ☎ 902 500 442
Fax 961 462 587 *Email* info@poblamarina.es
www.poblamarina.es

A large marina with plans for a major extension

A 835 berth parking lot built in front of a mass of high-rise buildings on a long stretch of sandy coast. The entrance silts and would be difficult or dangerous in strong E to S winds and swell. There is no club house but the club maintains an office. Large sandy beaches on each side of the harbour.

The Monastery of St Mary at El Puig lies about 2M inland. It was founded in the 12th century and remodelled in the 18th. It has a 6th-century Byzantine statue of St Mary.

Approach

From the south The huge outer breakwaters of Puerto de Valencia are conspicuous and easily recognised. 3M further N the low breakwaters of Puerto Saplaya which is backed by large apartment buildings should be identified. The breakwaters and blocks of high-rise buildings of Puerto de Farnals can be seen in the close approach with a red latticework tower near the entrance.

From the north The coast from Castellón de la Plana is low and flat with sandy beaches. The harbours of Burriana and Sagunto will be recognised by the industrial development behind them. The steelworks at Sagunto are particularly noticeable because of the smoke. The group of high-rise apartment blocks behind the breakwater of Puerto de Farnals will be seen in the closer approach.

Anchorage in the approach

Anchor in 10m, sand, with the harbour mouth ½M to NW. Do not anchor further out because of foul ground.

Entrance

The harbour mouth is subject to silting and though frequently dredged, depths are variable. Approach the head of the Escollera de Levante at slow speed, sounding. Keep 25m from the Muelle and do not veer to port into the shallow area off the beach.

Berths

On passing the Dique Sur turn to port and moor in the waiting berth (W of the fuel berth) while sorting out a berth with the *capitanía*. Max draft is 2·7m.

Facilities

Maximum length overall 18m.
Boat yard: hull and engine repairs.
80-tonne travel-hoist.
3-tonne crane.
A large 7,000m² hard-standing for yachts.
Slipways at entrance to the harbour.
Chandlery from AZA workshop in NE corner of the harbour.
Taps on quays and pontoons but drinking water by the pumps on Dique Sur.
220v AC points on quays and pontoons.
Gasoleo A and petrol.
Shops and supermarkets behind the harbour, more in Farnals 2M inland.

Communications

Bus and rail services (the station is 2M away). Taxi ☎ 961 470 434.

⊕114 39°33'3N 00°16'.8W App. Pobla Marina

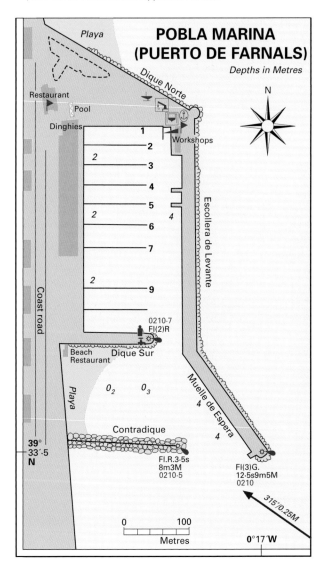

Pobla Marina from the N 2006   *Peter Taylor*

Pobla Marina   *Peter Taylor*

Pobla Marina plans   *Peter Taylor*

111. Puerto de Sagunto

39°39'N 0°12'W

Charts

British Admiralty *1515, 1701*. Imray *M13*
French *7296, 4720*
Spanish *4812, 481, 482*

⊕115 39°37'·6N 00°12'·4W

Lights

0210.75 **Dique de Abrigo head** Fl.G.5s20m5M Green & white tower 5m
0210.8 **Contradique S corner** Q(3)10s3M BYB tower
0211 **Contradique E corner** Fl.R.5s3M Red tower
0212.1 **Contradique head** Fl(2)R.7s3M Red tower
0210·8 **Contradique S corner** Q(3)10s3M Black tower, yellow band
0210·9 **Dique de Abrigo spur head** Q.G.2M Green tower
To the north
0212·6 **Pantalan Sierra Menera** Q(3)10s12m5M Card E tower 6m
0216 **Cabo Canet** 39°40'·5N 0°12'·5W Fl(2)10s33m23M Brick tower and house 30m

Port communications

VHF Ch 12, 16. *Capitanía* ☎ 963 233 272

An artificial commercial harbour

An artificial harbour built to serve an industrial and commercial complex capable of handling vessels up to 90,000 tons. There is a small section of the harbour set aside for fishing boats. Approach and entrance are easy but the harbour is open to S. It is not a place for yachtsmen to call (Siles is next-door) except possibly in an emergency. If here, however, a visit might be made to the very old town of Sagunto, 2M away, to see the many ruins and remains from the past including a castle and a Roman amphitheatre.

As of September 2004 the Escollera de Levante is being lengthened and a huge contradique has been constructed south of the old harbour. Dredging and infilling is still ongoing however and it is still recommended to keep well clear of this port until work has finished.

Approach

From the south The coast of Valencia is low, flat and sandy, lined with blocks of flats and villas. Sagunto can be spotted by the Pantalán de Sierra Menera stretching 1700m out to sea. Closer in, the entrance walls will be seen.

From the north South of Burriana, 15M up the coast and easy to miss, the coast is flat and sandy with groups and blocks of buildings. The Pantalán de Sierra Menera makes it easy to locate Sagunto but stand at least two miles offshore until it has been rounded.

Anchorage in the approach

Anchor 400m to SW of head of Escollera de Levante in 7m, sand. Depths in and adjacent to this harbour may be less than charted.

Entrance

Approach the entrance on a N course, passing between a red and a green buoy and then between the head of the Escollera de Poniente (Muelle Sur) and another G buoy.

There may be two port-hand buoys laid south of the contradique indicating the entrance channel. There may also be a line of small orange buoys laid between these two buoys and the end of the contradique.

Berths

It is usually possible to find a berth alongside or stern-to a rather dirty quay in the NE corner of the harbour in the small fishing boat harbour.

Facilities

Water points on Escollera de Levante and at the *lonja*.
There are some shops and a market in the village to the N of the harbour and a fair selection of shops in Sagunto.

Communications

Bus service to Sagunto where there is a rail service.

Puerto de Sagunto inner harbour (2004)- see plan for recent extension to Dique de Abrigo

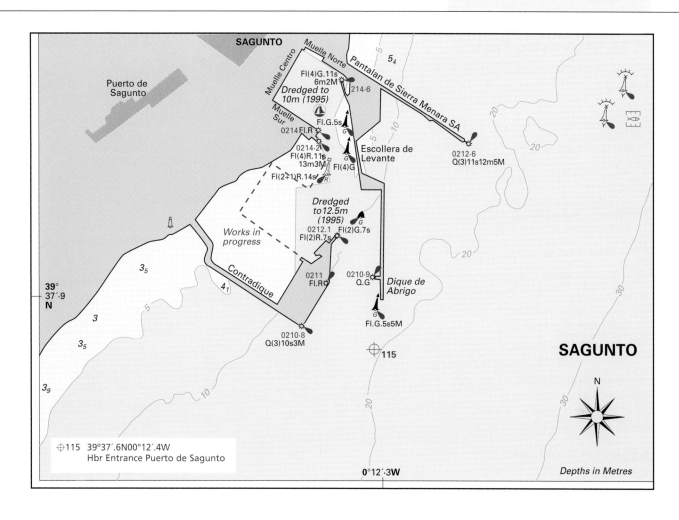

SAGUNTO

Puerto de Sagunto

Muelle Norte

Muelle Centro

Muelle Sur

Pantalan de Sierra Menara SA

Fl(4)G.11s
6m2M
214·6

Dredged to
10m (1995)

Fl.G.5s
0214 Fl.R
G
0214·2
Fl(4)R.11s
13m3M
G

Escollera de
Levante

0212·6
Q(3)11s12m5M

Fl(2+1)R.14s
R
Fl(4)G

Dredged
to12.5m
(1995)

Works in
progress

0212.1
Fl(2)R.7s

G
Fl(2)G.7s

Contradique

3₅

4₁

0211
Fl.R

0210·9
Q.G

Dique de
Abrigo

39°
37´·9
N

3

5

10

G
Fl.G.5s5M

3₅

3₅

0210·8
Q(3)10s3M

20

115

SAGUNTO

N

3₉

10

20

30

30

⊕115 39°37´.6N00°12´.4W
Hbr Entrance Puerto de Sagunto

0°12´·3W

Depths in Metres

Puerto de Sagunto. Typical port dredger *Robin Rundle*

112. Puerto de Siles (Canet de Berenguer)

39°40′N 0°12′W

Charts

British Admiralty *1701*. Imray *M13*
French *4720*
Spanish *4812, 481, 482*

⊕116 39°40′·25N 00°11′·9W. Steer 300°/0·15M to harbour

Lights

Approach
0216 **Cabo Canet** 39°40′·5N 0°12′·4W Fl(2)10s33m23M
Brick tower with house 30m
Harbour
0217 **Dique de Levante head** Fl.G.4s7m6M Green tower
on white base 3m
0217.5 **Contradique** Fl(2)R.5s4m3M Red tower on white
base 2m
To the north
0218 **Nules** 39°49′·5N 0°06′·5W Oc(2)11s38m14M Brown
square masonry tower 36m
Air radiobeacon
Sagunto/Cabo Canet c/s SGO (···/—·/———) 356kHz 50M
39°40′·52N 0°12′·4W

Port communications

VHF Ch 9. ☎/*Fax* 962 60 81 32.
Club Marítimo de Regates de Sagunto ☎ 962 608 132
Fax 963 624 900.

Subject to silt and swell

An artificial harbour which may make a good
alternative to the Puerto de Sagunto. Disadvantages
are that shallows make the entrance dangerous in
strong winds or swell from N-NE and the outer
berths are subject to swell in winds between E and S.
The Río Palencia debouches across the harbour
entrance and, like other harbours on this coast, it
silts up and is dredged periodically. There are sandy
beaches to N and S of the harbour.

The old town of Sagunto is worth visiting to see
the old walls, castle and arena. The original town
was Iberian, later Greek and then Roman. It put up
a famous nine months' defence against Hannibal
and his Carthaginian armies. When Rome
abandoned them to their fate the citizens built a
huge fire and the women, children, sick and old
threw themselves into it. The able-bodied men went
off to die in the last battle. The result was the
complete destruction of the town and its
fortifications so that five years later, when the
Romans re-occupied it, they called it Muri Veteres,
later corrupted to Murviedro, meaning literally Old
Walls. The Romans under Scipio Africanus the Elder
and later the Moors who called it Murbiter did a lot
of rebuilding, making use of the old stones. Traces of
these various occupations are to be found
everywhere despite further destruction during the
French occupation and then during the Spanish Civil
War.

Approach

From the south The harbour walls at Puerto de
Sagunto, 1 mile to the south of Siles, and the 1·5M

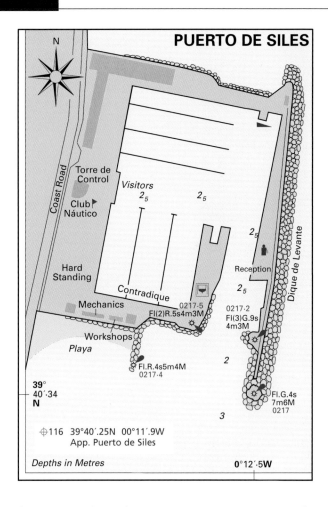

PUERTO DE SILES

Torre de Control
Visitors 2₅ 2₅
Club Náutico
Coast Road
Hard Standing
Contradique
Mechanics
0217·5 Fl(2)R.5s4m3M
Workshops
Playa
Fl.R.4s5m4M 0217·4
39° 40′·34 N
⊕116 39°40′·25N 00°11′·9W
App. Puerto de Siles
Reception 2₅
Dique de Levante
0217·2 Fl(3)G.9s 4m3M
2
3
Fl.G.4s 7m6M 0217
Depths in Metres
0°12′·5W

long Pantalán de Sierra Menera are easily
recognised.

From the north Puerto de Castellón and, to the SW,
the petrochemical works, which has two tall
chimneys with red and white bands, are
conspicuous. Puerto de Burriana can also be
recognised.

From either direction Cabo Canet light is
immediately behind the harbour and can be seen for
miles.

Anchorage in the approach

Anchor in 12m, sand, ½M to SE of the harbour
entrance.

Entrance

Depths can vary due to silting and dredging and as
of March 2001 the depth was 2m to 2·5m at the
entrance. Approach the entrance on a NW course,
sounding carefully. Round the head of the Dique de
Levante at 15m leaving it to starboard onto a N
course and enter between a short spur to starboard
and the SE corner of the *contradique* to port.
There may be two port-hand buoys laid south of the
contradique indicating the entrance channel. There
may also be a line of small orange buoys laid
between these two buoys and the end of the
contradique.

Puerto de Siles

Berths

The visitors' berths are at the second quay to port. Secure and confirm at the office. These outer quays are subject to swell in winds from E through S. Large vessels moor inside Dique de Levante.

Facilities

Maximum length overall 12m.
Workshop and mechanics on the *contradique*.
Slipway on the *contradique* and one near the root of the Dique de Levante.
25-tonne travel lift and a small crane near the root of the Dique de Levante.

Taps on all quays and pontoons.
Points for 220v AC on all quays and pontoons.
Small ice from the Club Marítimo.
Club Marítimo de Regates de Sagunto with bar, lounge, patio, restaurant, WCs, showers and swimming pool.
A supermarket 400m to N of the harbour with cash dispenser. More shops in Puerto de Sagunto 1M to SW.

Communications

Rail and bus services from Sagunto. Taxi ☎ 962 680 999.

Puerto de Siles entrance *Peter Taylor*

113. Puerto de Burriana

39°51'N 0°04'W

Charts

British Admiralty *1701*. Imray *M13*
French *7296, 4720*
Spanish *4822, 482*

⊕117 39°51'·2N 00°04'·05W. Steer 350°/0·25M to harbour

Lights

To the south
0216 **Cabo Canet** 39°40'·5N 0°11'·9W Fl(2)10s33m23M
  Brick tower with house 30m
Harbour
0219 **Dique de Levante head** Fl(2)G.8s12m5M Green
  tower 8m
0221 Dique de Poniente head Fl(2)R.8s10m3M Red
  structure on house 8m
0221·5 **Dique Exterior di Levante** Q(3)10s7m3M on tower
To the north
0226 **Castellón de la Plana** 39°58'·2N 0°01'·7E
  Oc(2+1)10s32m14M White round tower 27m

Port communications

VHF Ch 09. Club Nautico de Burriana ☎ 964 58 70 55
Fax 964 58 53 47 *Email* nautic@cnburriana.com
  www.cnburriana.com
Marina
VHF Ch 9 Burriananova Club de Mar
☎ 964 227 200 *Fax* 964 585 655
Email info@renosmaritima.com www.burriananova.com

A pleasant club and impressive new marina

An artificial harbour enclosed by two jetties. It is used by fishing craft and yachts. There is a small ship-breaking yard and a new, and welcoming, marina (Club de Mar Burriananova). The local village has limited facilities but more are available at the town some 3km away. The approach is easy but the entrance requires care owing to ever-extending sand bars. Good shelter is obtainable once inside the harbour. Entrance would be difficult with strong winds and swell from E through SW.

The town is worth visiting to see the original walls and gate and an important 16th-century church of Moorish origin. Excellent sandy beach to NE of the harbour.

Approach

From the south The flat, sandy coastal plain continues N from Sagunto for about 8M to Burriana. The town itself is some 2M inland but can seen as can the few blocks of flats near the harbour. In clear weather Pica Espadón (1105m) which lies 15M to WNW of this harbour may be seen. There is a fish farm at 39°50'.2N 0°03'.2E indicated by 4 buoys, Fl.Y.5s with cross topmarks.

From the north The main feature of this low, flat, dull coast are the two conspicuous tall, red and

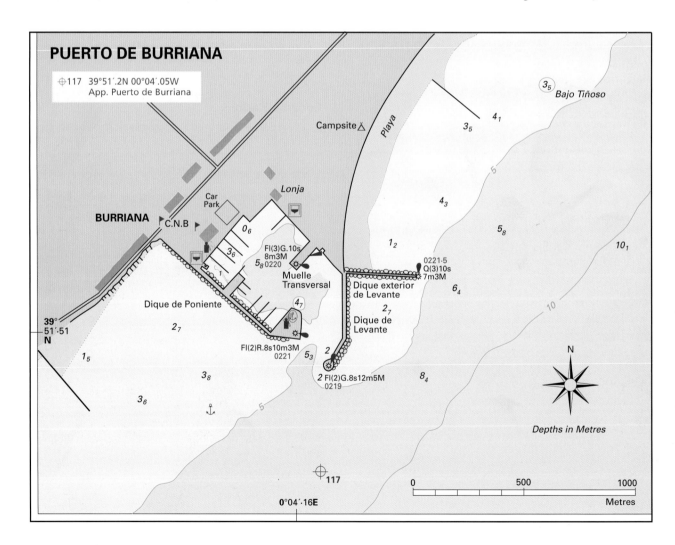

Puerto de Burriana (2004)

white banded chimneys of Castellón. Burriana itself, located some 2M inland, will be seen in the closer approach.

Anchorage in the approach

Anchor 200m to SW of the head of Dique de Levante in 6m, sand. Careful sounding is advisable.

Entrance

From a position 400m to SW of the head of Dique de Levante approach the entrance on a course of 30°. Pass some 15m to E of the head of Dique de Poniente. The approach to this harbour is tending to shoal and the sandbank that lies to the S of the head of the Dique de Levante is extending southwards.

Berths

The capitania and fuel berth are to port on entering. This modern marina has 378 berths and can accomodate vessels up to 30m.

Anchorage

Anchor NE of the Dique de Poniente, clear of any moorings off the *club náutico* piers, 5m, sand. Use a trip line.

Moorings

Private moorings may be available, apply to the club.

Facilities

Maximum length overall 17m.
Two slipways.

A small crane at the root of the Dique de Levante (5 tonnes) and a number of mobile cranes of greater power. A large one of unknown capacity on the Muelle Transversal.

Mechanic available.

Water from either end of the sheds on the Dique de Levante, from the *club náutico* and pontoons. Sample before filling tanks.

220v AC supplies from the *club náutico* and pontoons. *Gasoleo A.*

Ice is available at the *club náutico*.

The Club Náutico de Burriana has a bar, lounge, terrace, restaurant and showers.

Only a few shops near the harbour but many in the town where there is also a good market.

Communications

Bus service and rail service some 4M away.
Taxi ☎ 964 511 011.

Burrianova Capitania and fuel dock   *Peter Taylor*

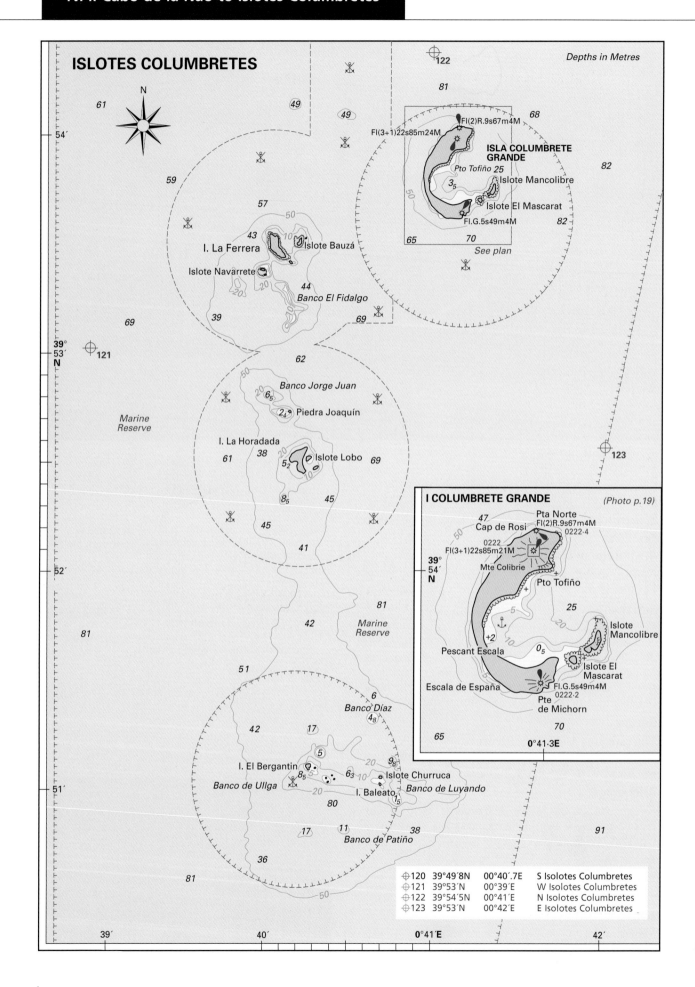

ISLOTES COLUMBRETES

Depths in Metres

N

61

⊕122

81

⊕49

49

68

54′

FI(2)R.9s67m4M

FI(3+1)22s85m24M

ISLA COLUMBRETE GRANDE

82

59

Pto Tofiño 25

Islote Mancolibre

3₅

57

50

Islote El Mascarat

82

43

I. La Ferrera

Islote Bauzá

FI.G.5s49m4M

65

70

See plan

Islote Navarrete

44

Banco El Fidalgo

39°
53′
N

⊕121

69

39

69

62

Banco Jorge Juan

50

6₅

20

2₄ Piedra Joaquín

Marine
Reserve

I. La Horadada

61

38

5₂ Islote Lobo

69

⊕123

8₅

45

52′

45

41

81

42

Marine
Reserve

I COLUMBRETE GRANDE

(Photo p.19)

Pta Norte

47

FI(2)R.9s67m4M

Cap de Rosi

0222·4

50

81

0222

FI(3+1)22s85m21M

39°
54′
N

Mte Colibrie

Pto Tofiño

5

25

51

20

Islote
Mancolibre

6

Pescant Escala

0₅

+2

Banco Díaz

42

17

4₈

Escala de España

FI.G.5s49m4M

Islote El
Mascarat

5

0222·2

Pte
de Michorn

51′

I. El Bergantin

8₅

6₃

Islote Churruca

65

70

Banco de Ullga

I. Baleato

Banco de Luyando

0°41·3E

80

1₅

17

11

38

91

Banco de Patiño

36

81

50

⊕120 39°49′8N   00°40′.7E   S Isolotes Columbretes
⊕121 39°53′N   00°39′E   W Isolotes Columbretes
⊕122 39°54′5N   00°41′E   N Isolotes Columbretes
⊕123 39°53′N   00°42′E   E Isolotes Columbretes

39′

40′

0°41′E

42′

114. Islotes Columbretes (Puerto Tofiño)

39°52'N 0°40'E

Charts

British Admiralty *1701*. Imray *M13*
French *4033, 4720*
Spanish *836, 483A, 4831*

⊕120   39°49'·8N 00°40'·7E
⊕121   39°53'N 00°39'E
⊕122   39°54'5N 00°41'E
⊕123   39°53'N 00°42'E

Lights

Columbrete Grande
0222 **Monte Colibri** 39°53'·9N 0°41'·2E Fl(3+1)22s85m21M
   White conical tower and dwelling 20m Racon
0222·2 **Punta Michorn** Fl.G.5s49m4M White 8-sided tower
   6m
0222·4 **Punta Norte** Fl(2)R.9s67m4M White 8-sided tower
   6m

Isolated and impressive islands

See photo on page 19.
Don't go without Spanish Chart *483A*.

Four isolated and barren groups of volcanic islets with outlying submerged rocks and shoals, Islotes Columbretes lie some 27M off the coast and opposite Castellón de la Plana. The four groups lie roughly N-S with an isolated shoal patch some 7M to WSW. The most northerly is Islote Columbrete Grande, 65m high, ½M in diameter, with high points to the N and S. This islet has the only lights. The next, Islote la Ferrera, a saddle-shaped island 44m high and 300m long, with a group of six smaller islets and shoal patches. Further S is Islote La Horadada, 55m high and 250m long, and a rough pyramid shape. It has two smaller rocky islets in its group and off-lying shoals. The most southern group consists of Islote El Bergantin 32m high and only 100m wide. It is the core of an old volcano. This group has at least eight smaller islets and several shoal patches. The area around these islands was renowned as one of the best fishing areas in the Mediterranean. Parts are now a marine reserve, interspersed with a rocket range and a target area for the air force.

The islets are inaccessible with the exception of the largest, Islote Columbrete Grande, which has a small military garrison. The islet is horseshoe-shaped and offers limited shelter in Puerto Tofiño where there is a mooring buoy but otherwise no facilities whatsoever. It is open to winds from N through to E and can be dangerous in these conditions. A walk over the arid island to the lighthouse is rewarding on a clear day with a view of the distant mainland.

Approach by day

Avoid Place de la Barra Alta, the shoal area some 7M WSW of the main group, a rocket range in an area W of Isla Columbrete Grande and the area 10M around Islote Bergantin, which is used for aerial exercises. Head for a position N to NE of Islote Columbrete Grande. It is possible to take the passages between the various groups of islets but streams are unpredictable and it can be rough.

Entrance

Approach the NE point of Islote Columbrete Grande on a SW course and follow this coast around at 150m into the anchorage.

Moorings

If free use the mooring buoy.

Anchorage

Anchor 150m from the W side of the harbour in 5m on rock and stone. An anchor trip-line is advisable. The holding is not good and should only be used in fair weather.

Landings

There are places to land at the head of the bay where the coast is lower.

Formalities

Check with the army on arrival.

Facilities

The island is barren and has no supply of water. Supplies are not available from the garrison except in an emergency.

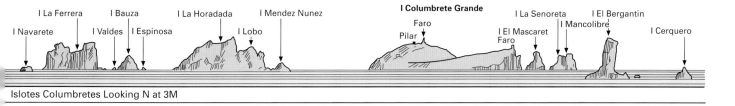

Islotes Columbretes Looking N at 3M

Islotes Columbretes Looking ENE at 7M

IV. COSTA DEL AZAHAR
ii. Islotes Columbretes to Río Ebro

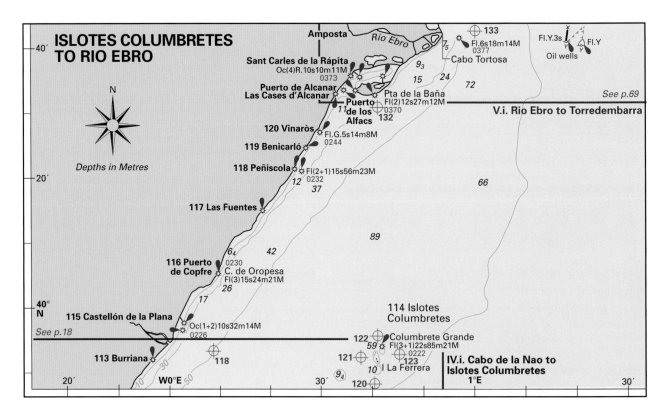

⊕120	39°49′8N	00°40′.7E	S Islotes Columbretes
⊕121	39°53′N	00°39′E	W Islotes Columbretes
⊕122	39°54′5N	00°41′E	N Islotes Columbretes
⊕123	39°53′N	00°42′E	E Islotes Columbretes

V. COSTA DORADA

⊕132	40°31′N	00°42′.3E	3M SE Punta de la Baña
⊕133	40°43′N	01°E	5.3M E Cabo Tortosa

Valencia oranges *Graham Hutt*

PORTS OF COSTA AZAHAR BETWEEN ISLOTES COLUMBRETES AND RÍO EBRO

115. **Puerto de Castellón de la Plana (Castelló)**
116. **Puerto Oropesa de Mar (Puerto Copfre)**
117. **Puerto de las Fuentes (Alcossebre)**
118. **Puerto de Peñíscola**
119. **Puerto de Benicarló**
120. **Puerto de Vinaròs**

Valencia. Almond trees   *Peter Taylor*

Ebro delta. Rice Fields   *Peter Taylor*

Vinaròs church   *Peter Taylor*

Beach Anchorage to the North of Peñiscola *(see page 61)*   *Peter Taylor*

IV. ii. COSTA DEL AZAHAR

115. Puerto de Castellón de la Plana (Castelló)

39°58'N 0°01'E

Charts

British Admiralty *1515, 1701.* Imray *M13*
French *7296, 4720*
Spanish *4821, 482*

⊕118 39°55'N 00°10'E 320°/0·4m to harbour

Lights

To the southwest: Oil Terminal
26700(S) **Safewater Buoy** 39°56'·2N 0°03'·7E LFl.10s3M
  Red and White Spherical
0224 **Oil Fuelling Berth** 39°56'·7N 0°01'·6E
  Oc(2)Y.14s13m4M Horn Mo(U) Yellow metal column
  6m
0224·2 **120m W** Oc(2)Y.14s9m1M Yellow post on dolphin
0224·4 **150m E** Oc(2)Y.14s9m1M Yellow post on dolphin
Harbour
0226 **Faro** Oc(2+1)10s32m14M White round tower 27m
  (Flare 1·8M SW)
0266·15 **Dique de Levante SE head** Q(3)10s6m3M Grey
  tower
0226·1 **Dique de Levante SW head** Fl(3)G.9s13m5M
  Green tower10m
0226·5 **Dique de Levante N corner** Q.7m5M Card N tower
To the northeast
0230 **Cabo Oropesa** 40°04'·9N 0°09'·0E Fl(3)15s24m21M
  White tower and house 13m

Port communications

Oil terminal and pilots. VHF Ch 16, 12, 13
  Harbour ☎ 964 28 11 40 *Fax* 964 28 14 11
Real Club Náutico Castellón
  ☎ 964 282 520 *Fax* 964 283 905
  Email capitania@rcncastellon.es
  www.rcncastellon.es
Marina Port Castelló.S.L.U
  ☎ 964 73 74 52 *Fax* 964 73 74 53
  Email marinaportcastello@marinaportcastello.es
  www.marinaportcastello.es

New yacht harbour within a commercial harbour

Large commercial and fishing harbour with an easy entrance and good shelter within. There is an oil terminal off shore with room to pass between it and the shore-line.

Work has been going on for some time now to extend the port, the Dique de Levante has been widened considerably and a new Dique Sur is being built to the SW of the present entrance. There are a number of buoys forming an access channel, which should be used for entering the port. Head N for the inner harbour.

The beach about a mile northeast of the harbour is good but approached along a noisy main road. The pleasant town some 2M inland was established by Jaime I of Aragón. It became the capital of the area and prospered as the centre of a fertile region, famous for its oranges and *azulejo* tiles.

Approach

From the south The harbours of Sagunto and Burriana are the only conspicuous features on this low, flat sandy coast. The two tall red and white banded chimneys just S of Castellón de la Plana (which are in line from this direction) are conspicuous as is the oil refinery flare (75m). A pipeline stretches out from the refinery ending about 2½M ESE where tankers anchor; the mooring is marked by a safewater buoy and has 5 mooring buoys (Fl(4)Y.10s). Along the line of the pipeline and a mile offshore is a floating fuelling berth with light and two lit dolphins. Navigation is prohibited between the safewater buoy and the floating berth but small craft may pass between the floating berth and shore. The lighthouse on the Dique de Levante should then be easy to spot as will the group of tall flats located just behind the harbour.

From the north The high Los Colls (420m) feature which extends to the sea at Cabo Oropesa is recognisable. The coast to the S is low, flat and sandy with a line of apartment blocks and houses. The features mentioned above at Castellón de la Plana are also easily seen from this direction.

Entrance

Approach from the S, pick up the port and starboard channel buoys and make for the Dique de Poniente buoy, leaving the Dique de Levante well to starboard.

Berthing

Yachts are welcome at both the RCN, to the southwest of the inner harbour, and the Marina in the northwest. Their large reception buildings are in the respective corners of the harbour.

Anchorages

As is common with most harbours on this coast at present, it is forbidden to anchor in the commercial harbour.

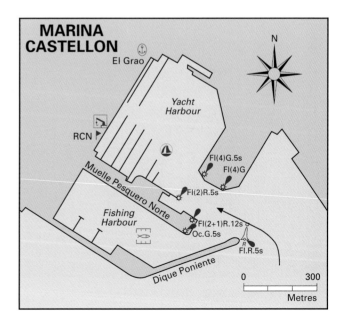

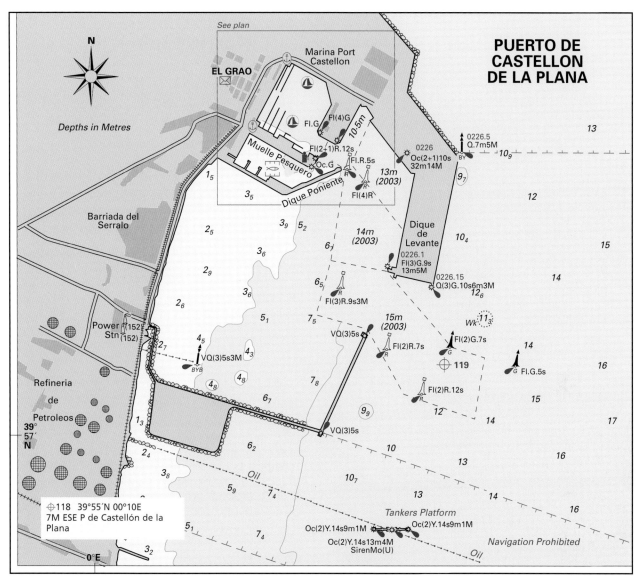

N

Depths in Metres

PUERTO DE CASTELLON DE LA PLANA

See plan

Marina Port Castellon

EL GRAO

Fl.G

Fl(4)G

10.5m

13

0226.5
Q.7m5M
BY

10₉

Fl(2+1)R.12s

Muelle Pesquero

Oc.G

Fl.R.5s

R

0226
Oc(2+1)10s
32m14M

9₇

12

1₅

13m
(2003)

Fl(4)R

R

Dique Poniente

3₅

Barriada del Serralo

3₉ 5₂

2₅

14m
(2003)

Dique de Levante

10₄

15

3₆

6₇

0226.1
Fl(3)G.9s
13m5M

2₉

3₆

6₅

R

0226.15
Q(3)G.10s6m3M

12₆

14

2₆

Fl(3)R.9s3M

5₁

7₅

15m
(2003)

Wk ᐧ11ᐧ

Power Stn (152)
(152)

2₇

4₅

VQ(3)5s

Fl(2)R.7s
R

Fl(2)G.7s
G

14

16

Refineria de Petroleos

VQ(3)5s3M

4₃

BYB

4₈

4₈

7₈

G 119

G Fl.G.5s

39°
57′
N

1₃

6₇

9₉

Fl(2)R.12s
R

12

15

2₄

VQ(3)5s

6₂

10

13

14

17

16

3₈

Oil

10₇

13

16

5₉

7₄

13

14

16

⊕118 39°55′N 00°10E
7M ESE P de Castellón de la Plana

5₁

7₄

Tankers Platform

Oc(2)Y.14s9m1M

Oc(2)Y.14s9m1M

Navigation Prohibited

0°E

3₂

Oc(2)Y.14s13m4M
SirenMo(U)

Oil

Puerto de Castellón de la Plana - See plan for pontoon layout in inner harbour

Facilities

Maximum length overall 20m.

A shipyard on the N side of the Muelle Pesquero where hull repairs can be carried out. Engine mechanics are also available.

Small slipway is located beside the *club náutico*, larger ones in the Dársena Pesquero.

32-tonne travel-lift.

12·5-tonne crane at the marina and large commercial cranes in Dársena Comercial.

Chandlery shop to the NW of the harbour.

Water and electricity 220v AC on the pontoons and the quays.

Gasoleo A and petrol at the fuel quay by the yacht club

Ice from the fuel quay.

The Club Náutico de Castellón clubhouse is in the W corner of the Dársena Comercial. It has a bar, lounge, terrace, restaurant, showers and a repair workshop.

A number of shops including a small supermarket near the harbour. Many more shops and a market in the town 2M away.

Launderette in the town.

Communications

Frequent bus service to the town where there is a rail service. Taxi ☎ 964 237 474.

⚓ OLLA DE BENICASIM 40°03′N 0°05′E

Open between NE and SE and to swell from the S. Daily requirements from shops serving the beach blocks or in the town of Bencasim.

Olla de Benicasim

⚓ S OF CABO OROPESA 40°04′.8N 0°08′.4E

A small anchorage tucked away under the cape open to SE. Use with care because of rocky patches. Anchor off sandy beach in 2m, sand. Houses and apartments ashore with road to the village of Oropesa on top of the hill (24m) where everyday supplies are available.

116. Puerto Oropesa de Mar (Puerto Copfre)

40°04′N 0°08′E

Charts

British Admiralty *1701*. Imray *M13*
French *4720*
Spanish *482*

⊕124 40°04′·36N 00°08′·13E 315°/0·08M to harbour

Lights

To the south
0226 **Faro** 39°58′·2N 0°01′·7E Oc(2+1)10s32m14M White round tower 27m
Harbour
0229·7 **Dique de Abrigo head** Fl(3)G.9s8m5M Green tower 3m
0229·8 **Contradique head** Fl(3)R.9s6m3M Red tower 2m
0230 **Cabo Oropesa** 40°04′·9N 0°09′·0E Fl(3)15s24m21M White round tower and house 13m

Port communications

VHF Ch 9. ☎ 964 313 055 *Fax* 964 310 000
Email cnom@cnoropesa.com
www.cnoropesa.com

Useful harbour – subject to silting

A useful harbour, easy to enter in bad weather and near to a busy seaside resort. It offers good protection though swell may enter the harbour from SE winds. Good facilities for laying up but there are no local shops. The main line railway is a bit noisy. A climb to the top of Cabo Oropesa is worthwhile for the coastal view. A small sand beach at the N side of the harbour, with a large beach at Oropesa del Mar.

Approach

From the south The huge petrochemical plant just to S of Puerto de Castellón which has two tall red and white banded chimneys is easily recognised as is Puerto de Castellón itself. The low, flat sandy coast is lined with apartment blocks. Cabo Oropesa (21m) is not prominent but the lighthouse and an old tower on its crest can be identified. The harbour is on the S side of the cape.

From the north Puerto de las Fuentes can be recognised by a small sail-shaped building. The shore to S is low flat and sandy. There are towers at Capicorp and the mouth of the Río Cuevas. This harbour is just beyond the collection of high-rise buildings at Oropesa del Mar.

Anchorage in the approach

The water is deep off this harbour. Anchor to S of Cabo Oropesa or in the Olla de Benicasim.

Entrance

Approach the head of the Dique de Levante on a NW course and round it, leaving it 15m to starboard onto a N course in to the harbour. Be prepared for dredging operations which are a continous activity.

Puerto Oropesa de Mar

Berths

Secure on the SW side of the harbour and ask at the *torre de control*.

Facilities

Maximum length overall 15m.
Hard-standing.
70-tonne travel-lift and 10-tonne crane.
Engine mechanic, painting, carpentry, sailmaking.
Chandlery.
Water taps on quays and pontoons.
Gasoleo A and petrol.
220v AC outlets on quays and pontoons.
Small ice from *club náutico*.
Club náutico with bar.
Stock up in Oropesa del Mar.

Communications

Bus and rail services at Oropesa del Mar. Taxi ☎ 964 310 616.

Note Red and green buoys in the entrance to the harbour are moved as the dredger works.   *Robin Rundle*

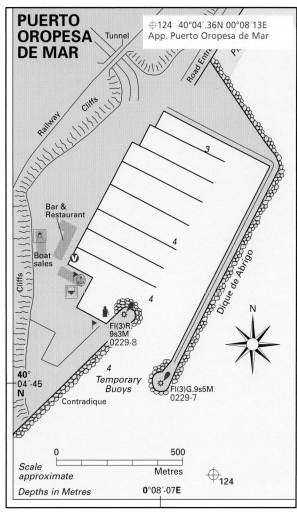

117. Puerto de las Fuentes (Alcocebre)

40°15'N 0°17'E

Charts
British Admiralty *1701*. Imray *M13*
French *4720*
Spanish *836*

⊕125 40°14'·75N 00°17'·35E 318°/0·11 to harbour

Lights
To the south
0230 **Cabo Oropesa** 40°04'·9N 0°09'·0E Fl(3)15s24m21M
  White round tower and house 13m
Harbour
0231 **Dique de Levante** 40°14'·8N 0°17'·2E Oc.G.4s6m4M
  Green concrete column 2m
0231·2 **Contradique** Fl(4)R.14s5m3M Red concrete column
  2m
Heads of pontoons and quays F.R and F.G – *see plan*.
To the north
0232 **Castillo del Papa Luna** 40°21'·6N 0°24'·6E
  Fl(2+1)15s56m23M White 8-sided tower and house
  11m 184°-vis-040°
0231·6 **Cabo de Irta** 40°15'·8N 0°18'·2E Fl(4)18s33m14M
  Square tower on white building 28m

Port communications
VHF Ch 9. ☎ 964 412 084 *Fax* 964 414 657
Email puertolf@telefonica.net

A pleasant yacht harbour
A pleasant medium-sized yacht harbour near a busy resort. Approach and entrance is not difficult except with strong SSE winds. Fine view from the church, San Benito, 2½M to W. Good but crowded sandy beach to N of harbour and rocky, stony one to S.

Approach
From the south Cabo Oropesa, though high (420m), is not prominent but can be easily recognised by its white round lighthouse and the old Torre del Rey alongside it. The coast is low, flat and marshy and can be closed to ½M. At Capicorp there are two *torres* and the mouth of Río Cuevas, 2½M further N lies the harbour with a number of apartment blocks behind it. The sail-like building of the *torre de control* is unique on this part of the coast and is easily recognised. Careful watch should be kept for floating cages 'Alcocebre' in approximate position 40°13'·9N 0°18'E with 4 yellow buoys (Fl.Y.5s).

From the north Peñíscola, surmounted by the Castillo del Papa Luna, is unmistakable. The coast to S is of low rocky cliffs and small sandy beaches at the mouths of the numerous small streams which descend from the Sierra San Benet (573m) a range of hills located 2M inland and lying parallel to the coast. The coast can be followed at ½M.

The harbour lies near the S end of this hill feature. The low breakwater and a number of apartment blocks are a short distance west of a conspicuous white tower and will be seen when close-to. The unique *torre de control* is not so obvious from this direction.

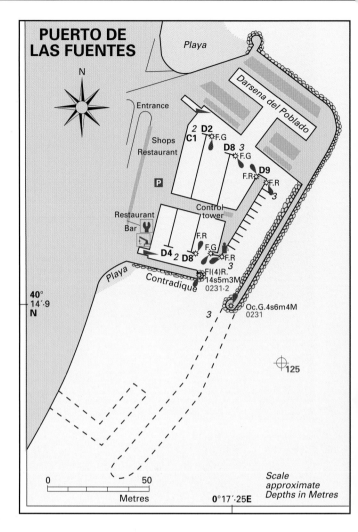

⊕125 40°14'75N 00°17'.35E App. Puerto de las Fuentes

Anchorage in the approach
Anchor 500m to E of the harbour in 8m, sand, or closer in, if weather is suitable, in 5m, sand.

Entrance
Straightforward.

Berths
Secure to the wide quay near the *torre de control*, a sail-like building, for allocation of a berth.

Facilities
Maximum length overall 20m.
Two slipways.
Travel lift. 8-tonne crane.
Engine mechanics.
Water taps and 220v AC on quays and pontoons.
Gasoleo A and petrol.
Some shops in the harbour, better in the village.
Small ice from the bar at SW corner of the harbour.

Communications
Bus service, rail 3M inland. Taxi ☎ 964 410 152.

Note There are plans to extend this harbour, as indicated, to provide 110 new berths for vessels up to 40m.

Las Fuentes

IV. ii. COSTA DEL AZAHAR

Las Fuentes entrance looking down Contradique   *Peter Taylor*

Las Fuentes fishermen   *Robin Rundle*

118. Puerto de Peñíscola

40°21'N 0°24'E

Charts

British Admiralty *1701*. Imray *M13*
French *7296, 4720*
Spanish *4841*

⊕126 40°21'·05N 00°24'·14E 330°/0·14M to harbour

Lights

0232 **Castillo del Papa Luna** 40°21'·6N 0°24'·6E
   Fl(2+1)15s56m23M White 8-sided tower and house
   11m 184°-vis-040°
27200(S) **Buoy** 40°21'·6N 0°24'·7E Q(3)10s3M
E cardinal BYB pillar (signals end of submerged
   breakwater)
Harbour
0234 **Dique de Levante head** Fl.G.4s15m4M Green
   column 7m
0234·4 **Espigón head** F.R.7m3M Red column 6m

Port communications

Harbour ☎/*Fax* 964 48 94 36
   Email puertos_peniscola@gva.es

An attractive small port

An attractive bay with a fishing harbour on its east
side which has very limited accommodation for
yachts. It is overlooked by a Knights Templars castle,
one of the more frequently visited sites on the east
coast of Spain. The approach and entrance are easy
but the bay is open to SE and winds from this
direction make it uncomfortable.

There is a good beach and anchorage on the N
side of the isthmus and another in the bay itself
which is often crowded. A holiday, the Fiesta of La
Virgen de la Ermitana, is held 8–9 September.

The Phoenicians called the harbour Tyriche,
because of its resemblance to Tyre. The Greeks
renamed it Chersonesos. Carthaginians and Romans
followed and later the Moors. The Moors were
driven out by Jaime I who gave the site to the
Knights Templars. The castle was completed by the
Montesianos in the 14th century. Pope Benedict XIII
(often referred to as Papa Luna), the last of the
schismatic Popes, retired here from Avignon in 1417
and remained until his death in 1423 at the age of
90. After a spell as part of the Holy See it reverted to
the crown of Aragón, withstanding an 11-day siege
by the French during the Peninsular War.

Approach by day

From the south After Cabo Oropesa, the coast is low
and flat. 10M north, Sierra Benet, a long line of
rocky hills, stretches as far as the harbour. From a
distance the castle at Peñíscola appears as an off-
lying island. Care should be taken to avoid a new
artificial reef in position 40°19'·6N 0°24'·8E.

From the north The harbours of Vinaroz and
Benicarló with their conspicuous harbour works are
easily identified on an otherwise featureless coast.
The castle at Peñíscola appears as an island.

A submerged breakwater (end marked by BYB lit
pillar buoy) extends 0·15 NM east from Escalera del
Papa Luna.

Puerto de Peñiscola

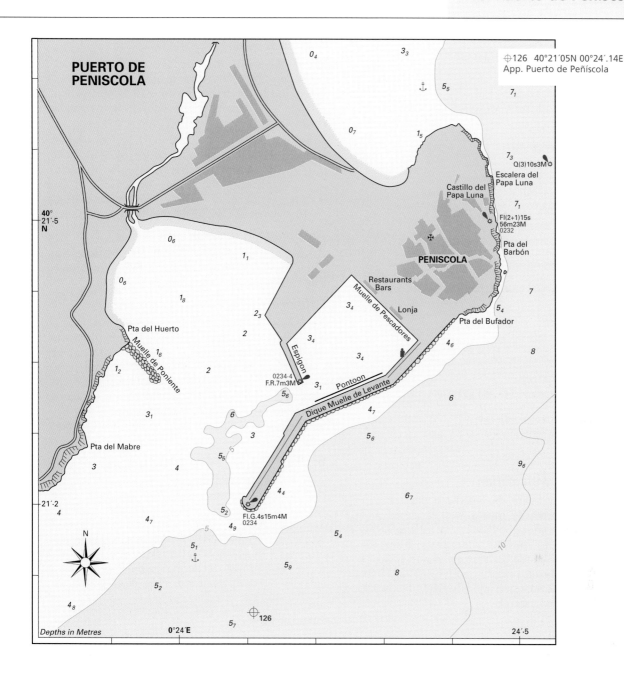

IV. ii. COSTA DEL AZAHAR

Anchorage in the approach

The bay may be marked as reserved for swimmers by a line of buoys between the Muelle de Poniente and the elbow of the *contradique*. If so, the options are to anchor near the line of the buoys, out of the fairway on the Muelle de Poniente side, or outside altogether either in the harbour approaches or north of Papa Luna.

Entrance

Straightforward but beware of fishing craft. After strong S winds the entrance can be quite shallow. It is dredged frequently but after strong winds from the S care must be exercised on entering. Avoid the head of Dique de Levante by 25m.

Berths

By day it may be possible to find a berth within the fishing harbour near the head of the *contradique* or alongside pontoons lying parallel to the Muelle de Levante. However, the fishing fleet which returns en masse at about 1700 hours usually requires all available berths.

Charges

Moderate charges in the harbour.

Facilities

Chandlery shop near the root of the jetty.
Water from the Lonja de Pescadores.
Ice available from the Lonja de Pescadores.
A number of small shops scattered around the village.

Communications

Buses.

⚓ N OF PENINSULA DE PEÑÍSCOLA
40°22′N 0°24′.6E

(*See photos on page 53 and 60*).

119. Puerto de Benicarló

40°25'N 0°26'E

Charts

British Admiralty *1701*. Imray *M13*
French *7296, 4720*
Spanish *4841, 837*

⊕127 40°24'·52N 00°26'·05E

Lights

To the south
0232 **Castillo del Papa Luna** 40°21'·6N 0°24'·6E
  Fl(2+1)15s56m23M White 8-sided tower and house
  11m 184°-vis-040°
Harbour
0238 **Dique de Levante head** Fl(2)G.5s13m5M Green
  tower 5m
0239·4 **Espigón head** Fl(2+1)G.15s7m3M Green round
  tower 3m
0238·5 **External Espigon head** Fl(2)R.6s8m3M Red tower
  5m
0239 **Dique Sur head** Fl(3)R.9s8m3M Red octagonal
  tower 4m
To the north
0370 **Punta de la Baña** 40°33'·6N 0°39'·7E
  Fl(2)12s27m12M White round tower, black bands 26m

Port communications

VHF Ch 9. Marina Benicarló ☎ 964 462 330
  Fax 964 462 317
  Email info@marinabenicarlo.com
  www.marinabenicarlo.com

Fishing harbour with marina

Over the last few years the northern part of this
harbour has been made into a well-sheltered and
impressive marina with good shoreside facilities. It is
situated about a 7 minute walk away from the
commercial centre of the thriving Valencian town of
Benicarlo, which is not over-run with tourists. There
is a sandy beach at the town and a long pebble beach
to the north of the harbour.

Approach by day

From the south Having passed the conspicuous
castle on the island-like feature at Peñíscola, the
town and harbour breakwaters of Benicarló will be
seen in the distance. The church in particular is
easily seen.

From the north From the harbour and town of
Vinaroz the coast consists of low broken rocky cliffs.
The town, church and harbour walls of Benicarló
are conspicuous from this direction. In heavy
weather avoid rocky shallows, Piedras de la Barbada
(6·4m), lying ½M to NE of the harbour entrance.

Anchorage in the approach

Anchor 200m to W of the head of Dique Sur in
3·5m, sand, or 400m further S, but sound carefully
due to silting.

Entrance

Round the head of Dique de Levante, leaving it 50m
to starboard as there are underwater obstructions
extending some 25 metres west of the head. Depths
may not be as charted due to silting and periodic
dredging so sound. Leave the Dique Sur head 50m to
port and head towards the conspicuous turning to
starboard to enter the marina. Notice one has to
leave the green light at the Espigon head to port to
enter the marina.

Berths

The water has been dredged from 3·7m to 2m near
the shore. It is recommended that one calls ahead by
radio or phone to ascertain whether a berth is
available. If so, one is usually met by an attendant
and shown to the berth. If one arrives unannounced
moor to a vacant berth and ask at the control tower
for a berth. Most berths have finger pontoons and
entry to the main pontoons is by electronic card.

Puerto de Benicarló

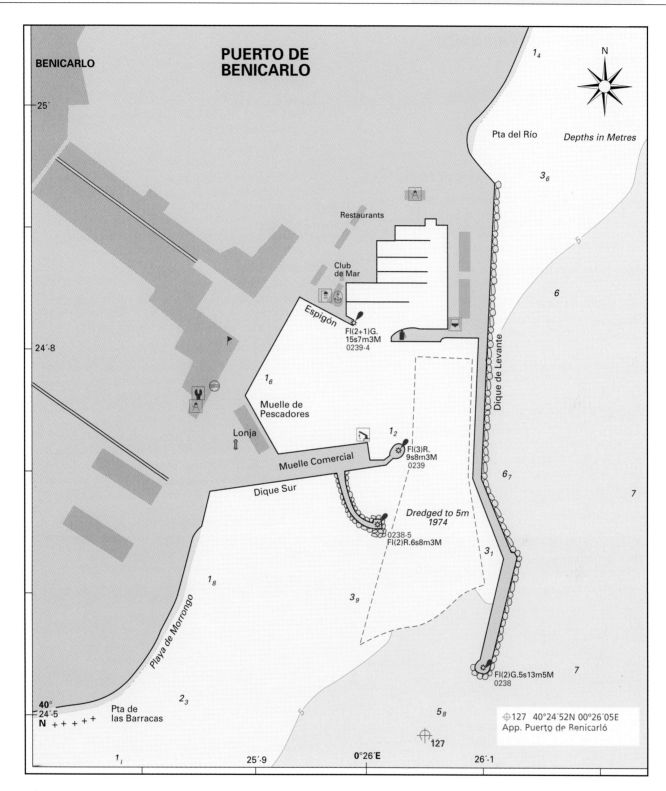

PUERTO DE
BENICARLO

BENICARLO

Depths in Metres

Pta del Río

Restaurants

Club
de Mar

Espigón
Fl(2+1)G.
15s7m3M
0239·4

Dique de Levante

Muelle de
Pescadores

Lonja

Fl(3)R.
9s8m3M
0239

Muelle Comercial

Dique Sur

Dredged to 5m
1974

0238·5
Fl(2)R.6s8m3M

Playa de Morrongo

Fl(2)G.5s13m5M
0238

Pta de
las Barracas

⊕127 40°24′52N 00°26′05E
App. Puerto de Benicarló

127

0°26′E

IV. ii. COSTA DEL AZAHAR

Charges

Medium to high.

Facilities

Maximum length 20m.
Water and electricity on pontoons.
24hr security staff.
Excellent showers in *Capitania* building.
Chandler.
32-tonne travel-lift and repair facilities.
5-tonne crane.

Local supermarket accepts telephone/email orders and will
deliver.
Shops and restaurant on site.
Fuel.

120. Vinaròs (Vinaroz)

40°27'·5N 0°28'·6E

Charts

British Admiralty *1515, 1701.* Imray *M13*
French *7296, 4720*
Spanish *4842, 485*

⊕128 40°27'·4N 00°28'·5E

Lights

0244 **Dique de Levante head** Fl.G.5s14m8M Green round
tower 10m
0244·5 **Knuckle** Fl(2)G.7s6m3M Green octagonal tower
3m
0246 **Dique de Poniente head** Fl.R.5s7m4M Red
octagonal tower 3m
0248 **Muelle Transversal head** Fl(3)G.9s8m3M Green
round tower 6m
0370 **Punta de la Baña** 40°33'·6N 0°39'·7E
Fl(2)12s27m12M White tower, black bands 26m

Port communications

☎/*Fax* 964 451 705 *Email* cnvinaros@telefonica.net
www.clubnauticovinaros.com

Storm signals

Shown from the root of Dique de Levante.

A large harbour with yacht facilities

A large artificial commercial fishing and yachting
harbour, easy to approach and enter. It is
periodically dredged and depths vary from time to
time. South to southwest swell may come in but
otherwise there is good protection.

Puerto de Vinaròs

The pleasant old town has good shops and a
church with a baroque portal. There are sand and
pebble beaches to the N of the harbour.

Approach

There are a number of fish farms off Vinaròs (both
N and S) and another artificial reef is being set up at
40°27'·8N 0°31'·7E.

From the south Having passed the conspicuous
castle at Puerto de Peñíscola and the harbour of
Benicarló, which can be recognised by its harbour
walls and town standing a little distance inland, the
coast from here on is of low sand-coloured cliffs.
The harbour walls of Vinaròs, some modern high-
rise buildings, a tall chimney and a tall crane will be
visible in the closer approach.

From the north The high range of hills, the Sierra de
Montsia, which backs the flat delta of the Río Ebro,
is easily recognised. Vinaròs lies in the flat plain to
the S of this feature. The blocks of flats, chimney and
crane are also visible from this direction.

Anchorage in the approach

Anchor 300m to NW of the head of the Dique de
Levante in 7m, sand, or 400m to E of this head in
11m, sand.

Entrance

Round the head of the Dique de Levante at 50m,
head between the knuckle and the head of Dique de
Poniente. When through, leave the head of the Dique
Transversal 50m to starboard. There are three black
mooring buoys on NE side of Dique de Poniente –
not for yachts.

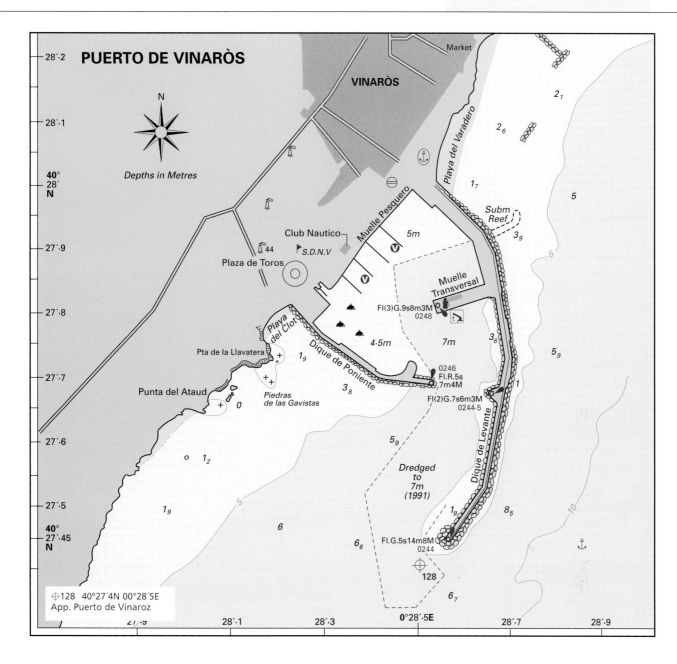

Berths

Call ahead on Ch 9 and secure to the visitors' berths as marked.

Moorings

Anchoring is not allowed. There are a few private moorings on the NW side of the inner harbour and some may be available; contact the *club náutico*.

Facilities

Hull repairs involving metal or woodwork can be carried out by the shipyards.

An engine workshop at the NW side of the harbour.

One small and two large slipways, one of 100-tonne capacity.

Two small cranes are on the NE side of the harbour. A powerful crane is located on the Dique Transversal

where there are a number of mobile cranes.

Chandlery shop near the harbour.

Water points on the pontoon and taps at the *lonja*, at the yacht club and on the Muelle Transversal.

220v AC on pontoons and quays.

Gasoleo A.

Ice available from the *lonja*.

The Sociedad Deportiva Náutica has a small clubhouse to the W of the harbour with restaurant, bar, lounge, terrace and showers.

A good range of shops and a market in the town.

Communications

Buses.

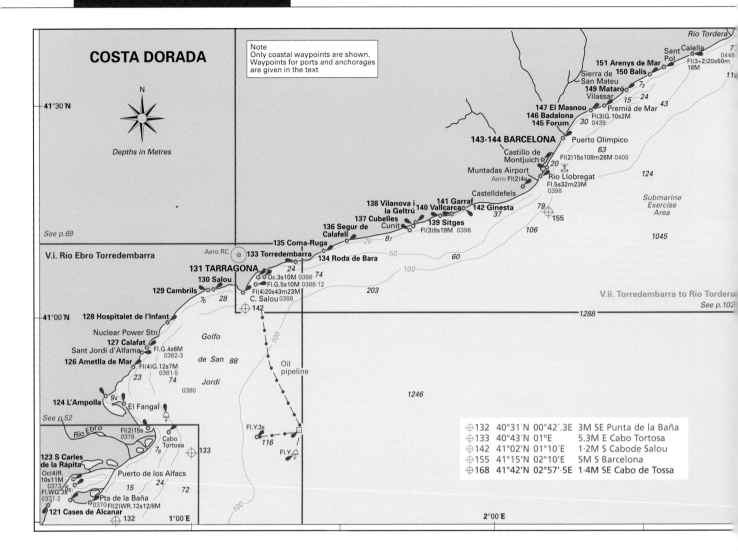

COSTA DORADA

N

Depths in Metres

Note
Only coastal waypoints are shown.
Waypoints for ports and anchorages
are given in the text

41°30′N

See p.69

V.i. Río Ebro Torredembarra

Aero RC

135 Coma-Ruga
133 Torredembarra
134 Roda de Bara

131 TARRAGONA
130 Salou
☼☼Oc.3s10M 0388 74
☼ Fl.G.5s10M 0388·12
Fl(4)20s43m23M
C. Salou 0386

24

129 Cambrils 7₅ 28

142

128 Hospitalet de l'Infant

41°00′N

Nuclear Power Stn
127 Calafat
Sant Jordi d'Alfama   Fl.G.4s6M
                       0382·3
126 Ametlla de Mar
☼ Fl(4)G.12s7M
  0381·5
23 74

Golfo

de San 88

Jordi

0380

124 L'Ampolla 9₄
El Fangal

See p.52

Río Ebro
Fl(2)15s
0376
Cabo
Tortosa 7₆

133

**123 S Carles
de la Ràpita**
Oc(4)R.
10s11M
0373
Fl.WG.3s
0371·2

Puerto de los Alfacs
15   24
72
Pta de la Baña
0370 Fl(2)WR.12s12/8M

121 Cases de Alcanar 132

1°00′E

**138 Vilanova i
la Geltrú**
137 Cubelles
Cunit
**136 Segur de
Calafell**

141 Garraf
140 Vallcarca☼ **142 Ginesta**

139 Sitges
Fl(3)8s19M 0396

20
8₇

37

50
60

100

203

FI.Y.3s
116

FI.Y
Y

151 Arenys de Mar
Sant Calella
Pol 0448
Fl(3+2)20s50m
18M

150 Balis
Sierra de
San Mateu 7₃
149 Mataró 15 24 43
Vilassar
147 El Masnou Premiá de Mar
146 Badalona Fl(3)G.10s2M
145 Forum 30 0439

143-144 BARCELONA

Puerto Olímpico
63
Fl(2)15s108m26M 0400
Castillo de
Montjuich☼ 20
Muntadas Airport
Aero Fl(2)4s
Río Llobregat
Fl.5s32m23M
0398

Castelldefels
79
155

106
1045

124

*Submarine
Exercise
Area*

1288

1246

V.ii. Torredembarra to Río Tordera
See p.102

⊕ 132   40°31′N 00°42′.3E   3M SE Punta de la Baña
⊕ 133   40°43′N 01°E   5.3M E Cabo Tortosa
⊕ 142   41°02′N 01°10′E   1·2M S Cabode Salou
⊕ 155   41°15′N 02°10′E   5M S Barcelona
⊕ 168   41°42′N 02°57′·5E   1·4M SE Cabo de Tossa

2°00′E

Río Tordera

Egrets follow the rice harvest in Ebro delta   *Peter Taylor*

V. Costa Dorada

Introduction

General description

The Costa Dorada (Golden Coast) is so called because of the golden sandy beaches between the mouths of the two large rivers, Ebro and Tordera. The 140 miles of coast varies considerably. At the south is the huge flat muddy delta of the Río Ebro which projects well out to sea. It is surrounded by extensive and dangerous shoals and should be given a wide berth. On either side of this delta are high ranges of hills leading down to broken rocky cliffs on the coast. Flat plains and low hills alternate along the coast from just S of Cabo Salou to beyond the delta of the Río Llobregat, backed by higher hills further inland. N of the Río Llobregat these higher hills follow the coastline with a narrow band of low-lying ground along the coast itself as far as the delta of the Río Tordera. In general the coastline is comparatively straight, broken only by the major promontory of the delta of the Río Ebro, Cabo Salou, Cabo Gros and the deltas of Ríos Llobregat and Tordera. Regular soundings follow the coast and with the exception of the areas around the river deltas, there is deep water close inshore. There are no outlying dangers except for a shallow bank, Banco de Santa Susana, parallel to the coast near Pineda and about ½ mile offshore.

Les Cases is the southernmost port of Catalunya. The province has some of the largest concentrations of industry in Spain which has resulted locally in some bad pollution of both air and sea. The sandy beaches are attractive to holiday-makers and there has been considerable development along the coastline for both Spanish and foreign tourists.

Visits

Apart from places mentioned in the harbour descriptions, the following sites are interesting but some distance inland. They can be reached by public transport or taxi.

Tortosa, an old Roman and Moorish city with many interesting buildings

Monasterio de Escornalou, in the Sierra Montsant behind Cambrils with a superb view.

Monasterio de Sants Creus, behind Tarragona, a 12th-century building.

Tamarit, a 12th-century castle and museum.

Arca de Bará, a Roman arch astride the old Via Maxima near Torredembarra.

Castelldefels, a 15th-century tower, the Torre del Homenaje.

Montserrat, an extraordinary saw-shaped mountain ridge behind Barcelona, has a fine view and an interesting monastery dating from the 1st century.

Monasterio de Sant Cugat del Valles, another very old monastery on the site of the Roman Castrum Octavianum located behind Barcelona.

Sierra del Montseny, a number of places with tremendous panoramas located inland from Arenys de Mar. (*See also page 79 for comments on the Ebro Delta*).

Pilotage and navigation

Shoaling

The deltas along this coast are constantly altering and their off-lying shoals steadily extend further out to sea. Allowance must be made for the possibility of changes when rounding such promontories – keep well off and sound.

Restricted anchorages

There is a small area near the atomic power station that is located between L'Ametlla and Cambrils, a large area just to the N of Barcelona, and a smaller area to the S, where anchoring is forbidden.

Prohibited areas

Oil wells and exploration drilling platforms are located in an area 15M E of Cabo Tortosa, each platform carrying a light Mo(U)15s+Fl.R. Additional sites may be occupied nearby. Navigation is prohibited within the areas concerned.

Harbours of refuge

Only the main ports of Tarragona and Barcelona offer refuge in really bad storms with onshore winds. In certain conditions one or the other side of the Río Ebro delta may provide shelter and, with offshore winds, the smaller harbours of L'Hospitalet, Castelldefels (Ginesta), Mataró, Cambrils, Vilanova i la Geltrú and Arenys de Mar could be entered.

Magnetic Variation

1°00'W (2008). Decreasing by 6' annually.

Planning Guide

Distances (Miles)

V. COSTA DORADA
i. Río Ebro to Torredembarra

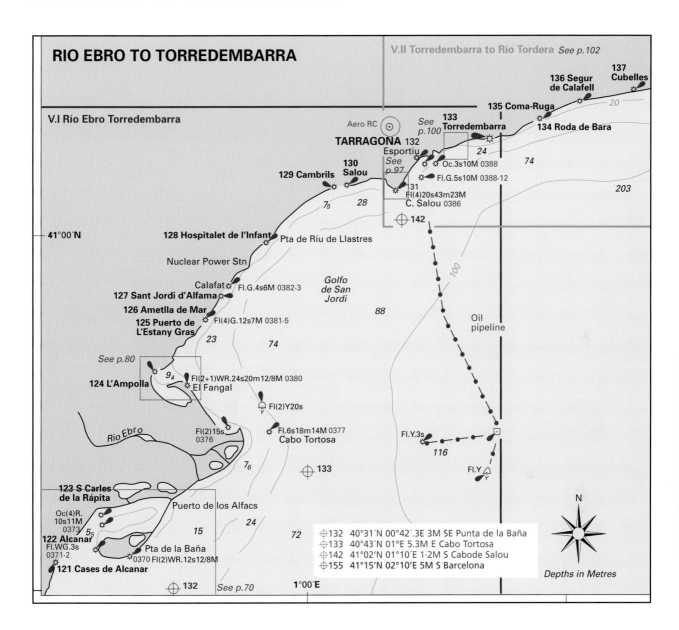

PORTS OF COSTA DORADA BETWEEN RÍO EBRO AND TORREDEMBARRA

121. Puerto de les Cases d'Alcanar
122. Puerto de Alcanar (La Martinenca)
123. Puerto de Sant Carles (San Carlos) de la Rápita & Marina
124. Puerto L'Ampolla
125. Puerto de L'Estany Gras
126. Puerto de L'Ametlla de Mar

127. Puerto de Calafat
128. Puerto de Hospitalet de L'Infant
129. Puerto de Cambrils
130. Puerto de Salou
131. Puerto de Tarragona
132. Port Esportiu

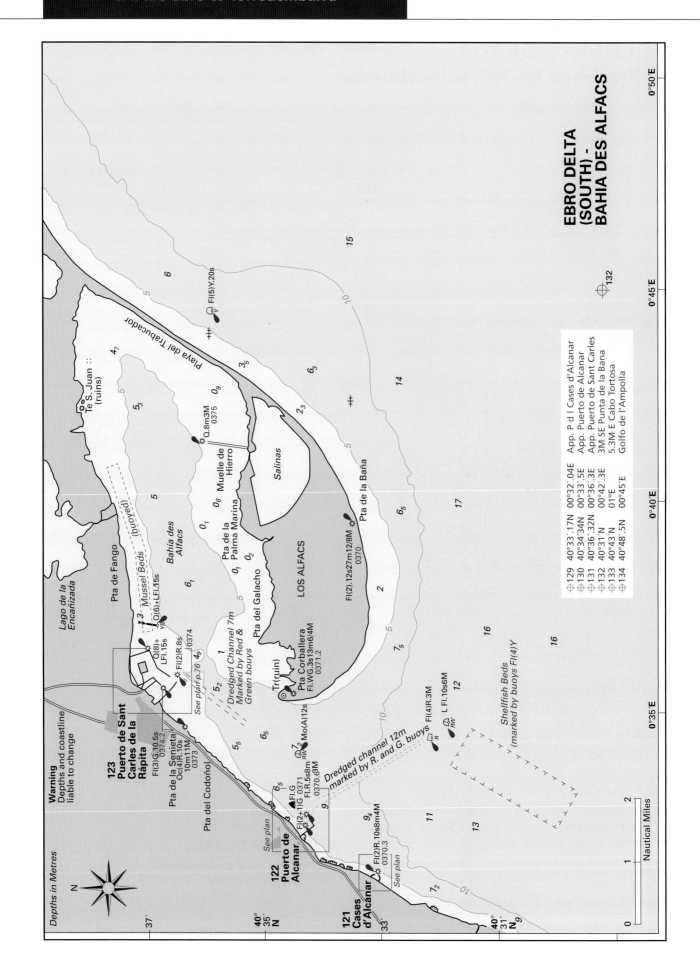

EBRO DELTA (SOUTH) - BAHIA DES ALFACS

⊕ 129	40°33'·17N	00°32'·04E	App. P d I Cases d'Alcanar
⊕ 130	40°34'·34N	00°33'·5E	App. Puerto de Alcanar
⊕ 131	40°36'·32N	00°36'·3E	App. Puerto de Sant Carles
⊕ 132	40°31'N	00°42'·3E	3M SE Punta de la Bana
⊕ 133	40°43'N	01°E	5.3M E Cabo Tortosa
⊕ 134	40°48'·5N	00°45'E	Golfo de l'Ampolla

Warning
Depths and coastline liable to change

Depths in Metres

Lago de la Encanizada

Pta de Fango

Te S. Juan :: (ruins)

Playa del Trabucador

Musel Beds (buoyed)

Pta de la Senieta

Pta del Codoñol

123 Puerto de Sant Carles de la Rápita

Fl(3)G.10.5s 0374.2
Oc(4)R.10s 10m11M 0373

Q(8)+LFl.15s
Q(6)+LFl.15s
Fl(2)R.8s 0374

See plan (p.76)

Bahia des Alfacs

Dredged Channel 7m
Marked by Red & Green bouys

Pta del Galacho

Tr(ruin)

Pta Corballera
Fl.WG.3s13m6/4M 0371.2

Q.8m3M 0375

Muelle de Hierro

Salinas

Pta de la Palma Marina

LOS ALFACS

Pta de la Baña

Fl(2).12s27m12/8M 0370

Fl(5)Y.20s

Fl.G
Fl(2+1)G 0371
Fl.R.5s8m 0370.6?M

Mo(A)12s

122 Puerto de Alcanar

See plan

Fl(2+1)R 0370.3
Fl(2)R.10s8m4M

121 Cases d'Alcanar

See plan

Dredged channel 12m marked by R. and G. buoys

Fl(4)R.3M
R

L Fl.10s6M
RW

Shellfish Beds (marked by buoys Fl(4)Y)

N

Nautical Miles

40°35'N

40°31'N

Ebro Delta South

Bahía des Alfacs

40°36'N 0°40'E

Charts

British Admiralty *1704, 1515.* Imray *M13*
French *7048, 4720*
Spanish *485*

Lights

0375 **Muelle de Hierro head** 40°36'·2N 0°41'·4E Q.8m3M
N card pole 082°-vis- 229°(this light is well inside the Bahía)
S card lights mark shellfish beds on the north side of the Bahía

General

This *bahía* is an inland lake blocked off to seaward by a spit formed from the wash-out of the Río Ebro (Ebre). It is some 6M long and 2M wide. The entrance, which has Sant Carles de la Rápita on its N side, is about 1M wide and is shoal on the S side. Depths within range from 6m to 0m, the shallows being on the S side; the sea level tends to increase with winds between NE and SE and decrease with winds from other directions. The area offers considerable scope for larger boats to anchor out of open sea and for smaller boats wishing to sail in sheltered waters.

Apart from two small villages with a road inland from the N coast, there is little activity in the area. There are many rice fields, *salinas* (saltpans) and a few factories dealing with the salt. One such factory on the S side has a long metal jetty, the Muelle de Hierro, extending 1M out from the shore. The N side of the area has a long line of mussel beds, marked by three S cardinal buoys. Keep clear of them. The surrounding area, largely marsh, is low and flat; squalls can descend without warning from the Sierra Montsiá.

Approach

⊕132 is some 3·5M ESE from the Puerto de Alcanos fairway buoy.

Harbours

121 Cases d'Alcanar - use ⊕129
122 Puerto de Alcanar - use ⊕130
123 Puerto de Sant Carlos de Rapita and Marina- use ⊕131

Anchorage

Anchorage is possible virtually anywhere in the Bahía des Alfacs in mud in depth to suit draught. Use an anchor light.

Fishing boats cutting the corner – Pta Corballeta into Bahía des Alfacs with Puerto de Sant Carles de la Rapita visible in the distance

121. Puerto de les Cases d'Alcanar (Casas de Alcanar)

40°33'N 0°32'E

Charts

British Admiralty *1458, 1701, 1515*. Imray *M13*
French *7048, 4720*
Spanish *485, 837*

⊕129 40°33'·17N   00°32'·04E 265°/0·03M to harbour

Lights

0370·3 **Fishing marina S pier head** 40°33'·0N 0°32'·0E
   Fl(2)R.10s8m4M Red pyramidal tower 4m
0370·35 **Dique de Levante head** Fl.G.4s7m3M Green
   pyramidal tower 3m
To the south
0370 **Punta de la Baña** 40°33'·6N 0°39'·7E
   Fl(2)12s27m12M White tower black bands 26m

Port communications

VHF Ch 9. Club Náutico ☎/*Fax* 977 735 001
   Email cncalcanar@hotmail.com (office, mornings only)
   ☎ 977 735 014 (club house and bar)
   www.cncaportlescases.com

A small boat harbour

A pleasant small artificial yachting and fishing harbour; there is not much depth alongside in the yacht harbour. The area has not been highly developed and the harbour may be useful for a vessel on passage wanting to stop before rounding Cabo Tortosa without diverting to Puerto de Sant Carles de la Rápita but space for visitors is limited to two berths. Entrance could be difficult with high winds and seas between NE and SE. In 1998 a new club house was built and a pump for *Gasoleo A* installed.

The town was an important staging place on the N-S coast road from pre-Roman days. Remains from this period are still being found. There are several Roman remains and many from the time of the Moorish occupation. The town suffered many attacks by sea pirates in the Middle Ages and also suffered during the War of the Succession in the 18th century. The Seven Years War and the Civil War also affected the town.

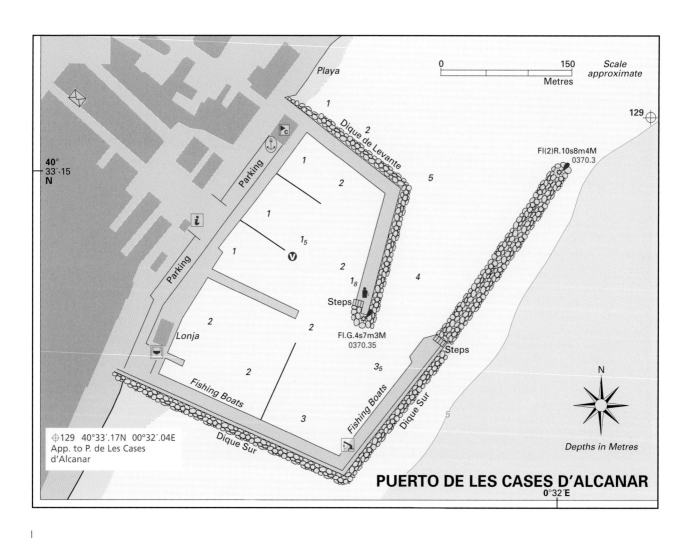

PUERTO DE LES CASES D'ALCANAR
0°32'E

Puerto de les Cases d'Alcanar

There are several interesting buildings, including the church in Alcanar and the remains of a Roman bridge. Fine views from the Sierra Montsiá. Details from the information office beside the harbour. Excellent sandy beach to S of the harbour. Local holidays include the *Remedio* in the second two weeks of October, in honour of the town's patroness.

Approach

There may be several oil rigs and oil wells located about 10M offshore in this area. They come and go as oil is found or used up. The areas are well marked by lights. Sometimes a tanker is kept moored to one of these wells.

From the southwest The coast from Vinaròs is flat with low sandy cliffs as far as this harbour where rocky cliffs commence, backed by the mountain range Sierra Montsiá. The tower Sol de Riv at the mouth of a small river can be identified. The group of houses and apartment blocks behind this harbour can be seen from afar.

From the northeast Round the large delta of the Río Ebro as far as Punta de la Baña which can be identified by its lighthouse. Approach the harbour on a W course and cross the line of 22 light buoys which mark a dredged channel leading to Puerto d'Alcanar (La Martinenca), 3M NW(except for the first and last buoys they are in pairs, red can and green conical). The buildings behind the harbour will now be seen.

Anchorage in the approach

Anchor in 5m, sand, 200m to S of the harbour.

Entrance

Approach the harbour on a W course and identify the head of Dique Sur. Note that the head of Dique Levante is well inside the head of Dique Sur. Give them both a 15m berth and enter.

Berths

Secure near head of fuel jetty and apply to *club nautico* for a berth.

Charges

High.

Facilities

Maximum length overall 15m.
Simple repairs only; mechanic in the town.
6-tonne crane and hard-standing on Dique Sur.
A slipway in W corner of the harbour.
Water taps on quays and pontoons.
220v AC points on quays and pontoons.
Ice from café/bars.
Club Náutico Cases d'Alcanar has a clubhouse at the N corner of the harbour.
Several shops in the area near the harbour and many in the town of Alcanar 2M inland where there is a market.

Communications

Bus service. Car Hire.

122. Puerto de Alcanar (La Martinenca)

40°34'N 0°33'E

Charts

British Admiralty *1701, 1704*. Imray *M13*
French *7048, 4720*
Spanish *3713, 485, 837*

⊕130 40°34'·34N 00°33'·5E 290°/0·15M to harbour

Lights

0370·6 **Muelle Exterior head** 40°34'·4N 0°33'·4E
   Fl.R.5s8m3M Square tower 2m
0371 **Muelle Interior head** Fl(2+1)G.14s8m3M Square
   tower, red and green top 3m

Port communications

Pilots Sant Carles Rápita Prácticos VHF Ch 11, 12, 14, 16.
   Continuous service.

A commercial harbour only

A commercial harbour which is a part of a large cement works. Not normally used by yachts but could be used as a shelter in the event of bad weather. The approach and entrance are easy and good shelter is obtained, though with N to NE winds it can be uncomfortable despite the shelter provided by the Ebro delta. Facilities for yachtsmen are very limited as might be expected from a purely commercial harbour but there are excellent sandy beaches on either side of the harbour.

Approach

From the south The flat coast with low sandy cliffs suddenly gives way to the high range of mountains, the Sierra Montsiá. At the foot of these mountains and close to the coast are the tall cement factory buildings usually with clouds of effluent pouring out from them. The harbour is located nearby. Close-to the dredged channel lightbuoys will be seen.

From the north Round the Ebro delta giving Cabo Tortosa a good berth and follow the low flat coast at 3M in a SW direction. Round Punta de la Baña onto a WNW course. The cement factory by the harbour will be seen from afar and the dredged channel lightbuoys will appear when closer in.

Approach channel
The approach channel 330° (dredged to 12m) has on its SE extremity a safewater buoy (Boya de Recalada 40°32'·0N 0°35'·4E LFl.10s6M) nearly 3M distant from the port. The NW end is marked by a green starboard-hand lateral buoy (Boya No.21 Fl.G.3s3M) about 400m NE of the harbour. Between these buoys lie ten pairs of R and G lightbuoys. A fish farm has been established about a mile SW of No.8 buoy.

Anchorage

Anchor with trip-line attached in 3m on sand about halfway between the shore and the Muelle Interior.

Entrance

Approach the head of the Muelle Exterior, round a red can lightbuoy Fl(3)R off it and then the head of the Muelle Interior at 25m.

Berths

Temporary berth alongside the quay on the land side of either Muelle.

Moorings

Temporary mooring available on the large mooring buoys in the inner harbour.

Formalities

Report to harbour officials on arrival and ask permission to stay while the bad weather lasts.

Facilities

Provisions from the town some 3M to SW.

Anchorage in the approach

Possible location for yachts is 600m to E of the entrance in 4m, mud.

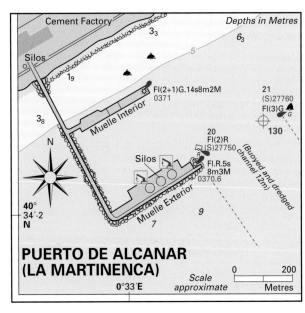

⊕130 40°34'34N 00°33'.5E   App. Puerto de Alcanar

Puerto de Alcanar

123. Puerto de Sant Carles (San Carlos) de la Rápita Yacht Harbour and Marina

40°36'N 0°36'E

Charts

British Admiralty *1515, 1701, 1704.* Imray *M13*
French *7296, 7048, 4720.* Spanish *485*

⊕131 40°36'·32N 00°36'·3E 000°/0·2M to harbour
entrance then 300°/0·45m to old harbour or
340°/0·4M to anchorage or new marina.

Lights

To the south by east
0371·2 **Punta Corballera** 40°34'·7N 0°35'·8E
Fl.WG.3s13m6/4M Black round tower 12m 000°-G-180°-
W-360°
To the west
0373 **Punta de la Senieta** 40°36'·4N 0°35'·1E
Oc(4)R.10s10m11M White round tower 7m
Harbour
0374 **Dique de Abrigo head** Fl(2)R.8s8m6M Red tower 5m
0374·1 **Dársena est Dique de Abrigo head** Q.G.3m1M
Green post 3m (note Este)
There are now 5 red cylindrical and 4 green conical
buoys forming an entrance channel with 3 more green
conical buoys indicating an area of dredging – keep
well clear of the latter 3 buoys.
0374·2 **Dique de Levante head** Fl(3)G.10·5s6m4M Green
tower 4m
0374·4 **Muelle de Poniente head** Oc.R.4s5m2M Red
truncated pyramidal tower 4m.
Cardinal lights mark shellfish beds between 0·65M and
3M ENE

Port communications

Pilots Sant Carles Rápita Prácticos VHF Ch 11, 12, 14, 16.
Hours various.
Port ☎ 977 741 103

Puerto de Sant Carles, yacht harbour left,
new marina top right

A busy harbour including a yacht harbour and developing major new marina

The harbour is well protected from winds and easy
to approach (once round the Ebro delta, if coming
from the north). The facilities are fair and the area is
attractive in a wild and unexploited way.

There are two sets of harbours. The older, to the
southwest, has the yacht harbour, a commercial
basin and a fishing harbour. The newer harbour to
the northeast has an inner and outer basin and was
developed for small fishing craft and yachts. This is
a good launching place for those who trail their
yachts and wish to visit the enclosed sea area to the
east, Puerto de los Alfacs. This is now being
developed into a major new marina.

The original harbour was founded by Carlos III
with the intention of making it into a large trading
port but this scheme never prospered and the
grandiose Plaza Carlos III is the sole reminder of it.
The Cerro de la Guardiola which lies behind the
town has a fine view.

Approach

From the south Pass the conspicuous harbours of
Benicarló and Vinaròs where the coastal plain is low.
Further to N the high range of the Sierra Montsiá
(764m) leads to this harbour. Follow the coast at 1M
or less passing through the line of red and green
lightbuoys leading to the conspicuous cement works
at Alcanar (La Martinenca). This course passes W of
the shallows off the low and inconspicuous Punta
Corballera and Punta del Galacho.

From the north round the large delta of the Río Ebro
and follow the S side round, keeping outside the
10m soundings. Careful navigation is necessary due
to the lack of identifiable features and the low flat
coast. When S of Punta Corballera cross over
towards the mainland shore and follow this in a NE
direction at 1M distance.

V. i. COSTA DORADA

Sant Carles Yacht Harbour (Club Náutico de Sant Carles)

40°37'N 00°35'·8E

⊕131 40°36'·32N 00°36'·3E 000°/0·2M to harbour entrance then 300°/0·45m to old harbour

Club Náutico de Sant Carles VHF Ch 9.
☎/Fax 977 741 103
Email cn.sant-carles@terra.es or clubnautic@larapita.com
www.cnscr.com

The southwest harbours

This is the old harbour area, no anchoring is permitted.

Entrance

Round the head of the Dique de Abrigo leaving it 50m to port onto a NW course and approach the entrance following the Dique de Abrigo at 50m.

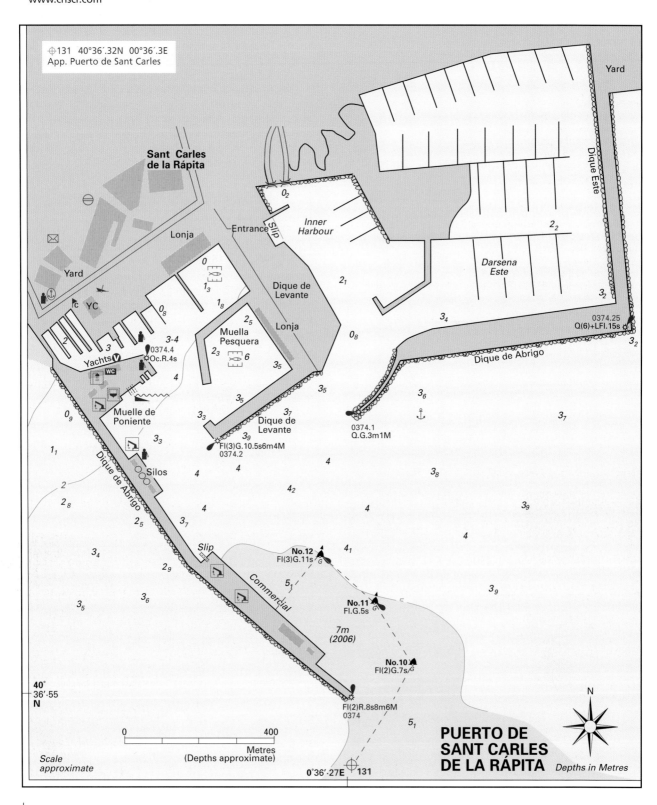

Berths

Go to the visitors berth on the N side of the Muelle de Poniente or moor at the fuel berth and arrange a berth at the newly enlarged club nautico. All berths have lazy lines running out from the quays/pontoons.

Harbour charges

Low.

Facilities in the southwest harbour

Maximum length overall 15m.
Shipyard to the NW of the harbour and an engine repair workshop nearby.
Several slipways in the complex.
100-tonne travel lift
Cranes up to 10 tonnes and a large mobile crane.
Several chandlery shops in town and near the harbour.
Water from the pontoons and the *lonja* and from the *club náutico*.
220v AC on the pontoons and at the *club náutico*.
Gasoleo A and petrol.
Ice from the *lonja* and *club náutico*.
Club Náutico de Sant Carles has a new clubhouse to the NW of the harbour with bar, lounge, terrace, showers and pontoon.
Shops of all kinds, supermarket, in the town nearby. A few shops near the harbour.
Launderette in town.

Communications

Rail and bus service. Taxi ☎ 977 741 317.

Sant Carles Marina

40°37′N 00°36′·22E
⊕131 40°36′·32N 00°36′·3E 000°/0·2M to harbour entrance then 340°/0·4M to anchorage or marina.

Lights

0374.1 Darsena Este Dique de Abrigo head Q.G.3m1M
    Green post 2m

Communications

VHF Ch not yet known
☎ 977 74 51 53 *Email* info@santcarlesmarina.es
www.santcarlesmarina.com

The northeast harbours

Entrance

To enter the Inner harbour round the head of the western Dique de Abrigo and steer for the Dique some 400m east of the main harbour entrance.

Anchorages

Anchoring is allowed in the NE harbour close outside Dique de Abrigo.

New Marina opening 2008

UK operators MDL are involved in a joint venture to open a 1000 berth Marina, Phase 1 in 2008 and Phase 2 in 2009. This will have full support facilities for visiting and permanently based yachts; the marina will offer additional recreational facilities as well as club house, bar and restaurant.

Approach

Approach as for Sant Carles de la Rapita and, after rounding Dique de Abrigo, head N for 0·35M towards the entrance to the marina (or to anchor).

Berthing

Boats up to 30m will be accommodated.

V. i. COSTA DORADA

Sant Carles from Abrigo looking NE   *Peter Taylor*

Looking out new marina entrance to anchorage
Peter Taylor

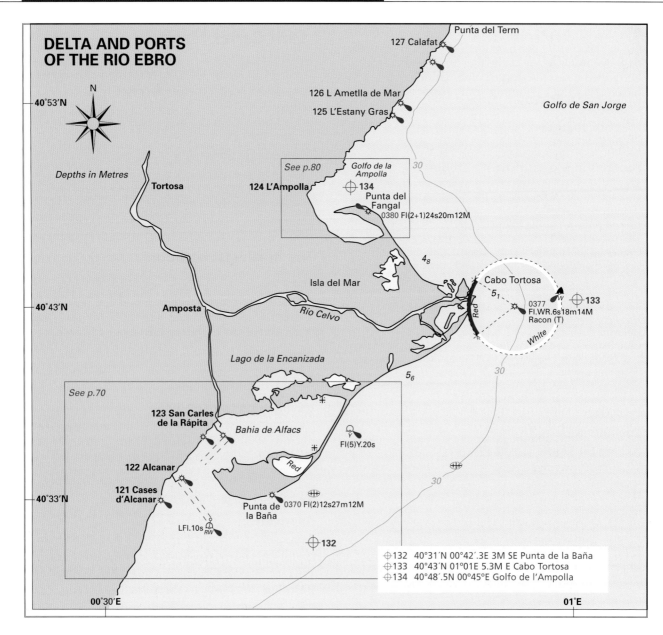

DELTA AND PORTS OF THE RIO EBRO

Depths in Metres

Tortosa

Golfo de San Jorge

Golfo de la Ampolla

See p.80

124 L'Ampolla

⊕ 134

Punta del Fangal
0380 Fl(2+1)24s20m12M

127 Calafat

Punta del Term

126 L Ametlla de Mar

125 L'Estany Gras

Isla del Mar

Cabo Tortosa

0377
Fl.WR.6s18m14M
Racon (T)

⊕ 133

Amposta

Río Celvo

Lago de la Encanizada

See p.70

123 San Carles de la Rápita

Bahia de Alfacs

Fl(5)Y.20s

Red

122 Alcanar

121 Cases d'Alcanar

Punta de la Baña
0370 Fl(2)12s27m12M

LFl.10s RW

⊕ 132

⊕132	40°31'N 00°42'.3E 3M SE Punta de la Baña
⊕133	40°43'N 01°01E 5.3M E Cabo Tortosa
⊕134	40°48'.5N 00°45°E Golfo de l'Ampolla

Rounding the Delta

Overview

Identifiable features on this low coast are few and far between. The coastline is constantly changing, as are the off-lying shoals. Navigational marks are not always on the coast and may be inland or out to sea. Sea levels tend to increase with winds between NE and SE and decrease with those from other directions. There is usually southerly current off the cabo.

From the S

From the area of Vinaròs set course for Punta de la Baña if necessary using the features on Sierra Montsi to keep a navigational fix. The industry at Alcanar (La Martinenca) may also be identified by the dust from the cement works. In the closer approach the lighthouse Punta de la Baña will be seen. Keeping about 1½M from the coast and outside the 10m contour, follow the coast in a NNE direction. The features marked on the plan will be seen in clear weather but in poor visibility little that can be identified will be seen. Do not cut the corner at Cabo Tortosa and keep at least 1M outside any visible land. The old lighthouse may be seen about a mile inland from the *cabo*. Continue outside the 10m contour which is about ½M off the coast.

Rounding the Ebro Delta from the N

It is normal to set course from the area of L'Ametlla de Mar direct for Cabo Tortosa. The houses at Ampolla and the lighthouse at Faro del Fangar will provide a position. The old lighthouse which lies about a mile inland to the W of Cabo Tortosa is difficult to spot even in good visibility. Do not approach the shore closer than the 10m contour. Do not attempt to round Cabo Tortosa within a mile of any visible land. Having rounded the *cabo* follow the coast about 1½M offshore, outside the 10m contour. If going up to Sant Carles, get into mid-channel between Alcanar and Punta Corballera.

Delta and Ports of the Río Ebro

Alfacs de Tortosa

40°43'N 0°54'E

Charts

British Admiralty *1701, 1704.* Imray *M13*
French *7048, 4720*
Spanish *485*

⊕132 40°31'N 00°42'·3E

Lights

0370 **Punta de la Baña** 40°33'·6N 0°39'·7E
   Fl(2)12s27m12M White tower black bands 26m
0377 **Cabo Tortosa** 40°42'·9N 0°55'·7E Fl.WR.6s18m14M
   Black metal framework tower, aluminium top 18m
   122°-W-052°-R-122°
0380 **El Fangal** 40°47'·4N 0°46'·1E Fl(2+1)24s20m12M
   White tower, red band, 18m Fl.2·5s Lts mark mussel
   beds 1·8M WSW

Buoys

There may be five wave measuring buoys Fl(5)Y.13s
stretching NW from near ⊕133.

The Ebro is the largest river in Spain depositing vast amounts of silt, building the delta out to sea. In some places the shore is advancing by 10m a year, sometimes leaving inland what were once coastal marks. In other places currents have washed away the shore and similar features have been left standing in water. Away from the sea, the delta consists of many small islands separated by canals, saltpans, pools, marshes and mud, all subject to flooding; it is hovercraft terrain. For some, and for fauna, it has its attractions. A large part of the delta on the NE side is a nature reserve and park.

This is a good area to hire a car or explore by cycle, to see rice being harvested or to spend an early evening in a bird hide. Large flocks of birds may be seen including; Great Egrets, Cattle Egrets, Little Egrets, various ducks and terns, Marsh Harrier, Osprey and Flamingos.

The shore line of the delta is probably the most dangerous section of this coast. It is featureless, very low-lying, it extends over 12M seawards from the general line of the coast and has unmarked, shifting, off-lying shoals. A peculiarity is that in good visibility, buildings etc. which are located some distance inland appear to be situated on the coast. A branch of the *tramontana* NW gale can come down the Ebro valley with considerable force and little warning. Altogether, from the point of view of the navigator, it is a place to be avoided.

Entry

It is possible for shallow draught vessels to enter and leave the river but very dangerous without a pilot (*práctico*) with up-to-date knowledge of the channels at the bar. The bar is itself dangerous if there is any sea running at the time.

Entrance to river

The River

There are two main ports on the lower section of the Río Ebro, Amposta 16M upstream from the river mouth and Tortosa a further 9M. Yachts with draught of 1·5m or less can ascend the river to Tortosa and for some miles more but again, a pilot (*práctico*) is essential. There are high tension wires, 13m or less above the water, just downstream of Isla Gracia, well before Amposta. Yachts with masts over 10m high will not be able to go beyond the three road bridges at Amposta. There are also rail and road bridges at Tortosa.

AMPOSTA

40°43'N 00°35'E

Amposta is a small old town with narrow streets and with 14,650 inhabitants. There is an old narrow road bridge and a series of quays alongside the river on the right (SW) bank. Below the town is a new wide bypass road bridge and above it is the new motor route bridge. There are a fair number of shops in town and everyday requirements can be met.

The Club Náutico de Amposta has a base with a pontoon and a small crane on the right bank of the Río Ebro just below the old road bridge. ☎ 977 701 824. There are showers, WCs and bar. A mechanic is available. This is a good place for motor boats.

TORTOSA

40°48'N 0°31'E

A very old town of 31,200 inhabitants with quays on the left bank, many interesting places and ruins to visit. This town had the first and only road bridge over the lower part of the Río Ebro and it was an important place from the point of view of commerce and defence. The Romans established the town and called it Dertosa Julia Augusta but they lost it to the Visigoths. They in turn lost it to the Moors in 714 who built the castle, now in ruins. It was then re-conquered by the Catalan, Ramon Bereguer IV, and for several centuries Catalans, Moors, Jews and others lived here together in peace. In 1938 there was a terrible battle here on the right (W) bank of the river between the Republicans and the Nationalists who triumphed; 150,000 died. A memorial stands in the middle of the river.

V. i. COSTA DORADA

Puerto del Fangar (Fangal)

Charts
British Admiralty *1701, 1704.* Imray *M13*
French *7048, 4720*
Spanish *485*

Lights
0380 **El Fangal** Fl(2+1)24s20m12M White tower with red
bands, 18m Fl.2·5s Lts mark mussel beds 1·8M WSW

A large shallow bay
This large stretch of water which is enclosed by the
N part of the Río Ebro (Ebre) delta. It is about 1M
by 2M with an entrance about 1M but space is
limited by *viveros*, fish farms, here raising mussels. It
is wide open to the N and with a NE wind a current
crosses the entrance. Depths, which ordinarily range
from 4m to 0m, may be raised as much as 0·6m by
easterly winds and lowered the same amount by
westerlies. The sides are very shallow. It is

surrounded by rice fields and *salinas* (saltpans)
ashore, together with a few barns and salt factories
but no roads or villages.

The *viveros* are all round the bay but there are
anchorages to be found, depending on draught.
Sound carefully.

⚓ ENSENADA DE CARTAPACIO 40°48′N 0°42′·4E

An anchorage in the W corner of the Golfo de
L'Ampolla in 1·8m, sand, open to NE-E. Sandy
beach. Road to L'Ampolla.

El Fangal lighthouse

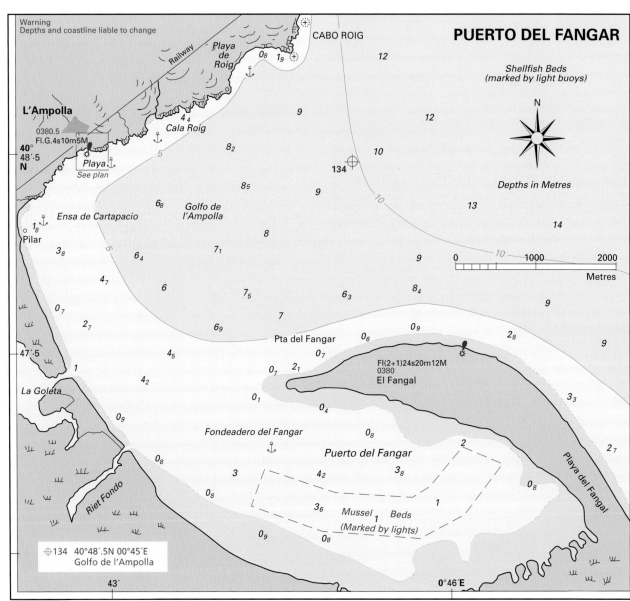

124. Puerto L'Ampolla

40°48'N 0°46'E

Charts

British Admiralty *1701.* Imray *M13*
French *7048, 4720*
Spanish *485, 838*

⊕134 40°48'·5N 00°45'E Steer 267°/1·8M to harbour

Lights

0380·3 **Dique jetty head** Fl(2)G.7s4m3M Green post 2m
0380·5 **Dique head** Fl.G.4s10m5M Green pyramidal tower 5m
0380·55 **Contradique head** Fl.R.5s4m3M Red truncated tower 3m
0380·6 **Contradique interior** Fl(2)R.7s4m1M Red square tower 3m

Port communications

VHF Ch 9. Club Náutico L'Ampolla ☎ 977 460 211
   Fax 977 593 007 *Email* port@nauticampolla.com
   www.nauticampolla.com

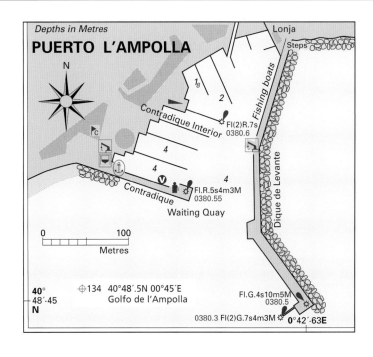

A reasonable port for yachts

A working fishing port with facilities developed for yachts and apparently a place favoured by Andorrans. The approach and entrance are easy but could be difficult if not dangerous in strong easterlies. Construction work is going on in the harbour and care should be taken on entering.

Approach

From the south Round the delta of the Río Ebro and from off the Faro del Fangar, go WNW towards the houses of L'Ampolla and look for the *dique.*

From the north Follow the steep rugged and indented coast at 400m. Punta Figuera and Cabo Roig will be identified, the latter having a reddish

streak of rock. The houses of L'Ampolla can be seen in the distance and, when close, the *dique.*

There are oyster beds marked by buoys Fl.Y.13s in the approaches to Ampolla.

Anchorage in the approach

Anchor off the Nuevo Contradique according to depth, with a line ashore.

Entrance

Approach the head of the Dique de Abrigo leaving it at least 30 metres to starboard and continue on that course to round the new jetty extension that protrudes WSW from just inside the Dique head. Round the end of the jetty and proceed to the fuel berth just inside the head of the contradique.

Puerto L'Ampolla

V. i. COSTA DORADA

Berths

Wait at the end of the *contradique* and ask at the *club náutico*.

Charges

High-ish but include showers, water, electricity and security.

Facilities

Maximum length overall 15m.
30-tonne travel-lift.
10- and 5-tonne cranes.
Slipway (but shallow approach).
Engine mechanics.
A small chandlery shop in the village.
Water from the *lonja* and taps on pontoons.
220v AC on piers, 380v AC on slipway.
Ice from the *club náutico* and the *lonja*.
Club Náutico L'Ampolla with terrace, swimming pool, showers and WCs.
Shops and supermarket nearby in the village.

Communications

Buses. Rail service to Barcelona. Taxi ☎ 977 490 386.

⚓ **CALA MONTERO** 40°48′·6N 0°43′·1E

A dry river mouth with rocky sides provides a small anchorage in 2m, mud, open between NE and S, stony beach.

⚓ **CALA DEL AGUILA** 40°50′·6N 0°45′·3E

A small anchorage off the mouth of a dry river open NE to S. The bottom is rocky 1 to 3m deep.

⚓ **ESTANY PODRIT** 40°51′·5N 0°47′·0E

An open anchorage off the mouth of a dry river open to NE to S. The bottom is 1 to 3·5m, weed, rocks and sand. A peak, Montaña del Aquila (159m), lies 1M to W.

⚓ **PLAYA DE ROIG** 40°49′·2N 0°44′·2E

125. Puerto de L'Estany Gras

40°52′N 0°47′E

Chart

British Admiralty *1701, 1704*. Imray *M13*
French *4720*
Spanish *838*

⊕135 40°52′·1N 00°47′·7E 295°/0·09M to harbour

Lights

0381 **North Point** 40°52′·4N 0°47′·7E Fl(3)G.10s14m3M
Green pyramidal tower 5m
0381·2 **Jetty** Fl(4)R.12s6m3M Red pyramidal tower 3m
Offshore, opposite entrance, there are a number of fish farms off the harbour which must be avoided when entering.

A very attractive small harbour

A small, most attractive, old natural harbour, now virtually deserted, which is located in a narrow deep rocky *cala*. A fish farm has been established opposite the entrance, about two miles out. The approach is easy but the entrance should not be attempted with onshore winds or swell. Facilities are limited to a broken quay. All supplies have to be obtained from L'Ametlla about 1M away to NE.

Approach

From the south Round the delta of the Río Ebro and set a NW course from off Cabo Tortosa. The town of L'Ametlla will be seen on approaching the mainland coast and the harbour lies 1M to the SW of this town. In the closer approach the two small lighthouses, 6m and 4m, will be seen.

From the north Follow the rocky broken coast in a SW direction past a conspicuous nuclear electric generating station near Cabo del Terme and the town of L'Ametlla. This harbour lies about 1M to SW of L'Ametlla. The two small lighthouses, 6m and 4m high, will be seen beside the entrance.

Playa de Roig (beyond the first headland): the S half of the bay is better than the N half where the bottom is mostly rock

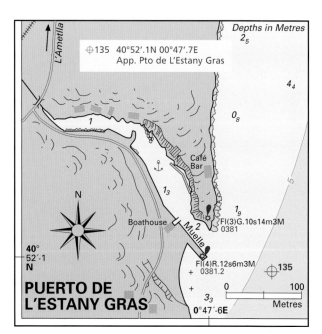

PUERTO DE L'ESTANY GRAS

Puerto de L'Estany Gras left, Calas central, Puerto de L'Ametlla de Mar, right

Entrance

Very tight. Approach on a NW heading and enter with care, towards the W side.

Anchorage

Depth off the quay is only 0·4m and ashlars and other underwater obstructions stick out from it. Anchor near the centre of the harbour in 1·5m, weed and rock, using an anchor trip-line. Lines can be taken ashore if others do not wish to get by.

Communications

A country road runs to L'Ametlla about 1M away where most requirements can be met.

⚓ CALA BON CAPO AND CALA BON CAPONET
40°52'·4N 0°47'·7E

⚓ CALA DE ARANGARET 40°53'N 0°48'E

A very small anchorage in 1·5m, sand, 400m to SW of Puerto de L'Ametlla de Mar. Open between NE, S and SE.

Note There are many small coves between Puerto de L'Ametlla and Cabo de Sant Jordi that may be used with care and prudence as day anchorages.

Puerto de L'Ametlla de Mar looking down harbour. Yachts turn to port at the fuel jetty *(page 84)* *Peter Taylor*

V. i. COSTA DORADA

126. Puerto de L'Ametlla de Mar

40°53'N 0°48'1E

Charts

British Admiralty *1701, 1704.* Imray *M13*
French *4720*
Spanish *838*

⊕136 40°52'·65N 00°48'·3E 340°/0·07M to harbour

Lights

0381·5 **Dique de Levante head** Fl(4)G.12s17m7M White
  post, green top 10m
0381·6 **Dique de Poniente head** Fl(2)R.7s9m4M Red
  truncated tower 4m
0381·7 **Contradique head** Fl(3)R.9s8m2M Red truncated
  tower 4m

Port communications

VHF Ch 9. Capitania ☎ 629 894 538
  Club Náutico ☎/*Fax* 977 45 72 40
Email cnam@pcserveis.com www.cnametllamar.com

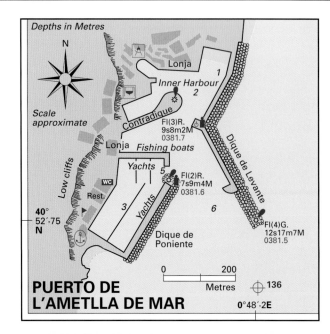

⊕136 40°52'.65N 00°48'.3E App. Pto de L'Ametlla de Mar

A busy harbour

An active fishing harbour with an area in the south
developed for yachts. The yacht quays are all new
and well equipped with water and electricity but are
some way from the old part of town which is well
worth a visit. There are a number of small beaches
in *calas* near the harbour.

Approach

From the south To the N of the Ebro delta the
mainland coast is of reddish rock and is of very
broken low cliffs with high ground further inland.
Punta Figuera with a red and white beacon on it is
easily recognisable but Punta del Aguila is not
conspicuous. The wide Cala de Santa Cruz and the
deep Puerto de L'Estany Gras, which has two small
lighthouse towers can be identified. The town of
L'Ametlla can be seen from afar.

From the north From the conspicuous promontory
Cabo de Salou the coast is low until Punta Llastres
where the high Sierra de Balaguer range reaches the
sea. The grey blocks of two nuclear power stations
just to the N of Cabo Terme are conspicuous; off
shore there are two buoys, one an E cardinal. The
town of L'Ametlla will be seen from afar.

Puerto de L'Ametlla de Mar

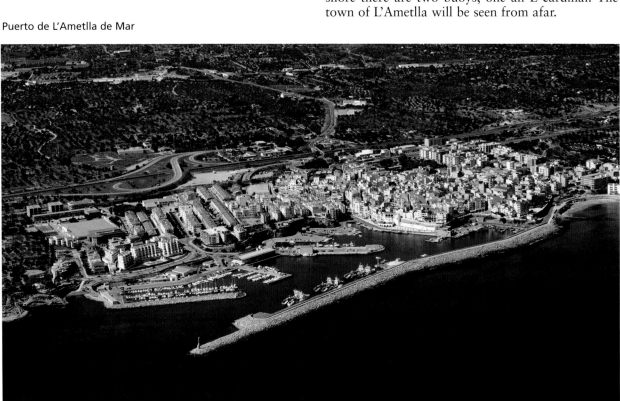

Entrance

Straighforward but give the Dique de Levante a reasonable (25m) berth as its foundations slope out into the water. Make for the head of the Dique de Poniente and turn to port around its head into the yacht basin.

Berths

The *capitanía* should be called (Ch 9 or phone) before entering to obtain berthing instructions. Failing this pick up a vacant berth (all berths have lines from the quay) and go ashore to the *capitanía* for further instructions. The inner harbour is now totally taken over by fishing vessels and a yacht should not proceed past the fuelling berth – and, as usual, no anchoring is permitted in the harbour.

Charges

Medium.

Facilities

Full repair facilities with slipway and 20-tonne crane.
Chandlery in NW corner.
Water and electricity on quays and pontoons.
Fuel and ice.
Club nautico has new building with WCs, showers, bar, restaurant and office.
Many shops near harbour and in town.

Communications

Rail and bus service.

⚓ PUERTO SANT JORDI D'ALFAMA

⊕ 40°54'·65N 0°50'·43E

Sant Jordi was developed back in the late nineties but ran out of money around 2000 and the harbour silted up and the lights were withdrawn. In 2007 it was reported that the Calafat Marina Company had taken over the badly silted site and would be developing it.

Puerto Sant Jordi d'Alfama

V. i. COSTA DORADA

127. Puerto de Calafat
40°56'N 0°51'E

Charts
British Admiralty *1701, 1704*. Imray *M13*
French *4720*
Spanish *838*

⊕138 40°55'·55N 00°51'·1E 300°/0·07M to harbour

Lights
Harbour
0382·3 **Dique de Abrigo head** Fl.G.4s9m6M Green tower 6m
0382·4 **Contradique** Fl(2)R.10s5m4M Red tower 4m
To the northwest
0386 **Cabo Salou** 41°03'·3N 1°10'·3E Fl(4)20s43m23M White tower with red bands, 11m

Port communications
Marina office VHF Ch 09 ☎ 977 48 61 84
Fax 977 48 60 23 *Email* info@portcalafat.com
www.portcalafat.com

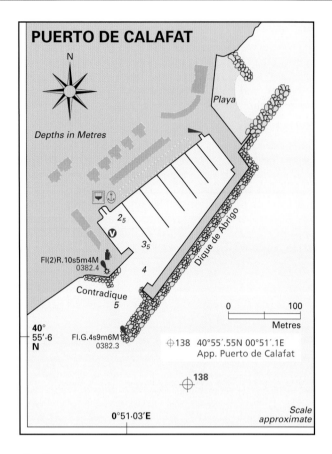

Yacht marina
A medium-sized yacht harbour built as part of a large residential development. Easy to approach and enter except in a gale in the south quadrant when the entrance is difficult and the harbour uncomfortable. Limited supplies. Sandy beach at NE side of the harbour.

Approach
From the south From Cabo Tortosa head NNW towards the two peaks of Es Frares (470m) and La Mamelleta (713m) which lie behind the harbour. The grey concrete buildings of the nuclear power station are about a mile beyond the harbour.

In the closer approach Cabo de Sant Jordi, with a ruined fort, and its near-by port may be seen, then the housing estate in the trees behind the harbour and its breakwaters will be recognised.

From the north from Cabo de Salou (79m) the coast to SW is of low rocky cliffs with concentrations of houses. Puerto de Cambrils has some tall apartment blocks and a long rocky breakwater which are easily recognised.

Puerto de Hospitalet de L'Infant can likewise be recognised by the high-rise buildings and the harbour breakwater. Punta de Ríu de Llastres is a low promontory and has shallow water off its point. The two large concrete buildings of the nuclear reactors can be seen from afar. In the close approach the housing estate and the harbour breakwaters will be seen.

Anchorage in the approach
Anchor ¼M to S of the harbour in 10m sand.

Entrance
Straightforward but if entering with a strong following wind, be prepared for some sharp manoeuvring once inside.

Berths
Secure to quay at port side of the entrance and ask. If no-one around, inquire at the *torre de control*.

Facilities
Maximum length overall 20m.
40-tonne travel-hoist.
5-tonne crane.
Limited hard-standing near travel-hoist.
Slipway.
Water from taps on quays and pontoons.

Calafat fuel berth *Robin Rundle*

Puerto de Calafat

Gasoleo A and petrol.
Some shops and a small supermarket near the harbour; probably better to go to Ametlla.

Communications

Bus and rail. Car hire. Taxi ☎ 977 456 468.

Cabo del Term 40°57'·07N 0°52'·45E
Two nuclear power stations, one inside a large square concrete building with no windows, the other inside a round tower-shaped building, are located 1 to 1½M respectively to NE of this *cabo* and are very conspicuous. A special spar light buoy lies 600m off the coast to NE and a S cardinal lightbuoy lies to SW marking water intakes.

V. i. COSTA DORADA

128. Puerto de Hospitalet de L'Infant

40°59'N 0°56'E

Charts

British Admiralty *1701, 1704*. Imray *M13*
French *4720*
Spanish *838*

⊕139 40 59'·2N 00°55'·6E 000°/0·04M to harbour

Lights

0382·5 **Dique SE head** Q(4)G.10s10m5M Green tower, 5m
0382·6 **Contradique head** Fl.R.2s5m3M Red tower on white base, 3m
28530(S) **Buoy** 40°59'·3N 0°55'·6E Fl(4)R.15s1M Port hand can topmark
To the northwest
0386 **Cabo Salou** 41°03'·3N 1°10'·3E Fl(4)20s43m23M White tower with red bands, white building 11m

Port communications

VHF Ch 9. ☎ 977 823 004 *Fax* 977 82 05 34
Email cnhv@cnhv.net www.cnhv.net

Medium-sized yacht harbour

An artificial yacht harbour of medium size controlled by the Club Náutico de L'Hospitalet-Vandellós. Entry is usually easy but difficult in S gales when swell enters the harbour. This is a tourist area and there are many apartment blocks and hotels. Quite a lot of walking to be done to get anywhere. Good large sandy beach to SW. A hospice was founded here in 1314. Its ruins and a tower can still be seen.

Approach

From the south The harbour is due N from Cabo Tortosa. As the coast is approached Vandellós nuclear power station, with two large grey concrete buildings 3M SW of the harbour, should be seen. The group of high-rise buildings behind the harbour and its breakwaters will appear in the close approach.

From the north From Cabo Salou, a prominent and easily recognised feature, the low rocky cliffs and sandy beaches stretch SW. The houses, breakwater and tower of Puerto de Cambrils will be recognised as will the high-rise buildings of L'Hospitalet and its harbour breakwaters in the close approach.

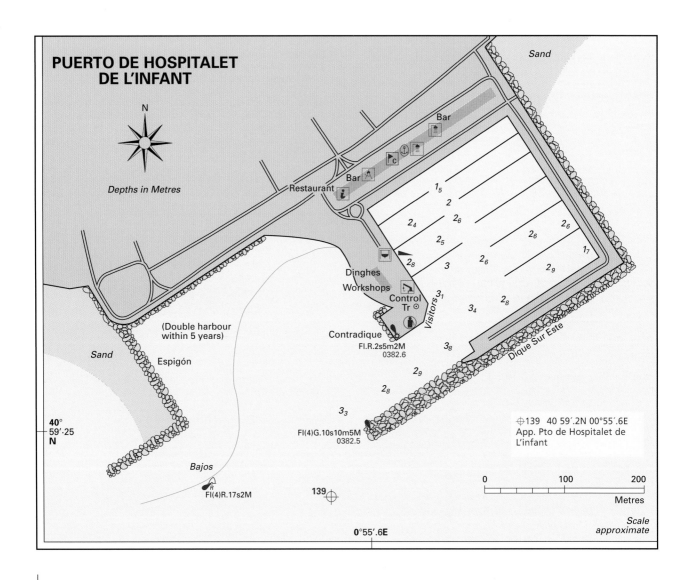

Puerto de Hospitalet de L'Infant (Vandellós)

Anchorage in the approach

Anchor in 8m, sand, ¼M to S of the harbour entrance.

Entrance

Approach on a N course, round Dique Sud Este and go to the waiting quay on the *contradique*, by the fuel pumps. Do not stray inshore on the west side of the *contradique*.

Berths

If no-one comes, ask at the *torre de control*. Berths have posts instead of mooring buoys or lines for securing the bow of the yacht. Berths for smaller yachts on pontoons have floating spurs.

Harbour charges

Medium.

Facilities

Maximum length overall 18m.
8-tonne crane.
Limited hard-standing.
Slipway.
Two chandlers beside the harbour.
Water on quays and pontoons.
Electricity 220v AC on quays and pontoons.
Small ice from the club and bars.
Gasoleo A and petrol.
Club Náutico de L'Hospitalet-Vandellós has a clubhouse
   on the NW side of the harbour with bar, showers,
      WCs etc. The club controls the harbour.
Food shops etc. in the village.

Communications

Road and rail. Taxi ☎ 977 810 363.

Hospitalet de L'Infant   *Robin Rundle*

129. Puerto de Cambrils

41°04′N 1°04′E

Charts

British Admiralty *1701, 1704. Imray M13*
French *4720*
Spanish *838*

⊕140 41°03′·57N 01°03′·52E 045°/0·06M to harbour

Lights

0383 **Dique de Levante head** Fl.G.4s15m5M Green
   pyramidal tower 11m
0384 **Dique de Poniente head** Fl(2)R.8s13m5M Red tower
   9m
0383·4 **Malecón Dársena Deportiva head** Fl(2)G.7s6m2M
   Green pyramidal tower 4m
To the west
0386 **Cabo Salou** 41°03′·3N 1°10′·3E Fl(4)20s43m23M
   White tower with red bands, white building 11m

Port communications

VHF Ch 9. *Club náutico* ☎ 977 360 531 *Fax* 977 362 654
   Email info@clubnauticcambrils.com
   www.clubnauticcambrils.com

Fishing harbour with yacht marina

Puerto de Cambrils is easy to approach and enter
and has good shelter. The area caters for a large
number of tourists in the season and a number of
ferries use the harbour for day trips. Facilities and
the shops are good.

The Monasterio de Escornalou some 5M inland
has a spectacular view. The Roman 'Oleaster', a
fortified church tower in the front of the town is of
interest. Good sandy beaches on either side of the
harbour, the better being to SW.

Approach

From the south The reddish rocky cliffs where the
Sierra de Balaguer lies alongside the coast end at
Punta de Ríu de Llastres and the coast becomes low,
flat and sandy. The houses and harbour works at
Cambrils can be seen from afar.

From the north Having rounded the rocky-cliffed
promontory of Cabo de Salou, which is covered with
large private houses and some high-rise buildings,
the coast becomes low, flat and sandy. The houses,
flats and light-coloured rocky breakwater of this
harbour can be seen from afar.

Anchorage in the approach

Anchor some 400m to W of the entrance in 5m on
sand.

Entrance

Round the head of the Dique de Levante, leaving it
25–30m to starboard and enter nearer to the head of
the Dique de Poniente which can be rounded at 15m.
Go across the harbour and round the head of the
Malecón Darsena Deportiva at about 15m.

Berths

Berth stern-to the pontoons with mooring buoy
from the bow in the E side of the yacht harbour and
check at the reception centre.

Harbour Charges

Low.

Moorings

A few private moorings are available in the main
harbour.

Puerto de Cambrils

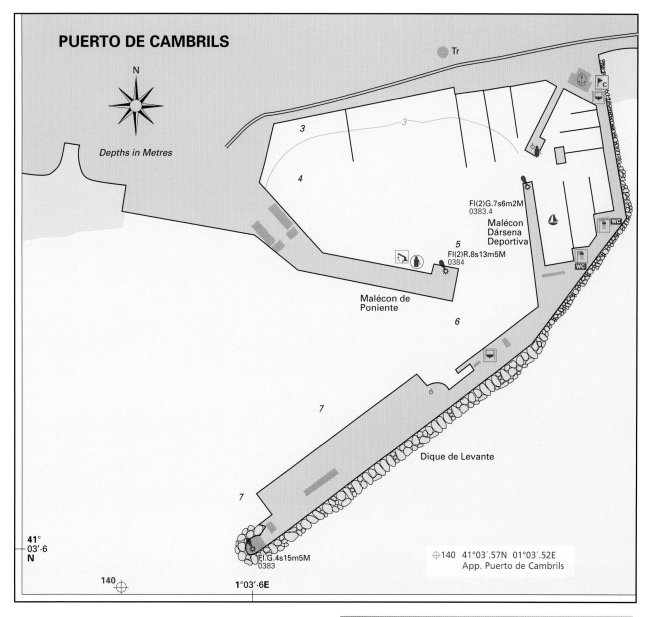

PUERTO DE CAMBRILS

N

Tr

Depths in Metres

3

3

4

5

Fl(2)G.7s6m2M
0383.4

Malécon
Dársena
Deportiva

Fl(2)R.8s13m5M
0384

Malécon de
Poniente

6

WC

WC

c

7

Dique de Levante

7

41°
03'·6
N

Fl.G.4s15m5M
0383

140

⊕140   41°03'.57N 01°03'.52E
App. Puerto de Cambrils

1°03'·6E

V. i. COSTA DORADA

Facilities

Maximum length overall 20m.

Limited repairs are possible and there are a number of engine mechanics in town.

140-tonne travel-lift and 12-tonne crane in port.

7·5-tonne crane.

Two slipways.

A chandlery shop in the town.

Water on the pontoons in the yacht harbour or from the *lonja*.

110v and 220v AC from the *club náutico*, pontoons and quay.

Gasoleo A and petrol.

Ice factory near the *lonja*.

Club Náutico de Cambrils with restaurant, bar, terrace, showers.

A number of shops alongside the harbour but many more in the town itself which is about ½M inland.

Launderette in the town.

Communications

Rail and bus service. Air services from Tarragona-Reus about 10M away. Taxi ☎ 977 362 622.

Cambrils: fuel and reception   *Peter Taylor*

EMBARCADERO DE REUS CLUB DE MAR
41°04'·2N 1°07'E

A jetty 100m long projecting from the shore ¾M to W of Puerto de Salou. Roads, railway and houses ashore. Can be used as a landing. Anchor in 2m, sand, to S of head of pier.

130. Puerto de Salou

41°07′N 1°07′E

Charts

British Admiralty *1701, 1704*. Imray *M13*
French *4720, 4827*
Spanish *4861, 487A, 838*

⊕141 41°04′·2N 01°07′·7E 010°/0·18M to harbour

Lights

0385 **Dique de Levante head** Fl(2)G.8s9m5M Green
    column 4m
0385·5 **Dique de Poniente head** Fl(2)R.8s4m3M Red post
    2m

Port communications

VHF Ch 9. ☎ 977 382 166/ 977 382 167 *Fax* 977 384 454
    Email club@clubnauticsalou.com or cnsalou@bitel.es
    www.clubnauticsalou.com

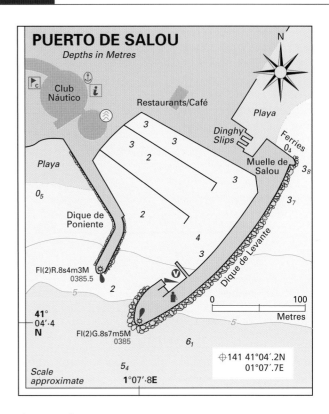

A small expensive port

Salou has been a fishing port since Roman times
when it was called Salauris; from it Jaime I (El
Conquistador) set forth to conquer Mallorca in
1229. It is now one of the more popular summer
resorts and the town is primarily concerned with the
mass tourist trade. It has an expensive, small
artificial harbour with very limited space for visitors
and limited facilities. The approach and entrance are
not difficult but would be dangerous in strong winds
and swell from SW. There are excellent sandy
beaches on each side of the harbour.

Approach

From the south The high Sierra de Balaguer gives
way to flat, sandy coasts at Punta de Ríu de Llastres.
The houses, flats and breakwater at Cambrils are
easily identified. The many high-rise buildings at
Salou can be seen from afar and the harbour will be
seen when closer in.

Puerto de Salou

From the north Cabo de Salou, a rocky-cliffed promontory, is easily identified. Apart from its lighthouse it has a number of high-rise buildings and large houses on it. Once rounded, the buildings of Salou will be seen about 4M further on. In the close approach the harbour will be seen.

Anchorage in the approach

Anchor 300m to W of the head of the Dique de Levante in 3m, sand.

Entrance

Straightforward, the visitors berth is immediately inside the entrance to starboard.

Charges

High.

Facilities

Engine mechanics.
10-tonne crane and a mobile 5-tonne crane.
Two slipways and dinghy slips.
Water points on the quays and pontoons.
220v and 380v AC on the quays and pontoons.
Ice from the *club náutico*.
Gasoleo A and petrol.
Club Náutico de Salou clubhouse has good facilities.
Supermarket and many shops in the town nearby.
Launderette in town.

Communications

Bus and rail. Tarragona airport 7M. Taxi ☎ 977 380 034.

Salou   *Robin Rundle*

Salou entrance – wide but shallow   *Peter Taylor*

V. i. COSTA DORADA

Cala de la Torre Nova (or del Lazareto): an anchorage in 2m, sand, open SE through to W. Sandy beach and high-rise buildings

⚓ **S OF SALOU** 41°04′N 1°08′·3E

A big ship anchorage ½M to S of Puerto de Salou in 11m, sand and weed. Open to SE through to W.

⚓ **CALA DE LA TORRE NOVA (OR DEL LAZARETO)** 41°04′N 1°08′·7E

⚓ **CALA PINATEL (OR GRAN)** 41°03′·7N 1°09′·2E

An open anchorage off a large sandy beach the Playa de Pinatell in 2m, sand. Open to SE through to W.

⚓ **N OF PUNTA DE PENY TALLADA** 41°03′·6N 1°09′·4E

A small bay open between S and W; anchor in 2m, sand.

⚓ **CALA DE LA FONT** 41°03′·5N 1°09′·5E

A small anchorage off a beach with a projecting rock. Open to S through to NW. Anchor in 2m, sand.

⚓ **CALA DEL CRANC** 41°03′·2N 1°10′E

A narrow bay with small bech and an isolated rock 0·5m deep in its mouth. Anchor in 2m, sand. Open S and SW

⚓ **CALA MORISCA** 41°03′·4N 1°10′·5E

A small bay open to NE through to S. Anchor in 2m, sand.

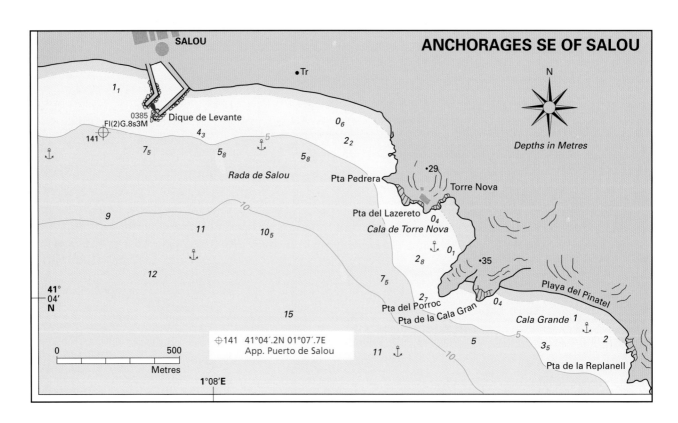

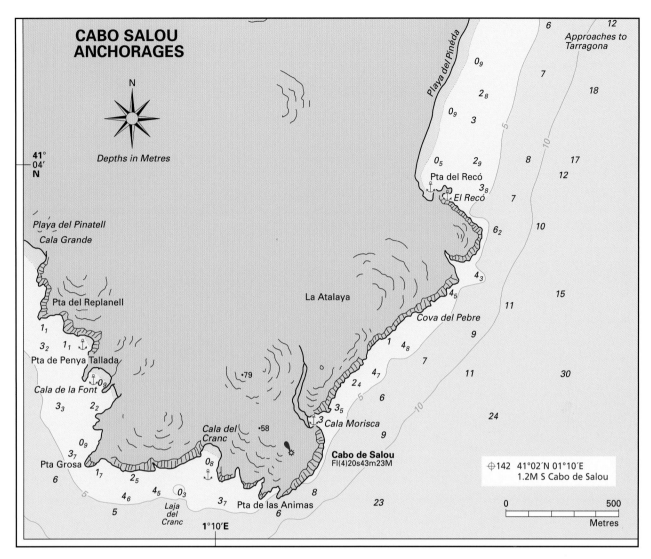

CABO SALOU ANCHORAGES

N

Depths in Metres

41° 04′ N

Playa del Pinatell
Cala Grande

Pta del Replanell

1_1

3_2 1_1

Pta de Penya Tallada

Cala de la Font 0_9

3_3 2_2

0_9

3_7

Pta Grosa 1_7 2_5

6

4_6 4_5 0_3

5 Laja del Cranc 3_7 Pta de las Animas

La Atalaya

•79

Cala del Cranc •58

0_8

Cova del Pebre

4_3

4_5

1 4_8

4_7

2_4

6

3_5

3 Cala Morisca

9

Cabo de Salou
Fl(4)20s43m23M

Playa del Pinéda

0_9

2_8

0_9 3

0_5 2_9

Pta del Recó

3_8 El Recó

6_2

8

9

7

11

11

6 12

Approaches to Tarragona

7

18

17
12

10

15

30

24

23

⊕142 41°02′N 01°10′E
1.2M S Cabo de Salou

0 500
Metres

41°10′E

⚓ **EL RECÓ** 41°04′·1N 1°10′·9E

A small bay open between N and E; anchor in 2m, sand. Two small rocky islets one each side of the bay.

⚓ **PLAYA DEL RECÓ** 41°04′·2N 1°11′E

An open anchorage off a long sandy beach. Anchor to suit draught, sandy bottom. Playa de Reco runs into Playa de Pineda which has a light on a breakwater at 41°04′N 1°11′E (Q(3)10s8m1M) on a cardinal E pole 6 metres high. Note pipeline on chart to W.

⚓ **CABO SALOU** 41°03′.3N 1°10′.3E

A built up and prominent headland with conspicuous lighthouse tower (11m) and a second tower (120m) NE of it on the top of the headland

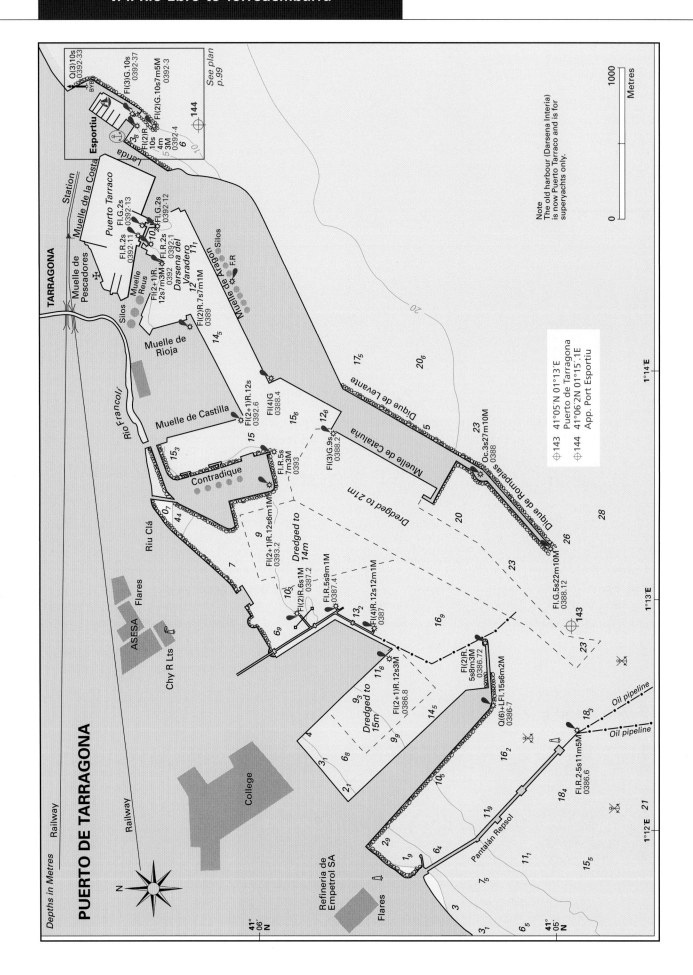

Depths in Metres   Railway

PUERTO DE TARRAGONA

TARRAGONA

Station

Muelle de la Costa

Lerida

Esportiu

See plan p.99

Note
The old harbour (Darsena Interia) is now Puerto Tarraco and is for superyachts only.

Q(3)10s
0392.33

Fl(3)G.10s
0392.37

Fl(2)G.10s7m5M
0392.3

Fl(2)R.10s 4m 3M
0392.4

144

1000 Metres

0

Puerto Tarraco

Fl.R.2s
0392.11   Fl.G.2s
0392.13   Fl.G.2s
0392.12

Muelle de Pescadores

Fl.R.2s
0392.1

Muelle Reus

Fl(2+1)R. 12s7m3M
0392

Darsena del Varadero

Fl(2)R.7s7m1M
0389

Muelle de Aragón   Silos   F.R

Muelle de Rioja

Silos

14₅

Río Francoli

Muelle de Castilla

Fl(2+1)R.12s
0392.6

Fl(4)G
0388.4

15₆   12₆

15₃   15   Fl(3)G.9s
0388.2

Contradique

Fl.R.5s -7m3M
0393

Muelle de Catalunya

17₅

20₆

Dique de Levante

Oc.3s27m10M
0388

23

5   5

Riu Clá

0₇   4₄

9   Fl(2+1)R.12s6m1M
0393.2

Dredged to 14m

Dredged to 21m

20

28

ASESA

Flares

7   Fl(2)R.6s1M
0387.2

10₁   Fl.R.5s9m1M
0387.41

13₂   Fl(4)R.12s12m1M
0387

23

26

Fl.G.5s22m10M
0388.12

143

Chy R Lts

6₉

6₈   Dredged to 15m   11₆   Fl(2+1)R.12s3M
0386.8

9₉   14₅   Fl(2)R. 5s8m3M
0386.72   16₉   23

College

4   3₁

2₁   9₃

Q(6)+Fl.15s6m2M
0386.7

18₃   Oil pipeline
Oil pipeline

16₂

10₅   Fl.R.2-5s11m5M
0386.6   21

Refineria de Empetrol SA

Flares

3₁   11₉   6₄   Pantalán Repsol   18₄

2₉   1₉   11₁   15₅

3   7₅   6₅   41° 05′ N

1°12′E   1°13′E   1°14′E

41° 06′ N

⊕143   41°05′N 01°13′E   Puerto de Tarragona
⊕144   41°062N 01°15′.1E   App. Port Esportiu

Puerto de Tarragona

131. Puerto Tarraco
132. Portu Esportiu

41°05'N 1°13'E
Note The old harbour is normally forbidden to yachts but might be used in stress of weather. In normal circumstances go to the Port Esportiu (Puerto Deportivo).

Charts

British Admiralty *1193, 1701, 1704.* Imray *M13*
French *7047, 4720, 4827*
Spanish *4871, 487A, 838*

⊕143 41°05'N 01°13'E

⊕144 41°06'.2N 01°15'.1E 340°/0·15 to harbour

Lights

To the south
0386 **Cabo Salou** 41°03'·4N 1°10'·4E Fl(4)20s43m23M
   White tower with red bands, white building
Approach main harbour
0386·2 **Repsol Pipeline buoy** 41°04'N 1°13'·2E
   Fl(4)Y.20s5M Spar with x topmark
0388·12 **Dique de Levante head** 41°05'N 1°13'·2E
   Fl.G.5s22m10M Green tower 11m
0386.72 **Contradique head** Fl(2)R.5s8m5M
0388 **Dique de Levante Faro de la Banya** Oc.3s1M Grey
   post on pilot house 27m
Port Esportiu
0392·3 **Outer breakwater** 41°06'·4N 1°15'·1E
   Fl(2)G.10s7m5M Green post 3m
0392.4 **Contradique head** Fl(2)R.10s4m3M Red post 1m
To the north
0393·6 **Altafulla Beach breakwater** 41°07'·8N 1°22'·2E
   Q(6)+LFl.15s5m5M s on black beacon, yellow top 4m
0393.7 **Punta de la Galera** 41°07'·9N 1°23'·7E
   Fl(5)30s58m19M White tower, bronze top 38m

Port communications

Tarragona Pilots – VHF Ch 9, 12, 14, 16.
Capitanía ☎ 977 226 611.
Real Club Nautico de Tarragona ☎ 977 240 360
   Fax 977 222 417 *Email* info@rcntarragona.com
   www.rcntarragona.com

Storm signals
Flown from a flagstaff on the Muelle de Pescadores.

An old port with two marinas

This is a very old port of a city with a fascinating history with a new yacht marina alongside. The old commercial and fishing port, greatly enlarged by the addition of huge breakwaters has an easy all weather approach and entrance. However, the old harbour (now Puerto Tarraco) is for super yachts only. All visiting yachts and pleasure craft should proceed to Port Esportiu outside the Dique de Levante. The Club Náutico de Tarragona is located there and is available to all visiting yachtsmen. Its facilities include a swimming pool. Entry may be difficult in strong S to SW winds.

Originally the Iberian stronghold of Cosse, Tarragona has been an important place since the Carthaginians built a fortress here called Tarchon in the 3rd century BC. Some of the walls can still be seen. Known under the Romans as Callipolis,

Terraco, Togata and later Colonia Julia Victrix Triumphans, the city flourished, only to be occupied by the Goths and later razed by the Moors in 714. It was subsequently rebuilt but damaged again by the French and later the British during Sir John Murray's retreat in the face of Soult's advance in 1813. There are so many interesting places to visit in Tarragona and the surrounding area that if a green *Michelin* or a *Guide Bleu* is not aboard, it is worth getting a guide from the local tourist board. Apart from all the historic monuments, there are good sandy beaches on either side of the harbour.

Approach

Commercial craft have right of way in the harbour and its approaches.

A special yellow pillar lightbuoy Fl(4)Y.20s marks the extremity of a pipeline about 1M SE of the harbour, with floating hose lines marked by buoys Fl.Y.

From the south The low, flat, sandy coast extends to the rocky-cliffed promontory of Cabo de Salou which is easily recognised by its conspicuous lighthouse, houses and some high-rise buildings. Once these are rounded the city of Tarragona on its hill, the large petrochemical works and factories to its W will be seen. In the closer approach the port breakwater, cranes and silos will become apparent. The entrance to the Port Esportiu lies outside the Dique de Levante, about 2M from its head.

From the north The long, flat, sandy beaches backed by low ranges of hills are only broken by the low yellow cliffs of Cabo Gros and Punta Mora. The city of Tarragona on its hill will be seen from afar, probably before passing Altafulla Beach breakwater marked by a S cardinal light. In the closer approach the yellow rocky harbour breakwater will be seen together with the smoke and flares from the factories beyond the port. The Port Esportiu lies on the way to the old harbour entrance, outside the harbour walls, just southwest of the point where the city buildings turn inland to skirt the harbour.

Anchorage in the approach

Anchor ½M to NE of the head of the Dique de Levante in 26m, sand, or about 200m to W of the *contradique* in 6 to 10m sand. Beware oil pipelines which run across the harbour from the entrance to the various terminals.

Entrance

Main harbour Round the head of the Dique de Levante, giving it a berth of at least 400m to starboard. Follow the NW side of this *dique* at 100m into the Dársena de Varadero which should be crossed on a NE course, entering the Dársena Interior between the heads of the two *muelles*. The *muelle* to starboard may be marked by a buoy.

Port Esportiu Straightforward but awkward and possibly dangerous in strong southerlies. There may be backwash from the harbour wall if there is a sea running.

V. i. COSTA DORADA

131. Puerto Tarraco

⊕142 41°02′N 01°10′E 1·2M S Cabo de Salou

Port communications

Puerto Tarraco
☎ 977 24 41 73 *Fax* 977 21 63 22
Email info@puertotarraco.com www.imt.es
VHF Ch 11,14 (bridge operator Ch 06)

A harbour for superyachts

Puerto Tarraco is managed by the company International Marine Tarragona. It is specifically designed for superyachts who must give notice of arrival 48 hours in advance. The port does not accept vessels of less than 24 metres length, except in emergency. Vessels entering Puerto Tarraco in an emergency should be aware of the air draft of 6·5 metres and the need to call the Mobil Bridge operator on Ch 6 to ask for an opening. They should also note that Tarragona Port control listen on Ch 16 and should be kept informed of the vessel's position and intentions.

Facilities

Major facilities to cater for the needs of superyachts are available in this harbour and are not listed here although they include one of the best yacht yards on the coast located in the W corner of the Dársena Interior. There are a number of engine repair workshops and one which repairs electronic equipment.

There is an abundance of restaurants on site or within easy reach of this harbour.

Port Tarraco looking S – restaurants on the left   *Peter Taylor*

Port Tarraco at Tarragona with Port Esportiu in foreground

132. Tarragona - Port Esportiu

⊕144   41°06'·2N 01°15'·1E 345°/0·15M to harbour

Port Communication

☎ 977 21 31 00 *Fax* 977 21 27 02
Email nautictg@portesportiutarragona.com
www.portesportiutarragona.com
VHF Ch 9

A modern marina

The Club Nautico is located in Port Esportiu, a modern purpose built marina which is managed by Nautic Tarragona SA. Visitors are welcome to use all the Club facilities.

Approach

Approach to the harbour is straightforward but care should be taken if swell builds up in S or SW winds. Call for berthing instructions on Ch 9 or go to the waiting pontoon just beyond the fuel dock.

Facilities

Engineering services in the old harbour may be arranged. 12-tonne crane.
Ice factory three streets behind the Muelle de Pescadores. There are many small shops near the port. There is a large market in the city, a short bus ride away.

Communications

Bus and rail service. Airport at Reus, 7M.
    Limited bus service to mountainous parts inland.
    Taxi ☎ 977 221 414.
British Consul: Calle Real 33 1°1a 43004 Tarragona
    ☎ 977 220 813 *Fax* 977 218 469.

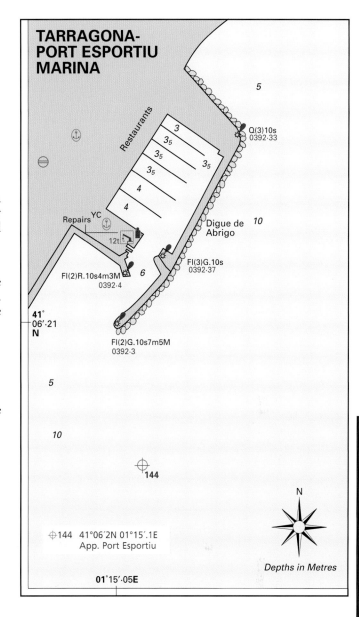

Port Esportiu restaurants *Robin Rundle*

Port Esportiu 12-tonne crane *Robin Rundle*

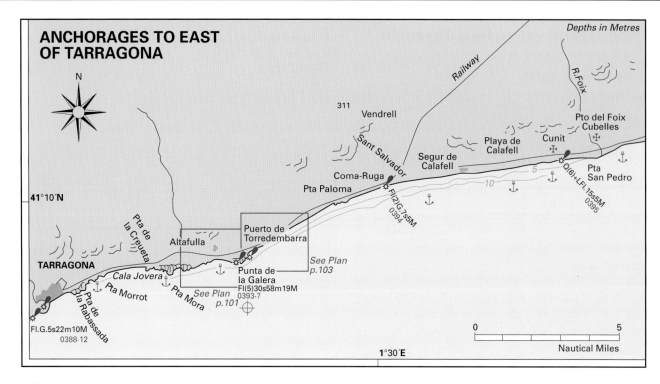

ANCHORAGES TO EAST OF TARRAGONA

Depths in Metres

N

311 Vendrell

Railway

R.Foix

Pto del Foix
Cubelles

Sant Salvador

Playa de Calafell

Cunit

Segur de Calafell

41°10′N

Coma-Ruga

Pta Paloma

Pta San Pedro

Q(6)+LFl.15s5M
0395

Fl(2)G.7s5M
0394

10

5

Pta de la Creueta

Altafulla

Puerto de Torredembarra

TARRAGONA

Cala Jovera

Pta Morrot

Pta Mora

Punta de la Galera
Fl(5)30s58m19M
0393.7

See Plan p.103

See Plan p.101

Fl.G.5s22m10M
0388·12

Pta de la Rabassada

1°30′E

0 5

Nautical Miles

⚓ **PLAYA DE LA RABASSADA** 41°07′N 1°16′·7E

⚓ **ANCHORAGE E OF RABASSADA**
41°07′·2N 1°17′·2E

Anchorage E of Rabassada: anchor to suit draught.
Open between E and SW

⚓ **CALA DE LA JOVERA** 41°07′·5N 1°20′·9E

A very small anchorage in 1.8m, sand, tucked away at the foot of the 12-13th-century castle of Tamarit which has three towers. Only for use by small yachts with care, open to E to S

⚓ **ALTAFULLA** 41°07′·8N 1°22′·8E

A deep-water anchorage ½M offshore to S of the town of Altafulla in sand open from E through S to W. Yacht club for dinghies ashore. Ruins of a Roman city. Sandy beach. There is now a breakwater off the beach with a 4m cardinal S tower at its seaward end. It is in 41°07′·7N 1°22′·3E and has characteristics Q(6)+LFl.15s5m5M.

⚓ RECO DEL FORTIN
41°07'·9N 1°23'E

An anchorage backed by holiday flats located where sandy Playa de Selmar meets the rocky mass of Cabo Gros. Anchor in 2m, sand. Open from S to W

⚓ W OF PUNTA LA GALERA (ROQUER)
41°07'·85N 1°23'·67E

A very small anchorage surrounded by rocky cliffs in 2m, sand, open to SE through W

⚓ CALA DEL CANADEL 41°07'·8N 1°23'·3E

An anchorage in front of a small sandy beach surrounded by low rocky cliffs in 2m, sand, open to SE through W.

PUNTA DE LA GALERA 41°07'·8N 1°23'·7E

A prominent rocky headland (20m) with a tall new lighthouse Fl(5)30s58m19M on its tip. The point has rocky cliffs with some houses on top.

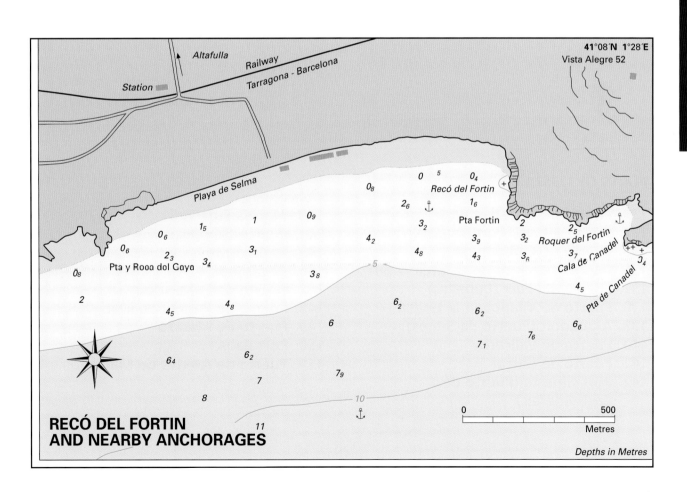

RECÓ DEL FORTIN
AND NEARBY ANCHORAGES

V. i. COSTA DORADA

V. COSTA DORADA
ii. Torredembarra to Río Tordera

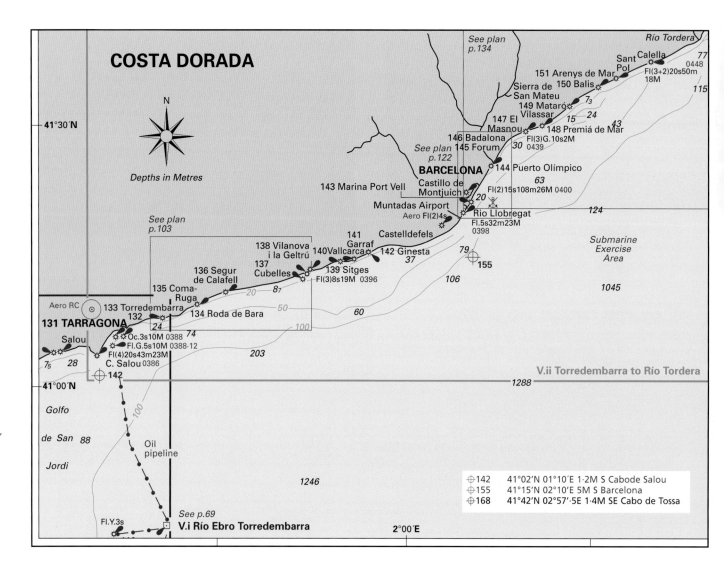

PORTS OF COSTA DORADA

133. Puerto de Torredembarra
134. Roda de Bara (Port Daurat)
135. Puerto de Coma-Ruga
136. Puerto de Segur de Calafell
137. Puerto del Foix (Cubelles)
138. Puerto de Vilanova i la Geltrú
139. Aiguadolç (Puerto de Sitges)
140. Puerto de Vallcarca
141. Puerto de Garraf
142. Port Ginesta (Puerto de Castelldefels)

143. Marina Port Vell
144. Puerto Olímpico
145. Port Forum
146. Badalona
147. Puerto de El Masnou
148. Puerto de Premiá de Mar
149. Puerto de Mataró
150. Port Balís
151. Puerto de Arenys de Mar

Port Vell Barcelona   *Robin Rundle*

Port Vell Barcelona   *Robin Rundle*

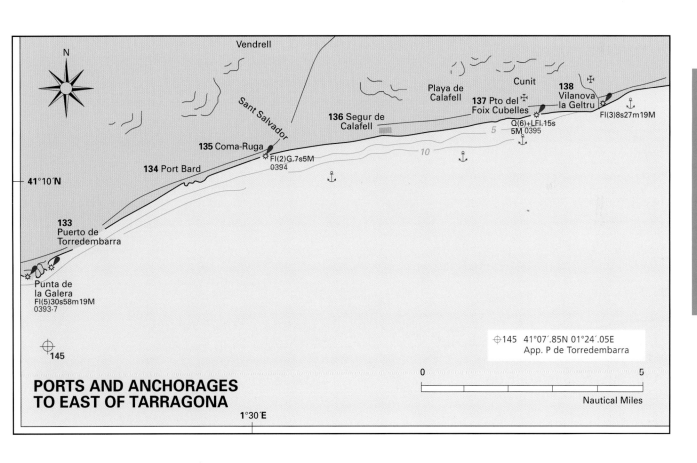

**PORTS AND ANCHORAGES
TO EAST OF TARRAGONA**

133. Puerto de Torredembarra

41°07'N 1°24'E

Charts

British Admiralty *1701, 1704.* Imray *M13*
French *4720, 4827*
Spanish *487A, 838*

⊕145 41°07'·85N 01°24'·05E 000°/0·12M to harbour

Lights

0393.7 **Punta de la Galera** 41°07'·9N 1°23'·7E
    Fl(5)30s58m19M Octagonal white tower, coppery top
    38m
0393.8 **Dique de Abrigo head** Q(4)G.10s10m5M Green
    post 5m
0393.82 **Inner Spur** Fl.G.5s4m1M Green post 2m
0393.83 Contradique corner Q(4)R.10s4m3M Red post
    0·5m
0393.84 **Contradique head** Fl.R.5s4m3M Red post 2m on
    short espigon jutting out of contradique
0393.85 **Dique de Abrigo corner** Q(3)10s9m3M BYB post
    E card topmark 3m

Port communications

VHF Ch 9. *Capitanía* ☎ 977 643 234 *Fax* 977 643 236
Email info@porttorredembarra.es
www.port-torredembarra.es

An excellent modern marina

Torredembarra is a first class marina with excellent shelter, all facilities but lacking only stores and provisioning which can be obtained in the town nearby. The marina has good chandlers, bars and restaurants.

Approach

From the south Cabo de Salou and the huge breakwater of Puerto de Tarragona are easily recognised. The old castle and towers at Tamarit near Punta de la Mora will be seen if close in, also the rocky-footed Punta de la Galera with its conspicuous 38m tall lighthouse at its tip. Torredembarra town may be visible inland.

From the north Pass the modern harbour at Aiguadolç with its old houses and new housing developments plus the large Puerto de Vilanova i la Geltrú close to SW. There is a tall white chimney at Cubello and a yellow generating station with breakwaters at Cunit. Puerto de Coma-Ruga which has a tall tower inland behind it may also be seen.

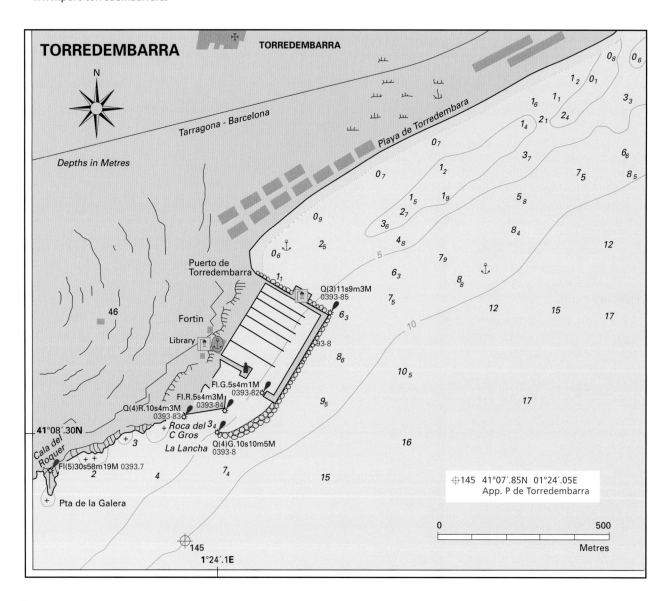

Puerto de Torredembarra

Entrance

The entrance (depth 6m) is at the SW end of the outer Dique de Abrigo and runs SW-NE. Round the head leaving at least 20m clear and proceed towards the head of the contradique. Note the light at its head is situated on a short *espigón* jutting SE.

Berths

Call the *capitanía* on Ch 9 (or phone) to arrange a berth before entering – otherwise go alongside the fuel berth and ask. All berths have lazy lines to the quay and anchoring is not permitted. Depths are generally 3·5m.

Anchorage in the approach

Anchor off the Playa de Torremdebarra NE of the harbour wall in a depth to suit.

Facilities

Maximum length overall 24m.
Full repair facilities including engine, welding, painting.
New *club náutico* has restaurant and bar.
45-tonne travel-lift.
6-tonne crane.
Chandlery.
Water on quays.
Showers.
220v AC on quays.
Gasoleo A and petrol.
Ice at the bar and at the petrol station.

Communications

Taxis ☎ 977 641 147/977 640 266.

Torredembarra *Capitania*   Peter Taylor

Torredembarra fuel jetty   *Peter Taylor*

V. ii. COSTA DORADA

134. Roda de Bara (Port Bará)

41°10'·0N 1°28'·5E

⊕146 41°09'·6N 01°28'E 020°/0·2M to harbour

Communications

VHF Ch9

☎ 977 138 169 Fax 977 803 566

Email mserra@novadarsenabara.es

www.novadarsenabara.es

Major marina opening 2008/2009

Although work started in 2000 the project stalled for a few years. In September 2007 work was proceeding fast with major stone, concrete and earth works well under way but no jetties or pontoons in position. The marina is due to be in operation in 2008 but this may be optimistic. By 2009 the full facilities of a modern marina (including a 100-ton travel lift) should be available. The plan is shown below.

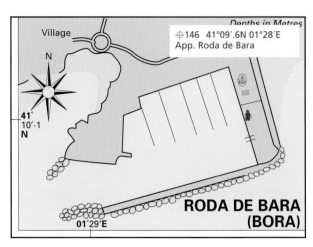

Roda de Bara: Outer breakwater and contradique
September 2007   *Peter Taylor*

Rada de Bará site of marina (2004)

Roda de Bara Point S of entrance   *Robin Rundle*

Coma Ruga *(page 108)   Peter Taylor*

V. ii. COSTA DORADA

135. Puerto de Coma-Ruga

41°11′N 1°31′E

Charts

British Admiralty *1701, 1704. Imray M13*
French *4827*
Spanish *838*

⊕147 41°10′·4N 01°31′·56E 000°/0·12M to harbour

Lights

0394 **Dique Oeste head** Fl(2)G.7s7m5M Green post 2m
0394·2 **Muelle Transversal W corner** Q(6)+LFl.15s9m3M s
   on yellow tower, black base 4m
0394·4 **E corner** VQ(6)+LFl.10s9m3M s on yellow tower
   black base 4m
0394·6 **Dique Este head** Fl.R.5s7m5M Red post 2m

Port communications

VHF Ch 9. *Capitanía* ☎ 977 680 120 *Fax* 977 681 753.
Email cnco@clubnautic.com www.clubnautic.com

An interesting small marina

An extraordinary harbour for small craft built at the
end of a 300m elevated road reaching out into deep
water. It has two entrances, one open to the East, the
other to the West. The water is shallow on either side
and the harbour is kept open by dredging. Facilities
are limited but everyday requirements can be met in
the town.

   The Arco Roman de Bará, a 2nd-century Roman
arch 1½M to SW of the town, is worth a visit and for
those interested in the 'cello, there is a Casals
museum. Excellent sandy beaches on either side of
the harbour.

Approach

From the south After the huge breakwaters of
Tarragona the old castle and towers at Tamarit near
Punta de la Mora will be seen if close in, as will the
rocky footed Punta de la Galera with its conspicuous
lighthouse. Torredembarra marina just N of Punta
de la Galera and the its inland town may be seen.
Puerto Coma-Ruga itself appears to be well out to
sea.

From the north The modern harbour at Aiguadolç
with its old houses and new housing developments
plus the large Puerto de Vilanova i la Geltrú close to
SW are easily seen. The power station and chimney
at Foix are conspicuous, followed by the Puerto de
Segur de Calafell which, like Coma-Ruga, is built
out to sea.

Anchorage in the approach

Anchor ¼M to SE of the harbour in 10m, sand and
mud, or closer in during good weather.

Future work: A major development of this port is planned
for completion around 2012.

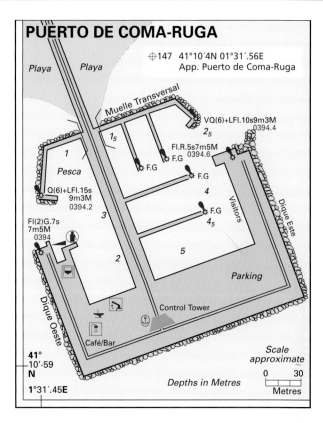

Entrance

Approach the E side of the harbour from the SE,
follow the Dique Este shorewards and enter by
rounding its head at 15m leaving it to port. Do not
use the entrance on the W side unless directed to do
so or to fill up with fuel. Sound as you go. The
entrance usually has about 2·5m but can be much
less.

Berths

Secure to the inner side of the Dique Este and ask at
the *torre de control* for a berth.

Facilities

Maximum length overall 15m.
Engineer on other side of the coast road.
A 10-tonne crane on the Dique Oeste.
A small slipway at the head of the Dique Oeste.
Chandlery in the town.
Water taps on quays and pontoons.
Showers and WCs at SW corner of the harbour.
220v AC from points on quays and pontoons.
Gasoleo A and petrol from pumps at the head of the
   Dique Oeste.
Small ice from the bar.
Club Náutico de Coma-Ruga has a temporary clubhouse
   at the junction of the harbour road with coast road.
Many shops including supermarkets in the town.

Communications

Bus and train services. Taxi ☎ 977 641 147.

Puerto de Coma Ruga

Coma Ruga W entrance   *Peter Taylor*

⚓ **SANT SALVADÓR** 41°10'·7N 1°32'·6E

An anchorage with 4 to 10m, sand, open from E to SW with a sandy beach ashore. There is a basic *club náutico* ashore for dinghies. A small town of 2000 inhabitants (approx) several hotels and some shops. See plan on page 102.

⚓ **CALAFELL** 41°11'N 1°35'E

An open anchorage in 4 to 10m, sand, off a sandy beach. Some houses ashore on the coast but the town of Calafell (4500 inhabitants) is 1½M inland, where there is a 12th-century castle. Two hotels, shops etc. There is a *club náutico* ☎ 977 69 03 37 which is a dinghy club with bar, restaurant, showers, WCs and a slipway. Not an attractive area. The anchorage is open between E and SW. See plan on page 102.

V. ii. COSTA DORADA

136. Puerto de Segur de Calafell

41°11'N 1°36'E

Charts

British Admiralty *1704*. Imray *M13*
French *4827*
Spanish *486*

⊕148 41°11'N 01°36'·25E 010°/0·2M to harbour

Lights

0394·8 Breakwater head Fl(4)G.12s8m5M Green post 4m
0394·84 **Contradique head** Fl(4)R.12s4m3M
  Red structure 1m

Port communications

VHF Ch 9 Capitania ☎ 977 159 119 *Fax* 977 162 666
Email capitania@portsegurcalafell.com
www.portsegurcalafell.com

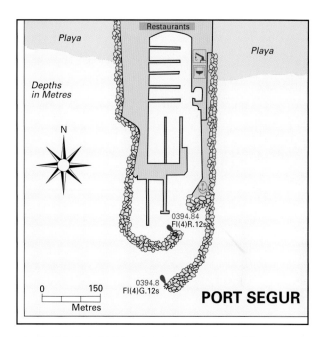

⊕148 41°11'N 01°36'.25E   App. P de Segur de Calafell

A first-class modern marina

The old port has been totally redeveloped with an entrance well out to sea. This should solve problems of silting which plagued the old harbour.

Facilities are much improved over the old Segur and the town is still there for supplies. There is a 12th-century castle at Calafell 2M inland. There are good sandy beaches on both sides of the harbour.

Approach

From the south North of Tarragona the coast has sandy beaches broken by the rocky Punta de la Galera just south of Torredembarra. Puerto de Coma Ruga, which is joined to the coast by a causeway is easily recognized as will be this harbour on closer approach.

From the north From the easily recognized Puerto de Vilanova i la Geltru the sandy beach stretches past the power station at Foix to this harbour which is easily seen on closer approach.

Anchorage in the approach

Anchor E or W of the harbour in a suitable depth in sand and mud.

Segur de Calafell   *Peter Taylor*

Puerto de Sugur de Calafell (2004) dredging and shoreside facilities are now complete

Segur de Calafell   *Peter Taylor*

Entrance

The new entrance is now in reasonably deep water. Approach the end of the Dique and enter on a northeasterly course.

Facilities

Engine repairs.
5-tonne crane.
50-tonne travel-lift.
Chandlery.
Water and electricity at all berths.
Cafés and restaurant on the N side of inner harbour.
24-hour security.

⚓ CUNIT

An anchorage open between E and SW off a sandy beach with T-shaped groynes. Anchor in 4 to 10m, sand. Ashore is a small town of some 1,000 inhabitants and a small *club náutico* for dinghies.

V. ii. COSTA DORADA

137. Puerto del Foix (Cubelles)

41°12'N 1°39'E

Charts

British Admiralty *1704*. Imray *M13*
French *4827*
Spanish *871, 487*

⊕149 41°11'·2N 01°38'·7E 010°/0·35M to harbour

Lights

0395 **Dique de Abrigo E end** 41°11'·6N 1°39'·4E
Q(6)+LFl.15s5m5M Black ꜛ on yellow concrete post,
black base 3m
F.R on conspicuous chimney 0.5M WNW

A simple harbour with no facilities

The harbour was built to service the Central Termica del Foix, a conspicuous power station with a very tall chimney. The outer part of the harbour forms a useful passage anchorage but the inner part should only be used in emergency. The harbour silts and is occasionally dredged; depths are unreliable. The entrance is dangerous in strong on-shore winds.

Approach

From the south Cabo de Salou and the large harbour of Tarragona are easily recognised. The coast eastwards is low and flat and lined with houses and summer apartment blocks. The small harbours of Coma-Ruga and Segur de Calafell jutting out into the sea are significant and the tall chimney and power station of Central Termica del Foix are conspicuous.

From the north The harbours of Aiguadolç and Vilanova i la Geltrú stand out and the Central Termica del Foix with its tall chimney will be seen from afar.

Entrance

The entrance to the outer harbour and anchorage is through a gap between the W head of the Dique de Abrigo which has a small post beacon and notice board and the E end of a groyne. The groyne and the Dique de Abrigo have recognisable regular crenellations.

The entrance to the inner harbour and quays lies to the E of the outer harbour behind and to N of the Dique de Abrigo.

Berths

Secure with care alongside one of the quays. There are some underwater projecting rocks and very few securing bollards. Keep well away from power station water intake at the NE corner of the harbour.

Anchorage

In the outer harbour near the centre of the bay about 2m, sand.

Facilities

None.

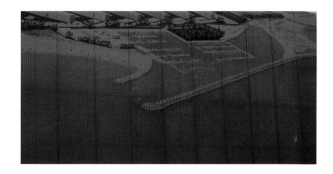

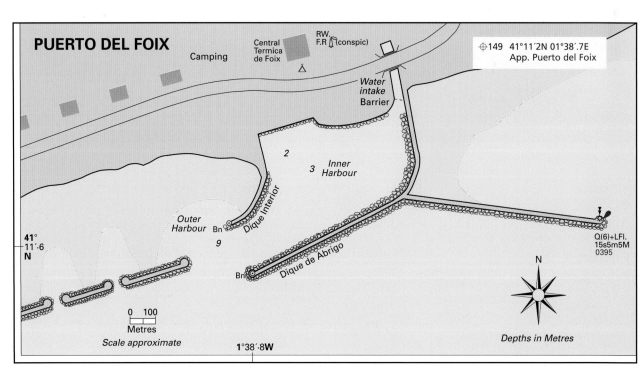

138. Puerto de Vilanova i la Geltrú (Villanueva y Geltrú)

41°13'N 1°44'E

Charts
British Admiralty *1704*. Imray *M13*
French *4827, 7298*
Spanish *488A, 4881*

⊕150 41°12'·3N 01°43'·6E 045°/0·1M to harbour

Lights
0396 **Punta San Cristobál** 41°13'·0N 1°44'·2E
Fl(3)8s27m19M Truncated conical stone tower, aluminium cupola, white house 21m 265°-vis-070°
0396.2 **Dique de Levante S head** Fl(2)G.7s18m5M Green tower on white base 10m
0396.12 **Nuevo Contradique head** Fl(2)R.7s15m3M Red pyramidal tower 5m

Port communications
Port VHF Ch 16.
Club Nautico VHF Ch 9 ☎ 938 150 267 *Fax* 938 156 469
Email cnv@cnvilanova.com www.cnvilanova.com
CN Marina Office ☎/*Fax* 938 153 453
Email oficinadeportiva@cnvilanova.com
Marina Far ☎ 938 105 611 *Fax* 938 154 770
Email mfv@marinafarvilanova.com
www.marinafarvilanova.com

Well-sheltered marinas
A large artificial fishing, commercial, ship-breaking and yachting harbour, easy to enter and with good protection. There are good facilities for yachtsmen and hotels, restaurants and good shops ashore.

Major works are in progress in the harbour just inside the Dique de Poniente, where a new marina for super yachts is being constructed.

Villanueva developed rapidly from a small fishing village in the 18th century when the Basque families who had been engaged in plundering the West Indies since the 16th century returned to Spain with their fortunes. They built large houses, set up some industries and are still occasionally referred to as *Los Indianos*.

The 10th-century castle and the two museums are worth a visit. Excellent sandy beaches on either side of the harbour.

Approach
From the south From Tarragona the coast has low cliffs with sandy bays and backed by hills. North of the steep cliffs of Cabo Gros are the three marinas of Torredembara, Coma-Ruga and Segur. The conspicuous power station and chimney at Foix is about 2½M W of Vilanova i la Geltrú. The harbour lies at the edge of a plain and has yellow rocky harbour breakwaters and a backdrop of factory chimneys, blocks of flats and houses.

From the north Barcelona is easily identified by the concentration of buildings, harbour works and smoke. The comparatively flat and featureless delta of the Río Llobregat is followed by a range of hills, the Sierra de la Guardia, which reach the sea in broken cliffs and small bays. South of this outcrop the harbour with its yellow rocky breakwater and factories, flats and houses will be seen, backed by a flat plain. A rocky patch lies on the W side of the Dique de Levante.

Anchorage in the approach
Anchor about 100m to W of the elbow of the Nuevo Contradique in 4m, sand.

Major works were in progress in late 2007 to alter the harbour within the existing breakwaters in order to provide more berths to larger yachts. Expect temporary lights to port during reconstruction

PUERTO DE VILANOVA
I LA GELTRÚ

⊕150   41°12´3N 01°43´.6E
App. P de Vilanova i la Geltrú

Entrance

Leave the head of the Dique de Levante 50m to starboard and round it onto a NE course then enter between the head of the Dique de Poniente and the root of the Dique de Levante.

Berths

Secure to pontoon near office of the *capitán de puerto* for allocation of a berth at Club Náutico or the new 'Marina Far'.

Charges

Medium.

Facilities

Maximum length overall 25m or 50m at new dock.
Repairs available by a local yard.
Mechanics and sailmakers.
100-tonne travel-lift.
25-tonne crane at the *club náutico* and several larger cranes at the ship breaking yard.
Slipway in the NW corner of the harbour, larger ones in the NE corner and the Dársena Comercial.

Puerto de Vilanova i la Geltrú prior to the ongoing work on Dique de Poniente.
Note new works on Plan page 114.

Three small chandlery shops near the harbour.
Water taps on the pontoons of the *club náutico* and the quays.
220v AC from points on the pontoons and quays.
Gasoleo A and petrol.
Ice at fuel quay or from a factory at the N end of the Dársena de la Pesca.
The Club Náutico de Vilanova i la Geltrú clubhouse, in the NW corner of the harbour, has bars, lounge, terrace, restaurant, showers and a swimming pool.
Good shops of most types in the town, also a market and supermarket.
Launderette at marina.
Weather forecast at *capitanía*.

Communications

Rail and bus services. Taxi ☎ 938 933 241.

Sitges Captania　　*Robin Rundle*

139. Aiguadolç (Puerto de Sitges)

41°14′N 1°49′E

Charts

British Admiralty *1704*. Imray *M13*
French *4827, 7298*
Spanish *871, 4882, 488A*

⊕151　41°13′·85N 01°49′·25E 045°/0·15M to harbour

Lights

0396·54 **Dique de Levante head** Fl.G.5s12m5M Green tower, white base 10m
0396·55 **Dique de Levante Spur** Fl(2)G.13s6m1M Green tower, white base 6m
0396·56 **Contradique head** Fl.R.5s4m3M Red house corner 4m

Port communications

VHF Ch 9. *Capitanía* ☎ 938 942 600 *Fax* 938 942 750
　Email info@portdesitges.com www.portdesitges.com
Club Nautic de Sitges ☎ 937 432 057 *Fax* 937 432 008
　Email cns@nauticsitges.com www.nauticsitges.com

A friendly marina

An artificial yacht harbour with good facilities. Approach and entrance are easy and good shelter obtained, but with wind from the SW swell will find its way into the harbour.

The town of Sitges nearby is very attractive and provides most facilities for visitors. There are three important museums here, some interesting old buildings and good sandy beaches near the town.

Sitges has been in occupation since Roman times, made popular by its climate. The area is well sheltered from the cold northeast winds. The painters Rusiñol and Utrillo worked here. The town holds a *fiesta* in the form of a flower show in late May or early June, on the first Thursday after Whitsun.

Approach

From the south The town and harbour of Vilanova i la Geltrú are easily recognised. The coast is low and flat as far as Sitges which has a small hill feature a little distance inland. Its concentration of flats and houses has a conspicuous church at its E end and the harbour lies 500m to the E.

From the north The rocky broken coast where the Sierra de la Guardia meets the coast gives way to the flat coastal plain near this harbour. A conspicuous cement works is located some 1·5M to the E of the harbour.

Anchorages in the approach

Anchor 200m to the S of the entrance in 8m, sand.

Entrance

Approach the entrance on a NE course and enter between the two *diques* and in mid-channel. Then round the head of the Contradique de Poniente leaving it 25m to port, secure to the pontoon inside the entrance to starboard – call Ch 9.

Aiguadolç (Puerto de Sitges). There is talk of extending the outer mole westwards

PUERTO DE AIGUADOLÇ

0   50
Metres
Scale approximate

Contradique de Poniente

2_7
1 2 3 4 5 6
3
2_8
FI.R.5s 10m3M 0396.56
FI(2)G.13s6m1M 4 0396.55
5
3_5
2_5

41° 13'.90 N
FI.G.5s 12m5M 0396.54

N

⊕151 ⊕151 41°13'.85N 01°49'.25E App. Aiguadolç

1°49'.4E
Depths in Metres

Charges

High and note high season begins is 1 April–1 October.

Facilities

Maximum length overall 32m.
A shipyard on the NE side of the harbour with two workshops and an engineer.
20-tonne travel-lift.
2-tonne mobile crane.
Slipway on the NE side of the harbour.

A hard-standing area for yachts to NE of the harbour.
Two chandlers at the harbour.
Water from taps on the pontoons.
Showers on W side of the harbour.
220v AC supply points on the pontoons.
Gasoleo A and petrol from the head of the Espigón Nord.
Ice available from bars and fuel berth.
Many shops in the town, also a market and supermarket. Shops also around the harbour.
Launderette in the town and one to be established at the harbour.
Weather forecasts posted at the *torre* daily.

Communications

Bus and rail services. Taxi ☎ 938 943 594/938 941 329. Car Hire ☎ Hertz 938 945 750, Avis 938 949 926.

Sitges – many restaurants by the quay   *Robin Rundle*

140. Puerto de Vallcarca

41°14'N 1°52'E

Charts

British Admiralty *1704*. Imray *M13*
French *4827, 7298*
Spanish *871, 488*

⊕152   41°14'·1N 01°51'·85E 015°/0·1M to harbour

Lights

0396·6 **Muelle head** 41°14'·3N 1°52'·0E Fl(4)G.13s10m4M
  Green tower, white base 5m

An unpleasant commercial port

A private harbour belonging to a huge cement works. It might be used in emergency but not when wind and swell are between W and S as it is wide open to that quarter. There are no facilities for yachtsmen other than water and a beach restaurant. The noise and dust created by the Fradera SA cement works which is in operation day and night makes it an unpleasant place to stay.

Approach

From the south The flat plains around the harbours at Vilanova i la Geltrú and Aiguadolç give way to the high mountainous feature, the Sierra de la Guardia, which reaches to the coast near this harbour. The cement works, two white silos on the harbour wall and the clouds of dust are all conspicuous.

From the north From Barcelona the coast is low and flat until the rocky cliffs where the Sierra de la Guardia meets the coast beyond the delta of the Río Llobregat. The cement works, two white silos and the dust near this harbour are also conspicuous from this direction.

Entrance

Round the head of the Muelle de Atraque leaving it 50m to starboard and follow this *muelle* in a NE direction.

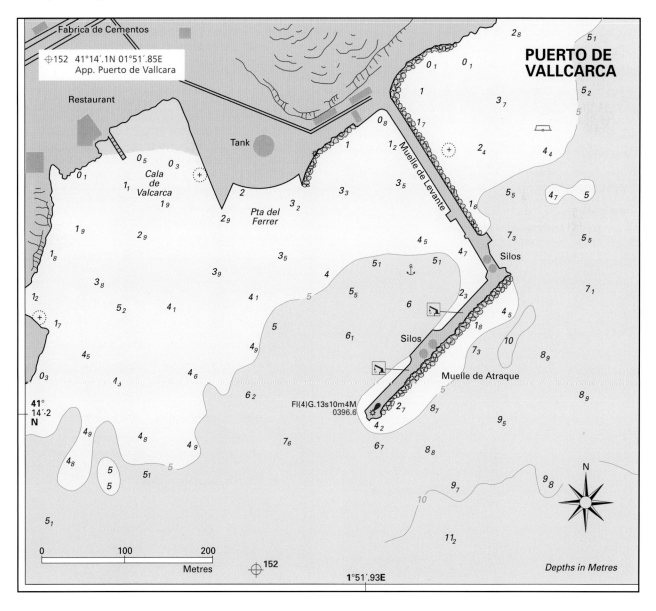

Puerto de Vallcarca

Berths

In calm weather, temporary berths may be available alongside the Muelle de Levante if not in use by commercial shipping.

Anchorage

Anchorage on a temporary basis is possible in the E corner of the harbour and also outside the harbour to the E or W if the swell is entering the harbour itself.

Mooring

Temporary moorings to one of the hauling off buoys might be possible.

Facilities

Water from a tap near root of *muelle*.
Small beach restaurant.

Communications

Bus and rail service.

Silos Vallcarca   *Robin Rundle*

141. Puerto de Garraf

41°15'N 1°54'E

Chart

British Admiralty *1704*. Imray *M13*
French *4827, 7298*
Spanish *871, 488A*

⊕153 41°14'·86N 01°53'·84E 035°/0·08M to harbour

Lights

0396·62 **Dique de Levante head** Fl(3)G.9s7m5M Green tower 3m
0396·63 **Espigon Interior head** Fl(4)G.20s2m1M Green column 1m
0396·64 **Dique de Poniente head** Fl(3)R.9s4m3M Red tower 3m

Port communications

VHF Ch 9. Capitanía ☎ 936 320 013 *Fax* 936 320 126
Email info@clubnauticgarraf.com
www.clubnauticgarraf.com

A quiet marina

A large marina but unaccompanied by the trappings (and traps) which surround most of the marinas along the coast. A few bars and restaurants can conveniently be reached by foot. Repair facilities are very limited but many are available at Port Ginesta, close by.

Approach

From the south After passing the flat coast around Vilanova i la Geltrú the coast becomes rocky and broken where the high Sierra de la Guardia reaches the sea. The harbour is located on this section of coast 1·7M beyond a conspicuous cement works and harbour at Vallcarca.

From the north South of the wide flat delta of the Río Llobregat, where Barcelona airport is located, is the rocky broken coast of the Sierra de la Guardia.

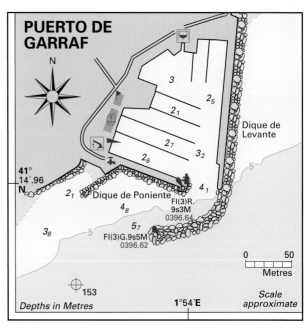

⊕153 41°14'.86N 01°53'84E   App. Puerto de Garraf

Puerto de Garraf

Port Ginesta is the first along that stretch, Garraf the second, in sight of the conspicuous Vallarca cement works.

Entrance

As is common along this stretch of coast, the entrance to Garraf silts up badly after any strong winds from the south quadrant. The mouth is dredged frequently but the sand returns almost as quickly. Usually there is a line of small red buoys laid from the head of the Dique de Poniente towards the beach parallel to the end of the Dique de Levante. These are to be left to port on entry and if they are missing, round the end of the dique and enter keeping close to the dique sounding carefully. Go right into the port and turn to come alongside the fuelling berth. Go to the Torre de control in the club nautico building to sort a berth out.

Garraf looking down Dique de Levante

Facilities

Workshop outside the marina with mechanic.
20-tonne travel-hoist.
6-tonne crane.
Hard-standing.
Water on the quays.
Gasoleo A and petrol.
Showers and ice at the *club náutico*.
220v AC on the quays.
Laundry in marina, limited shops in the town.

Communications

Bus and rail services. Taxi ☎ 936 653 557.

Garraf red buoys, Vallcarca silos beyond

V. ii. COSTA DORADA

142. Port Ginesta (Puerto de Castelldefels)

41°15′N 1°55′E

Charts

British Admiralty *1704*. Imray *M13*
French *4827*
Spanish *488*

⊕154 41°15′·3N 01°55′E 070°/0·14M to harbour

Lights

0396·8 **Dique de Abrigo head** Fl(2)G.10s8m5M Green tower 3m
0396·85 **Contradique head** Fl(2)R.10s5m3M Red tower 3m
0396·9 **Espigón de Levante** Q(6)+LFl.15s5m3M s on black beacon, yellow top 3m
To the north
0398 **Río Llobregat** 41°19′·6N 2°09′·2E Fl.5s32m23M Tower on building 31m 240°-vis-030°

Port communications

VHF Ch 9. *Capitanía* ☎ 936 643 661 *Fax* 936 650 166
Email info@portginesta.com www.portginesta.com

A first-class marina

A large modern yacht harbour, easy to enter and with good protection. There is a wide range of yacht repair and brokerage facilities besides chemist, restaurant, bars etc. and a crafts market at the weekend. The port is popular. A major expansion of the harbour has now been completed.

Castelldefels (originally Castrum de Fels) has fair shopping and its Romanesque church and the keep of the castle (1211 AD) are worth a visit. Barcelona, 12M away, is within striking distance. There is a good beach to NE.

Approach

From the south Aiguadolç and the cement works at Puerto de Vallcarca are conspicuous followed by Puerto de Garraf. Ginesta is at the end of the coastal cliffs.

From the north Barcelona is unmistakable, after which the delta of the Río Llobregat is low and flat with its light and radio antenna as features. Follow the sandy coast at ½M in 10m, sounding. The harbour is where the sandy beach stops and coastal cliffs commence.

Anchorage in the approach

Anchor 400m to S of the entrance to the harbour in 10m sand and mud. Not recommended in heavy weather because of undertow.

Entry

Approach the area where there is a large quarry in the background. The entrance between the breakwaters is straightforward. Most harbours along this coast are prone to silting. Although this has not been reported since Port Ginesta was extended caution is advised during the approach.

Facilities

Maximum length overall 30m.
Workshops with mechanics to NW of the harbour.
GRP, joinery, paintwork, sailmaking.
Slipway at NW side of the harbour (6m).
75-tonne travel-lift.
8-tonne crane.
Hard-standing for yachts at N side of the harbour.
Shops selling chandlery to N side of the harbour.
Water taps on quays and pontoons.
Showers and WCs in the *torre de control* complex.
220v AC points on quays and pontoons.
Gasoleo A and petrol.
Small ice from the café/bars and fuel station.
Some shops around the harbour, many more in the town 3M away. There is now a supermarket within the marina.
Laundry is now on site (24hrs) and not in town.
Weather forecasts posted daily at the *torre de control*.

Communications

Bus and rail service. Barcelona International Airport 5M Taxi ☎ 936 635 537.

⚓ GAVA

An open anchorage off a sandy beach about 1M to WSW of the airport, wide open to the S. Dinghy yacht club ashore. Coast road and road to Gava.

The new Port Ginesta   *Peter Taylor*

Ginesta harbour from entrance (interior jetty head)   *Peter Taylor*

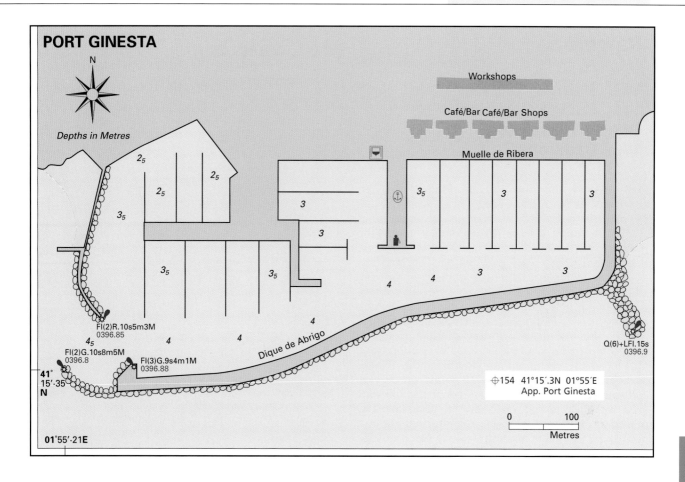

PORT GINESTA

N

Depths in Metres

Workshops

Café/Bar Café/Bar Shops

Muelle de Ribera

2_5

2_5

2_5

2_5

3_5

3

3

3_5

3

3

3_5

3_5

3

3

4

4

4

4

Fl(2)R.10s5m3M
0396.85

4_5

Fl(2)G.10s8m5M
0396.8

Fl(3)G.9s4m1M
0396.88

Dique de Abrigo

4

4

Q(6)+LFl.15s
0396.9

⊕154 41°15'.3N 01°55'E
App. Port Ginesta

41°
15'·35
N

01°55'·21E

0   100
Metres

Ginesta entrance   *Peter Taylor*

V. ii. COSTA DORADA

Barcelona

143. Marina Port Vell
144. Puerto Olimpico
145. Port Forum
146. Badalona

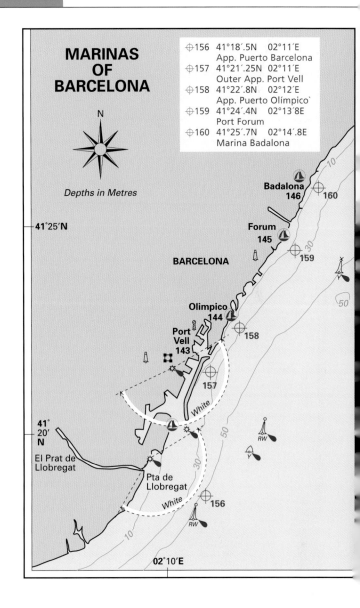

During 1999 the port of Barcelona started an enormous reconstruction programme, which is due to complete in 2010. The initial phase was to build a half-mile long Dique de Abrigo outside and at the root of the Dique del Este and to build a bridge, Puerta de Europa, joining Dique del Este and the Muelle de Poniente. Infill was poured to join the Dique de Abrigo to the Dique del Este and there is now a brand new harbour for the Barcelona fishing fleet at the root and outside the Dique del Este.

The phase of making a new entrance has now been completed and all pleasure craft should use the new northern entrance, just south of the fishing harbour.

Meanwhile at the southwest end of the harbour even more extensive works are in progress. The mouth of the Río Llobregat is being moved about a mile to the SW much infilling is taking place and the Dique del Este is being extended by nearly a mile with a new Dique Sur being built to make a new port to the SW of the present one.

With all this construction work in progress it is difficult to give timely advice on the changes that are happening almost daily.

Barcelona - capital of Cataluña

Barcelona is the largest city and port on this coast. The port of Barcelona itself (as distinct from Puerto Olímpico which is outside the main harbour walls) is easy to approach and enter in any weather, though winds may funnel at the entrance. There is good protection inside. Commercial traffic must be given right of way near and inside the port. Facilities for yachts and their crews are excellent and there are many attractions in the city and surrounding area. The marina at Port Vell is close to Las Ramblas and the city centre.

There are scores of places to see, such as 38 museums, 26 art galleries besides permanent trade fairs and exhibitions. To mention but three, visit Gaudi's cathedral, the Picasso Museum and walk along Las Ramblas at the hour of the *paseo*.

Though the area was probably occupied by the Iberians and later the Phoenicians, the first recorded history is of its occupation by the Carthaginian Hamilcar Barca in 230 BC when it was called Barcino. The Romans took over in about 200 BC and later called it Colonia Julia Augustus Pia Faventia. The town was destroyed by the Barbarians in AD 263 but was later retaken by the Romans who fortified it with a great wall. The Visigoths made it their capital of Gothalania in AD 415, from which name the province of Cataluña is thought to have originated.

The town surrendered to the Moors in AD 713; they were in turn driven out in AD 801, only to return in AD 985 for a short period during which the town was burnt. For the next 600 years, while still asserting her independence and rights, the town was ruled by the various royal and noble houses as their fortunes changed. An event of note was the royal reception of Columbus in June 1493 on his return from his discovery of America. In 1714 the city was sacked by the French because the inhabitants supported the cause of Archduke Charles against the French nomination of Philip V for the crown. The French also occupied the city from 1808 to 1813. From then until the Civil War the city was often the centre of agitation and revolt against the established order, insisting on its own rights and customs. In the 19th century the industrial revolution created a situation which caused the vast development of the city and its surroundings into one of the largest and most prosperous in Spain. It was the centre of Republican activity during the civil war and was badly bombed; the fall of Barcelona in January 1939 virtually marked the end of the war.

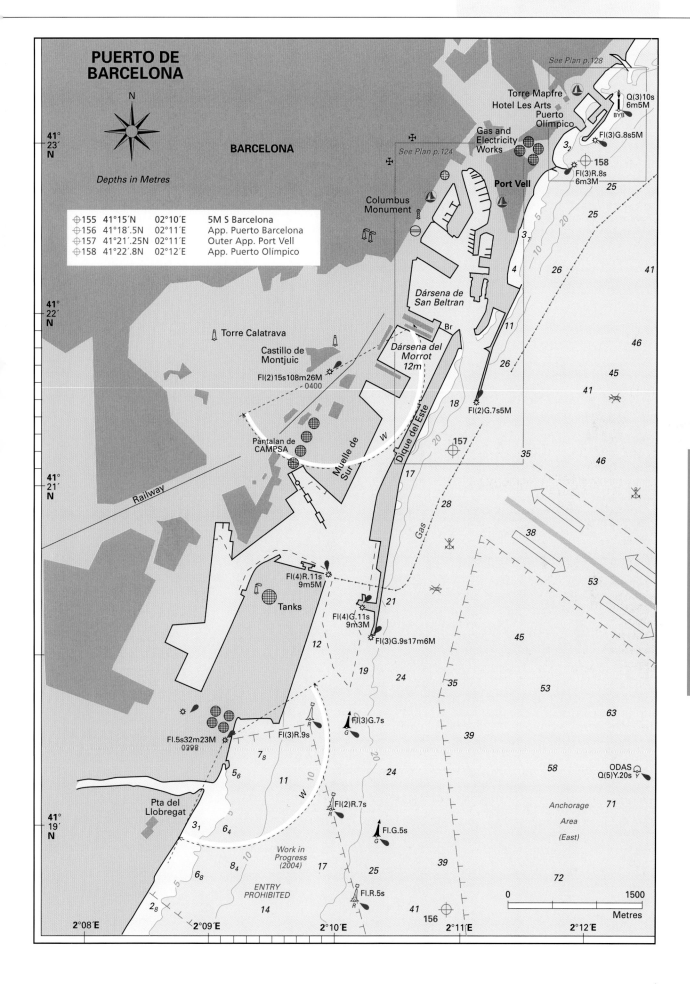

PUERTO DE
BARCELONA

N

BARCELONA

Depths in Metres

⊕155	41°15′N	02°10′E	5M S Barcelona
⊕156	41°18′.5N	02°11′E	App. Puerto Barcelona
⊕157	41°21′.25N	02°11′E	Outer App. Port Vell
⊕158	41°22′.8N	02°12′E	App. Puerto Olímpico

41°
23′
N

41°
22′
N

41°
21′
N

41°
19′
N

Torre Calatrava

Castillo de
Montjuic
Fl(2)15s108m26M
0400

Pantalan de
CAMPSA

Muelle de Sur

Railway

Fl(4)R.11s
9m5M

Tanks

Fl(4)G.11s
9m3M

Fl(3)G.9s17m6M

12

19

21

24

Fl.5s32m23M
0298

Fl(3)R.9s

7₈

5₆

11

Pta del
Llobregat

3₁   6₄

6₈

8₄

2₈

ENTRY
PROHIBITED

14

Work in
Progress
(2004)

17

Fl(2)R.7s
R

Fl.G.5s
G

Fl(3)G.7s
G

Fl.R.5s
R

25

24

See Plan p.124

Columbus
Monument

Port Vell

Dársena de
San Beltran

Br

Dársena del
Morrot
12m

Dique del Este

W

Fl(2)G.7s5M

18

157

17

28

Gas

11

26

3₇

4

5

3₂

See Plan p.128

Torre Mapfre
Hotel Les Arts
Puerto
Olímpico

Gas and
Electricity
Works

Q(3)10s
6m5M
BYB

Fl(3)G.8s5M

158
Fl(3)R.8s
6m3M

25

25

20

10

26

46

45

41

41

46

35

38

53

45

39

35

53

63

58

45

39

ODAS
Q(5)Y.20s
Y

Anchorage

Area

(East)

71

72

156

41

0   1500

Metres

V. ii. COSTA DORADA

2°08′E   2°09′E   2°10′E   2°11′E   2°12′E

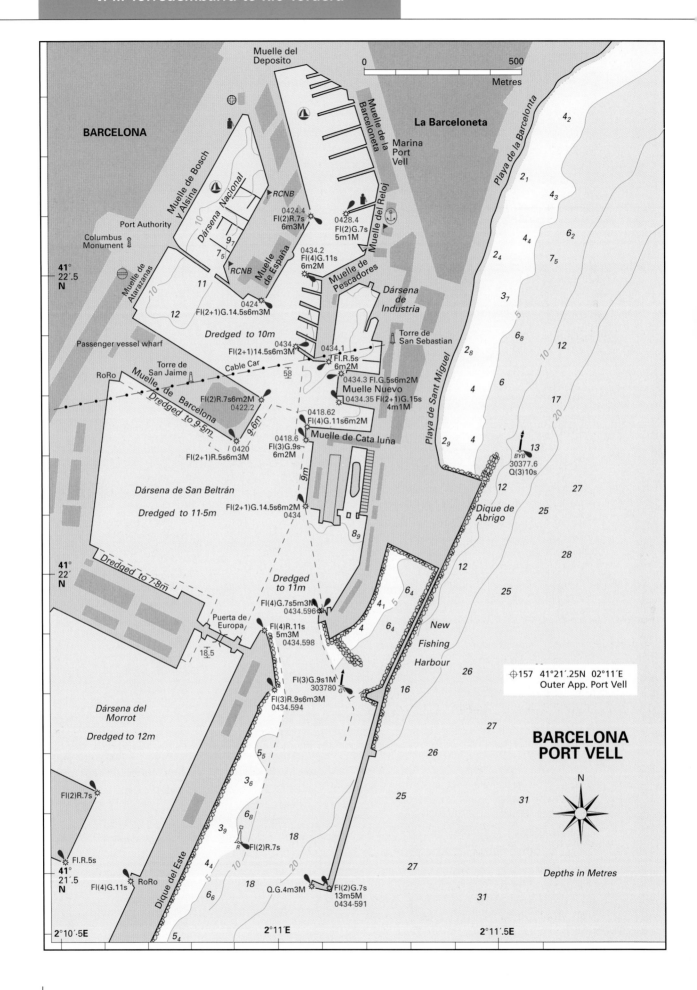

Muelle del
Deposito

0   500
Metres

BARCELONA

La Barceloneta

Muelle de Bosch
y Alsina

Dársena Nacional

Muelle de la Barceloneta

Marina
Port
Vell

Muelle del Reloj

Port Authority

Columbus
Monument

▶RCNB

0424.4
Fl(2)R.7s
6m3M

0428.4
Fl(2)G.7s
5m1M

41°
22´.5
N

Muelle de
Atarazanas

RCNB

Muelle
de España

0434.2
Fl(4)G.11s
6m2M

Muelle de
Pescadores

Dársena
de
Industria

11

12

0424
Fl(2+1)G.14.5s6m3M

Dredged to 10m

Torre de
San Sebastian

Passenger vessel wharf

RoRo

Torre de
San Jaime

Cable Car

0434
Fl(2+1)14.5s6m3M

Muelle de Barcelona

Dredged to 9.5m

Fl(2)R.7s6m2M
0422.2

0434.1
Fl.R.5s
6m2M

0434.3 Fl.G.5s6m2M
Muelle Nuevo
0434.35 Fl(2+1)G.15s
4m1M

Playa de Sant Miguel

9.6m

0418.62
Fl(4)G.11s6m2M
Muelle de Cata luña

0420
Fl(2+1)R.5s6m3M

0418.6
Fl(3)G.9s
6m2M

9m

BYB
30377.6
Q(3)10s

13

Dársena de San Beltrán

Dredged to 11.5m

Fl(2+1)G.14.5s6m2M
0434

8₉

Dique de
Abrigo

41°
22´
N

Dredged to 7.8m

Dredged
to 11m

Fl(4)G.7s5m3M
0434.596

Puerta de
Europa

Fl(4)R.11s
5m3M
0434.598

New

Fishing

Harbour

⊕157   41°21´.25N 02°11´E
Outer App. Port Vell

18.5

Fl(3)G.9s1M
303780

Fl(3)R.9s6m3M
0434.594

BARCELONA
PORT VELL

N

Dársena del
Morrot

Dredged to 12m

Fl(2)R.7s

Fl.R.5s

41°
21´.5
N

Fl(4)G.11s

RoRo

Dique del Este

Fl(2)R.7s

Q.G.4m3M

Fl(2)G.7s
13m5M
0434·591

Depths in Metres

2°10´·5E

2°11´E

2°11´.5E

143. Marina Port Vell

41°20′N 2°10′E

Charts

British Admiralty *1704, 1196, 1180.* Imray *M14*
French *4827, 7046*
Spanish *489A, 4891*

⊕157 41°21′·25N 02°11′E 000°/0·2M to harbour

Lights

Approach
41°19′·5N 2°09′·1E
0398 **Río Llobregat N side** 41°19′·5N 2°09′·1E
Fl.5s32m23M Octagonal tower on building 31m 240°-
vis-030°
0399 **S. Pier head** 41°17′·6N 2°08′·3E Q(3)10s6m5M Card E
post 2m
0400 **Montjuich** 41°21′·7N 2°10′·0E Fl(2)15s108m26M
Tower on red and white building 13m 240·5°-vis-
066·1°(this light is well within the harbour)
29655a(S) **Buoy** 41°17′·4N 2°09′E Q(3)10s5M Card E buoy
(this buoy advances as the Dique de Abrigo Sur is
constructed)
0401 **Dique del Este head** 41°20′·1N 2°10′·3E
Fl(3)G.9s17m6M Green post 7m

Harbour
0434·591 **Dique de Abrigo SE corner** Fl(2)G.7s13m5M
Green tower 4m
0434.594 **Dique del Este N head S corner** Fl(3)R.9s6m3M
Red column 3m

Port communications

Pilots VHF Ch 11, 12, 14, 16 (hours various).
Port VHF Ch 12, 14, 16 24hrs. ☎ 933 177 500.
Reial Club Maritim VHF Ch 09. ☎ 932 214 859
Fax 932 215 566 *Email* club@maritimbarcelona.org
www.maritimbarcelona.org
Real Club Nautico VHF Ch 09 ☎ 932 216 521
Fax 932 216 253 *Email* info@rcnb.com
www.rcnb.com
Marina Port Vell VHF Ch 68 ☎ 934 842 300
Fax 934 842 333 *Email* info@marinaportvell.com
www.marinaportvell.com

Port Vell is a first-class but expensive marina

Approach

From the south The high feature and broken rocky
cliffs of the Sierra de la Guardia suddenly give way
to the flat low delta of the Río Llobregat which has
the airport and a lighthouse. On a clear day the high
hill immediately behind the harbour (Montaña de
Montjuic), the harbour installations and the mass of
buildings of the city will be seen from afar. The two
towers of the aerial railway are also conspicuous.

From the north The coastline is backed by a series of
hills consisting of the Sierras del Corredó, de Sant
Mateu and de Matas, which fall back inland in the
area of Barcelona, leaving the isolated feature of
Montaña de Montjuic easily located. The coast is
lined with concentrations of houses and high-rise
buildings which extend across the delta of the Río
Bésos. The bridge over this river will be seen. The
concentration of buildings and harbour works
continues past Montaña de Montjuic, silos and the
two towers of the aerial railway. In clear conditions

the jagged peaks of Montaña de Montserrat some
20M inland can be seen from.

Entrance

From the south Leave the works and buoys off the
new Dique Sur well to port and proceed up the
outside of the Dique del Este and its new extension
and aim towards the conspicuous Puerta de Europa.
Keep steering northerly until the new Dique de
Abrigo is sighted and then shape a course towards a
small spur running ESE from the old Dique del Este.
When the new entrance opens up steer through and
enter the Darsena de San Beltran. Continue north
under the aerial cable car wire and enter the marina.

From the north Leave Puerto Olimpico and its off-
lying dangers well to starboard and proceed along
the new Dique de Abrigo. Round its south end and
proceed to steer a west of north course past the the
fishing harbour entrance when the new entrance will
open up. Proceed through the Darsena de San
Beltran to Port Vell.

Berths

For visitors berths at Port Vell call for a berth on Ch
68 or at the fuel quay. The Real Club Marítima may
accept visitors by arrangement; the Real Club
Náutico de Barcelona is for members only. An
alternative is to go to Puerto Olímpico but this has
less character and is further out of town.

Harbour charges

High.

Facilities

Barcelona can support all repairs, in or out of the water.
Many are close to Port Vell. Consult a marina or club
official if help is needed.
Chandlery shops near the port, one 200m SW of the
main post office and another between the two *clubs
náutico.*
Chart agent in Avenida Marques de l'Argentana.
At Port Vell
Maximum length overall 70m.
Water taps on the pontoons.
220v and 380v AC on the pontoons.
Gasoleo A and petrol.
Ice, ask at the fuelling berth.
In town:
Supermarket at 100m.
Thousands of shops of all kinds and a large market in
the city, many in the narrow streets near the port.
Launderette in the second road back from the NW side
of the Dársena Nacional, many others elsewhere in
the city.

Communications

International and national bus, rail and air services, car
hire etc. Shipping to most parts of the world. Taxi
☎ 933 912 222.
British Consulate-General: Edificio Torre de Barcelona
Avineda Diagonal 477, 13th Floor, 08036 Barcelona
☎ 934 199 044 *Fax* 934 052 411.

Puerto de Barcelona - Port Vell

Port Vell entrance   *Robin Rundle*

La Rambla   *Robin Rundle*

Statue Christopher Columbus   *Robin Rundle*

La Rambla   *Peter Taylor*

Puerto Olimpico dominated by two towers   *Robin Rundle*

Catalona History Museum Port Vell   *Robin Rundle*

Inside entrance Port Forum   *Robin Rundle*

V. ii. COSTA DORADA

144. Puerto Olímpico

41°23′N 2°12′E

Charts
British Admiralty *1704, 1196, 1180.* Imray *M14*
French *4827, 7046*
Spanish *489A, 4891*

⊕158 41°22′·8N 02°12′E 345°/0·2M to harbour

Lights
30384(S) Dique de Abrigo buoy Fl(4)G.8s1M Green conical topmark
0434·75 **Contradique head** Fl(4)R.8s3m1M Red post 2m
0434·6 Outer breakwater head Q.R.3m1M Red post
Submerged breakwater
0434·71 Fl(3)R.8s6m3M Red post
0434·72 Fl(3)G.8s6m5M Green post
0434·73 Q(3)10s6m5M ⊹ on black tower, yellow band
0434·74 Q(3)10s6m5M ⊹ on black tower, yellow band
(½M NE of 0434·73)

Port communications
VHF Ch 09 ☎ 932 25 92 20 *Fax* 932 25 92 21
Email portolimpic@pobasa.es www.portolimpic.es

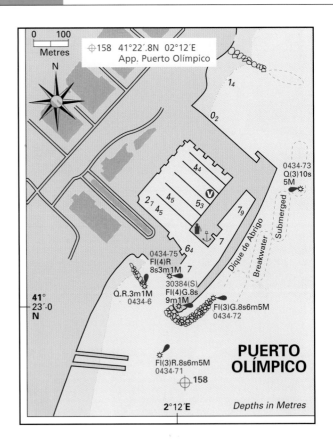

Olympic sailing village
This yacht harbour was built for the 1992 Olympic Games. The area of the city behind it formed the Olympic village. The metro is 10–15 minutes walk and the harbour is less convenient for shopping than Port Vell. But the place is tidy, secure and well sheltered.

Approach
From the south The low, flat delta of the Río Llobregat and the long breakwater of the Puerto de Barcelona are easily identified. Puerto Olímpico lies under a couple of skyscrapers (one marked MAPFRE) some 4M N of the S end of the outer breakwater of the old harbour.

From the north The harbour at El Masnou and the mouth of the Río Besós which has power and gas stations with tall chimneys either side of its mouth are easy to recognise. The harbour can be located by the two skyscrapers (one marked MAPFRE) immediately behind it.

Entrance
Approach the S end of the harbour passing between red and green beacon poles. Continue in towards the beach until the rocky extension at the head of the Dique de Abrigo can be rounded. A fairly sharp turn to starboard is needed to avoid running up on the beach.

Berths
Moor at fuel berth and obtain berth from *capitanía*.

Harbour charges
Low.

Facilities
Maximum length overall 30m.
Some maintenance facilities.
Travel-lift 50 tonnes.
Crane 6 tonnes.

Large hard-standing.
Gasoleo A and petrol.
Water on the quays.
Showers.
220v and 380v AC on the quays.
Shopping mall in basement of eastern skyscraper.
Tourist bus stop on main road N of marina.

Communications
Metro, buses. Taxi ☎ 933 581 111.

Puerto Olímpico

145. Port Forum

41°25'N 2°1 4'E

Charts
British Admiralty *1704.* Imray *M14*
French *4827*
Spanish *873, 4892, 489*

⊕159   41°24'·4N 02°13'·8E 310°/0·1M to harbour

Lights
0434·78 Dique de Abrigo SW head Fl(4)12s10m5M Green
   tower 6m
0434·782 Dique de Abrigo NE head Q(3)10s7m3M E
   Cardinal post BYB 6m
0434·784 Port hand entrance Fl(4)R.12s5m3M Red post
   3m
0434·786 Entrance port side Fl.R.5s5m1M Red column 4m
   (on submerged reef)
0434·788 Espigon Fl(2)R.10s4m1M Red column 2m
0434·79 Inner Pier head Fl(2+1)G.10s4m1M Green
   column, red band 2m
0434·795 Inner harbour pier head Fl.G.5s4m1M Green
   tower 2m.

Port communications
VHF Ch 73 & 09 ☎ 933 56 27 20/933 562 725
Fax 933 56 27 09
Email info@portforum.net www.portforum.net

A novel marina
Rather like London and the Dome, Barcelona cleared some waterfront area of the Besos suburb and built an exhibition hall and park area, which included a small darsena for dinghies and ribs etc. The exhibition itself finished in summer 2004 and the darsena was taken over by a private consortium who have developed part of the site into a first class marina for about 170 motor vessels (in the inner darsena (access is under a 10m bridge). Outside there are berths for vessels up to 80 metres and there is a 'dry' marina which is a shed which can hold up to 245 craft up to 9m in a stacking system. Obviously it is mainly for motor craft but it will take the strain off the other marinas of Barcelona.

Approach and entrance
The 800m breakwater just 3 miles NE of Puerto Olimpico is conspicuous and one can enter from the southern end but it is essential to make contact with the marina authorities to arrange a berth before entering.

Facilities
As befits a new modern marina the facilities are excellent and most services are available:-
150-ton travel lift
Water, electricity and internet connections at all berths.
Bunkering and provisioning.
Repairs and servicing.
Banking.
Security.
Ferries run to Plaza de Colon at the end of Ramblas.
There are numerous restaurants in this area.

Port Forum. Entrance to Harbour from within *Robin Rundle*

Port Forum. Outer harbour *Robin Rundle*

PORT FORUM

N

0434.782
Q(3)10s7m3M

Dique de Abrigo

10

0434.79
Fl(2+1)G.10s4m1M

Fl(2)R.
10s4m1M

Fl.R.
5s5m1M

0434.78
Fl(4)G.12s10m5M

41°
24'·55
N

Fl(4)R.
12s5m3M

5

10

159

⊕159 41°24'.4N 02°13'8E
Port Forum

10

Depths in Metres   **02°13'·7E**

5

20

V. ii. COSTA DORADA

146. Marina Badalona

41°26'N 2°14'·6E

Charts

British Admiralty *1704*
French *4827*
Spanish *4892, 489*
Navicarte *E05*

⊕160 41°25'·7N 02°14'·8E 300°/0·2M to harbour

Lights

0436 **Dique de Abrigo head** 41°25'·9N 2°14'·6E
  Fl(3)G.9s6m5M Green tower 2m
30452(S) Contradique S corner buoy Fl(4)R.11s1M

Port communications

VHF Ch 9 ☎ 933 20 75 00 *Fax* 933 20 75 28
Email port@marinabadalona-sa.es
www.marinabadalona-sa.es

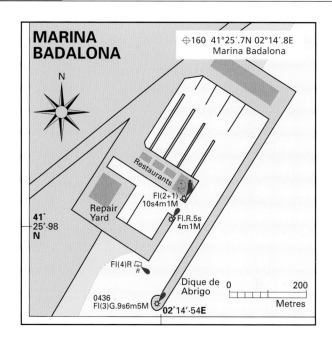

MARINA BADALONA

⊕160 41°25'.7N 02°14'.8E
Marina Badalona

A new and developing marina

Just over a mile northeast of Port Forum development continues at Badalona to produce a full service marina. The first phase is well underway and the marina is open for business. Captania, fuel and repair facilities are open as are some of the planned restaurants. Four main pontoons are in place and other mooring areas are also in use. 600 deep water berths will be available. Shops, more restaurants and a hotel are following. The second phase is to drive a canal into the town with motor boat moorings and properties on either side. This is planned to be completed by around 2012.

Badalona. Entrance *Peter Taylor*

Badalona model *Peter Taylor*

Badalona. Fuel and captania *Peter Taylor*

⚓ **MANGAT (MONGAT)** 41°28'N 2°17'·5E
Another open anchorage.

147. Puerto de El Masnou

41°28′N 2°18′E

Charts

British Admiralty *1704.* Imray *M14*
French *4827*
Spanish *873, 4892, 489*

⊕161 41°28′·32N 02°18′·5E 040°/0·14M to harbour

Lights

0439·3 **Dique de Levante head** Fl(2)G.12s10m5M Green tower 7m

0439·35 **Dique de Poniente head** Fl(2)R.12s3m3M Red post 2m

0439 **Dique de Levante corner** Fl(3)G.10s1m2M Square green tower 1m

0439·2 **Fuel jetty corner** Fl(3)R.10s1m2M Square red tower 1m

Port communications

VHF Ch 9. *Capitanía* ☎ 935 403 000 *Fax* 935 403 004 *Email* portmasnou@infonegocio.com
Club Náutico de El Masnou ☎ 935 550 605
 Fax 935 400 662 *Email* cnm@nauticmasnou.com
 www.nauticmasno.com

A well-run marina

A pleasant yacht harbour which has all facilities. Easy to approach and enter with excellent protection from even SW winds as the Dique de Levante has recently been lengthened by 70m. The modern seaside town has shops and restaurants and there are fine sandy beaches either side of this harbour.

Approach

From the south The mass of houses, harbour works and installations of Barcelona are unmistakable. Further N, and either side of the mouth of the Río Bésós, lie power stations with five tall chimneys and a jetty. The town of Badalona and many houses and flats line the coast, which is flat and sandy, backed by ranges of hills. The church at El Masnou and a tower, the Turó de Moná, on an isolated hill 1M inland are recognisable.

From the north The cliffs on either side of Arenys de Mar and its harbour can be recognised. Southwards the coast is flat and sandy with ranges of hills inland. The concentration of buildings at Mataró and its harbour can be identified, after which come the tower and church at El Masnou.

Anchorage in the approach

Anchor 200m to SW of the entrance in 5m, sand.

Entrance

The entrance is nearly at the west end of the harbour and runs ENE-WSW between the breakwaters. The gap won't be obvious until it bears about NE. Pass between the piers and proceed to the fuel quay by the new *torre de control.*

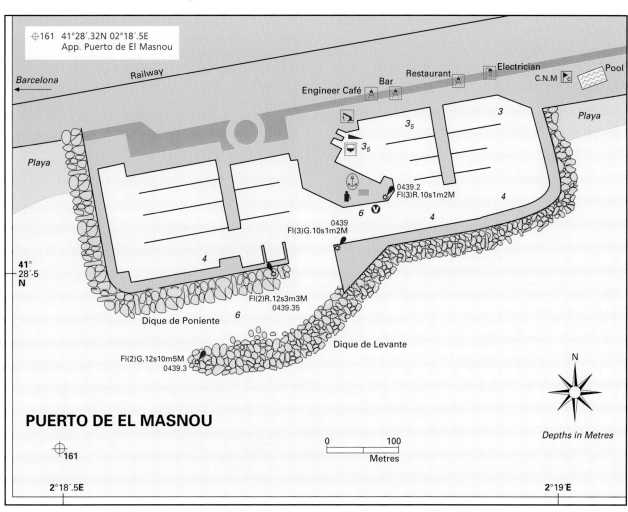

PUERTO DE EL MASNOU

V. ii. COSTA DORADA

Puerto de El Masnou (note the *capitanía* is not in the tower on the far jetty but in a new building on the fuel jetty and the *dique* on the right has been extended)

Berths

Ask at the *torre de control* for allocation of a berth.

Charges

Low off season, medium in high season.

Facilities

Maximum length overall 22m.
Practically all repair facilities including sailmaking.
50-tonne travel-lift.
4-tonne crane.
Two slips.
Three chandlery shops beside the harbour.
Water on the pontoons and quays.
Showers.
220v AC on the pontoons and quays.
Gasoleo A and petrol.
Camping Gaz.
Club Náutico de El Masnou has a clubhouse to the NE of the harbour with bar, terrace, showers and a pool. It is separate from the harbour. Ask the secretary.
Supermarket, shops in the town nearby and hypermarket at Mataró.
Laundry collects from the marina.

Port de El Masnou looking SW from Capitania   *Peter Taylor*

Communications

Bus and rail services. Taxi ☎ 935 402 492.

148. Puerto de Premiá de Mar

41°29'N 2°21'E

Charts

British Admiralty *1704*. Imray *M14*
French *4827*
Spanish *489*

⊕162 41°29'·2N 02°21'·8E 030°/0·1M to harbour

Lights

0439·5 **Dique de Abrigo head** Fl.G.3s6m5M Green post 3m
0439·52 **Contradique head** Fl.R.3s3m3M Red lantern on hut 1m

Port communications

VHF Ch 09 Capitania ☎ 937 54 91 19
Fax 937 54 91 18 *Email* info@marinapremia.com
www.marinapremia.com
Club Nautico de Premia de Mar ☎ 937 52 35 87
Fax 93752 41 11.

A developing marina

This marina has been struggling to establish itself for some years. In September 2007 it had a new and enthusiastic Capitane. All pontoons were in place and all services connected. Despite its proximity to Barcelona, and being only 20 minutes from the airport, there were many berths still available to rent. Visiting yachts should wait at the end of the first pontoon (G); the captania is at the root of the pontoon. Additional facilities, repairs and shops are only slowly becoming established. Visitors are not welcome at the members' only club in the NE corner of the complex.

Puerto de Premiá de Mar. This shows the overall situation, but see the plan for the significant changes which have taken place

The town, well known for its carnations which are sent all over Spain, has good supplies but is on the other side of the railway tracks which make it a bit of a hike. Entrance to the marina is normally simple but could be tricky in strong SW winds. There are long sandy beaches both sides of the harbour.

Approach

From the south After Barcelona there are two large power stations either side of the Río Besós. 2M further north east is Port Masnou; then the large white *torre de control* behind Premiá de Mar should be spotted.

From the north Puerto de Arenys de Mar and the smaller ports of El Balís and Mataró are easily recognised. The very small landing at Vilassar may also be seen. The white control tower of Puerto de Premiá is easily identified from this direction.

V. ii. COSTA DORADA

Anchorage in the approach

Anchor in 10m, sand, ½M to S of this harbour.

Entrance

The entrance is straightforward. However, the old harbour mouth, which was further inshore, used to silt up and the new one may do the same. Sound carefully both on the approach and inside the harbour.

Berths

Secure to end of the first (G) jetty and report to *torre* for allocation of berth.

Facilities

Mechanic with workshop.
A slipway on the NW side of the harbour.
A 1·5-tonne in the E corner.
Chandlery in town on road to Calvo Sotelo.
Water on quays and pontoons.
220v and 380v AC on slipway.
Ice at the bar.
A few local shops with many more in Badalona 5M and Mataró 5M.
Weather forecasts posted at *torre de control*.

Communications

Bus and rail services. Taxi ☎ 937 522 532.

⚓ VILASSAR DE MAR 41°29'·8N 2°23'·3E

Anchorage off sandy beach in 3m, sand, with a conspicuous yacht club and slipway enclosed by two rocky breakwaters with many small fishing boats on the hard. The Club Náutico de Vilassar de Mar has a restaurant, bar, water, showers, WCs and swimming pool. The village of 9,000 has many restaurants, café/bars, a chandler, post office, two hotels, bus and rail services and at 1½M the well preserved Castle Barbara and a flower-growing centre. Open between NE and SW.

Vilassar de Mar

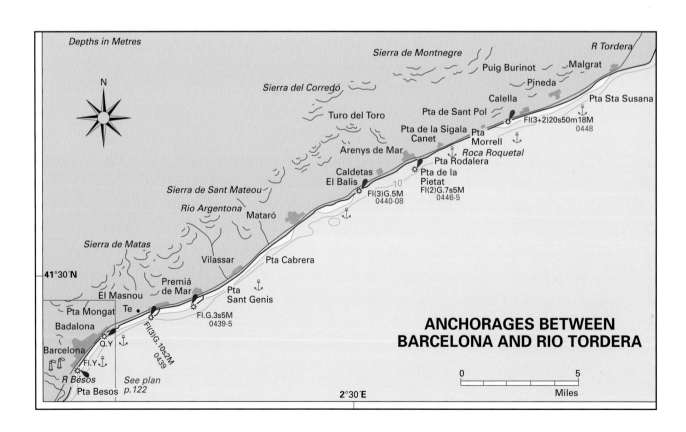

149. Puerto de Mataró

41°31′N 2°26′E

Charts

British Admiralty *1704.* Imray *M14*
French *4827*
Spanish *873, 489, 301A*

⊕163 41°31′·5N 02°26′·5E 040°/0·1M to harbour

Lights

0439·8 **Dique de Abrigo head** Fl(4)G.16s15m5M Green
  tower
0439·85 **Contradique head** Fl(4)R.8s5m4M Red tower

Port communications

VHF Ch 9. *Capitanía* ☎ 937 550 961 *Fax* 937 902 942
Email info@portmataro.com www.portmataro.com

A pleasant marina

A large artificial yacht harbour of 1,000 berths cut
off from the dreary town by the main road and
railway. It is a useful stop-over, handy for Barcelona
(20 minutes by train).

Mataró is the ancient Roman town of Iluro and
many remains of that period have been discovered
including the important Villa Torre Llauder. There
are also Moorish relics. The first railway in Spain
was laid from here to Barcelona in 1848. The town
expanded and became well known for its
shipbuilding. It is now equally well known for
growing and marketing carnations.

The church and the ruined castle of St Vincente de
Burriach, both 15th century, and the walled
medieval town of Argentona should be visited.
There are sandy beaches on both sides of the
harbour.

Puerto de Mataró

Approach

From the south Northeast of Barcelona the coast is
flat with a long sandy beach with a series of towns
and villages. The chimneys of the power stations at
the mouth of the Río Besós, the yacht harbours of El
Masnou and Premiá de Mar and the mouth of the
Río Argentona are easy to see. The town of Mataró
and the harbour breakwaters are large and easily
recognised.

V. ii. COSTA DORADA

From the north Blanes and the mouth of the Río Tordera can be identified. The coast is low and flat with a long sandy beach, lined with small villages and towns including Puerto de Arenys de Mar and Puerto de El Balís. The town and breakwaters of Mataró are conspicuous.

Anchorage in the approach

Anchor in 7m, sand, 50m to SE of the Dique de Levante.

Entrance

Approach the head of the Dique de Levante on a course between W and N and round the head at 20m.

Berth

Pass the *contradique* close to port and make for the waiting quay under the *torre de control*, next to the fuelling point, at the end of the first jetty to port. Moor and arrange a berth with the *capitanía* in the *torre*.

Charges

Lowish, no variation between high and low season.

Facilities

Maximum length overall 20m.
Almost all repair services.
100-tonne travel-lift.
12-tonne crane.
Two chandlers on the coast road.
Water on pontoons and quays.
Showers.
220v and 380v AC on pontoons and quays.
Gasoleo A and petrol.
Ice on fuel quay.
Shops, bars.
Supermarket and a weekly market in the town.
Laundry.

Communications

Bus and rail services. Taxi ☎ 937 986 060.

Lift and repair facilities Mataró   *Peter Taylor*

150. Port Balís

41°33′N 2°30′E

Charts

British Admiralty *1704*. Imray *M14*
French *4827*
Spanish *873, 489*
⊕164 41°33′·3N 02°30′·3E 030°/0·08M to harbour

Lights

0440 **Dique de Levante head** Fl(4)G.12s4m2M Green
   column 2m
0440·08 **Espigón head** Fl(3)G.10s10m5M Green tower 6m
0440.2 **Dique de Poniente head** Fl(3)R.10s6m2M Lantern

Port communications

Club Nautico El Balis VHF Ch 6 ☎ 937 929 900
Fax 937 927 261 *Email* info@cnelbalis.com
www.cnelbalis.com

A friendly and well-run marina

A pleasant yacht harbour, easy to enter and offering good protection though the swell from SW gales can enter the harbour. Facilities are good.

The nearby town of Caldetas with its hot springs and 13th-century church, and Mataró, the ancient Iluro, a walled town with many Moorish remains, can be visited. There are fine sandy beaches nearby.

Approach

From the south The chimneys of the power stations at the mouth of the Río Besós, the yacht harbours of El Masnou and Premiá de Mar and the mouth of the Río Argentona are easy to see. The town of Mataró and the harbour breakwaters are large and easily recognised. The harbour walls of El Balís will be visible in the closer approach.

From the north From the flat, low delta of the Río Tordera the coast has sandy beaches backed by ranges of hills with several small towns. A pair of towers near Calella and the harbour breakwater at Arenys de Mar will be seen.

Anchorage in the approach

Anchor 200m to SW of the entrance in 10m, sand and mud.

Entrance

Approach the head of the Dique de Levante on a N course and round it at 25m.

Berths

Secure to the fuel quay for allocation of a berth.

Facilities

Maximum length overall 25m.
50-tonne travel-lift. 5-tonne crane.
There is a slipway in the N corner of the harbour and on the beach outside the entrance.
A chandlery shop at the N of the harbour.
Water and 220v AC on pontoons and quays.
Gasoleo A and petrol. Ice on the fuel quay.

Communications

Bus and rail services. Taxi ☎ 937 958 390.

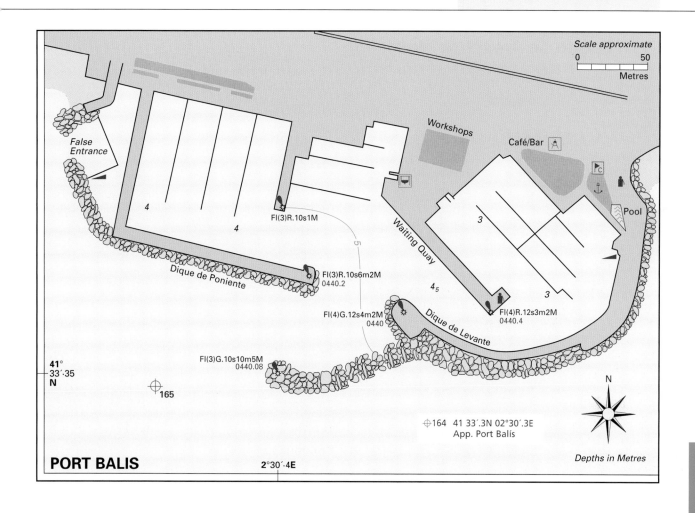

Scale approximate
0 ___ 50
Metres

Workshops

Café/Bar

False
Entrance

4

4

FI(3)R.10s1M

Waiting Quay

Pool

3

Dique de Poniente

FI(3)R.10s6m2M
0440.2

FI(4)G.12s4m2M
0440

4 5

Dique de Levante

FI(4)R.12s3m2M
0440.4

3

FI(3)G.10s10m5M
0440.08

41°
33´.35
N

⊕ 165

N

⊕164   41 33´.3N 02°30´.3E
App. Port Balís

PORT BALIS

2°30´.4E

Depths in Metres

Port Balís

V. ii. COSTA DORADA

151. Puerto de Arenys de Mar

41°34′N 2°33′E

Charts

British Admiralty *1704*. Imray *M14*
French *4827, 7298*
Spanish *489, 4911*

⊕165 41°34′·5N 02°33′·2E 065°/0·14M to harbour

Lights

0446·5 **Dique de Portiñol head** Fl(2)G.7s9m5M Green
  tower on white base 5m
0446 **Dique del Calvario head** Fl(2+1)R.21s5m2M Red
  tower, green band 3m
0446·2 **Dique de Portiñol elbow** Fl(3)G.10s7m2M Green
  tower 3m 025°-vis-185°
0446·3 **Contradique de Poniente head** Fl(2)R.7s8m3M Red
  tower 3m
To the northeast
0448 **Calella** 41°36′·4N 2°38′·7E Fl(3+2)20s50m18M White
  tower on building 10m (Aeromarine)

Port communications

VHF Ch 09 ☎ 937 92 16 00 *Fax* 937 92 07 44
Email administracio@cnarenys.com
www.cnarenys.com

A major fishing harbour

This fishing harbour now accommodates a large number of yachts in addition to the fishing fleet. Popular with French yachts, it becomes crowded in summer so book ahead. It is easy to approach and enter. Inside, protection is good though SW winds send in some swell.

Those interested in history might visit the Torre del Encantate, built on the site of a pre-Roman town, and a 16th-century church. The beaches on either side of the harbour are good but have coarse sand.

Approach

From the south The low and sandy coast is lined with towns and, a short distance inland, ranges of hills. El Masnou, the harbour at Mataró and a conspicuous tower just inland from Caldetas will be recognised. The cliffs either side of Arenys de Mar and the tall blocks of flats can be seen from afar and the harbour walls show up on the approach.

From the north After the low, flat delta of the Río Tordera the sandy coast is backed by ranges of hills and lined with a number of small towns. A breakwater (in ruins) at Malgrat and two towers at Calella may be seen. Arenys de Mar will be recognised by cliffs either side of the town, blocks of flats and, in the closer approach, by the harbour breakwaters.

Anchorage in the approach

There is no good anchorage. A pipe-line runs out to sea W of the Dique de Calvario.

Entrance

Approach the head of the Dique de Portinol on a N course and round it at 50m.

Berths

Berth stern-to pontoons with bows-to mooring buoy as directed by the club officials. Vacant berths have a red plaque around the bollard on the pontoons.

Charges

High.

Facilities

Maximum length overall 18m.
A yard to the N of the harbour and another larger one in the NE corner. Engine repair shops to the N of the harbour where there is also an electronic workshop.
Travel-lift in NE corner and two more, one of 100 tonnes near harbour entrance.
Two slipways in the NE corner and another on the N side of the harbour.
10-tonne crane at the NE side and another on the N side of the harbour.
Two chandlers in the road to the N of the harbour.
Water on the pontoons and at the *lonja*.
220v AC on the pontoons 380v AC in the workshops.
Gasoleo A and petrol.
Ice from a factory to the N of the harbour or from the *lonja*.
Club Náutico de Arenys de Mar has bars, lounges, terrace, restaurant, showers and a swimming pool.
The shops in the nearby town can supply most normal requirements.
Launderette in the town.

Communications

Bus and rail services. Taxi ☎ 937 958 390.

For ⚓ below, see plan on page 134.

⚓ **SANT POL DE MAR** 41°36′N 2°38′E

⚓ **PUNTA MORRELL** 41°36′N 2°38′E

A small anchorage in 4m, sand, protected by an L-shaped breakwater, open between E and SW with a sandy beach ashore and a large *club náutico*. Behind the coast road and railway line is the town of San Pol de Mar.

⚓ **CALELLA** 41°36′·5N 2°40′E

Another open anchorage off a sandy beach in 3m, sand, with another deep-water anchorage ½ M to SE of the town in 32m, sand, open between NE and SW. A yacht club ashore for dinghies. A large town backs up a variety of food shops. It is a centre of the hosiery trade. Rail and road connections.

⚓ **PINEDA DE MAR** 41°37′N 2°42′E

Again an offshore anchorage in 3m, sand, in front of a conglomeration with some facilities and a good sandy beach. Rail and road connections.

⚓ **RÍO TORDERA**

This small river is the boundary between Barcelona and Girona and also marks the junction between Costa Dorada and Costa Brava.

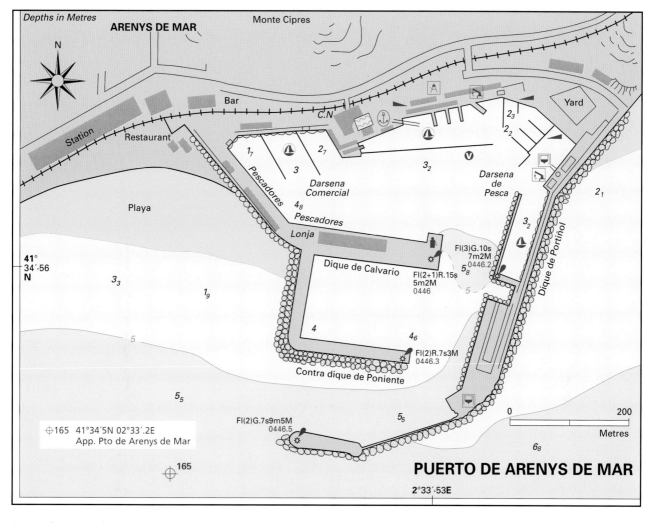

Depths in Metres
ARENYS DE MAR
Monte Cipres
N
Bar
Station
Restaurant
C.N
Playa
Pescadores
1₇
3
2₇
Darsena
Comercial
4₈
Pescadores
Lonja
Dique de Calvario
3₂
V
Darsena
de
Pesca
2₃
2₂
3₂
Dique de Portiñol
2₁

41°
34′·56
N
3₃
1₉
5

Fl(3)G.10s
7m2M
5₈ 0446.2
5
Fl(2+1)R.15s
5m2M
0446

4
4₆
Fl(2)R.7s3M
0446.3
Contra dique de Poniente
5₅

5₅
Yard

0   200
Metres

5₅
Fl(2)G.7s9m5M
0446.5
6₈

⊕165   41°34′5N 02°33′.2E
App. Pto de Arenys de Mar

⊕ 165

PUERTO DE ARENYS DE MAR

2°33′.53E

Puerto de Arenys de Mar

V. ii. COSTA DORADA

COSTA BRAVA

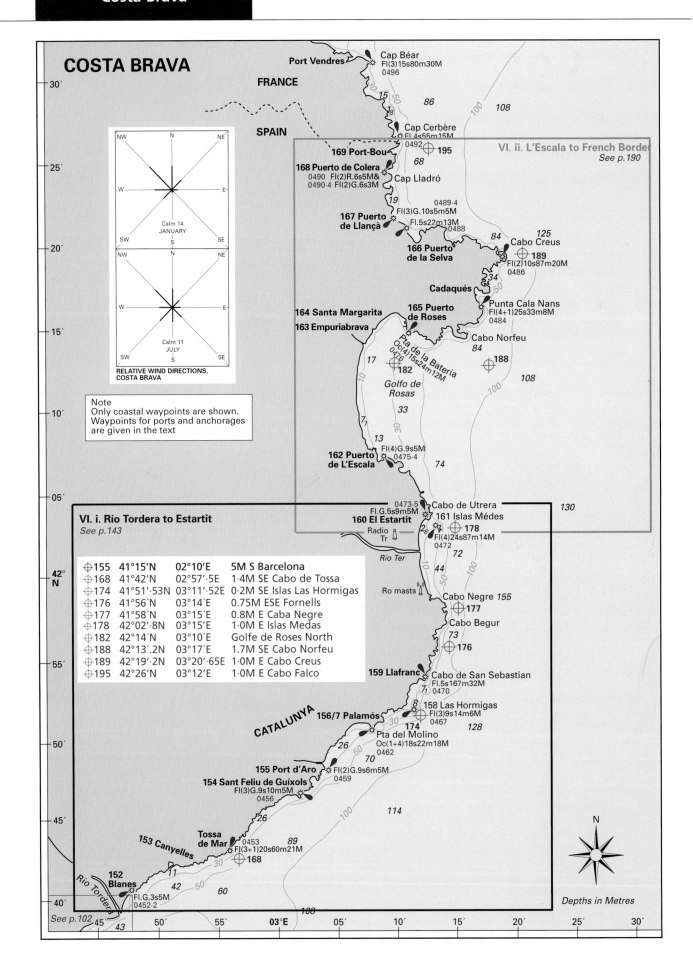

Port Vendres

Cap Béar
Fl(3)15s80m30M
0496

FRANCE

SPAIN

Cap Cerbère
Fl.4s55m15M
0492

169 Port-Bou

⊕ 195

VI. ii. L'Escala to French Border
See p.190

168 Puerto de Colera
0490 Fl(2)R.6s5M&
0490·4 Fl(2)G.6s3M

Cap Lladró

68

**167 Puerto
de Llançà**

19

0489·4
Fl(3)G.10s5m5M

Fl.5s22m13M
0488

**166 Puerto
de la Selva**

84

125
Cabo Creus
⊕ **189**
Fl(2)10s87m20M
0486

34

Cadaqués

Punta Cala Nans
Fl(4+1)25s33m8M
0484

164 Santa Margarita

**165 Puerto
de Roses**

163 Empuriabrava

Cabo Norfeu

84

⊕ **188**

108

Pta de la Batería
Oc(4)15s24m12M
0478
⊕ **182**

17

*Golfo de
Rosas*

33

7₁

13

Fl(4)G.9s5M
0475·4

**162 Puerto
de L'Escala**

74

0473·5
Fl.G.5s9m5M

Cabo de Utrera
⊕ **161 Islas Médes**

130

160 El Estartit

⊕ **178**
Fl(4)24s87m14M
0472

Radio
Tr

28₁

72

Río Ter

10

44

VI. i. Río Tordera to Estartit
See p.143

⊕155	41°15'N	02°10'E	5M S Barcelona
⊕168	41°42'N	02°57'·5E	1·4M SE Cabo de Tossa
⊕174	41°51'·53N	03°11'·52E	0·2M SE Islas Las Hormigas
⊕176	41°56'N	03°14'E	0.75M ESE Fornells
⊕177	41°58'N	03°15'E	0.8M E Caba Negre
⊕178	42°02'·8N	03°15'E	1·0M E Islas Medas
⊕182	42°14'N	03°10'E	Golfe de Roses North
⊕188	42°13'·2N	03°17'E	1.7M SE Cabo Norfeu
⊕189	42°19'·2N	03°20'·65E	1·0M E Cabo Creus
⊕195	42°26'N	03°12'E	1·0M E Cabo Falco

Ro masts

Cabo Negre 155
⊕ **177**

Cabo Begur

73

⊕ **176**

159 Llafranc

Cabo de San Sebastian
Fl.5s167m32M
7₁ 0470

8₁ **158 Las Hormigas**
⊕ Fl(3)9s14m6M
0467

156/7 Palamós
174

CATALUNYA

Pta del Molino
Oc(1+4)18s22m18M
0462

128

26

155 Port d'Aro
⊕ Fl(2)G.9s6m5M
0459

70

154 Sant Feliu de Guíxols
Fl(3)G.9s10m5M
0456

114

26

153 Canyelles

**Tossa
de Mar**

0453
Fl(3+1)20s60m21M

89

⊕ **168**

30

**152
Blanes**

Río Tordera

11

42

60

Fl.G.3s5M
0452·2

N

Depths in Metres

45' ... 43

50'

55'

03°E

05'

10'

15'

20'

25'

30'

See p.102

30'

25'

20'

15'

10'

05'

**42°
N**

55'

50'

45'

40'

RELATIVE WIND DIRECTIONS, COSTA BRAVA

NW N NE

W E

SW SE
S

Calm 14
JANUARY

NW N NE

W E

SW SE
S

Calm 11
JULY

Note
Only coastal waypoints are shown.
Waypoints for ports and anchorages
are given in the text

VI. Costa Brava

Introduction

General description

The 67M stretch of coast from Río Tordera to the French border is more dramatic than the other sections. *Brava* means wild, savage. Much of the coast is broken with steep rocky cliffs and can be scoured by *tramontanas* which blow up with little notice. It is backed by the eastern end of the Pyrénées. The scenery, the proximity of the rugged shores and the deep *calas* beneath steep-sided promontories make this the most attractive of all the *Costas* of Mediterranean Spain for cruising yachtsmen.

The rugged coast runs from Blanes to the wide, flat flood plain of the Río Ter. The hills and cliffs rise again at L'Estartit and continue for 5M as far as the second flood plain of the Ríos Fluviá and Muga. From Roses onwards to France the coast is even less hospitable with high mountains quite close to the sea.

Offshore are the two groups of islands, Islas Formigues and Islas Médes. There are also some islands off Cabo Creus and several groups of rocks close inshore. In general the coast is steep-to and can be approached to within 100m with care. The exceptions are the shallow waters at river-mouths which may extend 300–400m off-shore.

There are numerous attractive anchorages but all are open to the sea one way or another; none have all-round shelter and if the wind is from the wrong quarter, the swell comes rolling in. Often the sheltered places are occupied by moorings. Many of the better known anchorages are mentioned and, for some, details are given. For more adequate shelter, there are harbours and an increasing number of marinas.

Though tourism has been established for some time, development along the Costa Brava is not so raw and ugly as that along the coastline to the southwest. Moreover, there are no really large towns and very little industry. The price is paid in more literal terms. Prices for holiday properties increase along the coast of Spain from south west to north east: harbour dues in the Costa Brava are about double those in the Costa del Sol. Proximity to France adds to the demand on yachting facilities and it is more important to arrange a berth in advance of arrival on the Costa Brava than it is on the other coasts.

Meteorological

Winds

The main danger in this area comes from the sudden arrival of a NW *tramontana* (*tramuntana mestral*, *mistral*), a very strong cold dry wind which arrives with little warning from a clear blue sky and often reaches gale force in a quarter of an hour. In winter these winds can be severe and contingency plans should always be made when at sea and extra mooring or berthing lines used when in harbour in the expectation of their sudden onset. Many *calas* that offer good protection from this wind on an otherwise barren coast have been included and advice as to the best place to secure inside harbours under these conditions has been given where applicable.

On occasion this wind can blow from the N and also to a lesser extent the NE wind and the E *levanter (llevant)* may be experienced. These latter winds are usually preceded by a heavy swell and clouds with rain and poor visibility accompanying them. They rarely reach gale force but their seas can be dangerous.

Harbours of refuge

The following harbours can usually be entered with strong winds and gales from seaward although with some difficulty:
Puerto de Sant Feliu de Guíxols
Puerto de Palamós
Puerto de Port de la Selva
Puerto de Roses

Magnetic variation

0°0'W (2008). Decreasing 7' annually.

Tides

The maximum spring range is under 0·5m and its effects are small.

Currents

There is a permanent S going current of 1–2 knots. It is stronger off promontories and especially off Cabo Creus. Winds from N and E quarters tend to increase the flow and those from the S and W tend to reduce it.

Planning Guide

166 **Port de la Selva** (page 217)
   ⚓ Playa de la Ribera
   ⚓ Playa de la Vall
2.5M   ⚓ Playa d'en Vaques   Punta de la Sernella
   ⚓ Playa Cau de Llop
                                  Islas Falco
167 **Puerto de Llançà (Llansá)** (page 221)
   ⚓ Cala Grifeu
2M   ⚓ Cala Garbet
168 **Puerto de Colera** (page 224)
1.5M

169 **Puerto de Portbou** (page 226)
                                  Cabo Falco

Visits

Details of interesting local places to visit are listed with the harbour concerned. There are a number of places worth visiting located some distance inland which can be reached by public transport or taxi. These include:

Caldas de Malavella a small place inland from Tossa with ruins of old Roman baths and an old church.

Romany a de la Selva where there is a Megalithic tomb. The village is located behind San Feliu de Guíxols.

Girona the largest and most important town in the area, originally a Roman settlement where many old churches can be seen, together with old buildings and walls dating from the time of the Moors. There is a cathedral, several museums and a castle.

Ullastret not far from L'Estartit which has some Iberian and Greek remains and an 11th-century church.

Figueres a major town lying behind the Golfo de Roses, founded by the Romans on their Via Augusta. It has a castle almost intact, a museum and a monastery.

Empuries on the coast near L'Escala, is the most important archaeological site on the Costa Brava. It represents a microcosm of the history of this coast. The two Greek settlements of Paleopolis and Neapolis, sometimes called Emporion (c.500 BC) were taken over in 209 BC by the Romans and renamed Empuries. It co-existed with the nearby settlements of Iberian natives until it was first over-run by the Barbarians, then destroyed by the Moors and later ravaged by Norman pirates. The ruins were covered by sand and silt and in part built over by the small village of Sant Martí only to be rediscovered some 1,000 years later. These ruins are well worth a visit.

VI. COSTA BRAVA
i. Río Tordera to Estartit

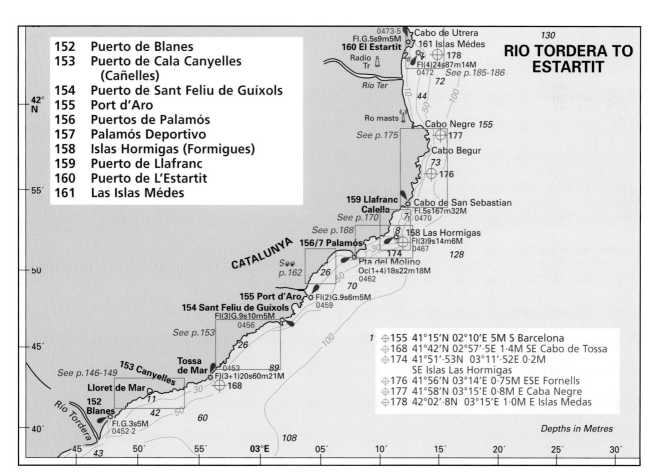

152 **Puerto de Blanes**
153 **Puerto de Cala Canyelles (Cañelles)**
154 **Puerto de Sant Feliu de Guíxols**
155 **Port d'Aro**
156 **Puertos de Palamós**
157 **Palamós Deportivo**
158 **Islas Hormigas (Formigues)**
159 **Puerto de Llafranc**
160 **Puerto de L'Estartit**
161 **Las Islas Médes**

RIO TORDERA TO ESTARTIT

1 ⊕155 41°15'N 02°10'E 5M S Barcelona
⊕168 41°42'N 02°57'·5E 1·4M SE Cabo de Tossa
⊕174 41°51'·53N 03°11'·52E 0·2M SE Islas Las Hormigas
⊕176 41°56'N 03°14'E 0·75M ESE Fornells
⊕177 41°58'N 03°15'E 0·8M E Caba Negre
⊕178 42°02'·8N 03°15'E 1·0M E Islas Medas

Depths in Metres

VI. i. COSTA BRAVA

152. Puerto de Blanes

41°40'N 2°47'E

Charts

British Admiralty *1704*. Imray *M14*
French *4827, 7298*
Spanish *873, 4913, 491*

⊕166 41°40'·25N 02°47'·8E 005°/0·11M to harbour

Lights

0452 **Dique de Abrigo elbow** Fl.G.3s7m3M White post,green top3m
0452·08 **Contradique head** Fl.R.3s7m5M White post, red top 4m
0452·2 **Dique de Abrigo head** Fl.G.3s7m5M White post, green top 3m
0452·1 **Diga Sur head** Fl(2)R.6s6m2M Red post 4m

Port communications

VHF Ch 9 Capitania ☎ 972 33 05 52 *Fax* 972 33 14 98
Email club@cvblanes.cat www.cvblanes.cat

An interesting port

A fishing and yachting harbour based on an old port and improved by breakwaters, quays and pontoons. The harbour is easy to approach and enter but heavy winds between SE and S may send swell into the harbour. The surrounding area is attractive and the town is pleasant. The harbour is crowded in summer.

The botanical garden and the 14th-century church and ruined palace are interesting. The view from Castillo de San Juan on the top of the hill behind the harbour is worth the climb. There is a fine sandy beach to the W of the harbour and to the northeast are a number of attractive small *calas* that can be visited by boat.

Originally a Roman port called Blanda, it once rivalled Barcelona and Tarragona but little remains of that era. The port did not develop at the same rate as its rivals and remained under the Counts of Cabrera whose ruined palace is beside the church.

Approach

From the south A narrow coastal plain backed by ranges of mountains gives way to the deep flat delta of the Río Tordera which projects about ½M out to sea and must be given a berth of at least ¼M because of shoals. The isolated conical hill topped by the Castillo de San Juan which lies just behind this harbour can be seen from afar. The small low rocky Islets de la Palomera and El Portell lie very close inshore just before this harbour is reached, they have deep water to seaward of them but are shoal either side.

From the north Cabo Tossa, a rocky-cliffed peninsula with a conspicuous lighthouse and castle with towers, is easily recognised. The coast remains broken and rocky-cliffed with a number of *calas* and small bays. The conical hill topped by Castillo de San Juan is conspicuous from this direction.

Punta de Santa Anna (or San Miquel) just to the NE of this harbour has outlying rocky islets and shoals. It should not be approached nearer than 300m and the harbour entrance should not be approached until the head of the Dique de Abrigo bears NW.

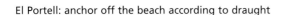
El Portell: anchor off the beach according to draught

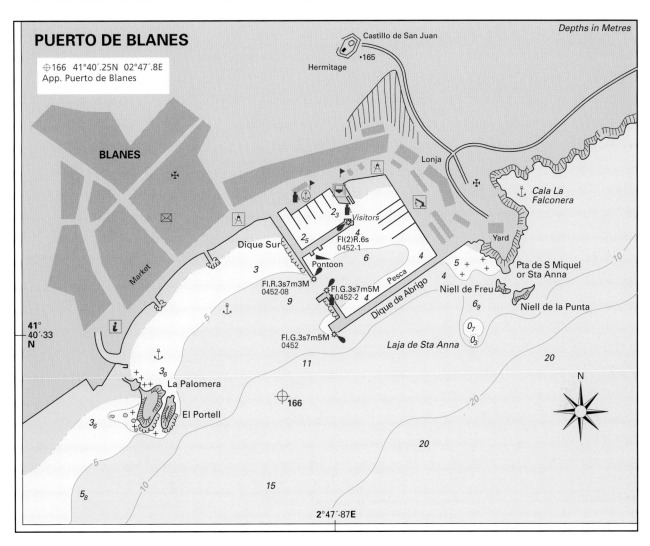

PUERTO DE BLANES

⊕166 41°40'.25N 02°47'.8E
App. Puerto de Blanes

Depths in Metres

Castillo de San Juan
·165
Hermitage
BLANES
Lonja
Cala La Falconera
Visitors
2₃
2₅
Dique Sur
4
Fl(2)R.6s
0452·1
Pontoon
6
3
Yard
5
4
Pta de S Miquel or Sta Anna
Fl.R.3s7m3M
0452·08
9
Fl.G.3s7m5M
0452·2
4
Niell de Freu
4
Pesca
Dique de Abrigo
6₉
Niell de la Punta
Fl.G.3s7m5M
0452
0₇
0₃
Laja de Sta Anna
11
20
La Palomera
3₆
166
El Portell
3₆
20
20
N
15
5₈
10
5

2°47'·87E

Anchorage in the approach

Anchor 300m to W of the head of the Dique de Abrigo in 6m, sand and weed. There are other anchorages in the area, see harbour plan.

Entrance

Approach the Dique de Abrigo on a northerly course, leaving it 50m to starboard and turn slowly to starboard to enter between the pier heads.

Berths

The *club náutico* controls the pontoons in the NW side of the harbour. It is advised to go round the end of the internal quay and moor to the fuelling berth for berthing instructions if it has not been possible to contact the *capitanía* previously.

Charges

High.

Facilities

Maximum length overall 15m.
A shipyard in the E corner of the harbour. Here or elsewhere in the harbour repairs to wood and GRP hulls, engines and sails.
50-tonne travel-lift.
3-tonne crane.
A slip in N corner of the harbour.

Chandlery on the front near the harbour and another beside the harbour.
Water on the quays and pontoons.
220v on the pontoons.
Gasoleo A and petrol.
Ice is delivered daily to a store behind the *lonja*.
Club de Vela de Blanes has a clubhouse beside the inner harbour with bar, lounge, restaurant, terrace, showers, etc.
Many shops and supermarkets in the town and a market every day except Sunday.
Launderette in the town.

Communications

Bus and rail service. Taxi ☎ 972 330 037.

Blanes. Visitors to inner harbour to the right   *Peter Taylor*

VI. i. COSTA BRAVA

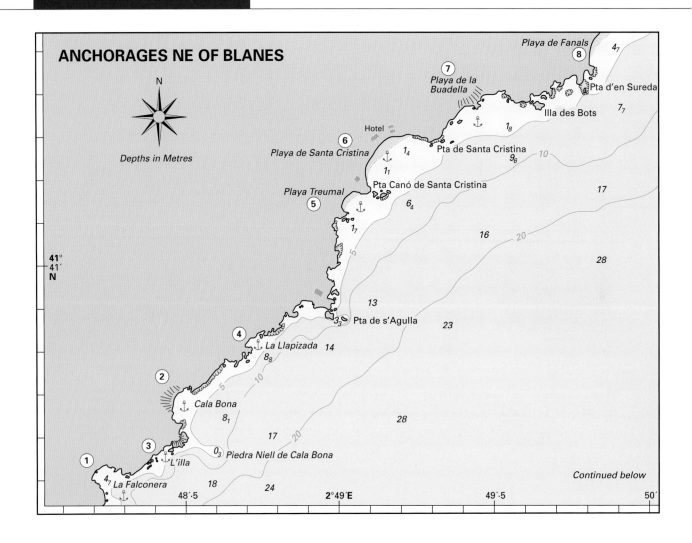

ANCHORAGES NE OF BLANES

N

Depths in Metres

Playa de Fanals
⑧ 4₇

⑦

Playa de la Buadella

Pta d'en Sureda
7₇

Hotel

Illa des Bots

⑥ Playa de Santa Cristina

1₈

1₄ Pta de Santa Cristina
9₆ 10

1₁

Pta Canó de Santa Cristina

17

Playa Treumal
⑤ 6₄

1₇ 16 20 28

13

3₃ Pta de s'Agulla 23

④ La Llapizada 14

8₈

②

Cala Bona 28

8₁

③ 17 20

0₃ Piedra Niell de Cala Bona

L'illa

① 4₇ La Falconera 18 24

Continued below

41°
41'
N

48'·5   2°49'E   49'·5   50'

1. ⚓ **LA FALCONERA** 41°40'·5N 2°48'·3E

An anchorage in a rocky-cliffed bay open between NE and SE.
Small stoney beach, crowded in season. Road and houses ashore.

2. ⚓ **CALA BONA** 41°40'·7N 2°48'·6E

Cala Bona: anchor off the beach in sand. Open between NE and SE.

3. ⚓ **L'ILLA** 41°40'·6N 2°48'·8E

Anchorage on S side of a hooked promontory in sand and stone with off-lying islets, open between E and S, road ashore.

4. ⚓ **CALA LA LLAPIZADA** 41°40'·8N 2°48'·9E

A rocky sided *cala*. Anchor in N corner under headland with house on its point and off-lying islet, Piedra Agulla, to its E. Anchor in sand and stone – open between E and S. Road ashore.

5. ⚓ **PLAYA TREUMAL** 41°41'·1N 2°49'·1E

Playa Treumal: anchor off either beach. Open between NE and SE

VI. i. COSTA BRAVA

153. Puerto de Cala Canyelles (Cañelles)

41°42'N 2°53'E

Charts

British Admiralty *1704*. Imray *M14*
French *4827*
Spanish *873, 492*

⊕167 41°42'·07N 02°52'·95E 315°/0·14M to harbour

Lights

0452·7 **Dique de Abrigo head** Fl(4)G.11s5m5M Green
  tower 3m
0452·9 **On cliff at entrance** Fl.R.5s1M Red hut
0452·8 **On cliff to south** Fl(4)R.11s3M Red hut
To the north
0453 **Cabo Tossa** 41°42'·9N 2°56'·0E Fl(3+1)20s60m21M
  White tower 11m 229·7°-vis-064·2°

Port communications

VHF Ch 9. *Capitanía* ☎ 972 368 818
Fax 972 36 15 35 *Email* info@cncanyelles.com
www.cncanyelles.com

A very small marina

A yacht harbour for smaller yachts (8m max) and
fishing boats. Built into the W end of a beach at the
side of an attractive *cala*. Entrance is normally easy
but could be difficult with strong winds between E
and SW. The swell from these winds also makes it
uncomfortable inside the harbour. Facilities are
limited, provisions are available from shops in the
nearby village.

The area around has been built over with large
private houses and the beach of fine sand to the E of
the harbour is crowded in summer with day-
trippers.

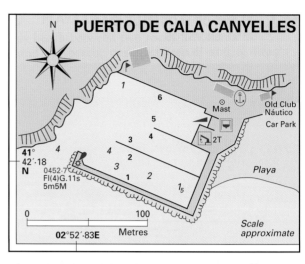

⊕167 41°.42'.07N 02°52'.95E App. Puerto de Canyelles

Approach

From the south Puerto de Blanes is unmistakable
with Castillo de San Juan on a hill behind it. Further
NE there are some eight *calas*, most with sandy
beaches at their head, the largest being the Playa de
Fanals and the Playa de Lloret which has the town
of Lloret de Mar behind it with a conspicuous
church tower. There are a few small *calas* to E of the
Playa de Lloret de Mar but the next large *cala* has a
sandy beach with the harbour at its west end.

From the north Puerto Sant Feliu de Guíxols is easily
recognised by its long breakwater and the prominent
Punta de Garbí on the W side. Broken rocky cliffs
with small *calas* extend 5·5M to Cabo Tossa which
has a conspicuous lighthouse and tower on its

Puerto de Cala Canyelles

summit. The harbour lies 2¼M to SW of Cabo Tossa. Do not mistake the large *cala* of Playa de Lloret (no connection with the Playa de Lloret de Mar which lies opposite the town of the same name which is only 1·5M from Cabo de Tossa). This stretch of coast has broken rocky cliffs with many small *calas*. The sandy beach and harbour of Cala de Canyelles are easily seen when S of the *cala*.

Anchorage in the approach

300m to S of the sandy beach of Cala de Canyelles in 10m, sand and stone.

Entrance

The entrance, which is only 12m wide, lies to the W side of the harbour between the head of the Dique de Abrigo and the red rocky cliffs.

Approach the head of the Dique de Abrigo and enter, keeping close to the head, at slow speed with a bow lookout because the channel is narrow.

Berths

Secure to a vacant berth and ask the *capitanía* for a berth.

Facilities

Maximum length overall 8m.
Mechanic for simple repairs.
2-tonne crane.
A small slip in NE corner of the harbour.
Small hard-standing.
Water on the quays.
Provisions from the village up the hill or in Lloret de Mar 3M away.
Club Náutico de Cala Canyelles now operates from a porta-cabin in low season and the restaurant/bar may now belong to a private concern.

Communications

Bus service on coast road 0·5M inland.

⚓ **CALA MORISCA** 41°42'·2N 2°53'·9E

A small V-shaped *cala* with stony beach at its head, anchor in mid-*cala* in rock and sand, open between SE–S–SW.

⚓ **PLAYA DE LLORELL** 41°42'·4N 2°54'·3E

Anchor off sand and pebble beach in sand open between SE and SW. Beach café/bar, road, some houses and apartment blocks.

⚓ **N OF ELS CARS** 41°42'·8N 2°55'·8E

A small bay open between E and S with rocky coast and cliffs. Anchor in sand and rock in middle.

⚓ **CALA ES CODOLAR** 41°42'·8N 2°55'·9E

Cala Es Codolar: open between SE and SW. A pre-Roman anchorage and harbour. *(See plan of Tossa, page 153.)*

VI. i. COSTA BRAVA

Puerto de Tossa de Mar

41°43'N 2°56'E

Charts

British Admiralty 1704. Imray *M14*
French *4827, 7505*
Spanish *873, 876, 491*
⊕169 310°/0·25M to anchor

Lights

0453 **Cabo Tossa** 41°42'·9N 2°56'·0E Fl(3+1)20s60m21M
  White tower 11m 229·7°-vis-064·2°

Anchorage only

Not actually a harbour but an important and very
attractive anchorage. Under Tossa it is well sheltered
from the prevailing winds though open between NE
and SE; further north up the bay the anchorages are
more exposed to the south. In the season the bay is
crowded with tourists.

Tossa is a very old harbour and town that has been
in occupation since pre-Roman times. The Romans
called it Turissa. It was, like the rest of the towns on
this coast, destroyed by the Vandals and rebuilt only
to be destroyed again. In the 10th century the
Castrum de Tursia, as it was then called, was given
by the Count of Barcelona to the monks of Ripoll.
Between the two world wars this town was
discovered by foreign tourists and became a popular
resort. There are many interesting places to visit
including a Roman villa, the old town (Villa Vella),
a Baroque church and a museum. The view from the
lighthouse is worth the climb.

Approach

From the south The coast from Blanes, which can be
recognised by the conical hill topped by a small
castle, is very broken and rocky-cliffed with many
calas. The concentration of houses and flats at Lloret
de Mar where there is a long sandy beach is easy to
identify. The lighthouse and tower on Cabo de Tossa
can be seen from afar.

From the north From Punta de Garbí the coast is
likewise very broken with rocky cliffs and ranges of
hills inland. The lighthouse and tower at Cabo Tossa
is also conspicuous from this direction.

Entrance

The easiest entrance is on a NW course towards the
river mouth where there is a gap in the line of
buildings.

From the northeast, the passage between Punta de
la Palma and Isla de la Palma should only be
attempted in good conditions with caution and then
only at the N side of the passage between Punta de
la Palma and the 0·3m shallows of Pedras del Freu.
Use in a NE-SW direction; minimum depth 3·0m.
When through, beware the unmarked rocky shoal
Llosa de la Palma, 2m, in the N half of the bay.

Anchorage

Anchor where indicated on the chart to suit
prevailing wind in 4m, sand. The nearest alternatives
are Es Codolar to the south or Playa de la Palma to
the north.

Puerto de Tossa de Mar

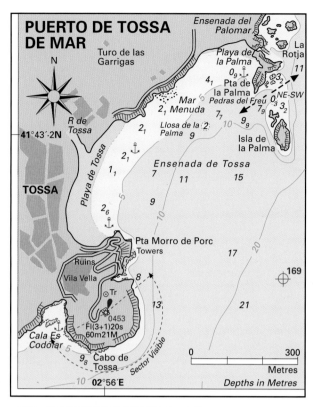

PUERTO DE TOSSA DE MAR

N

Turo de las Garrigas

Ensenada del Palomar

La Rotja

Playa de la Palma

0.9

Pta de la Palma

Pedras del Freu

NE-SW

4.1

Mar Menuda

2.1

7.7

7.9

0.3

3.2

R de Tossa

41°43′·2N

2.1

Llosa de la Palma

2.9

10

9.9

Isla de la Palma

TOSSA

Playa de Tossa

2.1

1.1

Ensenada de Tossa

7

11

15

2.6

9

10

Pta Morro de Porc

Towers

17

20

169

Ruins

Vila Vella

8

Tr

13

21

0453 Fl(3+1)20s 60m21M

Cala Es Codolar

5

9.8

Cabo de Tossa

Sector Visible

10

02°56′E

0   300

Metres

Depths in Metres

⊕168 41°42′N 02°56′.4E 1.4M SE Cabo de Tossa
⊕169 41°43′N 02°56′·4E App. Tossa Anchorages

Playa de la Palma: anchor in 5m, sand, stone and weed. Open to S.

Landings

On the sandy beach where and when swell allows.

Facilities

Many shops of all kinds in the town.

⚓ N OF PUNTA DE LA PALMA 41°43′·1N 2°56′·4E

A wide rocky bay with three small *calas*. Anchor in 5m sand, stone and weed in mid-bay, open between E and S.

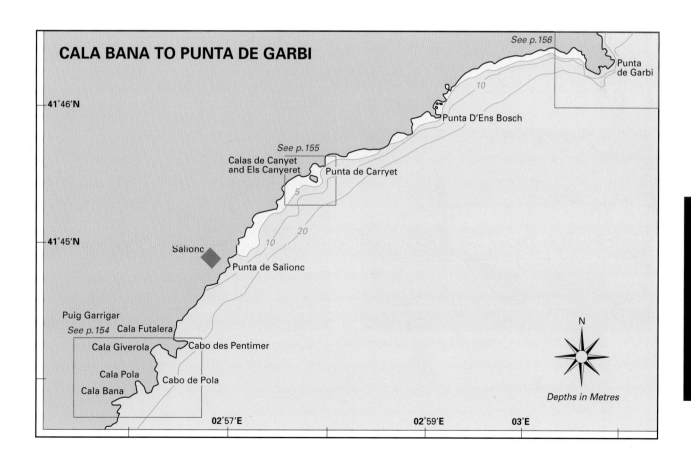

CALA BANA TO PUNTA DE GARBI

See p.156

Punta de Garbi

41°46′N

Punta D'Ens Bosch

See p.155

Calas de Canyet and Els Canyeret

Punta de Carryet

10

5

20

41°45′N

Salionc

10

Punta de Salionc

Puig Garrigar

See p.154 Cala Futalera

Cala Giverola

Cabo des Pentimer

Cala Pola

Cabo de Pola

Cala Bana

N

Depths in Metres

02°57′E

02°59′E

03°E

VI. i. COSTA BRAVA

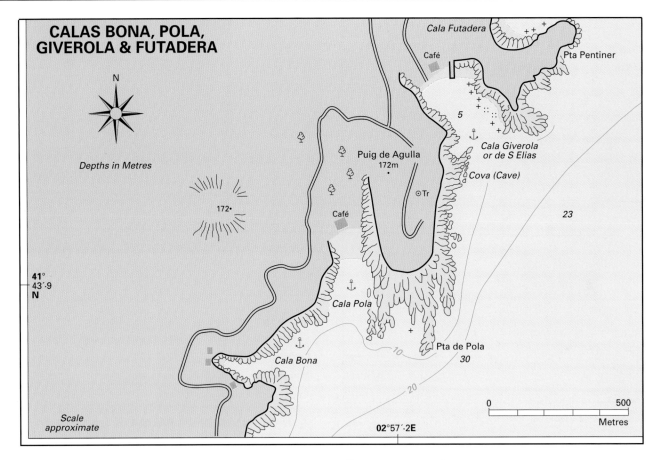

CALAS BONA, POLA, GIVEROLA & FUTADERA

Cala Futadera

Café

Pta Pentiner

N

Depths in Metres

172•

Puig de Agulla
172m

Café

⊙Tr

5

Cala Giverola
or de S Elias

Cova (Cave)

23

41°
43´·9
N

Cala Pola

Cala Bona

Pta de Pola

30

10

20

Scale
approximate

02°57´·2E

0   500

Metres

⚓ **CALA BONA** 41°43´·8N 2°57´E

A long narrow *cala* open between E and SE with rocky tree-covered sides and sandy beach at its head, with a beach café/bar. Anchor in mid-*cala*, sand and rock.

⚓ **CALA GIVEROLA (OR DE ST ELIAS)**
41°44´N 2°57´·4E

⚓ **CALA POLA** 41°43´·8N 2°57´·2E

⚓ **PUNTA DE POLA**

A rocky-cliffed, tree-covered headland with high ground inland, ending in a conspicuous hump. Dangerous rocks off the point but 5m depths nearby.

⚓ **CALA FUTADERA** 41°44´·3N 2°57´·6E

Cala Pola and Giverola with Cala Futadera at extreme right

Cala Futadera: anchor in the middle, sand and rock.
Open between NE and SE

⚓ CALAS DE CANYET AND ELS CANYERETS
41°45'·3N 2°58'·9E

Calas de Canyet and Els Canyerets: anchor off the beach of Els Canyerets (at the right of the photograph)

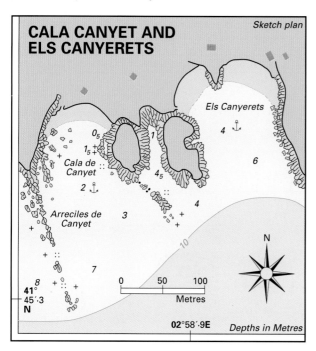

CALA CANYET AND ELS CANYERETS
Sketch plan

Els Canyerets

Cala de Canyet

Arreciles de Canyet

0 50 100
Metres

Depths in Metres

02°58'·9E

⚓ CALA DEL UIGUETÁ 41°46'·3N 03°01'·5E

A large *cala* with rocky-cliffed sides and inshore rocks, small sand and stone beach at its head. Ermita de Sant Elm (100m) a church with a small spire stands on top of the headland. There are several very small sub-*calas*. The main *cala* is open between S and W. Anchor in sand and rock near the head of the *cala*. It has been reported (2000) that in easterly winds effluent builds up around the small jetty in this *cala*.

⚓ CALA DE PORT SALVI 41°46'·2N 3°01'·9E

A small *cala* on the SE point of Punta de Garbí open between E and S. Unfortunately, throughout the summer season, a diving mark (Flag 'A' on yellow inflatable) is moored permanently in the middle of the *cala* and diving training by the Eden Roc Diving Centre takes place most days. For this reason it is

I CALA TO S OF PUNTA D'EN BOSCH
41°46'N 3°00'·3E

Punta d'en Bosch: this *cala* south of en Bosch does not welcome yachts in summer.

not recommended to anchor in this *cala*. There is a 1·1m shoal 50m to S of the mass of Punta Garbí.

PUNTA DE GARBÍ 41°46'·25N 3°01'·8E

A very prominent and conspicuous high headland with rocky cliffs which has rocky dangers extending 50m to SE and there is a 1·1m shoal 50m to S of point. The Ermita de Sant Elm stands on the crest and there are many houses and apartments.

⚓ CALA BETWEEN PUNTA DE GARBÍ AND PUNTA DE LAS PLANETES 41°46'·4N 3°01'·9E

A small *cala* open between NE and E with rocky sides. Anchor in mid-*cala*, rocks and stone.

⚓ CALA DE TETUÁN 41°46'·4N 3°01'·9E

Small *cala* open between N and E with rocky cliffs around it. Anchor in mid-*cala*, rocks and stone.

154. Puerto de Sant Feliu de Guíxols

41°46′N 3°01′E

Charts

British Admiralty *1704*. Imray *M14*
French *4827, 7008, 7505, 7298*
Spanish *4922, 492*

⊕168 41°42′N 02°57′·5E 343°/0·5M to harbour

Lights

0455 **Dique de Refuerzo W head** Fl(3)G.9s3M Green lantern on green/white post
0456 **Dique Rompeolas head** Fl(3)G.9s10m5M White tower, green top 5m
0458·1 **Anchorage Ldg Lts 343°**
Dir.Iso.WRG.3s14m4M Front unlit in line 343° 52m from rear 339°-G-342·3°-W-343·7°-R-345·3°

Port communications

VHF Ch 9. *Capitanía* ☎ 972 321 700 *Fax* 972 321 300
Email info@clubnauticsantfeliu.com
www.clubnauticsantfeliu.com

A popular and developing marina

A fishing, commercial and yachting harbour improved by the addition of a breakwater, quays and pontoons. The town and area are attractive but considerable tourist development continues apace and many old buildings are being pulled down. Swell from winds between E and S comes into the harbour.

This very old harbour, known to the Romans as Gesoria, came to fame by virtue of its monastery, originally built before the 8th century but then destroyed by the Moors and rebuilt in the 10th and 11th centuries. The abbot was feudal lord of the large area and the town and port prospered, becoming the most important town in the SE of Spain. During the Middle Ages the local people continuously fought against their overlords and eventually overthrew them. In the 18th century the cork trade brought further wealth and in recent years the tourist trade developed.

A new Club Náutico, offices and facilities is under contruction close to the root of the main breakwater; it opens in 2008. A line of pontoons

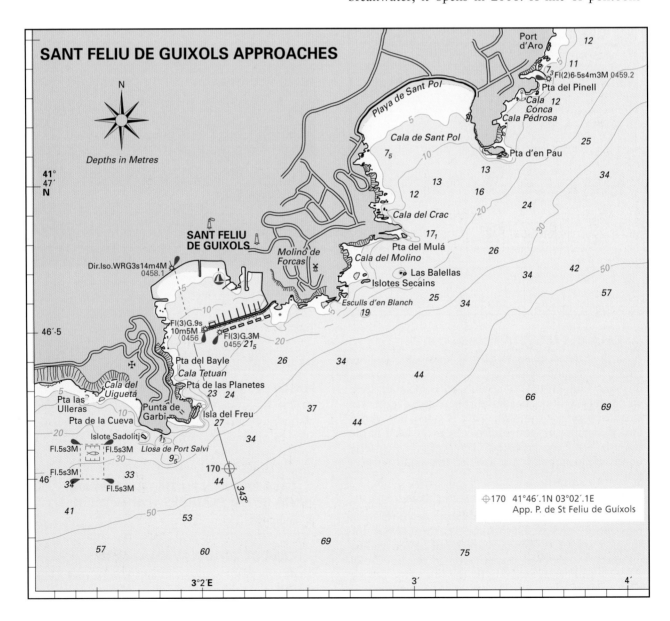

Puerto de Sant Feliu de Guíxols in 2004. Since then, a row of large, flat concrete blocks has been laid outside the outer breakwater to act as a wave breaker. The marina occupies the inner side of the main breakwater

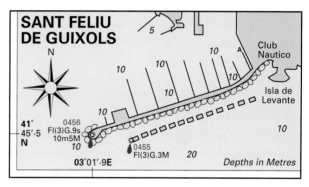

(lettered Q to A from seaward) is controlled by the Club who will fit visitors in as best they can. Two large box-shaped pontoons nearest the sea are for very large boats. Call ahead on Ch 9, visitors will be met. The inner harbour is not for visitors.

The museum in the old monastery and the 14th-century church can be visited and the view from the Ermita de Sant Elm is worth the climb. There is a pleasant beach ½M to E of harbour; the fine sandy beaches to the NW are very crowded in summer.

Approach

From the south From the conspicuous lighthouse and castle with tower on Cabo Tossa the very broken rocky-cliffed coast continues northeast. Punta de Garbí with the Ermita de Sant Elm is prominent and easily recognised. Round this promontory at 200m or more and the harbour entrance will be seen. Pay attention to a 1·1m rocky shallow, Llosa de Port Salvi, 50m to S of the massif of Punta de Garbí.

From the north From the Bahía de Palamós, which is easily recognised by virtue of its harbour wall and mass of houses and high-rise buildings, the rugged coast is broken by the wide sandy Bahía de Platja d'Aro and an almost square-shaped Cala de Sant Pol. Punta de Garbí is also prominent from this direction. Keep ½M off this section of coast to avoid off-lying shoals.

Entrance

Note that at night the leading lights have been replaced with a RWG directional light on the rear post. Steer to keep in the white sector on 343°. On a course of 343° enter the harbour leaving the head of the Dique Rompeolas 100m to starboard. It may be possible to see the leading marks, two sets of round white discs with black diagonal stripes located on white masts with black bands in the trees in front of the town.

The head of the Dique Rompeolas and that of the small *dique* on the E side of the harbour have been washed away several times and much rubble lies near their heads underwater; give them a berth of at least 30m. When clear of the head turn to a NE course.

Berths

Arriving craft must call ahead on Ch 9 and wait off the entrance to be met by staff and allocated a berth. These are generally equipped with lazy lines off the pontoon.

Anchorages

Anchoring is forbidden.

Facilities

Maximum length overall 15m.

Minor repairs can be carried out by the shipyard and there are a number of mechanics for engine repair.

50-tonne crane in port, 6-tonne crane at the *club náutico*

Small slips on either side of the Peñón de Guíxols and a slipway on the NE side of the harbour with 2m of water at its foot.

Chandlery: Hipocampo, a shop in the street which is one back from the N side of the harbour. There is another chandler on the Muelle Comercial.

Water from the quays, pontoons, *club náutico* and the *lonja*.

220v AC at the *club náutico* and the Dique Rompeolas.

Gasoleo A and petrol from pumps at the *club náutico* and from service station just to the N of this club.

Ice from the *club náutico*, from a shop behind the market or from an ice factory near the root of the Dique Rompeolas.

Many good shops in the town and a good market which is open on Sundays.

⚓ CALA DE SANT POL (S'AGARO)
41°47'·8N 3°03'·1E

Club Náutico de Sant Feliu de Guíxols has a clubhouse to the W of the Peñón de Guíxols with bar, lounge, terrace, restaurants, showers etc. Visitors using the club berths may use the club.

Launderettes in the town.

A weather forecast is posted daily at the *club náutico*.

Communications

Bus service. Taxi ☎ 972 320 934.

⚓ ANCHORAGES IMMEDIATELY E OF SANT FELIU DE GUÍXOLS

The ¾M section of coast from the root of the Dique Rompeolas to Cala de Sant Pol is very broken with many small islets, *calas* and passages. It is a most spectacular and attractive area. Explore in a powered dinghy or shallow-draught yacht. Spanish chart *305A* and a forward lookout are essential.

⚓ SE OF S'AGARO CALAS PÉDROSA, DE LA FONT, VAQUES, CONCA 41°47'·6N 3°03'·8E

Four *calas* in a rocky-cliffed coast with large private houses on top of the cliffs. Anchor with care in mid-*cala*, sand, rock and weed. Open between NE and SE.

Cala de Sant Pol (S'Agaro): open between E and S. S'Agaro is ½M to N and Sant Feliu 1M to SW. *See plan page 156*

155. Port d'Aro

41°48'N 3°02'E

Charts

British Admiralty *1704*. Imray *M14*
French *4827, 7505*
Spanish *876, 492*

⊕171 41°47'·9N 03°04'·07E 330°/0·16M to harbour

Lights

0459 **Playa de Aro Espigón head** Fl(2)G.9s6m5M Green
metal column 3m
0459·2 **Contradique** Fl(2)R.6·5s4m3M Red column on
pyramidal base 2m
To the northeast
0462 **Punta del Molino** 41°50'·6N 3°07'·8E
Oc(1+4)18s22m18M White round tower, grey cupola
8m
0460 **Bajo Pereira (La Llosa de Palamós)** 41°50'·1N
3°07'·2E Fl(2)7s10m5M Two black spheres on black
post, red band (isolated danger mark)

Port communications

VHF Ch 9. *Capitanía* ☎ 972 818 929 *Fax* 972 825 909
Email portdaro@cnportdaro.com
www.cnportdaro.net

Port d'Aro

A generally crowded marina

A holiday development with a yacht harbour built
on the delta of the Río Ridaura at the S end of the
Playa de Platja d'Aro. Approach and entrance is
simple but would be difficult and dangerous with
strong winds between NE and SE which also send
swell into the harbour. There are good facilities and
other shops are available at S'Agaró 0·7M (where
there is an interesting 14th-century cloister
incorporated into a modern church), Castillo d'Aro
1·2M and behind the Playa (Platja) d'Aro. The long
sandy beach to the N is very crowded in summer.

Approach

From the south Cabo de Tossa with its conspicuous
lighthouse, town and beach, are easily recognised.
Puerto de Sant Feliu de Guíxols with a long
breakwater and its prominent headland, Punta de
Garbi, are also easy to identify as is the wide deep
Cala de Sant Pol. The harbour lies 1M to NE of this
cala.

From the north Puerto de Palamós is unmistakable
as is the Bahía de Palamós which is lined with high-
rise apartment blocks. Cabo Roig is not prominent
but has shallows extending 500m towards SE and
with two small exposed rocky islets. The long sandy
Playa (Platja) d'Aro is backed by lines of high-rise

VI. i. COSTA BRAVA

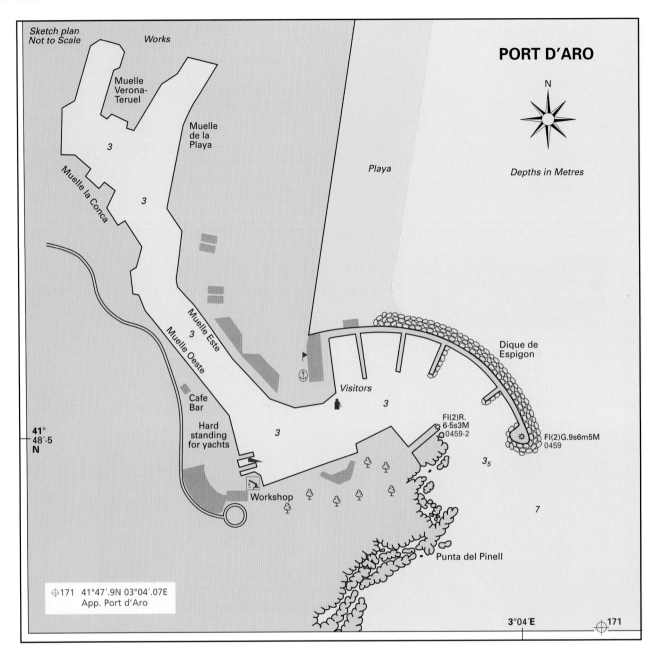

PORT D'ARO

N

Depths in Metres

Sketch plan
Not to Scale

Works

Muelle
Verona-
Teruel

Muelle
de la
Playa

Playa

3

3

Muelle la Conca

3

Muelle Este

3

Muelle Oeste

3

Cafe
Bar

Hard
standing
for yachts

3

3

Visitors

3

Dique de
Espigon

Fl(2)R.
6·5s3M
0459·2

Fl(2)G.9s6m5M
0459

3₅

7

Workshop

Punta del Pinell

41°
48′·5
N

⊕171   41°47′.9N 03°04′.07E
App. Port d'Aro

3°04′E   ⊕171

buildings. The harbour entrance lies at the S end of the beach.

Anchorage in the approach

Anchor in 15m, sand, 300m to NE of the harbour mouth.

Entrance

Approach the head of the Dique de Abrigo on a SW heading leaving it 20m to starboard.

Berths

If not directed by VHF, secure on the NW side of the second of the three spurs within the harbour on the starboard side, then ask. The SE side of the spur is protected by rocks.

Charges

Medium.

Facilities

Maximum length overall 15m.
Repairs to hull and engines possible at the yard in the
    SW corner.
20-tonne travel-lift.
8-tonne crane.
Slip.
Hard-standing.
Chandlery nearby.
Water on quays and pontoons.
220v AC on quays and pontoons.
Gasoleo A and petrol.
Ice from the *club náutico*.
Club Náutico de Port d'Aro with bar, ice, restaurant,
    launderette, showers, WCs, etc.
Provisions from S'Agaro ½M or behind the Platja d'Aro
    about 1M to N.
Weather forecast posted once a day at *oficina de capitán*.

Communications

Taxi ☎ 972 817 032.

Port d'Aro. Holding berth *Peter Taylor*

Port d'Aro. Club Náutico on right *Robin Rundle*

VI. i. COSTA BRAVA

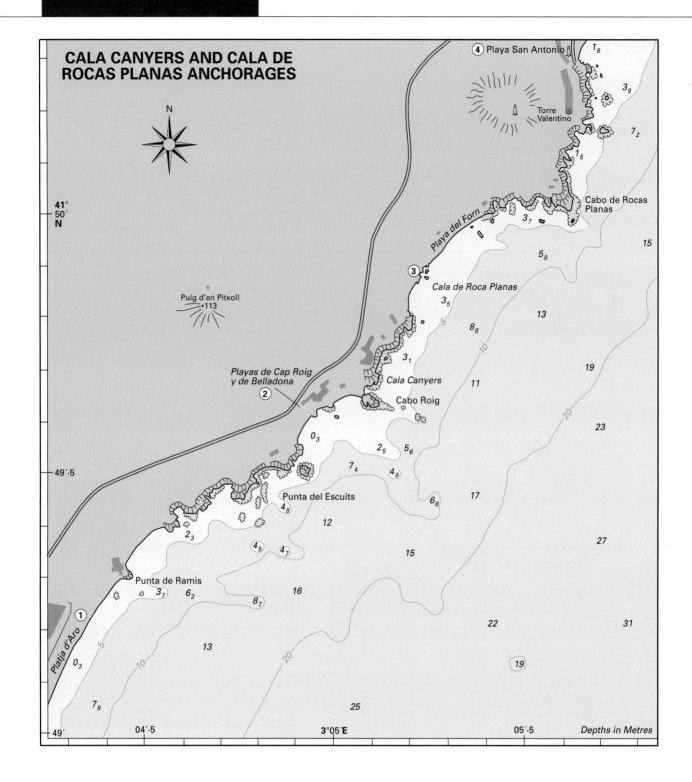

CALA CANYERS AND CALA DE
ROCAS PLANAS ANCHORAGES

N

41°
50′
N

Puig d'en Pitxoll
·113

Playas de Cap Roig
y de Belladona
②

Punta del Escuits

Punta de Ramis

Platja d'Aro

①

④ Playa San Antonio

Torre
Valentino

Cabo de Rocas
Planas

Playa del Forn

③

Cala de Roca Planas

Cala Canyers

Cabo Roig

49′·5

49′

04′·5

3°05′E

05′·5

Depths in Metres

1. ⚓ **PLAYA (PLATJA) D'ARO** 41°48'·6N 3°04'·3E

4. ⚓ **PLAYA SAN ANTONIO** 41°50'·4N 3°06'E

Playa (Platja) d'Aro: open between NE and S. A seaside resort with the usual facilities

2. ⚓ **PLAYAS DE CAP ROIG AND Y DE BELLADONA** 41°49'·4N 3°05'·3E

Playa de San Antonio: open between E and SE

⚓ **PLAYA DE PALAMÓS** 41°50'·7N 3°05'·3E

A long sandy beach backed by roads and lines of high-rise buildings. All facilities of a large seaside holiday town available. Anchor off the beach in sand, open between E and SW. Many stone groynes to trap the sand. (See plan on page 165).

Playas de Cap Roig and de Belladona: open between E and S with foul ground around (Cala Canyérs beyond)

3. ⚓ **CALA DE CANYERS AND ROCA PLANAS**
41°49'·7N 3°05'·3E

Cala Canyérs and Cala de Roca Planas beyond: open between NE and SE. Note the rocks off Cabo Roig

VI. i. COSTA BRAVA

Puertos de Palamós

156. Commercial
157. Deportivo

41°50'N 3°07'E

Charts

British Admiralty *1704*. Imray *M14*
French *7298, 4827*
Spanish *4923, 492*

⊕172   41°50'·1N 03°07'·75E 310°/0·15 to port
025°/0·600 to marina

Lights

0462 **Punta del Molino** 41°50'·6N 3°07'·8E
Oc(1+4)18s22m18M White round tower, grey cupola
8m
Commercial Port
0464 **Dique de Abrigo head** Fl.G.3s9m5M Grey globe
Marina – Puerto Deportivo
0466·7 **Dique de Abrigo head** Fl(4)G.10s11m5M Green
tower 8m
To the south
0460 **La Llosa de Palamós (Bajo Pereira)** 41°50'·1N
3°07'·2E Fl(2)7s10m5M 2 black spheres on black post,
red band (isolated danger mark) 197°-vis-165°
To the northeast
0467 **Hormiga Grande** 41°51'·7N 3°11'·1E Fl(3)9s14m6M
White round tower on hut 6m
0470 **Cabo San Sebastián** 41°53'·7N 3°12'·1E
Fl.5s167m32M White round tower on white building,
red roof 12m Aeromarine
Buoys
A black buoy marks Llosa del Molino, 1·9m, 100m SW of
Punta del Molino.

Port communications

See pages 166 & 167

Commercial harbour W, Marina E

There are two harbours at Palamós, one on either
side of the headland, Punta de Molino, which
catches the full force of the NW *tramontana* when it
blows. The harbour on the west side is used by
fishing and commercial craft. It is easy to approach
and enter. The Club Náutico Costa Brava is in the
old inner harbour and welcomes visitors. On the east
side, the Puerto Deportivo does not have a yacht
club (though a noisy disco has been noted). The
town serving both is pleasant but in the season is
crowded with tourists.

The museum and 14th-century church (much
altered in the 16th and 18th centuries) can be visited.
There are many attractive *calas* along the coast
which can be reached by boat. The ancient villages
of Ullastret (12M) and Calonge (1M) are worth a
visit. Fine beach to the N of the harbour.

Palamós rose to prominence in the Middle Ages
when it won an age-long struggle with Sant Feliu de
Guíxols to be the maritime outlet for Girona. In
1334 it became the maritime district of Girona and
prospered greatly. In 1534 it was sacked and burnt
by Barbarossa with the Turkish Fleet after which it
fell on hard times. With the development of the cork
industry and agriculture its fortunes revived but it
was again heavily damaged during the Civil War.
Today it depends largely on the tourist industry.

Puertos de Palamós Commercial left, Deportivo right

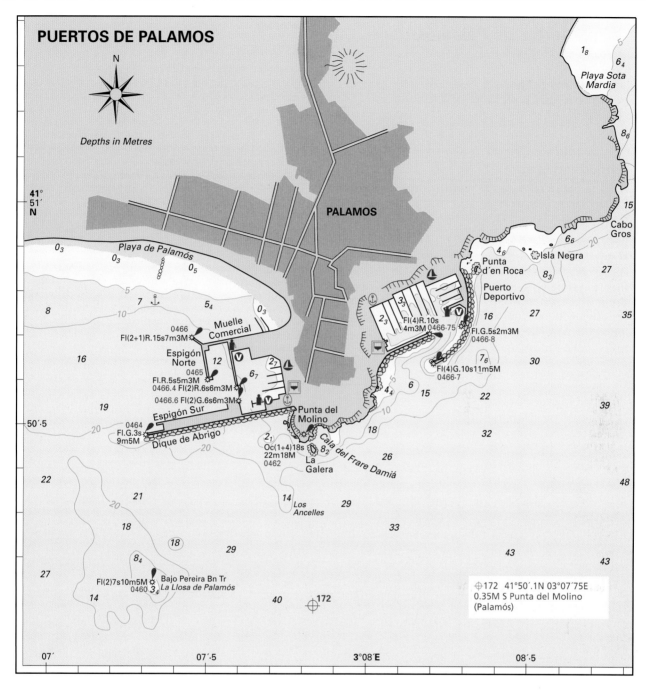

PUERTOS DE PALAMOS

N

Depths in Metres

41°
51′
N

PALAMOS

Playa de Palamós

Muelle
Comercial

0466
Fl(2+1)R.15s7m3M

Espigón
Norte
0465
Fl.R.5s5m3M
0466.4 Fl(2)R.6s6m3M

0466.6 Fl(2)G.6s6m3M

Espigón Sur

0464
Fl.G.3s
9m5M
Dique de Abrigo

Punta del
Molino

Oc(1+4)18s
22m18M
0462

La
Galera

Los
Ancelles

Fl(2)7s10m5M
0460
Bajo Pereira Bn Tr
La Llosa de Palamós

⊕172

Playa Sota
Mardia

Cabo
Gros

Isla Negra

Punta
d'en Roca

Puerto
Deportivo

Fl(4)R.10s
4m3M 0466.75

Fl.G.5s2m3M
0466.8

Fl(4)G.10s11m5M
0466.7

Cala del Frare Damiá

⊕172 41°50′.1N 03°07′75E
0.35M S Punta del Molino
(Palamós)

07′   07′.5   3°08′E   08′.5

Approach

From the south The prominent Punta de Garbí with the Ermita de Sant Elm on its summit and the harbour of Sant Feliu de Guíxols are easily recognised as is the deep square-shaped Cala de Sant Pol. The masses of high-rise buildings at Platja d'Aro and Palamós can be seen from afar. There are two high-rise buildings 500m due N of the harbour and in the close approach the grey rocky breakwater will be seen jutting out westwards from the Punta del Molino. Keep an eye out for La Llosa de Palamós. If going round to the Puerto Deportivo, keep ¼M off Punta del Molino and the breakwater will be seen to the E of the point.

From the north From the high prominent Cabo San Sebastián which has a conspicuous lighthouse, the coast is very rocky and broken. The lower wooded Capo de Planas, the small rocky Islas Hormigas should be easily recognised. There is a passage inside the Islas Hormigas (*see page 168*) but it is simpler to keep to seaward, especially in heavy weather. Later the two high-rise buildings located side by side 500m to N of the harbour at Palamós, should be spotted (they may appear as one). The coast should not be approached closer than ½M because of outlying dangers. If going to the old harbour, keep at least ¼M off Punta del Molino but beware of La Llosa de Palamós. Punta del Molino lighthouse is not conspicuous.

VI. i. COSTA BRAVA

156. Puertos de Palamós

41°59'·5N 03°07'·2E (Mole End)
⊕172 308°/0·6M

Port communications

Club Nautico Costa Brava (west) VHF Ch 09
☎ 972 31 43 24 *Fax* 972 31 54 17
Email cncb@cncostabrava.com www.cncostabrava.com

Outside anchorage

A possible anchorage is north of the Muelle Comercial in 10m or less.

Berths

Go alongside the fuel berth and ask for a berth or report to the *capitanía* nearby. Club Náutico rent a corner of the inner harbour for their own use and they welcome visitors for whom there are normally about 20 berths available. The Club building houses the offices, all facilities and a restaurant. Charges are higher than at Puerto Deportivo.

Facilities

Old Harbour

Maximum length overall 25m.

A large yard under the bridge behind the *club náutico* and a smaller one to the N of it. Repairs to hulls can be carried out. Engine shops.

5-tonne crane on the N side of the Muelle Comercial and three cranes, 3 to 10 tonnes, at the *club náutico*.

Large slip on the inner side of the Dique de Abrigo.

Small slipway by the *club náutico*.

A small hard alongside the *club náutico*.

Two chandlers in the town and a large one under the bridge behind the *club náutico*.

Water on the Dique de Abrigo, pontoons, the Muelle Comercial and at the *club náutico* and the *lonja*.

220v AC points on Dique de Abrigo, pontoons and the Muelle Comercial.

Ice from a factory behind the *lonja*.

Club Náutico Costa Brava is located at the root of the Dique de Abrigo with bar, lounge, terrace, restaurant, showers and swimming pool.

Weather forecast posted at *club náutico* once a day.

In town

Supermarket and other shops.

Fish can be bought from a market at the *lonja* in the evening.

Launderettes.

Communications

Bus service. Taxi ☎ 972 310 525.

Puerto de Palamós

157. Puerto Deportivo de Palamós

41°50'·65N 03°08'·14E

⊕172 024°/0·55M

Port communications

Marina Palamos (east) VHF Ch 09. ☎ 972 60 10 00 *Fax* 972 60 22 66 *Email* info@lamarinapalamos.es www.lamarinapalamos.es

Deportivo service block   *Peter Taylor*

Entrance

Aim to give the head of its Dique de Abrigo an offing of 30m or so, then turn in. The entrance is difficult in a south to southwest wind with swell.

Berths

The marina offers all modern facilities. If not met by a *Zodiac*, go to the fuel berth and ask. If no-one there, ask at the office. Charges are high.

Facilities

Puerto Deportivo
Maximum length overall on quays 18m but a vessel up
   to 25m can be fitted in.
Some repair and maintenance facilities on site.
Chandler.
35-tonne travel-lift.
6-tonne crane.
Water on pontoons.
Showers.
220v AC on pontoons, 380v AC on Contradique.
Gasoleo A and petrol.

Puerto Deportivo de Palamós

VI. i. COSTA BRAVA

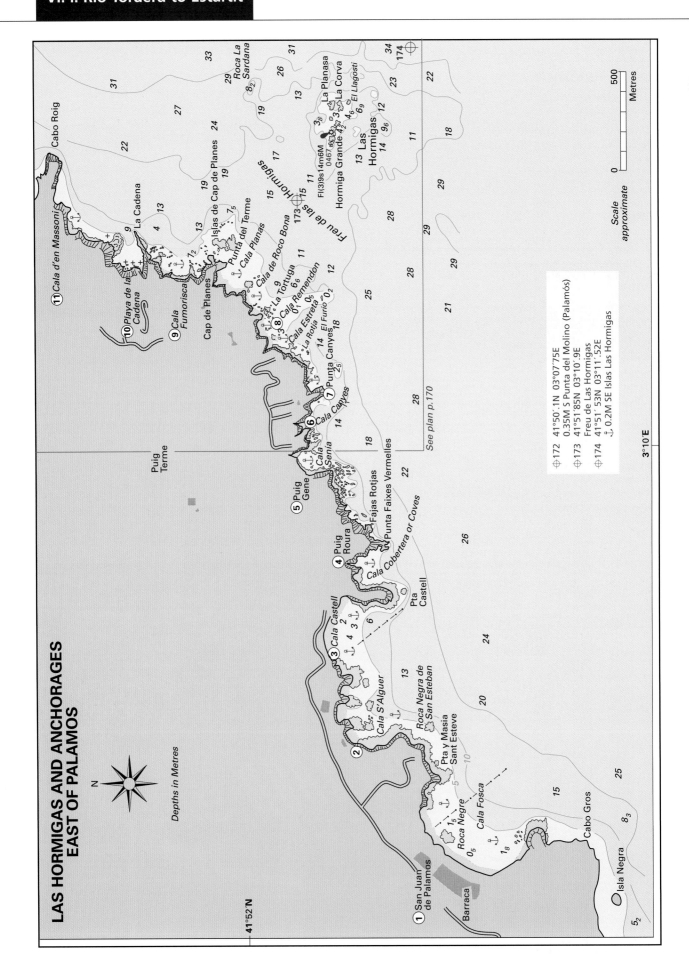

LAS HORMIGAS AND ANCHORAGES EAST OF PALAMOS

Depths in Metres

N

41°52'N

Scale approximate

500
Metres
0

3°10'E

⊕172   41°50'.1N 03°07'75E
       0.35M S Punta del Molino (Palamós)
⊕173   41°51'85N 03°10'.9E
       Freu de Las Hormigas
⊕174   41°51'.53N 03°11'.52E
       ⚓ 0.2M SE Islas Las Hormigas

Cabo Roig

Cala d'en Massoni ⑪

Playa de la Cadena ⑩

Cala Funorisca ⑨

La Cadena

Cap de Planes

Islas de Cap de Planes

Punta del Terme

Cala Planas

Cala de Roco Bona

La Tortuga

Cala Remendon

Cala Estreta

③⑧

La Rotja

El Furio

Punta Canyes ⑦

Cala Canyes

Cala Senia ⑥

Puig Gene ⑤

Puig Terme

Fajas Rotjas

Punta Faixes Vermelles

Cala Cobertera or Coves

Puig Roura ④

Cala Castell

③ Cala Castell

Pta Castell

Cala S'Alguer ②

Roca Negra de San Esteban

Pta y Masia Sant Esteve

Roca Negra

Cala Fosca

① San Juan de Palamos

Barraca

Isla Negra

Cabo Gros

Freu de las Hormigas

173 ⊕ 15

Fl(3)9s14m6M
0467

La Planasa
La Corva
El Llagosti
Las Hormigas
Hormiga Grande

174 ⊕

Roca La Sardana

See plan p.170

1. ⚓ **CALA FOSCA** 41°51'·3N 3°09'E

2. ⚓ **CALA S'ALGUER** 41°51'·5N 3°09'·2E

A small bay, the head of which is divided into three rocky beaches with a number of rocks lying off them. Anchor in the middle in 9m, stone, sand and rock. Open between SE and S.

3. ⚓ **CALA CASTELL** 41°51'·6N 3°09'·4E

4. ⚓ **CALA COBERTERA** 41°51'·5N 3°09'·7E

5. ⚓ **CALA SENÍA** 41°51'·7N 3°09'·9E

A rocky-cliffed bay with a rocky spur on the NE side. Approach on a NW course, enter with care and anchor in the middle in rock and stone. Open between E and S.

1. Cala Fosca. Open between E and S with foul ground on the south side of the bay. Mind the pipeline shown on the chart

2. Cala Castell: closed off for swimmers in summer. Open between SE and W.

4. Cala Cobertera (or Coves): anchor in the middle, stone and rock. Open between SE and SW

VI. i. COSTA BRAVA

158. Islas Hormigas (Formigues)

41°51'N 3°11'E

Charts
British Admiralty *1704*. Imray *M14*
French *4827, 7008, 7505*
Spanish *4924, 492*

⊕173 41°51'·85N 03°10'·9E

Also ⊕174

Lights
To the south
0462 **Punta del Molino** 41°50'·6N 3°07'·8E
  Oc(1+4)18s22m18M White round tower, grey cupola 8m
The islands
0467 **Hormiga Grande** 41°51'·7N 3°11'·1E Fl(3)9s14m6M
  White tower on hut 6m
To the north
0470 **Cabo San Sebastián** 41°53'·7N 3°12'·1E
  Fl.5s167m32M White round tower on white building, red roof 12m

A group of rocks and islands, best avoided

The Islas Hormigas (*hormiga* is Spanish for an ant) or Formigues are a group of unoccupied rocky islets which lie some ½M off Cap de Planas between Palamós and Llafranc. The islands are low, bare and foul. The highest, La Hormiga Grande, is only 12m high and 100m long. The mainland coast is also foul, notably the El Furió shoal and the rocks, Escuits del Cap de Planas, which extend to 400m from the shore. The area is generally foul and should be given a good berth especially in foul weather. However, Freu de las Hormigas, the passage between the islands and the mainland, about 400m wide, can be taken in fair weather.

Passage

From the south Approach the islands on a NE course and when level with Punta Faixes Vermelles bring Cabo San Sebastián onto 030°. This should lead through the Freu de les Hormigas about one third distant from the islands and two thirds from the mainland. Keep on this course until Cap de Planas is well past the beam.

From the north From Cabo San Sebastián make a course towards the islands. About 400m from them bring Punta del Molino on to 240° and pass through the Freu at a distance of about one-third of its width from the islands and two-thirds of its width from the mainland.

Landings

Hormiga Grande can be approached with care from the SW in deep water and landing is possible in calm weather.

6. ⚓ **CALA CANYES**
   41°51'·7N 3°10'·1E

7. ⚓ **CALA N OF PUNTA CANYES**
   41°51'·7N 3°10'·23E

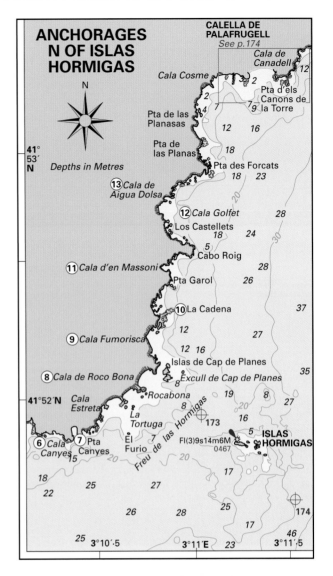

⊕173 41°51'85N 03°10'.9E   Freu de Las Hormigas
⊕174 41°51'53N 03°11'.52   ⚓ 0.2M SE Islas Las Hormigas

7. Cala N of Punta Canyes: enter with care and anchor in the middle. Open between E and S

8. Calas Estreta, Remendon, Roco Bona and Planas: divided by rocky outcrops and with sandy beaches at their heads, open between NE and S. Approach with great care and in good weather

8. ⚓ **CALAS ESTRETA, REMENDON, ROCO BONA AND PLANAS** 41°51'·9N 3°10'·7E

9. ⚓ **CALA FUMORISCA** 41°52'·2N 3°10'·8E

An open *cala* with rocky outcrops and reefs on either side. Open between N and SE. Enter with care on a W course.

10. ⚓ **PLAYA DE LA CADENA** 41°52'·4N 3°10'·8E

A medium-sized rocky-cliffed *cala* protected on its SE side by a long thin projection of rock, La Cadena. Open between NE and SE. Anchor in 5m, stone and rock. Rocks off head of *cala*.

11. ⚓ **CALA D'EN MASSONI** 41°52'·5N 3°10'·9E

A *cala* just to S of Cabo Roig, open between E and SE. Use the N half of the *cala*, the SW side has projecting rocks. Anchor in 3m, stone and rock.

12. ⚓ **CALA GOLFET** 41°52'·7N 3°10'·9E

13. ⚓ **CALA DEL AIGUA DOLÇA (in Cala Golfet)** 41°52'·7N 3°10'·9E

A small *cala* with low rocky cliffs and submerged rocks. Open between E and S. Anchor in mid-*cala* in rock and stone.

12. Cala Golfet: a wide rocky *cala* with a small pebble beach. Open between NE and SE

VI. i. COSTA BRAVA

Calella de Palafrugell

A collection of anchorages

A series of delightful little anchorages offering good shelter from all except winds and sea between NE and SE, Callela lies between Punta Forcat and Punta d'els Canons (or de la Torre). Care is necessary in the close approach owing to isolated submerged rocks and the anchorage is full of moorings. The village is most attractive but very crowded in the season. Facilities are reasonable for a large holiday village.

Cap Roig botanic gardens 1M away are worth a visit. On the first Saturday in July, there is a singing festival on the beach, *Cantada de Habaneras*.

The original town of Palafrugell was Roman, possibly Celebandica, and was greatly enlarged when the inhabitants of the coast moved there in the 8th and 9th centuries. It became Palaz Frugell, that is Palace of Fruits, from which its present name is derived. It is an interesting old town and has the remains of its original walls.

Approach

Because of submerged rocks near the coast, approach should be made with care, in calm weather and with a forward lookout.

From the south Pass between the Islas Hormigas (*see page 171*) and the mainland leaving Cabo Roig and Punta Forcat at least 200m to port. Approach the anchorage with the conspicuous church on a N heading.

From the north Having rounded the high Cabo San Sebastián with its conspicuous lighthouse and restaurant, the Cala de Llafranc with houses on its head will be seen. The Punta d'els Canons, a lowish rocky point with a tower, should be given a berth of at least 200m and the coast followed at this distance. When the conspicuous church at Calella de Palafrugell is due N, approach on that heading.

Anchorage

Anchor W of the very small rocky islet Cunill de Fora, opposite the centre bay but short of the rocky outcrops, in 5m sand, rock and stone (partly weed-covered). The holding ground is very patchy. Use a trip-line. Alternative anchorages exist opposite the other two bays but there are isolated rocks which restrict swinging room. It is also possible to anchor in the Cala del Canadell some 400m to the E but care is necessary.

Quays

There is a small quay on the W side of the centre bay with 1m alongside and another in the form of a miniature harbour on the E side of the E bay with 0·5m alongside.

Facilities

Water available from cafés.
Everyday supplies available from shops in the village and much greater variety from Palafrugell some 2M away.
Club Vela de Calella is a dinghy club with few facilities other than a terrace.

⚓ **CALA DEL CANADELL** 41°53'·2N 3°11'·3E

A wide bay divided by a projecting rocky point near the middle. Anchor on either side in 4m, sand. Open between SE and SW.

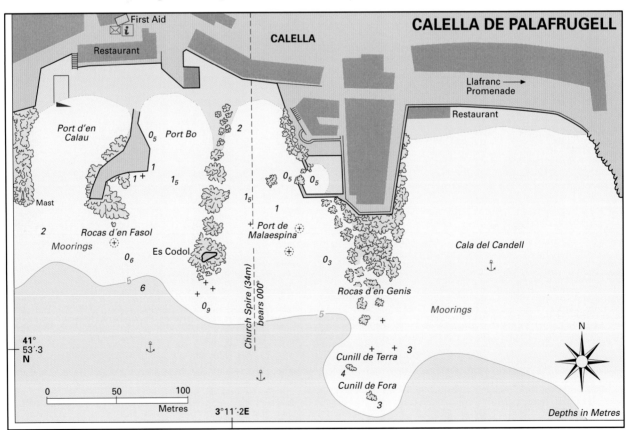

Calella de Palafrugell

159. Puerto de Llafranc (Llanfrach)

41°53'N 3°12'E

Charts
British Admiralty *1704.* Imray *M14*
French *4827, 7008, 7505, 7298*
Spanish *876, 492*
Navicarte *E04*

⊕175   41°53'·4N 03°11'·8E 340°/0·?19M to harbour

Lights
To the north
0470 **Cabo San Sebastián** 41°53'·7N 3°12'·1E
 Fl.5s167m32M White round tower on white building,
 red roof 12m Aeromarine
Harbour
0468 **Dique del Sur head** 41°53'·6N 3°11'·8E
 Fl(3)G.11s6m5M White metal post, green top 2m
Buoys
Red and white buoys mark the entrance channel, one
 port-hand buoy has a spar and one has a F.R light.

Port communications
VHF Ch 8. Club Náutico de Llafranc ☎/*Fax* 972 300 754
Fax 972 300 830 *Email* cnll@infopunt.com

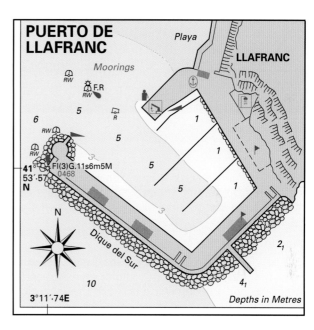

⊕175 41°53'.4N   03°11'.8E   App. Puerto de Llafranc

Small, attractive and expensive harbour
Small, attractive and expensive harbour. Puerto de Llafranc is under the high, steep-sided SW side of Cabo San Sebastián. It is an artificial yacht harbour established in a most attractive *cala* which has been used as a harbour since time immemorial. Approach and entrance need some care but, once inside, there is good protection though heavy swell coming from the SE can be tiresome. The hills around the harbour offer good protection against the NW *tramontana.* Everyday requirements can be met in the village and there are good shops and a market in Palafrugell 2M away. The area becomes very crowded and expensive in the season and, as the *capitanía* remarked, the harbour is always full.

The harbour is probably of Phoenician origin. It was certainly used by the Romans and is thought to

be the ancient port of Cypsela. In the 8th century the Normans razed the town to the ground and its inhabitants moved to Palafrugell. In recent years it has been redeveloped as a tourist resort. The excellent sandy beach is crowded in season. There is a fine view from the lighthouse of San Sebastián.

Approach
From the south A tree-covered promontory, Cap de Planas, and the Islas Hormigas, a group of low, jagged rocky islands are readily recognisable. If the weather is fair a passage inside these islands is possible (*see page 171*). The harbour wall will be seen under Cabo San Sebastián.

From the north Cabo Begur with its conspicuous signal station and the deep *calas* of Aiguafreda, Aiguablava and Tamariú are easily recognised. The

Puerto de Llafranc

high steep-sided Cabo San Sebastián with its lighthouse, restaurant and *ermita* on its summit can be seen from afar and the harbour will be found on its further side.

Anchorage in the approach

Anchor 200m off the centre of the sandy beach in 6m sand. Use a trip-line. In summer there are many moorings and a diving board between the anchorage and the beach.

Entrance

Enter the bay on a NW course and approach the head of the Dique del Sur with care. Round it at 10m leaving it to starboard. Note the head of the *dique* extends some 5m underwater. Leave a line of small red and white buoys to port and two similar buoys close to the head of the *dique* to starboard. There is little room to manoeuvre once inside the harbour.

Berths

Berth stern-to the inner side of the Dique del Sur; lazy lines are provided.

Facilities

6-tonne crane.
Small slip in the NW corner and another at the head of Dique del Sur.
Water from the pontoons and quays.
220v AC on the pontoons and quays.
Gasoleo A and petrol.
Club Náutico de Llafranc has a small office to the NW of the harbour. The clubhouse is on the NE side of the harbour with restaurant, bar, showers and WCs.
A limited number of shops near the harbour for everyday requirements. Many shops in Palafrugell 2M away.
Launderette in Llafranc.

Communications

Bus service.

Llafranc – visitors at end on left   *Peter Taylor*

LLAFRANC TO CALA DE SA RIERA

N

Depths in Metres

Cala de sa Riera
38
3₉   17₅
Pta de la Creu
17₁
65   87

Cabo Negre
Aiguafreda   Pta de la Sal   ⊕ 177   99
Cala de Aiguafreda
76
See p.180
Sa Tuna   Pta del Palom

5₅ *Bajo Furió Fito*
57

Area RC ⊙   Cabo Begur
95

18
65
See p.178
○ Isla Negra
Cala d'els Pins
24

Fornells   Isla Blanca
8₅   Hotel
59
Aiguablava   Punta del Mut
FI(2)G.10s4m5M ☆   21   42   ⊕ 176   114
0471·2 ⚓
Cova del Bisbé
81

27
9₈   68

Tamariú   *Cala d'Aigua Xelida*
⚓
⊙ *Furío de l'Aigua Xelida*

Cala de Tamariú
56   127
16₈
See p.176

Palafrugell
Pta de la Musclera Llanga   88
⚓ Pta de la Musclera Trencada
41°55'N
Cala Pedrosa
Punta Pedrosa

151
⚓ Punta S'Endavallada
54'   *Cala de Gens*
25   79
Llafranc   0470
FI.5s167m32M
Bahia de Llafranc   ☼   Cabo San Sebastián
10'   11'   12'   3°13'E   14'   15'

⊕176 41°56'N 03°14'E 0.75M ESE Fornells
⊕177 41°58'N 03°15'E 0.8M E Caba Negre

CABO SAN SEBASTIÁN (CAP DE SANT SEBASTIÁN) 41°53'·5N 3°12'E

A prominent, cliffed headland of reddish rock with a 12m lighthouse on the 167m high rounded summit. A number of houses are located near the summit. The headland is steep-to. There is also a restaurant and *ermita* on top.

⚓ CALA DE GENS 41°53'·9N 3°12'·12E

A small *cala* ½M to N of Cabo San Sebastián and a useful place if waiting to round the Cape. High rocky cliffs with houses. Anchor in 10m plus, stone and rock bottom. Hut on small stony beach.

⚓ **CALA PEDROSA** 41°54′·45N 03°12′·6E

Cala Pedrosa, S of Punta Tamariú: anchor in 10m, stone and rock. Open between E and S

⚓ **CALA TAMARIÚ** 41°54′·9N 3°12′·8E

![CALA TAMARIU map]
CALA TAMARIU
N
Cala Longa
Pta del Branch
Cala d´Aigua Xelida
Depths in Metres
TAMARIU
Furió de l'Aigua Xelida
Puig Rui •168
Tr⊙
20
Moorings Cala Tamariú
0   1000
Metres
Cala Putxeta
41° 55′ N
3°12′E   Scale approximate

Cala Tamariu: anchor in the middle, 5–10m, sand. Hotels and restaurants ashore. To the NE, Aigua Xelida, with its rocky islets, promontories and bays is fun to explore by dinghy

⚓ CALA AIGUA XELIDA 41°55'·2N 3°13'·2E

Cala Aigua Xelida

⚓ COVA DEL BISBÉ AND PORT D'ESCLANYA
41°55'·8N 3°13'·2E

Cova del Bisbe. Two very small square-shaped *calas* 80m apart, open between NE and SE with rocky cliffs. Anchor in 5m, rocks. There is a large cave at Bisbe

VI. i. COSTA BRAVA

Calas de Aiguablava y Fornells
41°56'N 3°13'E

Charts
British Admiralty *1704, 1705.* Imray *M14*
French *4827, 7008, 7505*
Spanish *876, 492*
⊕176 41°56'N 03°14'E 288°/0·75

Lights
To the south
0470 **Cabo San Sebastián** 41°53'·7N 3°12'·1E
  Fl.5s167m32M White round tower on white building,
  red roof 12m Aeromarine
Basin
0471 **Basin entrance port side** 41°56'·0N 3°12'·9E
  Fl(2)R.6s2m3M Red lantern
0471·2 **Starboard side** Fl(2)G.10s4m5M Green tower,
  white base 3m

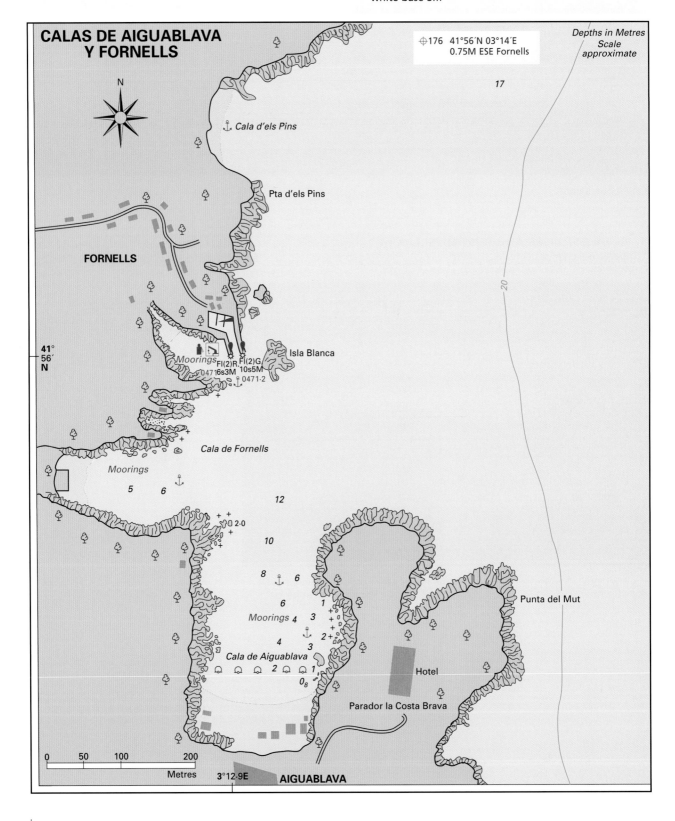

CALAS DE AIGUABLAVA Y FORNELLS

⊕176 41°56'N 03°14'E
0.75M ESE Fornells

Depths in Metres
Scale approximate

Puerto de Fornells

Port communications
Club Náutico Aiguablava VHF Ch 09. ☎/Fax 972 623 161
Email cnaiguablava@arrakis.es

Sheltered anchorage
A beautiful and sheltered anchorage with a small private harbour with protection from all but strong NE winds. Facilities are very limited and it is crowded in the season with many occupied moorings. Cala de Aiguablava has shelter from the NW *tramontana*.

There are fine sandy beaches. A visit to the old town of Begur is recommended.

Approach
From the south Pass the high prominent Cabo San Sebastián with its conspicuous lighthouse and restaurant and the deep Cala Tamariú with its houses. 1M to the N will be found the Punta del Mut with a large square-shaped hotel, the Parador la Costa Brava, on its summit. Follow the coast around into the anchorage.

From the north Round the prominent Cabo Negre and then Punta de la Sal where there is a very large hotel on the point and then in 1M round Cabo Begur which has a castle and a signal station. 1M to the S lies Punta del Mut with a large square-shaped hotel on its summit. Leave this point to port and the Isla Blanca to starboard and enter the anchorage.

Entrance
Enter the Calas de Aiguablava y Fornells on a W course nearer to the Punta del Mut than to Isla Blanca.

Anchorage
Anchor in 3m, sand and weed, in the E half of Cala de Aiguablava as near to the cliffs as draught will allow. There are ring-bolts on the cliffs and an isolated rock and there are also many moorings. In summer the southern part of Cala de Aiguablava is reserved for bathing.

Alternative anchorages are at the entrance to Cala Fornells and in a smaller *cala* 100m further to N but they do not have as good protection as Aiguablava.

Quays
There is a small stone quay in the SE corner of the Cala de Aiguablava with 0·5m alongside and a small pier in the Cala de Fornells at the entrance to the small private harbour.

Facilities
4-tonne crane at the entrance to the private harbour.
Slip at the N side of the private harbour.
Water from the beach restaurants and from the private harbour.
220v AC points at the private harbour.
Club náutico is located at the Playa de Fornells and is a dinghy club.
Limited supplies from two small shops at Fornells. More shops exist at Begur some 2M away.

Communications
A bus service to Begur in the season.

⚓ **CALA D'ELS PINS** 41°56'·5N 3°13'·2E
A small, narrow *cala* open between NE and E, surrounded by rocky cliffs. Anchor in rock and sand.

CABO BEGUR (CABO BAGUR) 41°57'N 3°14'E
A large hooked headland, 115m, with rocky cliffs and a conspicuous low yellowish coloured lookout station on its crest. The headland is steep-to.

Calas de Sa Tuna y Aiguafreda

41°58′N 3°14′E

Charts

British Admiralty *1704, 1705*. Imray *M14*
French *4827, 7008, 7505*
Spanish *492*

⊕177 256°/0·83M to anchor

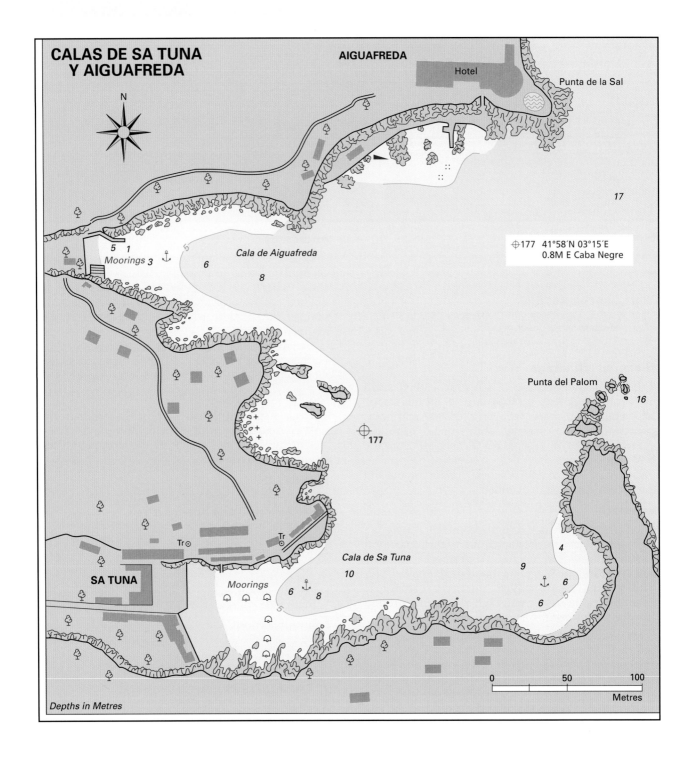

CALAS DE SA TUNA
Y AIGUAFREDA

AIGUAFREDA

Hotel

Punta de la Sal

N

17

⊕177 41°58′N 03°15′E
0.8M E Caba Negre

5 1
Moorings 3 ⚓
6
Cala de Aiguafreda
8

Punta del Palom
16

⊕ 177

4

9
Tr ⊙
Tr ⊙
Cala de Sa Tuna
10
⚓ 6
6
SA TUNA
Moorings
6 ⚓ 8
6

0   50   100
Metres

Depths in Metres

Generally good shelter

Two beautiful inlets, easy to enter and with good shelter from all but E wind which sends in a nasty swell; some shelter from this wind behind the Punta del Palom spur. Shelter from the NW *tramontana* is possible but not very effective with winter gales. Facilities are very limited. Though there are many visitors in summer it is not as crowded as some resorts. Many large houses have been built near these *calas* in recent years.

A visit to the ancient town of Begur is recommended. There is a sand and shingle beach at the head of each *cala*.

Approach

From the south Cabo Begur, a rocky headland can be recognised by a signal tower on its summit. Keep 400m from the coast to avoid the Furió Fito rocks. A very large hotel located on the Punta de la Sal at the far side of the entrance to this anchorage, visible over Punta del Palom, is very conspicuous. Round Punta del Palom at 50m and enter.

From the north Cabo Negre can be recognised by the very large hotel on Punta de la Sal just to its S. Round this at 100m and enter the anchorage.

Entrance

This is not difficult as there is deep water up to the cliffs. Cala Aiguafreda lies due W and Cala Sa Tuna to the SW of the outer entrance.

Anchorage

In winter, should an E wind arise, this anchorage should be vacated at once and shelter taken at Palamós. In summer, shelter behind Punta del Palom.

Anchor clear of moorings in 6m, sand and weed, near the centre of the Cala Sa Tuna with the tower bearing NNW. The W half of this *cala* is reserved for bathing and in the season, it is marked with yellow buoys.

In Cala Aiguafreda anchor in the centre of the *cala* about 100m from its head in 5m sand and stone clear of moorings. Alternative anchorages are possible in the little bay to SE and to S of the hotel. It is sometimes necessary to run a line ashore to keep the yacht head to swell, or use two anchors.

⚓ **CALA DA SA TUNA** 41°57'·7N 3°13'·8E

Cala de Sa Tuna

VI. i. COSTA BRAVA

⚓ **CALA AIGUAFREDA** 41°57'·8N 3°13'·8E

Cala Aiguafreda

Quays

There are three small quays and slips on the N side of Cala Sa Tuna and a longer one with 1m depth alongside on the N side of Cala Aiguafreda.

Facilities

There is a spring close to the beach at Cala Aiguafreda.
    Water is also available from the restaurant at Sa Tuna.
Very limited provisions from two small shops in Sa Tuna, many more in Begur 1M away.

Communications

Bus service to Begur in the season.

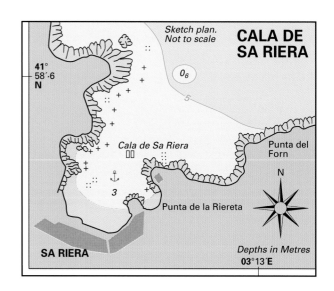

⚓ CALA DE SA RIERA (CALA DE LA RIERATA)
41°58'·6N 3°13'E

A *cala* with a sandy beach. Open between N and NE. Small village around the head of the *cala* with the beach. Anchor off the beach in sand. The old town and castle of Begur are 1M up the road

⚓ PLAYA DE PALS 41°59'N 3°13'E

The southern end of Playa de Pals, a 2·5M stretch of sandy beach backed by low, flat plains. A group of tall, red and white (F.R) aerial masts are conspicuous at the S end and the mouth of the Río Ter is at the N end. Anchor off the beach in 5m, sand. Open between N and SE

VI. i. COSTA BRAVA

160. Puerto de L'Estartit

42°03'N 3°12'E

Charts

British Admiralty *1704, 1705*. Imray *M14*
French *7008, 7505, 7298*
Spanish *876, 493*

⊕179 42°02'·8N 03°12'·5E 335°/0·22M to harbour

Lights

To the southeast
0472 **Isla Méda Grande, summit** 42°02'·8N 3°13'·2E
Fl(4)24s87m14M Tower on brick building 11m
Harbour
0473·5 **Dique de Levante head** Fl.G.5s9m5M White tower,
green top 4m
0474 **Dique interior head** Fl(2)G.13s4m3M White post,
green top 1m
0474·2 **Contradique corner** Fl.R.5s8m5M Red post 4m
0474·4 **Contradique head** Fl(2)R.13s3m3M Red lantern on
masonry base 4m
0474·5 **Fuel jetty head** Fl(3)R.13s2m1M White post red
top 1m

Port communications

VHF Ch 9, 16. *Capitanía* ☎ 972 751 402 *Fax* 972 751 717.
Email info@cnestartit.es www.cnestartit.es

Mainly a yachting harbour

A fishing and yachting harbour in an attractive
setting protected by a breakwater and with
reasonable shelter from the NW *tramontana*. Space
for visiting yachts on the pontoons is limited. The
town and surrounding areas have been developed as
a tourist resort and are crowded in the season.

The 14th-century church at Torroella de Montgrí
and the 13th-century castle may be visited (2M). The
view from the Castillo de Santa Catalina is
spectacular. Excellent sandy beach to SW of the
harbour.

Approach

The Río Ter brings down heavy deposits which tend
to silt up the harbour and its mouth. Sound carefully.
The pontoons on the SW side of the harbour are
sometimes removed during winter months.

From the south Cabo Begur with its signal station,
Cabo Negre with a large hotel, the group of seven
radio masts just to N of it, the Islas Médes close to
the harbour and a very tall orange and white radio
tower behind it are easily recognisable.

From the north Punta Trenca Braços can be
identified by a conspicuous tower and the deep wide
Cala Montgó to its S. The coast is very broken but
the Islas Médes are easily seen as is the tall orange
and white banded radio tower on the top of
Montaña de la Barra just to the N of this harbour.
Keep over 200m from the shore.

Anchorage in the approach

Anchor 100m to S of the *contradique* in 6m, sand.

Entrance

Straightforward but some sharp manoeuvring once
inside.

Berths

On arrival secure to the head of the *espigón* near the
fuel berth for allocation of a berth. The inner side of
the Dique Interior is reserved for diving vessels
whilst the outer side is for local ferries.

Charges

High.

Facilities

Maximum length overall 25m.
Repairs can be carried out to hull and engines by local
craftsmen.
Hard-standings in NW corner of harbour.

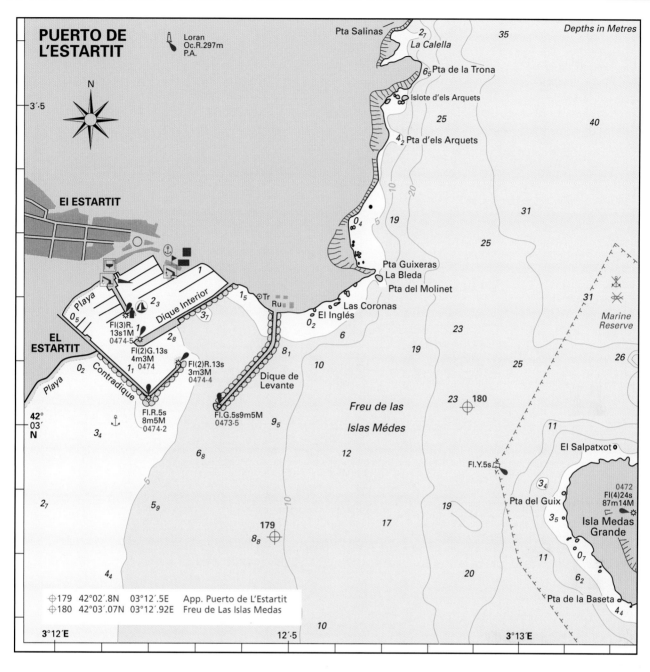

PUERTO DE L'ESTARTIT

Loran
Oc.R.297m
P.A.

Depths in Metres

Pta Salinas

La Calella
2₇

35

Pta de la Trona
6₅

Islote d'els Arquets

25

40

Pta d'els Arquets
4₂

3´·5

N

El ESTARTIT

Pta Guixeras
La Bleda
Pta del Molinet

31

0₄
19

25

EL ESTARTIT

Playa

Dique Interior
1
2₃
1₅
3₇
Tr
Ru

Las Coronas
El Inglés
0₂

6

23

31

Marine Reserve

Fl(3)R.
13s1M
0474·5

2₈

Fl(2)G.13s
4m3M
0474

Fl(2)R.13s
3m3M
0474·4

8₁

10

19

25

26

0₅
Contradique
1₁
0₂

Playa

Dique de Levante

Fl.R.5s
8m5M
0474·2

Fl.G.5s9m5M
0473·5

9₅

Freu de las Islas Médes

23 180

11

El Salpatxot

Fl.Y.5s

3₄

0472
Fl(4)24s
87m14M

42° 03´ N

3₄

6₈

12

Pta del Guix

3₅

Isla Medas Grande

2₇

5₉

179
8₈

17

19

20

11

0₇

6₂

Pta de la Baseta
4₄

4₄

⊕179 42°02´.8N 03°12´.5E App. Puerto de L'Estartit
⊕180 42°03´.07N 03°12´.92E Freu de Las Islas Medas

3°12´E

12´·5

3°13´E

10

30-tonne travel-lift.

7·5-tonne and 3-tonne cranes.

Chandlery to NE of the harbour and another to W of the town.

Water taps at the *club náutico* and on quays and pontoons.

Showers.

Gasoleo A and petrol.

220v AC from the Muelle de Ribera and on quays and pontoons.

Ice is available in the season from the *oficina de capitán*.

Club Náutico Estartit with a bar, lounge, terrace, restaurant, showers.

A fair number of shops in the town.

Launderette in the town.

Weather forecast posted at *club náutico* once a day.

Communications

Bus service. Day trips to the Islas Médes by ferry.

L'Estartit Fuel and waiting berth   *Peter Taylor*

VI. i. COSTA BRAVA

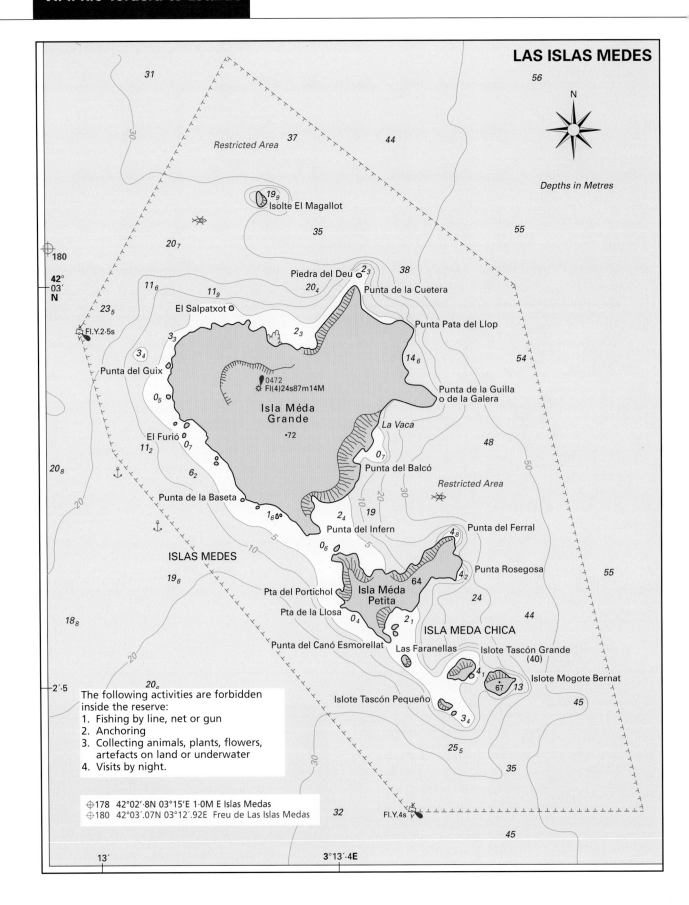

LAS ISLAS MEDES

56

N

Depths in Metres

31

Restricted Area

37

44

55

19₉
Isolte El Magallot

35

20₇

⊕180

42°
03′
N

Piedra del Deu 2₃

38

23₅

11₆

11₉

20₄

Punta de la Cuetera

⊟ Fl.Y.2·5s

El Salpatxot ⊙

Punta Pata del Llop

3₃

3₃

2₃

14₆

54

3₄

Punta del Guix

0472
✷ Fl(4)24s87m14M

Punta de la Guilla
o de la Galera

0₅

Isla Méda
Grande

La Vaca

48

El Furió ⊙
0₇

11₂

·72

0₇

20₈

6₂

Punta del Balcó

Restricted Area

⚓

Punta de la Baseta ⊙

50

1₆ ⊙ₒ

2₄

19

ISLAS MEDES

⚓

Punta del Infern

Punta del Ferral

4₈

19₆

Isla Méda
Petita

4₂

Punta Rosegosa

55

0₆

64

Pta del Portichol

24

Pta de la Llosa

0₄

ISLA MEDA CHICA

44

18₈

2₁

Punta del Canó Esmorellat

Las Faranellas

Islote Tascón Grande
(40)

2′·5

20₆

4₁

67 13

Islote Mogote Bernat

The following activities are forbidden
inside the reserve:

Islote Tascón Pequeño

45

1. Fishing by line, net or gun

3₄

2. Anchoring

3. Collecting animals, plants, flowers,
   artefacts on land or underwater

25₅

4. Visits by night.

35

⊕178 42°02′·8N 03°15′E 1·0M E Islas Medas
⊕180 42°03′.07N 03°12′.92E Freu de Las Islas Medas

32

Fl.Y.4s

45

13′

3°13′·4E

161. Las Islas Médes

42°03′N 3°13′E

Charts

British Admiralty *1704, 1705.* Imray *M14*
French *7298, 7505*
Spanish *4931*

⊕180   42°03′·07N 03°12′·92E

⊕178   42°02′·8N 03°15′E 1·0M E Islas Medas

Lights

0472 **Isla Méda Grande, summit**   42°02′·8N 3°13′·2E

Marine reserve

The Islas Médes are a group of uninhabited islands about ½M off Punta del Molinet near L'Estartit. They are a marine reserve with restricted access – *see chart*. The largest island, Isla Méda Grande is some 500m across and 79m high; there are splendid views from the lighthouse on its summit. To the S of this island lies Isla Méda Petita, 250m long and 67m high. Islote Mogote Bernat, the most SE island, is only 80m across but is 72m high, with almost vertical sides. To the N of the group and nearly 300m away is Islote El Magallot, 24m high. There are a number of low and inconspicuous smaller islets. The islands are in general steep-to but there are some groups of rocky shoals close inshore. The passage between this group of islands and the mainland is deep and clear of obstructions and can be taken under almost any conditions.

Approach

There is no difficulty in navigating the Freu de las Islas Médes as there is a deep-water passage some 600m wide and dangers only exist within 100m of the islands and the mainland shore. The passage is best taken in a NE-SW direction. There is a very narrow passage, 0·6m deep, between Islas Meda Grande and Petita in a NE-SW which is not recommended.

Moorings

Many mooring buoys are laid for visitors inside the restricted area on the SW side of Isla Méda Grande. Small boats use these by day but most are available overnight. Anchoring in this area is prohibited.

Anchorages

The area to the SW of the Isla Méda Grande outside the restricted area is a recognised anchorage. Yachts can anchor 100m to the SW of the landing in 10m weed over sand and stones. Note that there is an isolated rock 50m to SW of this landing which is not shown on all charts. Anchorage is also possible in deep water some 100m further to SE in 16m, sand.

Landing

There is a small landing pier on the SW side of the Isla Méda Grande and one on the NW corner of Isla Méda Petita. These should only be used in calm weather and ferry boats should not be obstructed. Landing from a dinghy in calm weather is also possible on the N and SE sides of the Isla Méda Grande.

Islas Medes looking SSE with L'Estartit partly hidden by headland

VI. i. COSTA BRAVA

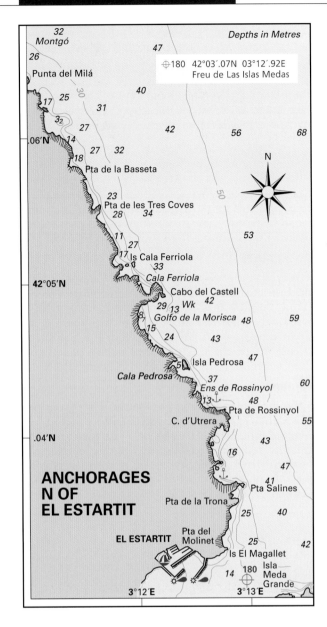

Depths in Metres

⊕180 42°03'.07N 03°12'.92E
Freu de Las Islas Medas

32
Montgó
26
Punta del Milá
17 25
31
3₂
27
.06'N 14
18 27 32
Pta de la Basseta
23
Pta de les Tres Coves
28 34
11 27
17 Is Cala Ferriola
33
Cala Ferriola
Cabo del Castell
29 13 Wk 42
8 Golfo de la Morisca 48
15
24 43
Isla Pedrosa 47
5
Cala Pedrosa 37
Ens de Rossinyol
13 48
Pta de Rossinyol
C. d'Utrera 55

42°05'N

.04'N
43
16
47
41
ANCHORAGES Pta Salines
N OF
EL ESTARTIT Pta de la Trona
25 40
Pta del
EL ESTARTIT Molinet 25 42
Is El Magallet
Isla
14 180 Meda
Grande
3°12'E 3°13'E

47
40
42 56 68
N
50
53
59
60

⚓ **ENSENADA DEL ROSSINYOL** 42°04'·3N 3°12'·6E

Ensenada del Rossinyol: Anchorage surrounded by rocky cliffs (110m), open between N and E. Anchor in over 10m on rock

⚓ **GOLFO DE LA MORISCA** 42°04'·7N 3°12'E

Golfo de la Morisca: anchor in 10m, rock. Open between E and SE. There is foul ground at the NW corner of the bay.

⚓ **CALA FERRIOLA** 42°05'·1N 3°12'E

Cala Ferriola: the anchorage is in 10m behind the two islets. There is a small shingle beach. Open between N and E

⚓ **N OF PUNTA SALINES** 42°03'·8N 3°12'·8E

A small anchorage in over 10m rock with high rocky cliffs. Open between N and E. There is foul ground behind the two islets to N of the anchorage.

CABO D'UTRERA 42°04'N 3°12'·73E

A double-pointed headland with high rocky cliffs (110m). There is a small islet off the north point but otherwise it is steep-to.

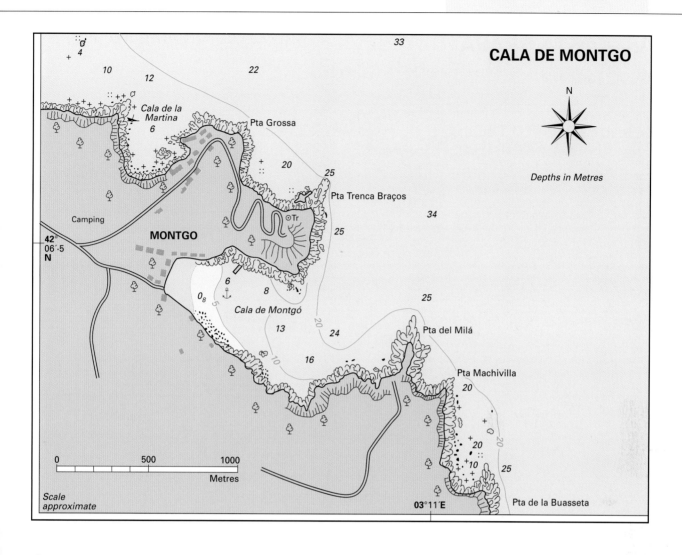

CALA DE MONTGO

N

Depths in Metres

33

10

22

12

4

Cala de la Martina
6

Pta Grossa

20

25

Pta Trenca Braços

Camping

MONTGO

42°06'·5 N

Tr

25

34

6

8

25

Cala de Montgó

13

24

Pta del Milá

16

Pta Machivilla

20

25

20

10

25

Pta de la Buasseta

0   500   1000
Metres

Scale approximate

03°11'E

⚓ **CALA DE MONTGO** 42°06'·5N 3°11'E

Cala de Montgó: anchor in 5m off the beach

PUNTA TRENCA BRACOS 42°06'·7N 3°10'·6E

A major steep-to headland (96m), located at the S end of the Golfo de Roses and on the N side of Cala de Montgó. The Torre de Montgó on the crest is conspicuous

VI. i. COSTA BRAVA

VI. COSTA BRAVA
ii. L'Escala to the French border

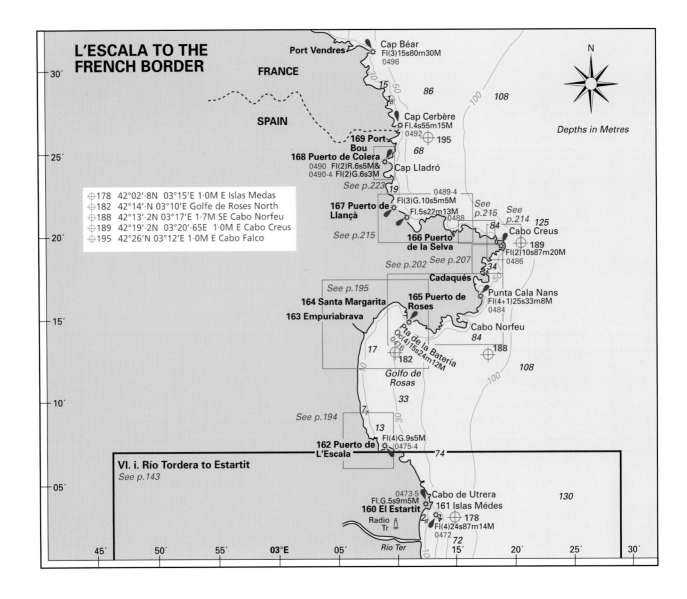

PORTS OF COSTA BRAVA BETWEEN PUERTO L'ESCALA AND PORT BOU

162. Puerto de L'Escala (La Clota)
163. Puerto de Empuriabrava (Ampuriabrava)
164. Puerto de Santa Margarida (Margarita)
165. Puerto de Roses (Rosas)
166. Port de la Selva
167. Puerto de Llançá (Llansá)
168. Puerto de Colera
169. Port de Portbou

Note
Marine reserve officers may
deny yachts access to many of
the anchorages shown between
Roses and Cabo Creus.

Hill top village of Pals   *Peter Taylor*

Hill top village of Pals   *Peter Taylor*

Last anchorage before France (NE of Portbou) *Robin Rundle*

Llançà looking E   *Peter Taylor*

VI. ii. COSTA BRAVA

162. Puerto de L'Escala (La Clota)

42°07'N 3°08'E

Charts

British Admiralty *1704, 1705*. Imray *M14*
French *4827, 7008, 7505*
Spanish *493A*

⊕181 42°07'·4N 03°08'·53E 180°/0·28M to harbour

Lights

0475·3 **Dique de Abrigo head** Fl(4)R15s12m5M Red post, 3m
0475·4 **Espigón de la Clota head** Fl(4)G.9s5m3M White post, green top 2m
0475·41 **Jetty head** Fl.R.3s4m3M White post, red top 3m
0475·42 **Espigón de defensa** Q.6m1M YB post on white base n card topmark
0475·44 **Dique interior W head** Fl(2+1)G.11s6m3M Green post, red band 3m
0475·45 **Dique interior E head** Fl(2)G.6s6m1M Green post 3m

Port communications

VHF Ch 9. ☎ 972 770 016 *Fax* 972 770 158
Email club@nauticescala.com www.nauticescala.com

A redeveloped marina

The original fishing and yacht harbour was created by the construction of a breakwater in Cala de la Clota on the east side of the bay. A new breakwater has been built to the north of the old harbour and now houses the fishing fleet and small local craft. Visitors should proceed into the old harbour, which is still susceptible to northerlies which can make the entrance difficult and send in swell.

The Greco-Roman remains at Empuries should be visited as they are unique on this coast and are only 2M away. The old church, Santa Maria de Vilabertran, at L'Escala can also be visited. There are sandy beaches to the W of the harbour.

Approach

The approach and entrance require care due to unmarked off-lying rocky shoals.

From the south the wide and deep Cala de Montgó and Punta Trenca Braços with a tower on its N side are easily recognisable. Punta de la Clota, a low feature with a small fort, is located just to NE of the harbour. Follow round the circular breakwater of the new marina at about 200m until the harbour entrances are clear.

From the north From the massive and mountainous promontory of Cadaqués/Roses the coast becomes

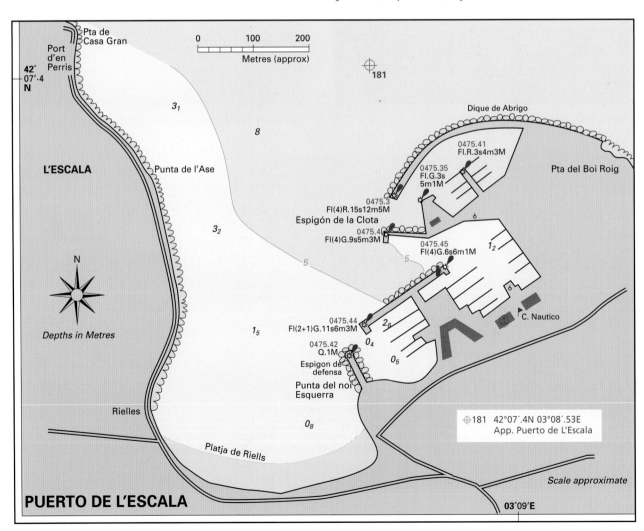

L'Escala

low and flat with a gently curving sandy beach. The marinas of Sta Margarita and Ampuriabrava and the inland towns of Sant Pere and Castelló de Empuries will be seen. The coast town of L'Escala will also be recognised.

Do not cut the corner by L'Escala town and, keeping well out from the coast on the west side, make for the head of the Espigón de la Clota on a southerly course.

Anchorage in the approach

Anchor to W of the old harbour near the centre of the *cala* in 10m, sand. An anchor light should be used. It is also possible to anchor off L'Escala in calm weather.

Entrance

Approach the end of the Espigón de la Clota on an easterly heading leaving it 20 to 25 metres to port. Moor to the fuelling point at the E end of the Dique Interior and arrange a berth with the staff there or at the *capitanía* in the club náutico. There is a second *capitanía* (with showers!) being built at the angle of the Espigón de la Clota and one may, in future, be able to moor on the S side of the *espigón* near the new *capitanía* to receive berthing instructions.

Berths

All berths are due to have lazy lines from the quays/pontoons. Go to the fuel berth and await instructions.

Moorings

Some private moorings to the SW of the harbour, some of which may be available.

Facilities

Maximum length overall 25m.
Mechanics and shipwrights available.
Two cranes of 8 and 10 tonnes and a 5-tonne mobile crane.
Slip to the SW of the harbour.
Water on the quay and the *espigón*.
Gasoleo A and petrol.
220v AC points by the *club náutico* and on pontoons and quays.
Ice from a factory in the NE corner of the harbour or from fuel station at head of Quai Norte.
Club Náutico L'Escala has a bar, lounge, restaurant, showers and WCs.
A limited number of shops near the harbour. Many more are available in L'Escala.
Launderette in the town.
Weather forecast posted twice a day at the *club náutico*.

Communications

Bus service ☎ Area code 972. Taxi ☎ 77 09 40.

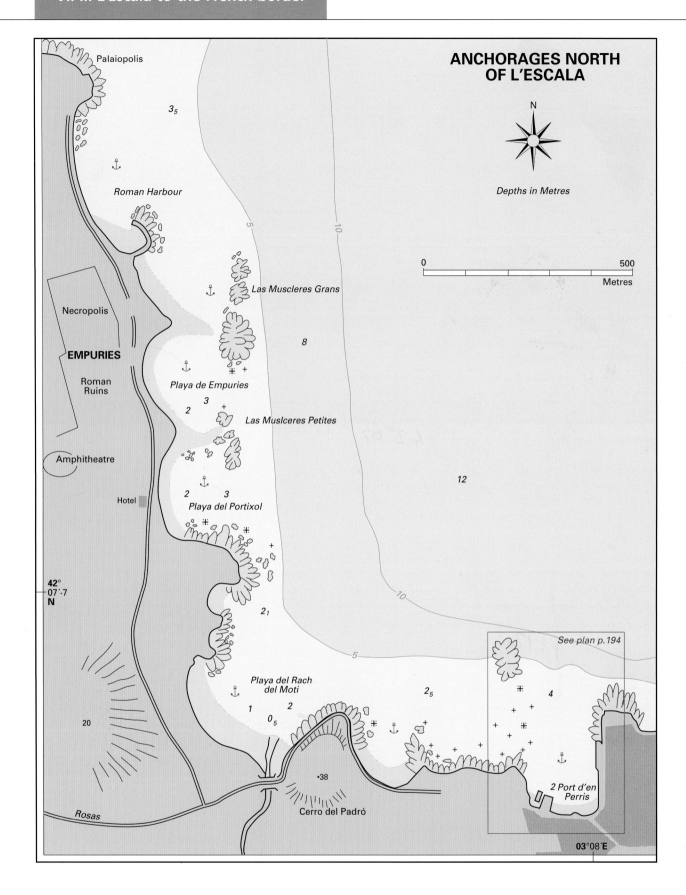

ANCHORAGES NORTH OF L'ESCALA

Depths in Metres

Palaiopolis

Roman Harbour

Necropolis

EMPURIES

Roman Ruins

Amphitheatre

Hotel

Las Muscleres Grans

Playa de Empuries

Las Muslceres Petites

Playa del Portixol

42°
07′·7
N

Playa del Rach del Moti

Rosas

Cerro del Padró

See plan p.194

2 Port d'en Perris

03°08′E

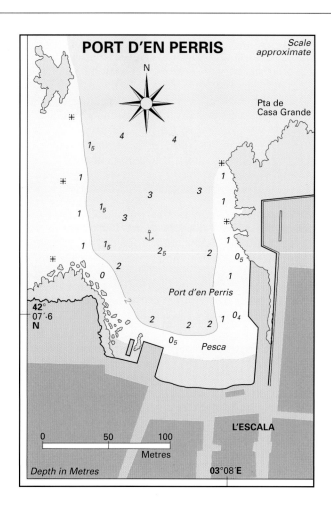

PORT D'EN PERRIS

Scale approximate

N

Pta de Casa Grande

Port d'en Perris

Pesca

42°07'·6 N

L'ESCALA

0   50   100
Metres

Depth in Metres

03°08'E

⚓ **CALAS DE L'ESCALA (TOWN)** 42°07'·8N 3°08'E

Two small *calas* on the N side of the town of L'Escala, the *cala* to E is used as a harbour for small fishing boats under the name of Port d'en Perris. Anchor in 3m, sand, near the centre of the *cala*, open between N and E. The W *cala* has rocky shallows on the E side and has a sandy beach. Use both *calas* with caution. There is an off-lying rocky islet.

⚓ **LAS CALAS DE EMPURIES** 42°08'N 3°07'·6E

A series of five *calas* lying between natural rocky projections from a sandy coast. The famous ruins of the Greco-Roman port and town of Empuries (3rd century BC) lies inland. The beach continues, backed by marshes, to the mouth of the Río Fluviá. 2·5 miles S of Empuriabrava.

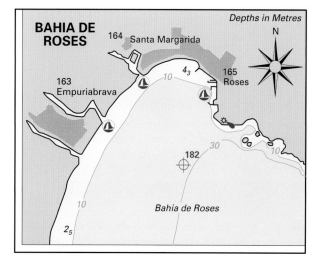

BAHIA DE ROSES

Depths in Metres

N

164 Santa Margarida
163 Empuriabrava
165 Roses
182
Bahia de Roses

⊕182   42°14'·N 03°10'E Golfe de Roses North

Playa del Portitxol and Playa de Empuries

163. Puerto de Empuriabrava (Ampuriabrava)

42°14'N 3°08'E

Charts

British Admiralty *1705*. Imray *M14*
French *7008, 7505*
Spanish *493, 4932*

⊕183 42°14'·63N 03°08'·32E 310°/0·15M to harbour

Lights

0475·5 **Dique de Levante head** Fl(3)G.7s8m5M Green
tower, white base 4m
0475·52 **Dique de Poniente head** Fl(3)R.7s8m4M Red
tower, white base 4m
0475·53 **Dique Transversal head** Fl(4)R.8s3m3M Red
tower, white base 1m
0475·54 **Dique Paralelo head** Fl(4)G.8s4m3M Green
tower, white base 1m

Port communications

VHF Ch 09 *Capitania* ☎ 972 45 12 39 *Fax* 972 45 61 61
Email info@empuriaport.com
www.marinaempuriabrava.com

A huge inland development

Miles of canals lined with blocks of flats, houses, shops and hotels on land reclaimed from the marshes between the Ríos Muga and Salinas. The marine side of the business meets most if not all maintenance requirements. Approach is easy but entering in strong winds between NE and SE is difficult. Once inside there is good protection from the sea, but not entirely from the NW *tramontana* which blows with considerable force in this area, and eddies around the buildings. Only the first part of this complex of canals can be used by yachts with masts because of low road bridges. There is a special harbour called *port interior* for visiting yachtsmen who may stay up to 15 days. When checking in, get a plan of the complex to locate shops etc.

Visits to the famous Greco-Roman remains at Empuries 6½M, and to Castelló de Empuries 2·5M and Sant Pere Pescador, 4M, are recommended. There are miles of sandy beaches on either side of the entrance.

Approach

From the south Cross the wide Golfo de Roses which has a low flat sandy shore. The towns of Sant Pere Pescador (32m) and Castelló de Empuries (69m) which stand a short distance inland will be seen. The high lighthouse-like building and other high-rise buildings at this harbour can be seen from afar. In the closer approach the breakwaters at the entrance will be seen.

From the north Round the prominent Punta de la Creu which has a small off-lying island and, keeping at least ½M from the shore, round Punta de la Batería onto a W course which leads towards the mass of buildings and a lighthouse-like building at this harbour. In the closer approach the breakwater at the entrance will be seen. Do not mistake Santa Margarita, 1·5M NE which has similar high-rise buildings, for this harbour.

Anchorage in the approach

Anchor to NE or SW of the entrance in 5m, sand.

Puerto de Empuriabrava

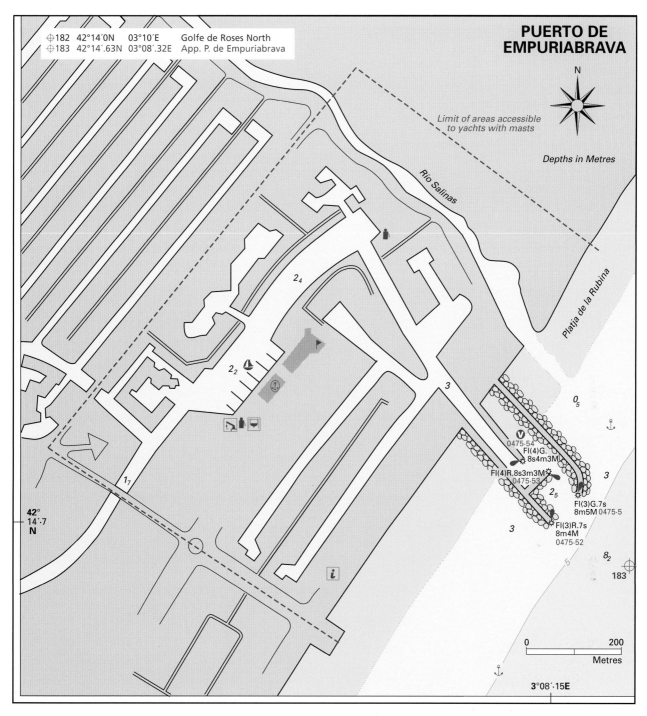

PUERTO DE EMPURIABRAVA

⊕182 42°14′0N   03°10′E   Golfe de Roses North
⊕183 42°14′.63N 03°08′.32E App. P. de Empuriabrava

N

Limit of areas accessible
to yachts with masts

Depths in Metres

Rio Salinas

Platja de la Rubina

0₅
0475·54
Fl(4)G.
8s4m3M
Fl(4)R.8s3m3M
0475·53
2₅
Fl(3)G.7s
8m5M 0475·5
Fl(3)R.7s
8m4M
0475·52
8₂
183

2₄

2₂

1₇

42°
14′.7
N

3

3

3

0   200
Metres

3°08′.15E

Entrance

Approach and enter on a NW course. Inside the entrance, the track is on an S-bend, starting to starboard, round a pier. The corners are blind because of the height of the piers and sand builds up off the pier heads so go slowly and do not cut corners. The waiting dock is to starboard at the start of the entrance canal, immediately after the S bend.

Harbour Charges

High.

Facilities

Maximum length overall 25m.
Shipyard and workshops.
50-tonne travel-lift.
10 and 7-tonne cranes.

Slip for boats less than 5m.
Several chandlers.
Water points on the quays and pontoons.
220v AC points on quays and pontoons.
Showers and WCs near the *capitanía*.
Gasoleo A and petrol from pumps at the SE corner of the yacht harbour, Port Interior, and at the NW end of the entrance canal.
Ice from the *club náutico*.
Club Náutico Empuriabrava with bar, restaurant, lounge, terrace and showers.
Many shops and a supermarket to SW of the yacht harbour.
Two launderettes within 10 minutes' walk.
Weather forecast posted at the *club náutico* 0900 daily.

Communications

Bus service. Car Hire and Taxi ☎ 972 451 218.

VI. ii. COSTA BRAVA

164. Puerto de Santa Margarida (Margarita)

42°15'N 3°09'E

Charts

British Admiralty *1705*. Imray *M14*
French *7008, 7505*
Spanish *876, 493A, 4932*

⊕184 42°15'·3N 03°09'·16E 320°/0·16M to harbour

Lights

0475·6 **Dique de Abrigo** 42°15'·5N 3°09'·1E
   Q(2)G.4s8m5M White tower, green top 6m
0475·7 **Contradique** Q(2)R.4s6m3M White tower, red top
   3m

Port communications

☎ 972 257 700 *Fax* 972 151 178.

An inland development

A large development on the flood plain of the Río Muga with buildings along the banks of dredged canals. The marina caters primarily for residents but accepts visitors. The various buildings are run as separate entities with their own offices. The office handling the marina is located at one of the entrances off the main road, at the edge of the complex.

Approach could be dangerous in heavy seas or strong winds between E and S though once inside there is complete protection. The NW *tramontana*, however, is very strong in this area and there is little shelter except in the lee of tower blocks which themselves generate gusts.

For visits, in addition to Roses, Castelló de Empuries about 3M away has an attractive 11th-

PUERTO DE SANTA MARGARIDA (MARGARITA)

Ⓐ to Ⓓ = Visitor's Moorings

Depths in Metres

Isla Gran

Workshops

Workshops

Gran Canal

SANTA MARGARIDA

Hotel

Hotel

Hotel

Contradique
Q(2)R.4s3M
0475·7

Dique de Abrigo

Q(2)G.4s5M
0475·6

⊕182 42°14'N   03°10'E   Golfe de Roses North
⊕184 42°15'·3N 03°09'·16E App. P. de Santa Margarida

3°09'E ⊕184

Puerto de Santa Margarida

century church and other remains. There are miles of sandy beaches on either side of the entrance.

Approach

From the south Cross the wide Golfo de Roses which has a low, flat sandy coast. The two towns of San Pedro Pescador (32m) and Castelló de Empuries (69m) can be recognised as well as the high *torre* at Empuriabrava, to the S of this harbour. The breakwater at the entrance will be seen in the closer approach with a mass of high buildings behind.

From the north Round the prominent Punta de la Creu which has a small off-lying island. Follow the coast round to Punta de la Batería keeping ½M offshore. Set a NW course from this point towards a mass of high buildings. In the closer approach the breakwater will be seen. Do not mistake Empuriabrava for this harbour.

Anchorage in the approach

Anchor to NE or SW of the entrance in 5m, sand.

Entrance

There appears to be no VHF contact. Approach the entrance from a position ½M to the S and enter close to the Dique de Abrigo on the starboard hand, follow it as it curves around the harbour at 20m. There may be red conical buoys and/or red-topped posts to leave port.

The entrance silts and is periodically dredged. Approach with due caution and sound.

Berths

Secure stern-to the quay by the yacht club area which will be seen ahead or in areas marked A, B, C or D on the plan, with bows-to mooring buoy, or when built, to the pontoons in the yacht harbour on the port hand, just inside the entrance. Then wait developments.

Harbour charges

Low.

Facilities

Maximum length overall 15m.
A shipyard and repair workshop in the repair and maintenance area can carry out minor repairs.
50-tonne travel-lift.
5-tonne crane.
12-tonne slipway.
Slips.
Hard-standing in the repair and maintenance areas.
Chandlery shop.
Water points on the pontoons and quays at A and B.
Showers and WCs.
220v AC at A and B quays.
Club Náutico de Santa Margarida.
A number of shops and supermarkets in the complex.
Ice from supermarket.

Communications

Bus service.

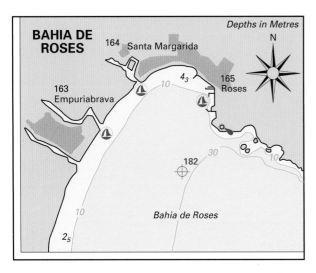

BAHIA DE ROSES
164 Santa Margarida
163 Empuriabrava
165 Roses
4₃ → 4_3
182
Bahia de Roses
Depths in Metres
N

⊕182   42°14'·N 03°10'E Golfe de Roses North

⚓ **BAHÍA DE ROSES** 42°15'·7N 3°09'·9E

There is an anchorage in the N corner of Bahía de Roses, 5–15m in sand, mud and weed, with the ruins of the Ciutadella bearing N to NNW. Open between SE and S.

Puerto de Rose

165. Puerto de Roses (Rosas)

42°15'N 3°10'E

Charts

British Admiralty *1705*. Imray *M14*
French *7008, 7505*
Spanish *493, 4932*

⊕185 42°15'·15N 03°10'·4E 090°/0·15M to harbour

Lights

To the south
0476 **Punta de la Batería** 42°14'·8N 3°11'E
   Oc(4)15s24m12M White round tower on building 11m
Harbour
0479 **Dique de Abrigo** Fl.G.4s8m5M Green tower 4m
0479.5 **New contradique head** Fl.R.4s3M Red post

Port communications

VHF Ch 09, 16 *Capitania* ☎ 972 20 14 27
Club Nautico VHF Ch 09. ☎ 972 15 44 12
Fax 972 15 37 68 *Email* info@portroses.com
www.portroses.com

Old harbour with a fine new marina

A very old fishing harbour with a mole and an L-shaped breakwater which offer good protection. Approach and entrance are easy and protection from the NW *tramontana* can be obtained but the harbour is subject to swell from winds from S to SW. The new marina to the north of the Muelle Comercial is now fully functional with a smart new

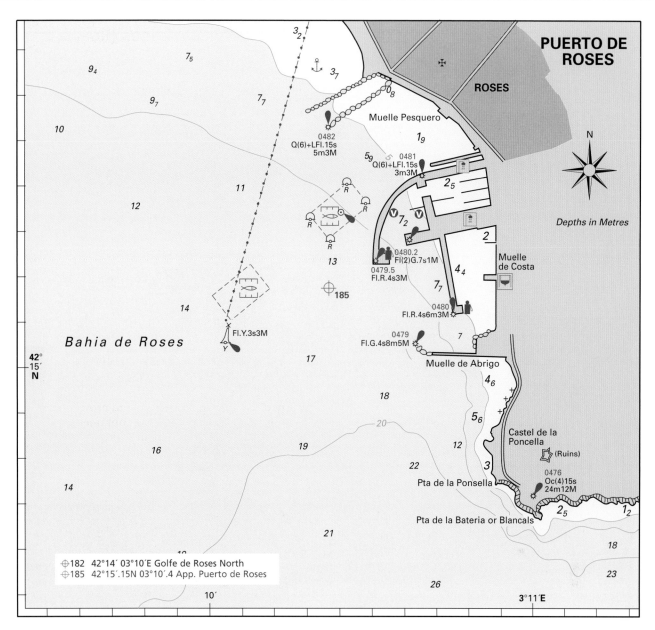

PUERTO DE ROSES

ROSES

Muelle Pesquero

Depths in Metres

N

0482
Q(6)+LFl.15s
5m3M

0481
Q(6)+LFl.15s
3m3M

Muelle
de Costa

0480.2
Fl(2)G.7s1M

0479.5
Fl.R.4s3M

185

0480
Fl.R.4s6m3M

0479
Fl.G.4s8m5M

Bahia de Roses

Muelle de Abrigo

42°
15′
N

Castel de la
Poncella

(Ruins)

0476
Oc(4)15s
24m12M

Pta de la Ponsella

Pta de la Bateria or Blancals

⊕182   42°14′ 03°10′E Golfe de Roses North
⊕185   42°15′.15N 03°10′.4 App. Puerto de Roses

10′

3°11′E

club house and all the usual facilities one expects from a normal marina.

Yachts may be allowed alongside the east quay opposite the entrance. Space is allotted by the *guarda de puerto* (the *capitán de puerto,* in overall charge, delegates berthing arrangements to the *guarda de puerto*). If a *tramontana* blows up, the quay has to be vacated for the fishing fleet and the *guarda* will suggest alternatives.

Facilities are good. The town which is about ½M away has good shops. The area is under development as a tourist centre.

A harbour has been in use here since the earliest times, its origins being connected with Emporion (Empuries). Greek and Roman records refer to Rhodus which was probably Roses, but there is a long gap in its history from the times of the Visigoths, whose remains have been found, until the Middle Ages when it was known to be a part of the domains of the Counts of Empuries and a naval port. The fort built at this time was blown up by

Suchet in 1814 as was the fort on the Punta de la Batería.

There are a number of sites to visit, from Megalithic to more recent times, including a church consecrated in 1022 and the fort that surrounds it which was built in 1543. Excellent sandy beaches to NW of the harbour.

Approach

From the south From the low hills around L'Escala the coast of the wide Golfo de Roses is flat and sandy. The two inland towns of Sant Pere (33m) and Castelló de Empuries (69m) and the marinas of Ampuriabrava and Santa Margarita are the only recognisable landmarks until the massive foothills of the SE end of the Pyrenees that lie behind Roses are visible. The harbour and anchorage are located in the extreme NW corner of this gulf.

From the north After rounding the very prominent but low Cabo Creus the coast is broken with a number of deep *calas* of which Cadaqués is the

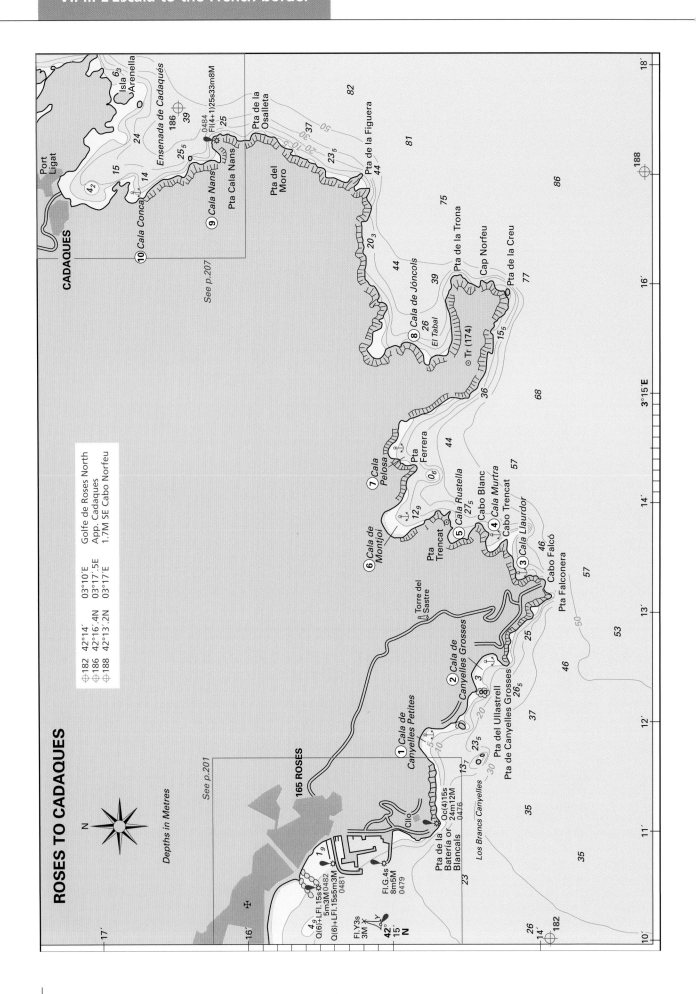

ROSES TO CADAQUES

N

Depths in Metres

⊕182	42°14'	03°10'E	Golfe de Roses North
⊕186	42°16'.4N	03°17'.5E	App. Cadaques
⊕188	42°13'.2N	03°17'E	1.7M SE Cabo Norfeu

See p.201

165 ROSES

CADAQUES

Port Ligat

Isla Arenella 6₃

Ensenada de Cadaqués

186 39

24

25₅

15

14

4₂

⑩ *Cala Conca*

See p.207

⑨ *Cala Nans*
Pta Cala Nans

0484
Fl(4+1)25s33m8M
25

Pta de la Osalleta

82

Pta del Moro

20 10₅ 37

50

23₅

44

Pta de la Figuera

81

Pta de la Trona

75

Cap Norfeu

Pta de la Creu

77

20₃

44

⑧ *Cala de Jóncols*
El Tabal 26 39

15₅

⊙ Tr (174)

36

68

86

3°15'E

⑦ *Cala Pelosa*
Pta Ferrera
0₆ 44

⑥ *Cala de Montjoi*
12₉

Pta Trencat
⑤ *Cala Rustella* 27₅
Cabo Blanc
④ *Cala Murtra*
Cabo Trencat 57
③ *Cala Llaurdor*
46
Cabo Falcó

Pta Falconera

57

50

53

35

† Torre del Sastre

② *Cala de Canyelles Grosses*
3
Pta del Ullastrell
26₅
Pta de Canyelles Grosses

25

37

46

① *Cala de Canyelles Petites*

5
23₅

20

10

30

13₇

23

35

Los Brancs Canyelles

Pta de la Batería or Blancals
Oc(4)15s 24m12M 0476

6

CIlo

0481
0482

0479
Fl.G.4s 8m5M

4₉
Q(6)+LFl.15s
5m3M0482
Q(6)+LFl.15s5m3M

Fl.Y.3s
3M

42°
15'
N

⊕ 182
26
14

largest and most easily recognised by virtue of the town at its head. Having rounded Punta de la Creu, which has a small island off its point, keep at least ½M from the coast to avoid rocky shoals. Pay special attention to Los Brancs Canyelles which is over 300m from the shore and has a wide passage inside it. The harbour is not seen until Punta de la Batería has been rounded.

Anchorage in the approach

Anchor 400m to W of the head of the Muelle Comercial in 10m mud and weed, or further to N in more shallow water. Anchor lights should be shown.

Entrance

Straightforward, but see below for berths.

Berths

This modern marina, in the northern part of the harbour, has all facilities. On approach, call ahead on Ch 9 and wait off the fuel berth for a *zodiac* to guide in. Visitors are normally berthed on the inside of the outer northern breakwater, larger vessels on the pontoons opposite.

Charges

Average.

Facilities

Repairs can be carried out by two yards and there are also engine mechanics.
Crane on the S side of the Muelle Comercial.
150-tonne slipway at root of the Muelle Abrigo.
Chandlery shop behind the yard at the head of the Muelle Comercial and two more in the town.
Water from the Club de Mar and taps on the Muelle Comercial and on pontoons.
Ice from the factory located behind the *lonja* and from fuel station.
Club de Mar de Roses has a small clubhouse with bar, lounge and showers.
A fair number of shops of all types in the town about ½M away.
Launderette in the town.

Communications

Bus service.

1. ⚓ CALA DE CANYELLES PETITES
42°14'·7N 3°11'·7E

Calas de Canyelles, Grosses in centre foreground with Petites in upper centre, looking NW with Los Branca Canyelles foul ground visible in left centre. Anchor in middle of each cala in 5m sand

2. ⚓ CALA DE CANYELLES GROSSES
42°14'·3N 3°12'·3E

Cala de Canyelles Grosses: This *cala* is very similar to Petites except that it is open between SE and W and the foul ground around Brancs Canyelles is ½M to W

PUNTA FALCONERA AND CABO FALCO
42°13'·9N 3°13'·1E

A prominent rocky-cliffed headland, steep-to with a small beacon on the Punta. A 5m-deep rocky shoal lies 600m ENE of Canbo Falco which is usually marked by breakers.

3. ⚓ CALA LLAURADOR 42°14'·1N 3°13'·4E

A small cala just to N of Cabo Falco, similar to Cala Murtra. Enter in mid-cala, anchor in 5m, rock and sand. Open between NE and S.

4. ⚓ CALA MURTRA 42°14'·3N 3°13'·7E

Cala Murtra: anchor in the middle to suit draught. Open between NE and S

5. ⚓ **CALA DE RUSTELLA** 42°14'·5N 3°13'·8E

Cala Rustella: similar to the two previous *calas* but with a larger beach and a road behind it. Open between NE and S

6. ⚓ **CALA DE MONTJOI** 42°18'·8N 3°14'E

Cala de Montjoi: anchor in 5m, sand and weed, in mid-*cala*. Open between SE and S. There is a shoal (0.5m) 200m to S of Punta Ferrera. Keep to W side of the *cala* when entering

7. ⚓ **CALA PELOSA** 42°14'·8N 3°14'·5E

Cala Pelosa: the bottom is rocky. A tower on Punta de la Creu/Cap Norféu is conspicuous. Beware the shoal (0·5m) off Punta Ferrera

VI. ii. COSTA BRAVA

⚓ **PUNTA DE LA CREU** 42°14'·2N 3°15'·8E

Punta de la Creu: a large rocky conspicuous headland (148m) with a tower, the Torre de Norféu (174m) 0.7M to NW of the point. A small islet, Carai Bernat, lies off its point, otherwise it is steep-to

8. ⚓ **CALA DE JONCOLS (JONTULLS)**
42°14'·9N 3°15'·6E

9. ⚓ **CALA NANS** 42°16'·4N 3°17'·2E

Cala Nans: anchor in 5m, sand and weed. Open between N and E. The light is Punta de Cala Nans

10. ⚓ **CALA CONCA** 42°16'·7N 3°16'·9E

Cala Conca: keep to the middle and anchor to draught. Open to SE

Puerto de Cadaqués
42°17'N 3°17'E

Charts
British Admiralty *1705*. Imray *M14*
French *4827, 7008, 7505, 7298*
Spanish *876, 493*

⊕186 42°16'·4N 03°17'·5E 322°/1·0M to anchor

Lights
0484 **Punta Cala Nans** 42°16'·1N 3°17'·1E
Fl(4+1)25s33m8M White round tower on house 7m
0485 **Los Farallones** 42°16'·9N 3°17'·3E Fl.G.4s 5m5M
Black stone tower

A sheltered anchorage
Cadaqués is a large anchorage, easy to approach, with complete protection from the seas created by the NW *tramontana* and partial protection from the wind itself. It is, however, wide open to winds between from E and S. The surroundings are beautiful and impressive and the old town is very attractive. The area has become a very popular place for tourists and holiday-makers.

Once the only route to town was by sea. In the 14th century, with some 600 inhabitants, it was prosperous after a troubled past but in the 16th century the troubles returned. The town was taken over by a succession of masters: Turkish Corsairs, the French, Algerian pirates, the French again in the 17th century followed by the British in the 18th century and again by the French during the Peninsular War. The church of Santa Maria (1662) is rare in that it has not been damaged as were most others in Spain during the various revolutions, wars and invasions. The baroque reredos is quite exceptional and should be seen.

A short walk to Port Lligat, with the summer residence of renowned surrealist Salvador Dali, is worth the effort. As an alternative, there are a number of small sandy beaches at the heads of the *cala*.

Approach
From the south The coast of the wide Golfo de Roses is low, flat and sandy but near Roses it becomes high broken rocky cliffs with many *calas*. This type of coast stretches to Cadaqués and beyond. Punta de la Creu, a prominent point, can be recognised by a small outlying island and the town of Cadaqués with a church spire will be seen at the head of the bay.

From the north The very prominent but low Cabo Creus which has a lighthouse and two smaller towers with off-lying islands can be recognised from afar. The coast to S is very rocky and broken. The Illa Messina, just to the N of the entrance to Cadaqués, is conspicuous and can be passed either side.

From both directions the twin white radomes on the top of Montaña de Cadaqués (610m) 1·5M to W of the town can be seen from far off.

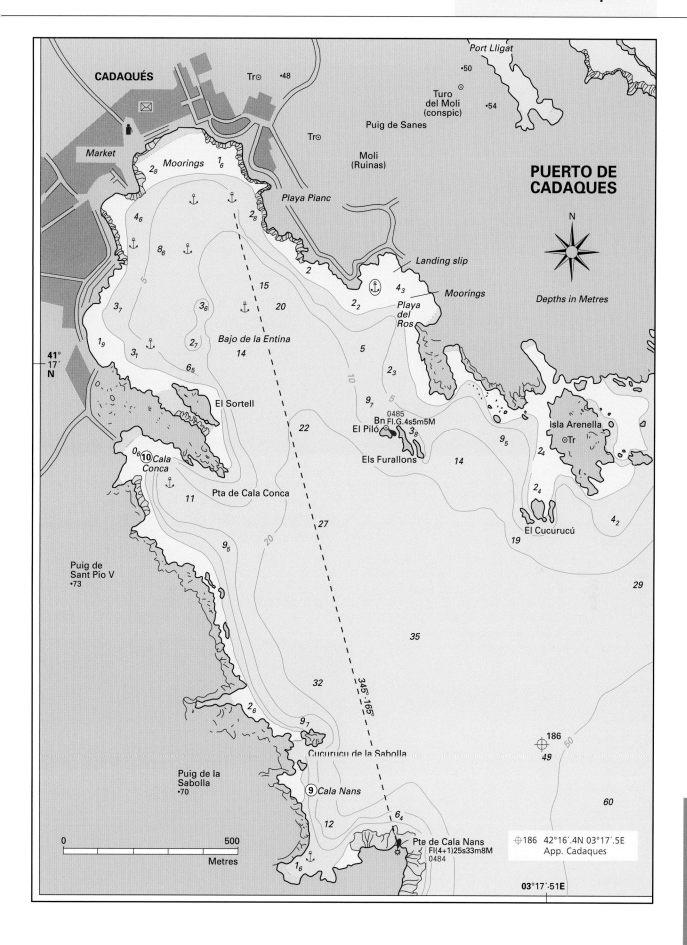

CADAQUÉS

Tr⊙   •48

Market

2₈ Moorings 1₆

4₆

8₆

3₇   3₆

1₉   3₁

6₅

41°
17′
N

Port Lligat

•50

Turo
del Moli
(conspic)   •54

Puig de Sanes

Tr⊙

Moli
(Ruinas)

Playa Pianc

2

Landing slip

4₃   Moorings

2₂   Playa
del
Ros

15

20

Bajo de la Entina
14

El Sortell

0₆ ⑩Cala
Conca

11   Pta de Cala Conca

Puig de
Sant Pio V
•73

22

27

9₅

20

**PUERTO DE
CADAQUES**

N

Depths in Metres

5

2₃

9₇

0485
Bn Fl.G.4s5m5M
El Piló   3₈

Els Furallons   14

Isla Arenella
⊙Tr

9₅   2₄

2₄

El Cucurucú   4₂

19

29

35

32

2₆

9₇

Cucurucu de la Sabolla

Puig de la
Sabolla
•70

⑨Cala Nans

12

6₄

1₆

0   500

Metres

6₄

Pte de Cala Nans
Fl(4+1)25s33m8M
0484

186
49

⊕186   42°16′.4N 03°17′.5E
App. Cadaques

50

60

03°17′·51E

VI. ii. COSTA BRAVA

Looking NW with Cadaqués just left of centre with Isla Arenella in centre foreground and Pta. Oliguera in bottom right corner. Port Lligat is the body of water on the right side

Entrance

Follow the centre line of the bay on a NW course leaving the lit beacon tower, El Piló, about 200m to starboard, steering towards the concentration of houses and a church spire at the head of the bay. In a *tramontana*, in order to obtain shelter it is necessary to make nearly 1M to windward inside the bay before the harbour is reached.

Moorings

Many private moorings will be found near the head of the bay and in the Playa del Ros, some of which may be available.

Anchorages

There are a number of anchorages around the head of the bay which may be used to suit the prevailing wind direction; these are shown on the chart. The bottom is sand, mud and weed with occasional patches of stone; use of a trip-line is advised. In the event of a NW *tramontana*, anchor as close inshore as draught permits opposite the town or in one of the small *calas* such as Cala Conca or Playa del Ros.

Landings

Land by dinghy on sandy beach in front of the town or in Playa del Ros.

Facilities

Water from local bars.
A number of small shops can supply everyday needs. There is also a small open-air market.

Communications

Bus service to Figueres and Roses.

ISLA ARENELLA 42°16′·8N 03°17′·5E

This is an interesting area to explore by dinghy. There are many small *calas,* some with stony beaches, and many islets and passages, good for fantastic photos.
Use Spanish chart *493*

Cala de Port Lligat

42°17'·6N 3°17'·5E

Charts

British Admiralty *1705*. Imray *M14*
French *4827, 7008, 7505, 7298*
Spanish *493*

⊕187 42°17'·9N 03°18'E 240°/0·5M to anchor

A sheltered anchorage

An attractive anchorage in impressive surroundings where Salvador Dali had a large summer residence. Approach and entrance are simple with good shelter except from NE winds. There is protection from the seas of the NW *tramontana* and limited protection from the effects of the wind itself. Facilities are limited to a small quay for landing from dinghies (0·6m). Many new holiday homes have recently been built around the area and more moorings have been put down. A visit to Cadaqués is worth the short walk.

It appears there is now a small enclosed area at the head of this cala with

0495·5 W entrance head 42°17'·8N 03°17'·8E Fl(2)R.7s3M
Red pillar in water
0485·7 E entrance head Fl(2)G.7s3M Green post 1m

There are also 2 port and 3 starboard buoys forming an entrance channel.

Approach

From the south Round the prominent Punta de la Creu which has a small off-lying island, cross the wide and deep Cala de Cadaqués which has houses at its head. Pass inside the Illa Messina, round Isla de Port Lligat leaving it at least 100m to port to avoid a submerged rock off the N point of Isla Farnera.

Do not attempt the narrow channel Paso de las Boquelles which lies to the S of Isla de Port Lligat. It has isolated and unmarked rocks. The shores of the bay are shallow.

From the north Round the very prominent but low Cabo Creus with its lighthouse, two towers and off-lying islands. The entrance to this cala is wide open from this direction and is to WNW of the Illa Messina. From both directions the two white radomes on Montaña Cadaqués are conspicuous.

Entrance

Enter on a SW course in mid-*cala*, then follow the starboard-hand shore around at 100m into the inner part of the *cala*. The houses are not visible until well inside.

Anchorage

Anchor 100m to SE of Punta de Sant Antoni in 4m, weed over sand and stones. Yachts with less draught may anchor further to the NW.

Facilities

Water from the local small hotel.

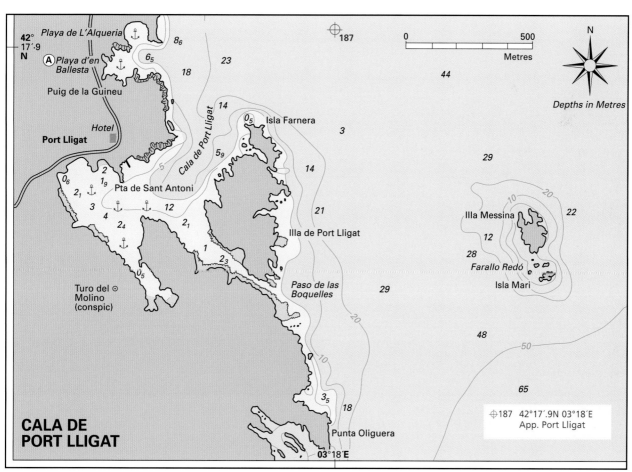

VI. ii. COSTA BRAVA

A. ⚓ **PLAYA D'EN BALLESTA Y PLAYA DE L'ALQUERIA** 42°17'·9N 3°17'·6E

C. ⚓ **CALA BONA** 42°18'·5N 3°18'·3E

Playa d'en Ballesta y Playa de l'Alqueria: the inner *calas* are banned to boats

Cala Bona: anchor in 3m, rock and stone. Open to the S. *See plan page 212*

B. ⚓ **CALA GUILLOLA & CALA JONQUET**
42°18'·2N 3°17'·7E

Cala Guillola showing Cala Jonquet, Playa d'en Lluis and Playa Guillola. Anchor in about 3m, stone, rock and sand. Open to the SE with parts open to E and S. *See plan page 212*

D. ⚓ **CALA D'ILLES** 42°18'·6N 3°18'·7E

E. ⚓ **CALA JUGADORA** 42°18'·7N 3°18'·9E

Cala d'Illes: open between E and S. Beware the rocks along the eastern shore. *See plan page 212*

Cala Jugadora, just S of Popa de Vaixell: anchor in 5 to 10m, rock. Open between SE and S. *See plan page 212*

F. ⚓ **CALA FREDOSA (COVA DEL INFERN)**
42°18'·9N 3°19'·3E

Looking into Cala Fredosa (Cova del Infern), immediately S of Cabo Creus: anchor in 5m, rock, but only in calm weather. There is a much visited rocky tunnel nearby. Cala Jugadora is at the left of the photograph. *See plan page 212*

CABO CREUS Y FREUS

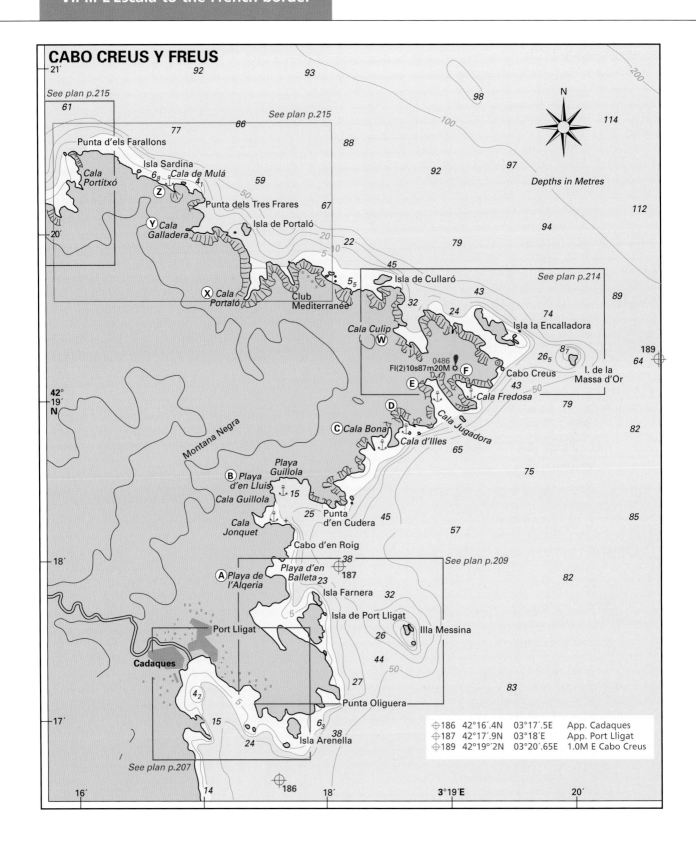

21′

92

93

98

N

See plan p.215

61

77

66

See plan p.215

114

Punta d'els Farallons

88

Depths in Metres

Isla Sardina

Cala de Mulá

Cala
Portitxó

6₈

4₁

59

92

97

Ⓩ

Punta dels Tres Frares

67

112

20′

Ⓨ Cala
Galladera

Isla de Portaló

20

22

79

94

10

5

45

See plan p.214

89

Isla de Cullaró

43

Ⓧ Cala
Portaló

5₅

74

Isla la Encalladora

64

189

Club
Mediterranée

32

24

26₅

8₇

Cala Culip

Ⓦ

I. de la
Massa d'Or

0486
Fl(2)10s87m20M ☆ Ⓕ

Cabo Creus

42°
19′
N

Ⓔ

43

Cala Fredosa

50

79

82

Ⓓ

Cala Jugadora

Montana Negra

Ⓒ Cala Bona

Cala d'Illes

65

75

Playa
Guillola

Ⓑ Playa
d'en Lluis

⚓ 15

45

85

Cala Guillola

25

Punta
d'en Cudera

Cala
Jonquet

⚓ +

57

Cabo d'en Roig

18′

38

See plan p.209

Playa d'en
Balleta

⊕ 187

Ⓐ Playa de
l'Alqeria

23

Isla Farnera

32

82

5

Isla de Port Lligat

Port Lligat

26

Illa Messina

Cadaques

44

50

27

4₂

83

17′

Punta Oliguera

15

6₃

⊕186 42°16′.4N 03°17′.5E App. Cadaques
⊕187 42°17′.9N 03°18′E App. Port Lligat
⊕189 42°19′2N 03°20′.65E 1.0M E Cabo Creus

38

24

Isla Arenella

See plan p.207

⊕ 186

16′

14

18′

3°19′E

20′

Cabo Creus y Freus

42°19′N 3°19′E

Charts

British Admiralty *1705*. Imray *M14*
French *4827, 7008, 7505*
Spanish *493*

⊕189 42°19′·2N 03°20′·65E

Lights

0486 **Cabo Creus** 42°19′·0N 3°18′·9E Fl(2)10s87m20M
  White round tower on a house 11m. Aeromarine
Beacons
Two white beacon towers (false lighthouses) are located
  on this headland, the one furthest to E is very
  conspicuous.

A major headland

A separate section is devoted to this very prominent
headland as it is located at the extreme E end of the
Pyrenees and represents a major obstacle to be
rounded. It is one of the most dangerous points on
the whole of the E coast of Spain because it is in the
centre of the path of the NW *tramontana*. This, with
its seas, can be worse here than on any other section
of the coast and can arise without warning in a very
few minutes. In such circumstances it may be
necessary to seek immediate shelter in the local *calas*
or harbours described in this section. However in
good weather it represents an excellent, unspoilt and
attractive cruising ground with many deserted
anchorages to visit.

The *cabo* is of dark rock (76m) sloping inland to
the two peaks of Els Puigs de Portas (127 and 120m)
and on up to Montaña Negra (433m) behind them.
To the NE of the *cabo* is the long, thin rocky Illa de
Encalladora (38m) separated from the *cabo* by the
inner passage which is 90m wide. There is a small
rocky islet close to its SE extremity with a rocky reef
extending onto SE. Illa de la Massa d'Or (19m) lies
800m to SE of the SE end of Isla La Encalladora.
This *islote* has a rocky reef extending 150m to W
leaving the middle passage 250m wide between these
two reefs.

Readers may wonder why there are 'false'
lighthouse towers, one of which is a horn. These

Isla La Encalladora and Cabo Creus

were built for a film about 'wreckers'. The situation
could not have been bettered.

Currents

A S-going current of up to 1·5 knots is a normal
feature of the area though in 1977 it was reported as
N-going.

Passages

(See plan on page 214). There are three possible
passages round this headland.

Inner passage This passage leads between Isla La
Encalladora and the mainland. It is deep but very
narrow, being under 90m wide in places. It is
shallower at the NW end where the seas break right
across it in strong winds between NW and W. The
wind buffets and funnels through this passage; be
ready to use the engine in emergency. In no
circumstance should the passage be attempted in bad
weather.

The passage runs WNW-ESE. Approach should be
made by closing the mainland coast and following it
along into the passage. The outer white beacon
tower (one of the false lighthouses) is very
conspicuous from either direction.

Middle passage This is between Cabo Creus and Illa
de la Massa d'Or passing outside the Isla La
Encalladora. It should not be used in very strong
winds because the seas break in this area but is quite
safe in normal weather. Attention must be paid to
the shoal patches which extend into the passage on
both sides from the Isla La Encalladora and from the
Illa de la Massa d'Or leaving a gap some 250m wide.
The passage lies midway between the two islands
and should be taken in a N-S direction. It is only
about 50m long and is 20 to 30m deep.

Outer passage In bad weather Cabo Creus must be
rounded at least 5M out to sea because savage seas
can arise close inshore. With very strong SW winds
a race develops off the headland. The outer passage
is the only safe one to use at night.

Calas to the SW of Cabo Creus are shown on pages
210 and 211 Letters A–F.

Calas to the NW of Cabo Creus are shown on pages
214 and 215, and Letters W–Z.

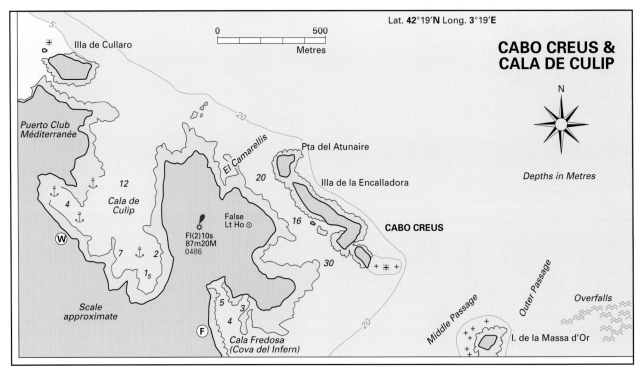

Lat. **42°19′N** Long. **3°19′E**

0 — 500
Metres

**CABO CREUS &
CALA DE CULIP**

N

Depths in Metres

Illa de Cullaro

Puerto Club
Méditerranée

El Camarellis

Pta del Atunaire

Illa de la Encalladora

12

Cala de
Culip

4

7   2

1₅

False
Lt Ho ⊙

Fl(2)10s
87m20M
0486

20

16

30

CABO CREUS

Scale
approximate

5   3

4

Cala Fredosa
(Cova del Infern)

20

Middle Passage

Outer Passage

Overfalls

I. de la Massa d'Or

W. ⚓ **CALA CULIP** 42°19′·7N 3°18′·7E

X. ⚓ **CALA PORTALÓ** 42°20′N 3°17′·5E

Cala Culip: open to the north and susceptible to a
tramontana. The small crowded harbour on the NW side
belongs to the Club Méditerranée

Cala Portaló: anchor in 5 to 10m, rock and sand. Open
between N and NE with swell from NW. Club Méditerranée
has a holiday village nearby. There is foul ground around
Isla del Portaló. See plan on page 215

Y. ⚓ **CALA GALLADERA** 42°20′·1N 3°17′E

Cala de Galladera: anchor in 5 to 10m, rock and
sand. Open between N and E and to swell from
N. There is foul ground around Isla del Portaló.
See plan on page 215

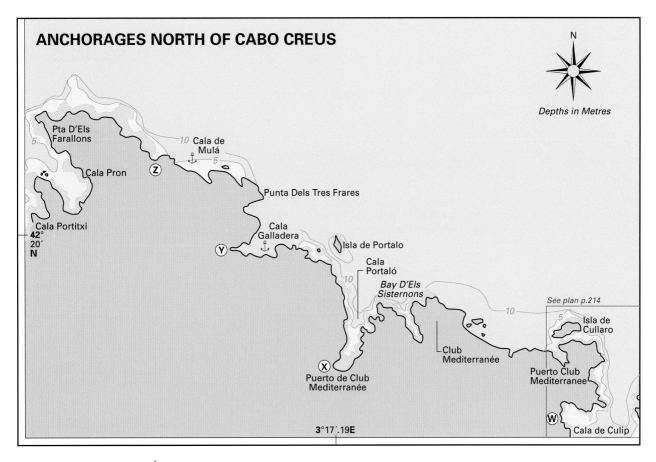

ANCHORAGES NORTH OF CABO CREUS

N

Depths in Metres

Pta D'Els Farallons

10 Cala de Mulá
5

Cala Pron (Z)

Punta Dels Tres Frares

Cala Portitxi

Cala Galladera (Y)

Isla de Portalo

42° 20' N

Cala Portaló

Bay D'Els Sisternons

See plan p.214

10

Isla de Cullaro

5

10

Club Mediterranée

Puerto Club Mediterranée

(X)
Puerto de Club Mediterranée

(W)

Cala de Culip

3°17'.19E

Z. ⚓ CALA DE MULÁ 42°20'·3N 3°16'·5E

A small cala with rocky-cliffed sides for use with care in calm weather. The bottom is rock. Open between NW and N.

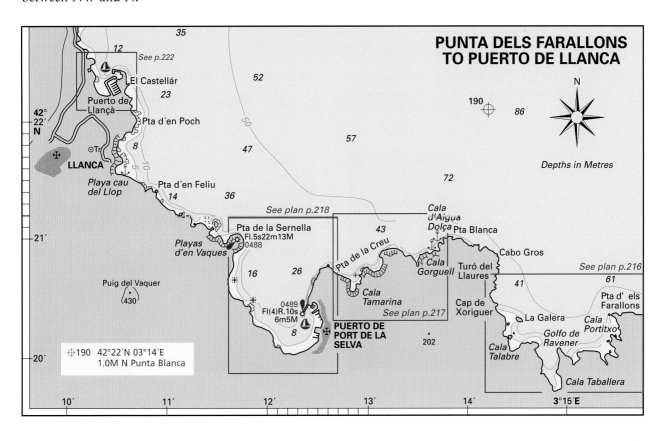

35

12

See p.222

El Castellár

23

PUNTA DELS FARALLONS TO PUERTO DE LLANCA

52

N

190 ⊕ 86

Puerto de Llançà

Pta d'en Poch

42° 22' N

⊙Tr

50

LLANCA

8

Playa cau del Llop

Pta d'en Feliu

14

36

47

57

Depths in Metres

72

21'

Cala J'Aigua Dolça
Pta Blanca

See plan p.218

Pta de la Sernella
Fl.5s22m13M
0488

Playas d'en Vaques

43

Pta de la Creu

Cala Gorguell

Cabo Gros

See plan p.216

Puig del Vaquer

(430)

16

26

Cala Tamarina

Turó del Llaures

41

61

Pta d' els Farallons

Cap de Xoriguer

La Galera

Cala Portitxo

0489
Fl(4)R.10s
6m5M

See plan p.217

8

PUERTO DE PORT DE LA SELVA

202

Golfo de Ravener

⊕190   42°22'N 03°14'E
1.0M N Punta Blanca

Cala Talabre

Cala Taballera

20'

10'   11'   12'   13'   14'   3°15'E

VI. ii. COSTA BRAVA

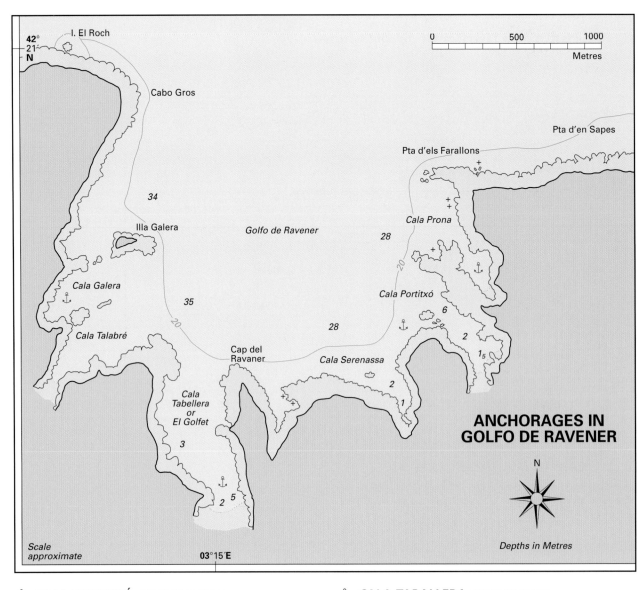

ANCHORAGES IN GOLFO DE RAVENER

Map labels: I. El Roch, Cabo Gros, 34, Illa Galera, Golfo de Ravener, Pta d'els Farallons, Pta d'en Sapes, Cala Prona, 28, Cala Galera, Cala Portitxó, 35, 20, 6, Cala Talabré, 28, 2, Cap del Ravaner, Cala Serenassa, 1 5, Cala Tabellera or El Golfet, 3, 2, 1, 5, 2

Scale approximate

03°15′E

Depths in Metres

N

⚓ **CALA PORTITXÓ** 42°20′·3N 3°15′·5E

A pair of sub-*calas* in the SE Golfo de Ravener with high rocky cliffs. Anchor in 5 to 10m. Open between NW and N.

⚓ **CALA TABALLERA** 42°20′·3N 3°15′E

⚓ **CALAS TALABRE AND GALERA** 42°20′·3N 3°14′·8E

Cala Taballera: anchor in 3 to 10m, rock and sand. Open to the N and to swell between NW and NE

Calas Talabré and Galera: anchor in 5 to 10m, rock and sand. Galera is better protected than Talabré; both get swell between NW and NE

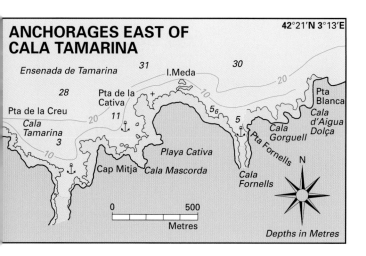

ANCHORAGES EAST OF CALA TAMARINA

42°21'N 3°13'E

Ensenada de Tamarina · 31 · I.Meda · 30 · 20
28 · Pta de la Cativa · 20 · 5₆ · 5 · Pta Blanca · Cala d'Aigua Dolça
Pta de la Creu · 20 · 11 · Cala Gorguell
Cala Tamarina · 3 · 10 · Playa Cativa · Pta Fornells · N
Cap Mitja · Cala Mascorda · Cala Fornells

0   500
Metres
Depths in Metres

⚓ **CALA D'AIGUA DOLÇA** 42°21'N 3°13'·5E

A small *cala* to SW of Punta Blanca with rocky sides. Anchor in 3m sand in mid-*cala*, open between W and N.

⚓ **CALA GORGUELL** 42°21'N 3°13'·4E

A small *cala* anchorage with rocky cliffs both sides. Anchor in 3m, stone and sand. Open between NW and N.

⚓ **CALA FORNELLS** 42°21'N 3°13'·3E

A long narrow *cala* with rocky-cliffed sides. Anchor in 5m, rocks, near the head of the *cala* where there is a shingle beach. Open between NW and N. *See plan*.

⚓ **PLAYA CATIVA AND CALA MASCORDA (LATIUS)** 42°20'·9N 3°12'·8E

Two very narrow *calas* with rocky cliffs in a wide bay to E of Cap Mitjá. Enter with care when sea is calm and no onshore wind. Anchor in 3m rocks and sand. Open between NW and N. *See plan*.

⚓ **CALA TAMARINA** 42°20'·9N 3°12'·6E

Two very narrow *calas* with rocky cliffs in a wide bay to E of Cap Mitjá. Enter with care when sea is calm and no onshore wind. Anchor in 3m rocks and

Cala Tamarina: anchor in 3m, sand, off the beach. Open between NW and NE. See plan

166. Port de la Selva

42°20'N 3°12'E

Charts

British Admiralty *1705*. Imray *M14*
French *7008, 7505, 7298*
Spanish *4934, 493*

⊕191 42°20'·8N 03°11'·7E 150°/0·45M to harbour

Lights

0489 **Muelle de Punta del Trench** 42°20'·5N 3°12'·0E
    Fl(4)R.10s6m5M Red concrete tower, white base 5m
0489·1 **Wharf head** Fl(4)R.11s Red structure
0489·15 **Jetty S head** Fl(2)G.7s Green structure.
31791(S) **Buoy** Fl.G.5s Green conical
31793(S) **Bifurcation buoy** Fl(2+1)G.12s GRG con
To the northwest
0488 **Punta Sernella** 42°20'·9N 3°11'·2E Fl.5s22m13M
    Grey square tower and building 176°-vis-272° and
    inside harbour
To the north
0492 **Cap Cebère** 42°26'·4N 3°10'·6E Fl.4s55m15M Grey
    tower red top 10m
0496 **Cap Béar** 42°30'·9N 3°08'·2E Fl(3)15s80m30M Pale
    red tower, grey corners 27m 146°-vis-056°

Port communications

VHF Ch 9, 13. *Capitanía* ☎ 972 387 000 *Fax* 972 387 001
Email nautic@cnps.es www.cnps.cat

sand. Open between NW and N. *See plan*.

A marina open to the NW winds

The port is at the side of a large bay and surrounded by mountains which has been developed into a fishing and yachting harbour. The approach and entrance are easy. There is very little shelter from the wind of the NW *tramontana* although good shelter from its seas can be had behind the Muelle de Punta del Trenc. Facilities are fair. The town and surrounding area are most attractive but there has been a considerable amount of building, fortunately mostly at low-level, for the tourist market.

The port was named after the extensive forest that surrounded the area in times past. It has been occupied since Neolithic times. Besides Neolithic remains, traces of Greek and Roman settlers have been found. The 11th-century monastery of Sant Pere de Roda, founded by the Benedictines and consecrated in 1022, kept strict control over the area despite constant incursion by the Counts of Ampuries. It was abandoned in 1798 and only recently has restoration commenced.

The local church, partly destroyed in the civil war, is interesting as it is half old and half modern. The monastery of Sant Pere de Roda and Sant Salvadó castle on the Sierra de Roses should be visited. The view from these points is fantastic.

Approach

From the south Round the very prominent Cabo Creus which has a lighthouse, two towers and off-lying islands. The coast is very broken and rocky with three major *calas* and many smaller ones. The wide bay at La Selva is easily recognised and the harbour will be found tucked away on its E side

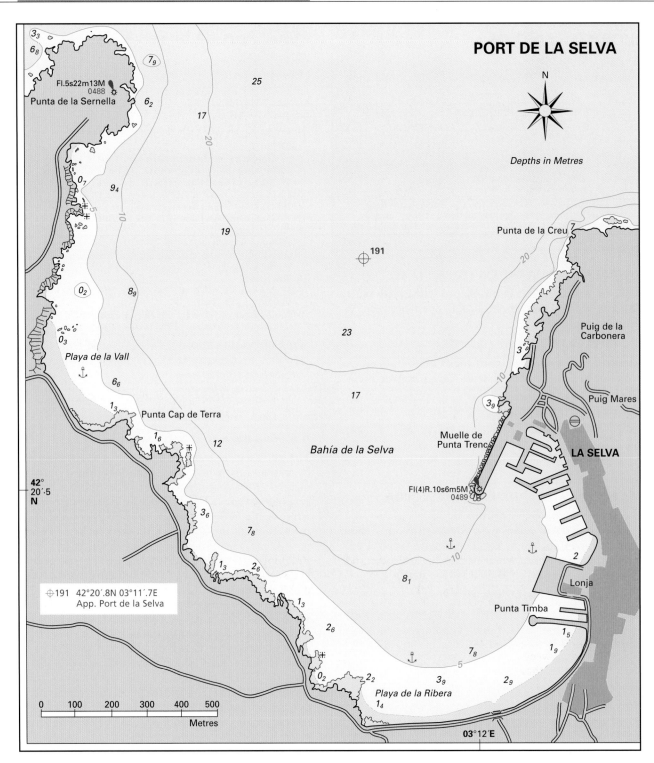

PORT DE LA SELVA

Depths in Metres

Fl.5s22m13M
0488
Punta de la Sernella

Punta de la Creu

Puig de la Carbonera

Puig Mares

Playa de la Vall

Punta Cap de Terra

Bahía de la Selva

Muelle de Punta Trenc

LA SELVA

42°
20'.5
N

Fl(4)R.10s6m5M
0489

⊕191 42°20'.8N 03°11'.7E
App. Port de la Selva

Lonja

Punta Timba

Playa de la Ribera

0 100 200 300 400 500
Metres

03°12'E

when Punta de la Creu has been rounded.

From the north From Cap Béar (France) with its conspicuous lighthouse, fort, radio and signal station the coast is high and rugged with a series of similar bays and headlands. Follow this coast to S, having passed Punta de la Sernella with its lighthouse, thence into the Bahía de la Selva where the harbour will be found on the E side.

On a clear day the two radomes on Montaña Cadaqués and the monastery Sant Pere de Roda on the mountain behind La Selva will be seen.

Anchorage in the approach

Anchor 200m to SE of the head of the Muelle de Punta del Trenc in 5m, weed over sand, or in deeper water further W. These anchorages are open to the NW *tramontana*.

Entrance

Approach the centre of the Bahía de la Selva on a S course. When level with the head of the Muelle de Punta del Trenc, turn onto an E course and enter leaving the head of the *muelle,* which has foul ground around it, at least 50m to port.

Port de la Selva

Berths

Visitors are likely to be allocated a place on the pontoons at the south end of the quay where the Club Náutico is situated. Call Club Náutico on Ch 9 to seek directions and a berth.

Moorings

Some private moorings may be available; contact *club náutico* officials for advice.

Anchorage

Anchor 200m to the E of the head of the Dique del Muelle in 5m, weed and sand, or in deeper water further W. Note that all anchorages are exposed to the NW *tramontana*.

Facilities

Maximum length overall 27m.
Minor repairs to hull and engines can be carried out by local craftsmen.
A small crane 1 tonne in the inner harbour and a larger one of 12·5 tonnes on the *muelle*.
A very small slip in the inner harbour and another to S of the harbour.
Chandler near the harbour and another in the town.
Water on the quays and pontoons.
220v AC on quays and pontoons.
Gasoleo A and petrol.
Club Náutico de Puerto de la Selva clubhouse with bar, restaurant, lounge, terrace, swimming pool and showers.
A fair selection of shops in and around the town.
Weather forecasts posted once a day.

Communications

Bus and rail service from Llançá 4M away.
Taxi ☎ 972 387 392.

Selva anchorage with harbour beyond   *Peter Taylor*

⚓ **PLAYA DE LA RIBERA** 42°20'·2N 3°11'·8E

A long, crescent-shaped sandy beach to S of La Selva. Anchor in 3m, sand, off the beach, open between NW and NE. Road and houses ashore. The W end of the beach has a rocky bottom. Dangerous during a NW *tramontana*.

⚓ **PLAYA DE LA VALL** 42°20'·7N 3°11'·3E

Playa de La Vall: anchor in 3m, sand. Open between N and E. *See plan on page 218*

⚓ **PLAYA CAU DEL LLOP** 42°21'·6N 3°10'E

A large bay with a sandy beach. There is foul ground on the N side of the *cala*. Anchor in the middle, 5m, sand. Open between N and E. See plan page 215 and photo on page 221.

⚓ **PLAYAS DE'N VAQUÉS** 42°21'·2N 3°11'·2E

Playas de'n Vaqués: two *calas* to N of Punta de la Sernella and largely hidden in this photograph. Anchor in 5m, rock and stone, in mid-*cala*. Open between N and E. *See plan page 215*

Playa Cau del Llop

Llançá entrance   *Robin Rundle*

167. Puerto de Llançà (Llansá)

42°22′4N 3°09′E

Charts

British Admiralty *1705*. Imray *M14*
French *6843*
Spanish *876, 493*

⊕192 42°22′·6N 03°09′·7E 176°/0·15M to anchor

Lights

0489·2 **Breakwater head** Fl(3)R.10s8m5M Red concrete tower, white base 3m
0489·3 **N entrance jetty** Fl(4)R.12s2M White tower, red top
0489·4 **Contradique head** Fl(3)G.10s5m5M White concrete tower, green top 2m

Port communications

VHF Ch 9 ☎ 972 38 07 10 *Fax* 972 38 07 06
Email club@cnllanca.cat www.cnllanca.cat

Llançá

VI. ii. COSTA BRAVA

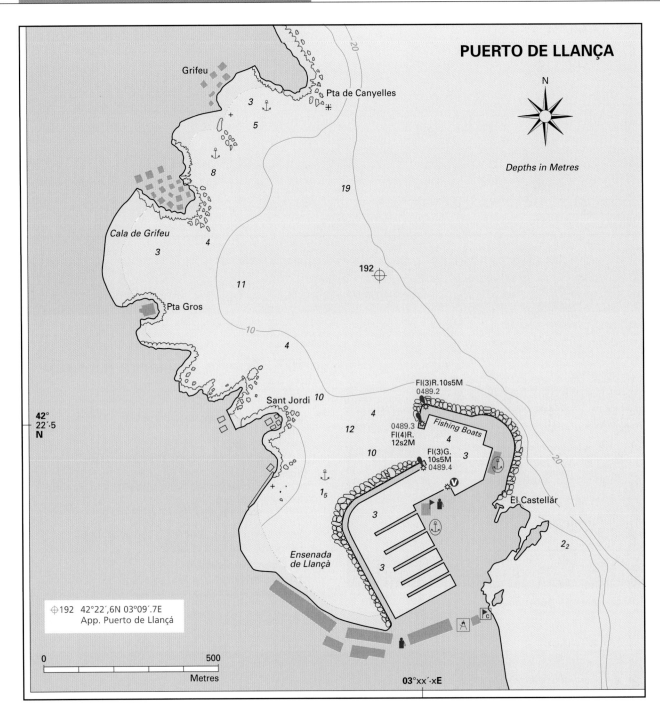

PUERTO DE LLANÇA

N

Depths in Metres

Grifeu

Pta de Canyelles

3

5

8

19

Cala de Grifeu

3

4

11

192

Pta Gros

10

4

Sant Jordi 10

Fl(3)R.10s5M
0489.2

4

0489.3
Fl(4)R.
12s2M

12

Fishing Boats

10

Fl(3)G.
10s5M
0489.4

3

El Castellár

1₅

3

2₂

3

Ensenada
de Llançà

42°
22′·5
N

⊕192   42°22′,6N 03°09′.7E
App. Puerto de Llançá

0   500

Metres

03°xx′·xE

Resort and yacht harbour

Resort and yacht harbour. A former fishing harbour and anchorage now developed as a resort with a good yacht harbour. Approach and entrance are easy and it has better protection than Selva or Portbou. The area is attractive. This harbour was called Deciana in Roman times. In the 17th and 18th centuries it exported a large amount of marble, olive oil and wine. The local wine is still one of the strongest to be found. There is an interesting 18th-century church and it is possible to visit the Benedictine monastery of Sant Pere de Roda and Sant Salvadó Castle, 670m above sea level with a fantastic view. There are also the Dali and the Toy Museums and excellent bathing beaches around the bay.

Approach

All the headlands in this bay have tongues of rocks projecting from the outer ends which are just below sea level.

From the south Cross the mouth of the deep Bahía de la Selva, which has Port de la Selva on its E side, and round Punta de la Sernella which has a lighthouse near the point. Keep at least 500m from the shore until the Ensenada de Llançà is fully opened up, then round El Castellár, which has a small castle on its top and follow the breakwater round.

From the north This harbour lies in the third large bay 3M to the S of Portbou. It can be recognised by El Castellár with its small castle lying just behind the harbour and the houses of the Puerto de Llançà can

⚓ CALA GRIFEU 42°23'N 3°09'·7E

Cala Grifeu: anchor in the middle; there is foul ground on both sides. Open between E and SE. See plan on page 222

also be seen from this direction. The harbour lies in the S corner of the bay.

Entrance

Round the breakwater head with caution prepared for a sharp turn to starboard.

Berths

Go alongside the visitors quay and ask for a berth.

Anchorages

NW of the harbour in 3m, sand and weed, but it is very exposed. Keep clear of the harbour entrance and use an anchor light. There are two other anchorages which may have better shelter on the N side of the *ensenada* (*see plan*).

⚓ CALA GARBET 42°23'·7N 3°10'E

Cala Garbet: large bay open between NE and SE. Anchor in 10m, rock and sand. The NW corner of the bay is foul

Facilities

Maximum length overall 15m.
Mechanics.
12-tonne crane.
Water on the quays.
230v AC on quays.
Gasoleo A and petrol.
Club Náutico de Llançà has the weather forecast posted daily.
Shops in the village and more at Llançá town some ½M away.

Communications

Railway to Barcelona and France. Taxi ☎ 972 381 344/972 380 317.

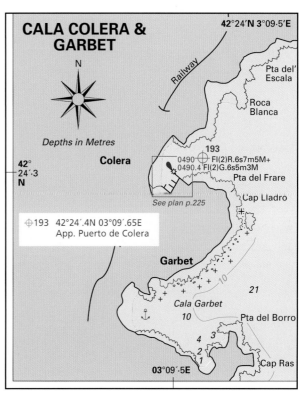

CALA COLERA & GARBET

42°24'N 3°09·5'E

Railway

N

Depths in Metres

Pta del' Escala

Roca Blanca

42°
24'·3
N

Colera

193
0490 ⊕ Fl(2)R.6s7m5M+
0490.4 Fl(2)G.6s5m3M
Pta del Frare

Cap Lladro

See plan p.225

⊕193 42°24'·4N 03°09'·65E
App. Puerto de Colera

Garbet

21

Cala Garbet
⚓ 10

Pta del Borro

4 3
2
1

Cap Ras

03°09'·5E

VI. ii. COSTA BRAVA

Colera *Peter Taylor*

168. Puerto de Colera

42°24'N 3°9'E

Charts

British Admiralty *1705*. Imray *M14*
French *7008, 7505*
Spanish *493*

⊕193 42°24'·4N 03°09'·65E 235°/0·16M to harbour

Lights

0490 **Dique de Levante head** Fl(2)R.6s7m5M Red tower
on white base 3m
0490·4 **Contradique head** Fl(2)G.6s5m3M Green tower
white base 3m
To the north
0492 **Cap Cerbère** 42°26'·4N 3°10'·6E Fl.4s55m15M Grey
tower red top 10m

Port communications

Club Náutico ☎ 972 38 90 95 *Fax* 972 38 70 01
Email piuspujades@hotmail.com

A very small harbour

A small fishing harbour and village originally called
St Miquel which was also used as a staging post on
the main coast road. It has a small harbour for
yachts and fishing craft tucked away on the S side of
the *cala*. It is a useful harbour with better protection

Puerto de Colera

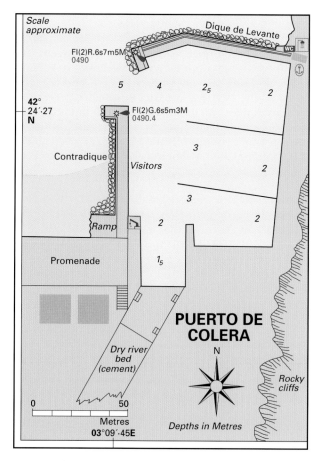

Scale approximate

Fl(2)R.6s7m5M
0490

Dique de Levante

WC

5   4   2₅   2

42°
24'·27
N

Fl(2)G.6s5m3M
0490.4

Contradique

Visitors

3

2

3

2

Ramp

2

Promenade

1₅

PUERTO DE COLERA

N

Dry river bed (cement)

Rocky cliffs

0   50

Metres
03°09'·45E

Depths in Metres

⊕193   42°24'·4N 03°09'·65E   App. Puerto de Colera

than the quay at Portbou though a NW *tramontana* creates a chop inside parts of the harbour. The area is impressive with high mountains all around. Harbour facilities are limited. There are a few shops in the village for everyday requirements and a beach of sand and stone to W of the harbour.

Cabo Falcó and Cabo Cerbère

Approach

From the south Leave the Bahía de la Selva and follow the coast at 500m to N. The following are easy to identify: Punta Sernella with a lighthouse, Puerto de Llançá which appears behind the Islote and Punta del Castellá, Cabo Rose with the wide Cala Garbet to its N and Cabo Lladró with a detached islet. Cala Colera lies to its N but the harbour remains hidden until mid-*cala* is reached.

From the north Port de Cerbère, Cap Cerbère with a small white building on its summit and the Cala de Portbou are easily recognised. Cala Colera is the next *cala* to S. From this direction the harbour may be seen in the early approach.

Anchorage in the approach

Anchor in 10m, stone and sand, near the centre of the mouth of Cala Colera. The head of the *cala* is shallow and has outlying spurs either side of the mouth of the river.

Entrance

Go west towards the head of the *cala* and when harbour bears S turn towards the entrance. Round the Dique de Levante at 15m.

Berths

Secure on the inner (E) side of the *contradique* where there is a notice, 'Amarres Servicio Publico' and ask the *capitanía* for a berth. Some of the quays have shallow rocky feet.

Facilities

Maximum length overall 15m.
Ramp from beach to *contradique*.
2-tonne crane.
Water taps on quays and pontoons.
Showers and WCs in NE corner of the harbour.
220v AC on quays and pontoons.
Club Náutico Sant Miquel de Colera.
Provisions from village shops in Colera about 500m.

Communications

Buses. Rail to Barcelona and Perpignan.

VI. ii. COSTA BRAVA

169. Puerto de Portbou

42°26'N 3°10'E

Charts

British Admiralty *1705*. Imray *M14*
French *7008, 7505*
Spanish *493*

⊕194 42°25'·69N 03°10'·25E 255°/0·17M to harbour

Lights

0491 **Dique de Abrigo head** Fl.R.5s7m5M Red post 3m
0491·5 **Contradique head** Fl.G.5s4m3M Green post 2m

Port communications

VHF Ch 09 Marina ☎/*Fax* 972 39 07 12
Email portdeportbou@telefonica.net
www.portdeportbou.com

A small, simple harbour

This inlet which forms a natural harbour is located close to the frontier with France. Approach and entrance are easy and good protection is offered from all directions except between NE and SE. The force of the NW *tramontana* is somewhat reduced by the ranges of mountains inland but can still descend on the harbour in strong gusts. With a strong wind between NE and SE a heavy swell enters this harbour. Shelter should be taken at Selva or Port Vendres.

The marina to the west of the town has been recently totally remodeled and the breakwaters massively strengthened, the surrounds all leveled and 6 pontoons laid in the marina. The shore side facilities are still rudimentary but it is now a well sheltered harbour for some 300 craft. The town is not especially attractive but the surrounding countryside is spectacular, with high mountains.

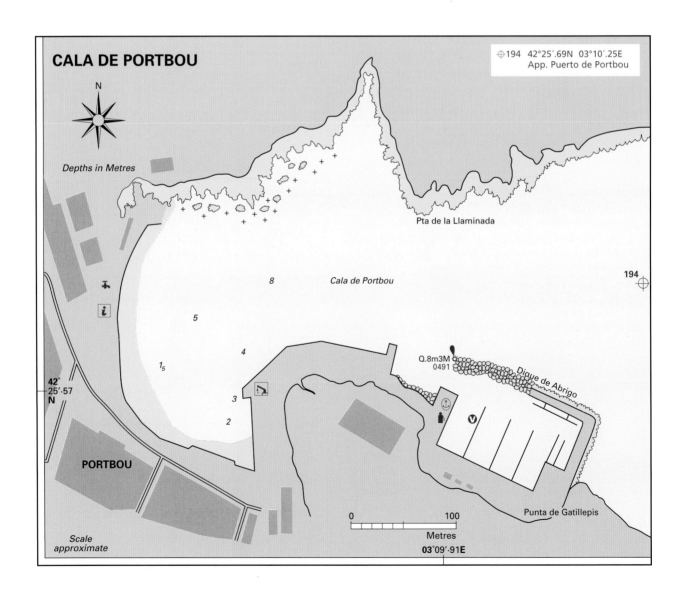

Puerto de Portbou

Approach

From the south From the wide and deep Bahía de la Selva, the coast which is rugged and broken consists of a series of deep *calas* with rocky headlands between. These rocks are of a very dark colour just to the S of this harbour. Cap Cerbère which is ½M to N of this harbour is the most prominent of the headlands and can be identified if coasting close in. At the head of the Cala de Portbou can be seen the long railway customs shed on an embankment, the lighthouse-like spire of the church to the N of it, and there is a prominent fort-like building with a small square tower on the inner point on the S side of the harbour.

From the north Round Cap Béar, a prominent point with a lighthouse, signal and radio station and fort. Banyuls-sur-Mer can easily be identified at the head of a wide bay. Port de Cerbère has a multi-arched railway embankment, Cap Cerbère just to S of it will be seen, if coasting close in, as a prominent headland. Cabo Falcó is triangular-shaped and has a small white customs shed on its summit. Portbou will be recognised as detailed in the section above.

Entrance

Enter down the centre of the cala on a W course. If making for the marina round the end of the breakwater at a reasonable (25m) berth as there are obstructions running south and east from the head.

Berths

Berth first at the fuel dock beside the office. There is excellent berthing for visitors in deep water on the first pontoon inside the entrance. Hauling off lines are provided.

Anchorages

It is no longer permitted to anchor off the quays. It is likely that buoys will be provided in the bay for larger vessels. Otherwise temporary anchorage may be found to the south of Cabo Falco.

Facilities

Small slip on the S side of the harbour.
Water tap on the NW side of the harbour.
Some small shops in the village.
Club Náutico de Portbou.

Communications

Rail to Barcelona and Perpignan. Bus service.
☎ Area code 972.

Appendices

I. WAYPOINT LIST

Way points 1-99 have been allocated to the sister volume *Mediterranean Spain Costas del a Sol and Blanca*.

Harbour WPs have generally been selected approaching the hbr up to the 5m line (sometimes further out to allow for headlands or known silting problem).

Coastal WPs are in **bold**.

Ch IV COSTA AZAHAR
100	38°44'N 00°16'E 1·5M E Cabo de la Nao
101	38°37'·5N 00°11'·5E App. Puerto de Javea 300°/0·3M
102	38°48'N 00°13'E 1M E Cabo San Antonio

Longitude W/E change
103	38°50'·95N 00°07'·68W App. Puerto de Denia 227°/0·01M
104	38°55'·97N 00°05'·4W App. Puerto de Oliva 280°/0·09M
105	8°59'·65N 00°08'·55W App. Puerto de Gandía 290°/0·1M
106	**39°10'N 00°10'W 2·6M ESE Cabo Cullera**
107	39°09'·05N 00°13'·9W App. Puerto de Cullera 280°/0·08M
108	39°16'·65N 00°16'W App. Puerto El Perelló 275°/0·27M
109	39°18'·6N 00°17'·2W App. Puerto El Perellónet 250°/0·24M
110	**39°25'N 00°15'W 3·0M ESE Valencia Hbr**
111	39°25'·3N 00°19'·4W App. Valencia Yacht Hbr 296°/0·5M
112	39°25'·82N 00°18'·2W Hbr Entrance Puertos de Valencia
113	39°30'·5N 00°18'·85W App. Puerto de Saplaya 300°/0·2M
114	39°33'3N 00°16'·8W App. Pobla Marina 315°/0·25M
115	39°37'·6N 00°12'·4W Hbr Entrance Puerto de Sagunto 350°/0·25M
116	39°40'·25N 00°11'·9W App. Puerto de Siles 300°/0·15M
117	39°51'·2N 00°04'·05W App. Puerto de Burriana 350°/0·25M

Longitude W/E change
118	**39°55'N00°10'E 7M ESE P de Castellón de la Plana**
119	39°57'·3N 00°01'·8E App. Castellón de la Plana 322°/0·05M
120	**39°49'8N 00°40'·7E**
121	**39°53'N 00°39'E W Isolotes Columbretes**
122	**39°54'5N 00°41'E N Isolotes Columbretes**
123	**39°53'N 00°42'E E Isolotes Columbretes**
124	40°04'·36N 00°08'·13E App. Puerto Oropesa de Mar 315°/0·08M
125	40°14'·75N 00°17'·35E App. Puerto de las Fuentes 318°/0·11M
126	40°21'·05N 00°24'·14E App. Puerto de Peñíscola 330°/0·14M
127	40°24'·52N 00°26'·05E App. Puerto de Benicarló 350°/0·03M
128	40°27'·4N 00°28'·5E App. Puerto de Vinaroz 355°/0·01M

Ch IV COSTA DORADA
129	40°33'·17N 00°32'·04E App. P. de l Cases d'Alcanar 265°/0·03M
130	40°34'·34N 00°33'·5E App. Puerto de Alcanar 290°/0·15M
131	40°36'·32N 00°36'·3E App. Puerto de Sant Carles 001°/0·2M
132	**40°31'N 00°42'·3E 3M SE Punta de la Bana**
133	**40°43'N 01°E 5·3M E Cabo Tortosa**
134	40°48'·5N 00°45'E Golfo de l'Ampolla 267°/1·8M
135	40°52'·1N 00°47'·7E App. Pto de L'Estany Gras 295°/0·09M
136	40°52'·65N 00°48'·3E App. Pto de L'Ametlla d Mar 340°/0·07M
137	40°54'·65N 00°50'·43E 0·25M SE Puerto de Sant Jordi (Closed)
138	40°55'·55N 00°51'·1E App. Puerto de Calafat 300°/0·07M
139	40°59'·2N 00°55'·6E App. Pto de Hospitalet de L'infante 000°/0·04M
140	41°03'·57N 01°03'·52E E App. Puerto de Cambrils 045°/0·06M
141	41°04'·2N 01°07'·7E App. Puerto de Salou 010°/0·18M
142	**41°02'N 01°10'E 1·2M S Cabode Salou**
143	41°05'N 01°13'E Puerto de Tarragona
144	41°06'·2N 01°15'·1E App. Port Esportiou 340°/0·15M
145	41°07'·85N 01°24'·05E App. P de Torredembarra 000°/0·12M
146	41°09'·6N 01°28'E App. Roda de Bara 020°/0·2M
147	41°10'·4N 01°31'·56 App. Puerto de Coma-Ruga N/0·12M
148	41°11'N 01°36'·25E App. P. de Segur de Calafell 010°/0·2M
149	41°11'·2N 01°38'·7E App. Puerto del Foix 010°/0·35M
150	41°12'·3N 01°43'·6E App. P. de Vilanova la Geltrú 045°/0·11M
151	41°13'·85N 01°49'·25E App. Aiguadolç 045°/0·15M
152	41°14'·1N 01°51'·85E App. Puerto de Vallcarca 015°/0·1M
153	41°14'·86N 01°53'·84E App. Puerto de Garraf 035°/0·08M
154	41°15'·3N 01°55'E App. Port Ginesta 070°/0·14M
155	**41°15'N 02°10'E 5M S Barcelona**
156	41°18'·5N 02°11'E App. Puerto Barcelona
157	41°21'·25N 02°11'E Outer App. Port Vell
158	41°22'·8N 02°12'E App. Puerto Olímpico 345°/0·2M
159	41°24'·4N 02°13'·8E Port Forum 310°/0·1M
160	41°25'·7N 02°14'·8E Marina Badalona 300°/0·2M
161	41°28'·32N 02°18'·5E

App. Puerto de El Masnou 040°/0·14M
162	41°29'·2N 02°21'·8E App. Puerto de Premiá de Mar 030°/0·1M
163	41°31'·5N 02°26'·5E App. Puerto de Mataró 040°/0·1M
164	41 33'·3N 02°30'·3E App. Port Balís 030°/0·08M
165	41°34'·5N 02°33'·2E App. Pte de Arenys de Mar 065°/0·14M

COSTA BRAVA

166	41°40'·25N 02°47'·8E App. Puerto de Blanes 005°/0·11M	
167	41°42'·07N 02°52'·95E App. Puerto de Canyelles 315°/0·14M	
168	**41°42'N 02°57'·5E 1·4M SE Cabo de Tossa**	
169	41°43'N 02°56'·4E App. Tossa Anchorages	
170	41°46'·1N 03°02'·1E App. P de St F de Guíxols ldg ln/0·5M	
171	41°47'·9N 03°04'·07E App. Port d'Aro 330°/0·16M	
172	**41°50'·1N 03°07'·75E 0·35M S Punta del Molino (Palamós)**	
173	**41°51'·85N 03°10'·9E Freu de Las Hormigas**	
174	**41°51'·53N 03°11'·52E 0·2M SE Islas Las Hormigas**	
175	41°53'·4N 03°11'·8E App. Puerto de Llafranc 340°/0·19M	
176	**41°56'N 03°14'E 0·75M ESE Fornells**	
177	**41°58'N 03°15'E 0·8M E Caba Negre**	
178	**42°02'·8N 03°15'E 1·0M E Islas Medas**	
179	42°02'·8N 03°12'·5E App. Puerto de L'Estartit 335°/0·22M	
180	**42°03'·07N 03°12'·92E Freu de Las Islas Medas**	
181	42°07'·4N 03°08'·53E App. Puerto de L'Escala 180°/0·28M	
182	42°14'N 03°10'E Golfe de Roses North	
183	42°14'·63N 03°08'·32E App. P de Empuriabrava 310°/0·15M	
184	42°15'·3N 03°09'·16E App. P de Santa Margarida 320°/0·16M	
185	42°15'·15N 03°10'·4E App. Puerto de Roses 090°/0·15M	
186	42°16'·4N 03°17'·5E App. Cadaques 322°/1·0M	
187	42°17'·9N 03°18'E App. Port Lligat 240°/0·5M	
188	**42°13'·2N 03°17'E 1·7M SE Cabo Norfeu**	
189	**42°19'·2N 03°20'·65E 1·0M E Cabo Creus**	
190	42°22'N 03°14'E 1·0M N Punta Blanca	
191	42°20'·8N 03°11'·7E App. Port de la Selva 150°/0·45M	
192	42°22'·6N 03°09'·7E App. Puerto de Llançá 176°/0·15M	
193	42°24'·4N 03°09'·65E App. Puerto de Colera 235°/0·16M	
194	42°25'·69N 03°10'·25E App. Puerto de Portbou 255°/0·17M	
195	**42°26'N 03°12'E 1·0M E Cabo Falco**	

II. CHARTS

Charts and other publications may be corrected annually by reference to the Admiralty *List of Lights and Fog Signals Volume D (NP 77) and E (NP78)* or weekly via the Admiralty *Notices to Mariners*.

Note A few charts appear twice in the following list under different island headings. The index diagrams only shows large-scale charts where the diagram's scale permits.

British Admiralty charts

Chart   Title   Scale
Note Index references refer to sections in Admiralty World Catalogue NP131 Index E Bay of Biscay, Spain, Portugal and Western Mediterranean

45	Gibraltar harbour	3,600
142	Strait of Gibraltar	100,000
	Tarifa	25,000
144	Gibraltar	10,000
165	Menorca to Sicilia including Malta	1,100,000
469	Puerto de Alicante	10,000
473	Approaches to Alicante	25,000
518	Approaches to Puerto de Valencia	27,500
562	Valencia	10,000
773	Strait of Gibraltar to Isla de Alborán	300,000
774	Motril to Cartagena including Isla de Alborán	300,000
	Isla de Alborán	15,000
1180	Barcelona	10,000

1193	Puerto de Tarragona and approaches	10,000
1194	Puerto de Cartagena	12,500
1196	Approaches to Puerto de Barcelona	30,000
1448	Gibraltar bay	25,000
1455	Algeciras	12,500
1515	Ports on the east coast of Spain	25,000
1700	Cartagena to Cabo de San Antonio including Isla Formentera	300,000
1701	Cabo de San Antonio to Villanueva y Geltrú including Islas de Ibiza and Formentera	300,000
1702	Ibiza, Formentera and southern Mallorca	300,000
1703	Mallorca and Menorca	300,000
1704	Punta de la Bana to Islas Medas	300,000
1705	Cabo de San Sebastian to Îles d'Hyères	300,000
1780	Barcelona to Napoli including Islas Baleares, Corse and Sardegna	1,100,000
1850	Approaches to Málaga	25,000
1851	Malaga	10,000
1854	Motril and Adra	7,500
2717	Strait of Gibraltar to Barcelona and Alger including Islas Baleares	1,100,000
2761	Menorca	60,000
2831	Mallorca: Punta Salinas to Cabo de Formentor including Canal de Menorca	120,000
	Puerto de Alcudia	20,000
2832	Mallorca: Punta Salinas to Punta Beca including Isla de Cabrera	120,000
2834	Ibiza and Formentera	120,000
	Ibiza	10,000
	San Antonio Abad	20,000
	Channels between Ibiza and Formentera	50,000
3034	Approaches to Palma	25,000
3035	Palma	10,000
3132	Strait of Gibraltar to Arquipélago da Madeira	1,250,000
3578	Eastern approaches to the Strait of Gibraltar	150,000

Spanish charts

6A	Isla de Menorca	96,000
7A	Isla de Ibiza y Formentera	97,500
44	De cabo de San Vicente al Estrecho de Gibraltar	350,000
44C	Costa Sur de España y Norte de Marruecos. De Broa de Sanlúcar a Estepona y de Larache a cabo Mazarí	175,000
45	Estrecho de Gibraltar y Mar de Alborán	350,000
45A	De punta Carnero a cabo Sacratif y de punta Cires a cabo Negro	175,000
45B	De cabo Sacratif a cabo de Gata	175,000
46	De cabo de Gata a cabo de las Huertas y de cabo Milonia a cabo Ivi	350,000
	Plano inserto: Puerto de Gazaouet (Nemours)	10,000
46A	De cabo de Gata a cabo de Palos	175,000
	Plano inserto: Fondeaderos de Palomares y Villaricos	25,000
47	De cabo Tiñoso a cabo Canet, con las islas Ibiza, Formentera, Cabrera y costa SW de Mallorca	350,000
48	De cabo de la Nao a Barcelona con las islas Baleares	425,000
48E	Islas de Mallorca y Menorca	175,000
105	Estrecho de Gibraltar. De cabo Roche a punta de la Chullera y de cabo Espartel a cabo Negro	100,000

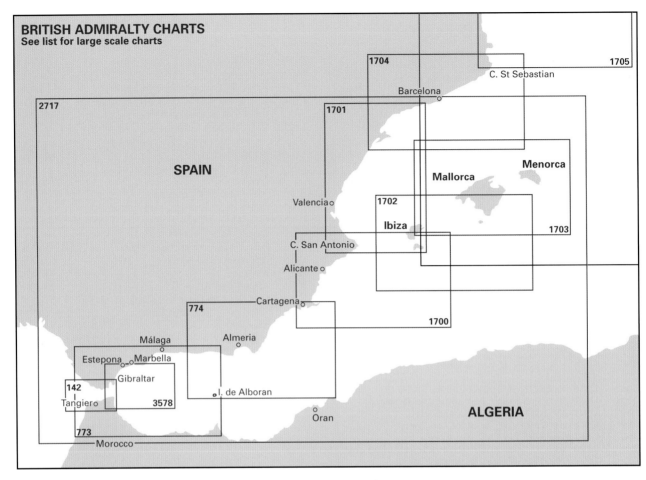

BRITISH ADMIRALTY CHARTS
See list for large scale charts

1704

1705

C. St Sebastian

Barcelona

2717

1701

SPAIN

Menorca

Mallorca

Valencia

1702

Ibiza

1703

C. San Antonio

Alicante

Cartagena

774

1700

Málaga

Almeria

Estepona   Marbella

Gibraltar

142

I. de Alboran

Tangier

3578

Oran

ALGERIA

773

Morocco

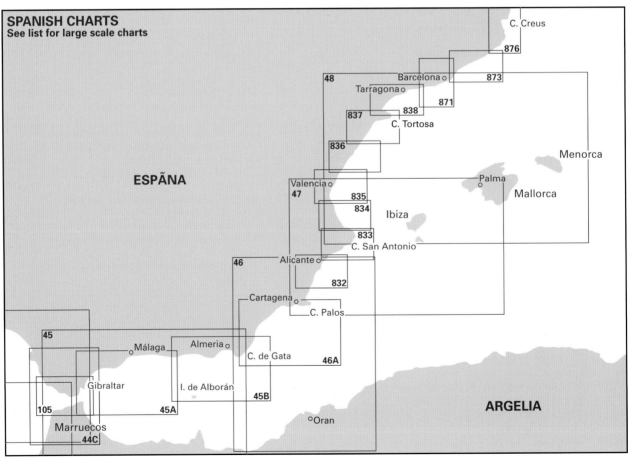

SPANISH CHARTS
See list for large scale charts

C. Creus

876

48

Barcelona

873

Tarragona

871

837

838

C. Tortosa

836

ESPAÑA

Menorca

Valencia

Palma

47

835

Mallorca

834

Ibiza

833

C. San Antonio

46

Alicante

832

Cartagena

C. Palos

45

Málaga

Almeria

C. de Gata

46A

Gibraltar

I. de Alborán

45B

105

45A

Oran

ARGELIA

Marruecos

44C

Chart	Title	Scale
215	De cabo Trafalgar a punta Europ y de Ceuta a Kenitra (Port Lyautey)	350,000
287A	Ensenada y puerto de Benidorm	16,400
288A	Ensenada y puerto de Altea	11,600
289A	Puerto y fondeadero de Calpe	17,000
291A	Ensenada de Morayra	11,700
292A	Ensenada y puerto de Jávea	13,000
301A	Fondeadero de Mataró	10,000
309A	Puerto de Cadaqués	10,000
421	De isla Dragonera a cabo Blanco	50,000
421A	Bahía de Palma. De Islote El Toro a cabo Regana	25,000
422	De Cabo Regana a punta Salinas	50,000
422A	Freu de Cabrera	25,000
423	De punta Plana a Porto Colom con la isla de Cabrera y adyacentes	50,000
424	De cala Llonga a cabo Farrutx	50,000
425	De cabo Pera a cabo Formentor	50,000
425A	Bahía de Alcudia	25,000
426	De la bahía de Alcudia al puerto de Sóller	50,000
427	De cala de la Calobra a Isla Dragonera	50,000
428A	De punta Binibeca a cabo Favaritx	25,000
435	Isla de Alboran	50,000
445	Estrecho de Gibraltar. De punta Camarinal a punta Europa y de cabo Espartel a punta Almina	60,000
445A	Bahía de Algeciras	25,000
451	De punta Leona a cabo Mazarí	50,000
453	De Punta Europa a la torre de las Bóvedas	50,000
	Planos insertos: Fondeadero de Estepona	12,500
	Fondeadero de la Sabinilla	12,500
454	De Estepona a punta de Calaburras	50,000
	Plano inserto: Fondeadero de Marbella	10,000
455	De punta de Calaburras a la ensenada de Vélez Málaga	50,000
	Plano inserto: Fondeadero y puerto de Fuengirola	10,000
455A	Aproches del puerto de Malaga	25,000
456	De punta de Torrox a cabo Sacratif	50,000
457	De Motril a Adra	50,000
458	De Adra a Almería	50,000
459	Golfo de Almería. De punta del Sabinal a cabo de Gata	50,000
	Plano inserto: Roquetas de Mar	5,000
461	De cabo de Gata a Mesa de Roldán	50,000
	Planos insertos: Puerto Genovés y ensenada de San José	15,000
	Ensenada de los Escullos	25,000
	Cala de San Pedro	25,000
462	De Mesa de Roldán a isla de los Terreros	50,000
	Plano inserto: Puerto de Garrucha	7,500
463	De punta de Sarriá a cabo Tiñoso	50,000
	Plano inserto: Puertos de Aguilas y el Hornillo	12,500
463A	De monte Cope a punta de la Azohía	30,000
464	De cabo Tiñoso a cabo de Palos	50,000
464A	Del puerto de Mazarrón a cabo del Agua	30,000
471	De cabo de Palos a cabo Cervera	50,000

Chart	Title	Scale
471A	De cabo de Palos a punta de la Horadada	40,000
	Planos insertos: San Pedro del Pinatar	7,500
	Cabo de Palos	15,000
	Puerto de Tomás Maestre	10,000
472	Bahías de Santa Pola y Alicante	50,000
472A	Aproches del puerto de Alicante	25,000
474	De la Punta de Hach al Río Bullent	50,000
476	De cabo Culleria al puerto de Valencia	50,000
478	De cabo Negret a cabo Berbería	50,000
479	De cabo Berbería a punta Arabí	50,000
479A	Freus entre Ibiza y Formentera	25,000
481	Del puerto de Valencia al puerto de Sagunto	50,000
481A	Aproches del puerto de Valencia	25,000
482	Del puerto de Sagunto al cabo de Oropesa	60,000
482A	Aproches del puerto de Casellón	25,000
483A	Aproches de les Islas Columbretes	25,000
485	De puerto de Vinaroz a puerto de La Ampolla	60,000
485A	De Vinaroz al puerto de los Alfaques	30,000
485B	Delta del río Ebro, puerto del Fangal y golfo de La Ampolla	30,000
487A	Aproches del puerto de Tarragona	85,000
488	Del puerto de Villanueva y Geltrú al puerto de Barcelona	50,000
488A	De puerto de Villanueva y Geltrú a puerto de Garraf	25,000
	Planos insertos: Puerto de Vallcarca	5,000
	Puerto de Garraf	5,000
489	Del puerto de Barcelona al puerto de Arenys de Mar	50,000
489A	Aproches del puerto de Barcelona	25,000
491	De puerto de Arenys de Mar a puerto de San Feliú de Guixols	50,000
492	De cabo de Tossa a cabo Begur	50,000
493	De cap Negre a cap Cerbere	10,000
	Planos insertos: Puerto de Llançà	10,000
	Fondeadero de Cadaqués	20,000
493A	Golfo de Rosas	25,000
729	Puerto de Villajoyosa	9,450
772	De cabo Callera al puerto de Valencia	35,600
832	De cabo Roig a cabo de las Huerta	99,000
833	De cabo de las Huertas a cabo de San Antonio	98,500
834	De cabo de San Antonio a la Albufera de Valencia	97,800
835	De la Albufera de Valencia al Grao de Moncófar	97,000
836	De Moncófar a Alcocebre	96,300
837	De cabo de Irta a cabo Tortosa	95,600
838	De cabo Tortosa a punta Paloma	94,900
871	De punta Paloma al río Llobregat	94,700
	Plano inserto: Puerto de Vallcarca	4,500
873	Del rio Llobregat a cabo de Tossa	94,000
876	De cabo de Tossa a cabo Cerbére	93,700
900	De Cabo Blanco a punta de Amer	100,000
965	De punta de Amer al Morro de la Vaca	100,000
970	De Morro de la Vaca a cabo Blanco	100,000
	Plano inserto: Surgidero de la Foradada de Miramar	12,000
3550	Puerto de Motril	5,000
	Fondeadero de Calahonda	5,000
	Puerto de Adra	5,000
	Ensenada de las Entinas	25,000
3713	Puerto de San Carlos de la Rápita	5,000
4211	Bahía de Palma. De las Illetas a islote Galera	10,000

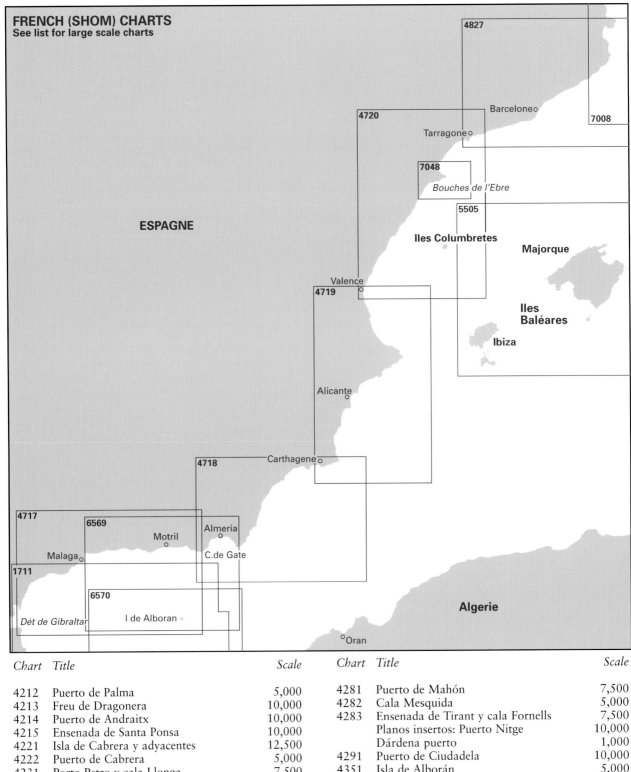

FRENCH (SHOM) CHARTS
See list for large scale charts

4827

Barcelone○

4720

7008

Tarragone○

7048

Bouches de l'Ebre

5505

ESPAGNE

Iles Columbretes

Majorque

Valence

4719

Iles
Baléares

Ibiza

Alicante

Carthagene○

4718

4717

6569

Almeria

Motril

1711

Malaga○

C.de Gate

6570

Algerie

Dét de Gibraltar

I de Alboran

○Oran

Chart	Title	Scale
4212	Puerto de Palma	5,000
4213	Freu de Dragonera	10,000
4214	Puerto de Andraitx	10,000
4215	Ensenada de Santa Ponsa	10,000
4221	Isla de Cabrera y adyacentes	12,500
4222	Puerto de Cabrera	5,000
4231	Porto Petro y cala Llonga	7,500
	Cala Figuera	2,500
4241	Porto Colom	5,000
	Porto Cristo o Cala Manacor	5,000
	Cala Ratjada	5,000
4251	Puerto de Pollensa	7,500
4252	Bahía de Alcudia. De playa de Sas Escortjas a isla de Aucunada	12,500
4253	Bahía de Alcudia. De cabo Farrutx a playa de Sas Escortjas	12,500
4254	Puerto de Alcudia	5,000
4271	Puerto de Sóller	5,000

Chart	Title	Scale
4281	Puerto de Mahón	7,500
4282	Cala Mesquida	5,000
4283	Ensenada de Tirant y cala Fornells	7,500
	Planos insertos: Puerto Nitge	10,000
	Dárdena puerto	1,000
4291	Puerto de Ciudadela	10,000
4351	Isla de Alborán	5,000
4451	Bahía de Algeciras - zona oeste	10,000
4452	Bahía de Algeciras - zona este	10,000
4551	Puerto de Málaga	5,000
4591	Puerto de Almería	10,000
4621	Puertos de Carboneras y Hornos Ibéricos	7,500
4631	De punta de Calnegre al puerto de Mazarrón	12,500
4632	Rada de Mazarrón	12,500
4642	Puertos de Cartagena y Escombreras	10,000
4711	Puerto de Torrevieja	50,000
4721	Bahía de Santa Pola	10,000

Chart	Title	Scale
4722	Puerto de Alicante	10,000
4741	De la ensenada de Javea al Puerto de Denia	15,000
4751	Puerto de Denia	10,000
4752	Puerto de Gandía	10,000
4781	Puerto de San Antonio Abad	5,000
4791	Puerto de Ibiza	10,000
4811	Puerto de Valencia	10,000
4812	Puerto de Sagunto	7,500
4821	Puerto de Castellón	10,000
4822	Puerto de Burriana	10,000
4831	Islas Columbretes	10,000
4841	Puertos de Banicarló y Peñíscola	10,000
4842	Puerto de Vinaroz	10,000
4861	Rada de Salou y Pto Cambrils	10,000
4871	Puerto de Tarragona	10,000
4881	Puerto de Villanueva y Geltrú	7,500
4882	Puerto de Sitges	10,000
4891	Puerto de Barcelona	10,000
4892	De Puerto de Masnou al Puerto de Premiá de Mar	10,000
4911	Puerto de Arenys de Mar	10,000
4913	Puerto de Blanes	10,000
4922	Ensenada y puerto de San Feliú de Guixols	10,000
4923	Fondeadero y puerto de Palamós	10,000
4924	Cabo San Sebastián e islas Hormigas	10,000
4931	Fondeadero de las islas Medas y puerto de El Estartit	10,000
4932	Bahia de Rosas	10,000
4934	Puerto de la Selva	10,000

French charts
Service Hydrographique et Oceanographique de la Marine (SHOM)

Chart	Title	Scale
4033	Iles Columbretes	18,000
4717	De Gibraltar à la pointe del Sabinal	250,000
	Cartouche: Port de Motril	10,000
	Mouillages de la Herradura, Los Berengueles, Almunecar, Belilla et Salobrena	80,000
4718	De la Pointe del Sabinal à Carthagène	247,000
	Cartouche: Port Genoves et anse de San Jose	25,000
	Cartouche: Anse de los Escullos	25,000
	Cartouche: Port de San Pedro	25,000
4719	De Carthagène à Valence	242,000
4720	De Valence a Tarragone	236,000
4827	De Tarragone au cap de Creux	231,000
5505	Iles Baléares	319,000
6515	Ports de la côte Est d'Espagne – Port d'Alicante	10,000
	Cartouche: Port de Torrevieja	15,000
6569	Mer d'Alboran, feuille Nord	202,000
6570	Mer d'Alboran, feuille Sud	203,000
6775	Baie de Palma, de las Illetas a l'ilot Galera	10,000
6843	Du Cabo Creus à Port-Bacarès	50,000
7008	Du Cabo de San Sébastian à Fos-sur-Mer	25,000
7042	Détroit de Gibraltar	100,000
7046	Port de Barcelona	10,000
7047	Du Cabo de Salou à Tarragona	10,000
7048	Du port de Vinaroz au port de la Ampolla - Delta de l'Ebre (Ebro)	60,000

Chart	Title	Scale
7114	Ibiza Formentera	
	Cartouche: Ibiza et Formentera	100,000
	Cartouche: Puerto de San Antonio Abad	20,000
	Cartouche: Puerto de Ibiza	10,000
	Cartouche: Passages entre Ibiza et Espalmador Abords de Puerto de Ibiza	30,000
7115	Mallorca – Partie Ouest – De Punta Beca à Punta Salinas	100,000
7116	Mallorca – Partie Est – De Punta Salinas à Cabo Formentor	100,000
7117	Menorca – Ports et Mouillages de Menorca, Ciudadela, Tiranet Cala Fornells, Máhon	100,000
7118	Abords de Palma – De Isla Dragoner à Cabo Blanco, Andraitx, Santa Ponsa	40,000
7119	Ports et Mouillages de Mallorca et Cabrèra Pollensa, Alcudia, Soller, Colom Ratjada, Surgidero de, Foradada, Figuera, Cristó ou Calá Manacor, Cala Llonga	12,500
7276	Abords de Valencia	25,000
7295	Ports et Mouillages entre Cabo de la Nao et Cabo de Palos Tomás Maestre, Palos, Villajoyosa, Mar Menor	15,000
7296	Ports et mouillages entre Tarragona et Alicante Peñiscola, Castellón de la Plana, Burriana, Jávea, Benìcarlo, Sagunto, Denia, San Carlos de la Rápita, Calpe, Gandia	15,000
	Altea	20,000
7298	Ports et mouillages entre la frontière franco-espagnole et Tarragona	
	Puerto de la Selva	10,000
	Puerto de Cadaqués	15,000
	Bahía de Rosas	15,000
	Puerto de El Estartit	15,000
	Puerto de Palamos	15,000
	Puerto de Arenys de Mar	10,000
	Puerto de San Feliú de Guíxols	10,000
	Cala de Llafranc	10,000
	Puerto de Blanes	15,000
	Puerto de Villanueva y Geltrú	15,000
	Sitges et puerto Vallcarca	20,000
	Puerto de Garraf	5,000
7304	Abords de Alicante	10,000
7504	Abords de Almeria	25,000
7505	Du Cabo de Tossa au Cap Cerbère	93,700
7642	Ports de Carthagène et d'Escombreras	10,000

Imray M series charts

M11 Mediterranean Spain – Gibraltar to Cabo de Gata & Morocco
1:440,000 WGS 84
Plans Strait of Gibraltar, Gibraltar, Ceuta, Almeria, Estepona, Puerto de Almerimar

M12 Mediterranean Spain – Cabo de Gata to Denia & Ibiza
1:500,000 WGS 84
Plans Mar Menor, Alicante, Dénia, Torrevieja, Altea, Villajoyosa

M13 **Mediterranean Spain** – Dénia to Barcelona
1:440,000 WGS 84
Plans Dénia, Tarragona, Valencia Yacht Harbour,
Barcelona Harbour, Barcelona Port Vell, San
Antonio (Ibiza)

M14 **Mediterranean Spain** – Barcelona to Bouches du
Rhône
1:440,000 WGS 84
Plans St-Cyprien-Plage, Puerto de l'Escala, Sète,
Cap d'Agde, Roses, Palamos, Port Vendres,
Barcelona Harbour, Barcelona Port Vell

M10 **Western Mediterranean** 1:2,750,000

III. FURTHER READING

Many navigational publications are reprinted annually, in
which case the latest edition should be carried. Others,
including most cruising guides, are updated by means of
supplements available from the publishers (see
Correctional Supplements, page ii). Further corrections or
amendments are always welcome).

Admiralty publications
Mediterranean Pilot Vol I (NP 45) and *Supplement*
covers the south and east coasts of Spain, the Islas
Baleares, Sardinia, Sicily and the north coast of Africa
List of Lights and Fog Signals, Vol E (NP 78)
(Mediterranean, Black and Red Seas)
List of Radio Signals
Vol 1, Part 1 (NP281/1) Coast Radio Stations (Europe,
Africa and Asia)
Vol 2 (NP 282) Radio Navigational Aids, Electronic
Position Fixing Systems and Radio Time Signals
Vol 3, Part 1 (NP 283/1) Radio Weather Services and
Navigational Warnings (Europe, Africa and Asia)
Vol 4 (NP 284) Meteorological Observation Stations
Vol 5 (NP 285) Global Maritime Distress and Safety
Systems (GMDSS)
Vol 6, Part 2 (NP 286/2) Vessel Traffic Services, Port
Operations and Pilot Services (The Mediterranean,
Africa and Asia)

Yachtsmen's guides, almanacs etc
English language
Imray Mediterranean Almanac, Rod Heikell (Imray). A
biennial almanac with second year supplement, packed
with information. Particularly good value for yachts on
passage when not every cruising guide is likely to be
carried.
Mediterranean Cruising Handbook, Rod Heikell (Imray).
Useful information on techniques such as berthing bow
or stern-to, clothing, storing up etc. General
information on cruising areas, passages etc.
Islas Baleares RCC Pilotage Foundation - Graham Hutt
(Imray 2006).
Mediterranean Spain – Costas del Sol and Blanca, RCC
Pilotage Foundation - John Marchment (Imray 2005).
Mediterranean France and Corsica Pilot, Rod Heikell
(Imray 2007).
North Africa, RCC Pilotage Foundation - Graham Hutt
(Imray 2005). The only yachtsman's guide to the coast
between the Strait of Gibraltar and Tunisia.

Spanish
La Guía del Navegante – La Costa de España y el Algarve
(The Yachtsman's Guide). Spanish and English, revised
annually.(PubliNáutic Rilnvest SL,). Not a full scale
pilot book, but an excellent source of up-to-date
information on local services and facilites (partly via the
advertisements) with phone numbers etc.

Guia Náutica Turistica y Deportiva de España by the
Asamblea de Capitánes de Yate. An expensive and
colourful guide book covering all the Spanish coasts and
including some useful data on harbours but no pilotage
information. The plans are in outline only. Written in
Spanish with a partial English translation. Because
symbols are lavishly used, much of it can be understood
with only a limited knowledge of Spanish.
*Guia Náutica de España. Tomo II, Costa del Azahar,
Blanca and Baleares.* One of a series of books featuring
attractive colour pictures, some of which are out of
date, and some text. Written in Spanish but an English
version is sometimes available.
El Mercado Nautico (The Boat Market). A free newspaper
published every two or three months and available from
yacht clubs, marina offices etc. Written in Spanish,
English and German it includes, amongst other things, a
useful (though by no means comprehensive) listing of
current marina prices.

French
Votre Livre de Bord – Méditerranée (Bloc Marine). French
almanac covering the Mediterranean, including details
of weather forecasts transmitted from France and
Monaco. An English/French version is also published
which translates some, though by no means all, the text.
Published annually.

German
Spanische Gewässer, Lissabon bis Golfe du Lion, K
Neumann (Delius Klasing). A seamanlike guide and
semi-pilot book, which includes sketch plans of most
harbours. Harbour data is limited but it contains much
good general advice on sailing in this area.

Background
The Birth of Europe, Michael Andrew (BBC Books). An
excellent and comprehensive work which explains in
simple terms how the Mediterranean and surrounding
countries developed over the ages from 3000 BC.
The First Eden, David Attenborough (William Collins). A
fascinating study of 'The Mediterranean World and
Man'.
The Inner Sea, Robert Fox (Sinclair-Stevenson, 1991). An
account of the countries surrounding the Mediterranean
and the forces which shaped them, written by a well
known BBC journalist.
Sea of Seas, H Scott (van Nostrand). A half-guidebook
half-storybook on the western Mediterranean. Very out
of date and now out of print, but a delight to read.

IV. SPANISH GLOSSARY

The following limited glossary relates to the weather, the
abbreviations to be found on Spanish charts and some
words likely to be useful on entering port. For a list
containing many words commonly used in connection
with sailing, see Webb & Manton, *Yachtsman's Ten
Language Dictionary* (Adlard Coles Nautical).

Weather
On the radio, if there is a storm warning the forecast starts
aviso temporal. If, as usual, there is no storm warning, the
forecast starts *no hay temporal*. Many words are similar to
the English and their meanings can be guessed. The
following may be less familiar:

Viento **Wind**
calma calm
ventolina light air
flojito light breeze
flojo gentle breeze

bonancible moderate breeze
fresquito fresh breeze
fresco strong breeze
frescachón near gale
temporal fuerte gale
temporal duro strong gale
temporal muy duro storm
borrasca violent storm
huracán, temporal
  huracanado hurricane
tempestad, borrasca thunderstorm

El Cielo The sky
nube cloud
nubes altas, bajas high, low clouds
nubloso cloudy
cubierto covered, overcast
claro, despejado clear

Names of cloud types in Spanish are based on the same
Latin words as the names used in English.

Visibilidad Visibility
buena good
regular moderate
mala poor
calima haze
neblina mist
bruma sea mist
niebla fog

Precipitación Precipitation
aguacero shower
llovizna drizzle
lluvia rain
aguanieve sleet
nieve snow
granizada hail

Sistemas del Tiempo Weather Systems
anticiclón anticyclone
depresión, borrasca depression
vaguada trough
cresta, dorsal ridge
cuna wedge
frente front
frio cold
cálido warm
ocluido occluded
bajando falling
subiendo rising

Lights and Charts – major terms and abbreviations:

A	*amarilla*	yellow
Alt	*alternativa*	alternative
Ag Nv	*aguas navegables*	navegable waters
Ang	*angulo*	angle
Ant	*anterior*	anterior, earlier, forward
Apag	*apagado*	extinguished
Arrc	*arrecife*	reef
At	*atenuada*	attenuated
B	*blanca*	white
Ba	*bahía*	bay
	bajamar escorada	chart datum
Bal	*baliza*	buoy, beacon
Bal. E	*baliza elástica*	plastic (elastic) buoy
Bco	*banco*	bank
Bo	*bajo*	shoal, under, below, low
Boc	*bocina*	horn, trumpet
Br	*babor*	port (ie. left)
C	*campana*	bell
Card	*cardinal*	cardinal

Cañ	*cañon*	canyon
	boya de castillete	pillar buoy
cil	*cilíndrico*	cylindrical
C	*cabo*	cape
Cha	*chimenea*	chimney
Cno	*castillo*	castle
cón	*cónico*	conical
Ct	*centellante*	quick flashing (50-80/minute)
CtI	*centellante interrumpida*	interrupted quick flashing
cuad	*cuadrangular*	quadrangular
D	*destello*	flash
Desap	*desaparecida*	disappeared
Dest	*destruida*	destroyed
	dique	breakwater, jetty
Dir	*direccional*	directional
DL	*destello largo*	long flash
E	*este*	east
edif	*edificio*	building
	ensenada	cove, inlet
Er	*estribor*	starboard
Est	*esférico*	spherical
Esp	*especial*	special
Est sñ	*estación de señales*	signal station
ext	*exterior*	exterior
Extr	*extremo*	end, head (of pier etc.)
F	*fija*	fixed
Fca	*fabrica*	factory
FD	*fija y destello*	fixed and flashing
FGpD	*fija y grupo de destellos*	fixed and group flashing
Flot	*flotador*	float
Fondn	*fondeadero*	anchorage
GpCt	*grupo de centellos*	group quick flashing
GpD	*grupo de destellos*	group flashing
GpOc	*grupo de ocultaciones*	group occulting
GpRp	*grupo de centellos rápidos*	group very quick flashing
hel	*helicoidales*	helicoidal
hor	*horizontal*	horizontal
Hund	*hundida*	submerged, sunk
I	*interrumpido*	interrupted
Igla	*iglesia*	church
Inf	*inferior*	inferior, lower
Intens	*intensificado*	intensified
Irreg	*irregular*	irregular
Iso	*isofase*	isophase
L	*luz*	light
La	*lateral*	lateral
	levante	eastern
M	*millas*	miles
Mte	*monte*	mountain
Mto	*monumento*	monument
N	*norte*	north
Naut	*nautófono*	foghorn
NE	*nordeste*	northeast
No	*número*	number
NW	*noroeste*	northwest
Obst	*obstrucción*	obstruction
ocas	*ocasional*	occasional
oct	*octagonal*	octagonal
oc	*oculta*	obscured
Oc	*ocultatión sectores*	obscured sectors
Pe A	*peligro aislado*	isolated danger
	poniente	western
Post	*posterior*	posterior, later
Ppal	*principal*	principal
	prohibido	prohibited

Obston	*obstrucción*	obstruction
Prov	*provisional*	provisional
prom	*prominente*	prominent, conspicuous
Pta	*punta*	point
Pto,	*puerto*	port[1]
PTO	*puerto deportivo*	yacht harbour
	puerto pesquero	fishing harbour
	puerto de Marina de Guerra	naval harbour
R	*roja*	red
Ra	*estación radar*	radar station
Ra+	*radar + suffix*	radar + suffix (Ra Ref etc.)
RC	*radiofaro circular*	non-directional radiobeacon
RD	*radiofaro dirigido*	directional radiobeacon
rect	*rectangular*	rectangular
Ra	*rocas*	rocks
Rp	*centeneallante rápida*	very quick flashing (80-160/min)
RpI	*cent. rápida interrumpida*	interrupted very quick flashing
RW	*radiofaro giratorio*	rotating radiobeacon
s	*sugundos*	seconds
S	*sur*	south
SE	*sudeste*	southeast
sil	*silencio*	silence
Silb	*silbato*	whistle
Sincro	*sincronizda con*	syncronized with
Sir	*sirena*	siren
son	*sonido*	sound, noise, report
Sto/a	*Santo, Santa*	Saint
SW	*sudoeste*	southwest
T	*temporal*	temporary
Te	*torre*	tower
trans	*transversal*	transversal
triang	*triangular*	triangular
troncoc	*troncocónico*	truncated cone
troncop	*troncopiramidal*	truncated pyramid
TSH	*antena de radio*	radio mast
TV	*antena de TV*	TV mast
U	*centellante ultra-rápida*	ultra quick flashing (+160/min)
UI	*cent. ultra-rápida interrumpido*	interrupted ultra quick flashing
V	*verde*	green
Vis	*visible*	visible
	vivero	shellfish raft or bed
W	*oeste*	west

1. 'puerto' can be applied to any landing place from a beach to a container port.

Ports and Harbours
a popa stern-to
a proa bows-to
abrigo shelter
al costado alongside
amarrar to moor
amarradero mooring
ancho breadth (see also manga)
anclar to anchor
botar to launch (a yacht)
boya de amarre mooring buoy
cabo warp, line (also cape)
calado draught
compuerta lock, basin
dársena dock, harbour
dique breakwater, jetty
escala ladder
escalera steps

esclusa lock
escollera jetty
eslora total length overall
espigón spur, spike, mole
fábrica factory
ferrocarril railway
fondear to anchor or moor
fondeadero anchorage
fondeo mooring buoy
fondo depth (bottom)
grua crane
guia mooring lazy-line (lit. guide)
nudo knot (ie. speed)
longitud length (see also eslora), longitude
lonja fish market (wholesale)
manga beam (ie. width)
muelle mole, jetty, quay
noray bollard
pantalán jetty, pontoon
parar to stop
pila estaca pile
pontón pontoon
práctico pilot (ie. pilot boat)
profundidad depth
rampa slipway
rompeolas breakwater
varadero slipway, hardstanding
varar to lift (a yacht)
vertedero (verto) spoil ground

Direction
babor port (ie. left)
estribor starboard
norte north
este east
sur south
oeste west

Phrases useful on arrival

¿Donde puedo amarrar?	Where can I moor?
¿A donde debo ir?	Where should I go?
¿Que es la profundidad?	What is the depth?
¿Que es su eslora	What is your length?
¿Cuantos metros?	How many metres?
¿Para cuantas noches?	For how many nights?

Administration and stores
aceite oil (including engine oil)
aduana customs
agua potable drinking water
aseos toilet block
astillero shipyard
capitán de puerto harbour master
derechos dues, rights
duchas showers
dueño, propietario owner
efectos navales chandlery
electricidad electricity
gasoleo, diesel diesel
guardia civil police
hielo (cubitos) ice (cubes)
lavandería laundry
lavandería automática launderette
luz electricity (lit. light)
manguera hosepipe
parafina, petróleo, keroseno paraffin, kerosene
patrón skipper (not owner)
gasolina petrol
título certificate
velero sailmaker (also sailing ship)

V. CERTIFICATE OF COMPETENCE

1. Given below is a transcription of a statement made by the Counsellor for Transport at the Spanish Embassy, London in March 1996. It is directed towards citizens of the UK but doubtless the principles apply to other EU citizens. One implication is that in a particular circumstance (paragraph 2a below) a UK citizen does not need a Certificate of Competence during the first 90 days of his visit.

2. a. British citizens visiting Spain in charge of a UK registered pleasure boat flying the UK flag need only fulfil UK law.
   b. British citizens visiting Spain in charge of a Spanish registered pleasure boat flying the Spanish flag has one of two options:
   i. To obtain a Certificate of Competence issued by the Spanish authorities. See *Normas reguladore para la obtención de titulos para el gobierno de embarcaciones de recreo* issued by the Ministerio de Obras Publicas, Transportes y Medio Ambiente.
   ii. To have the Spanish equivalent of a UK certificate issued. The following equivalencies are used by the Spanish Maritime Administration:
   Yachtmaster Ocean *Capitan de Yate*
   Yachtmaster Offshore *Patron de Yate de altura*
   Coastal Skipper *Patron de Yate*
   Day Skipper *Patron de Yate embarcaciones de recreo*
   Helmsman Overseas[1] *Patron de embarcaciones de recreo restringido a motor*
   1. The Spanish authorities have been informed that this certificate has been replaced by the International Certificate of Competence.

3. The catch to para 2(a) above is that, in common with other EU citizens, after 90 days a UK citizen is technically no longer a visitor, must apply for a *permiso de residencia* and must equip his boat to Spanish rules and licensing requirements.

   In practice the requirement to apply for a *permiso de residencia* does not appear to be enforced in the case of cruising yachtsmen who live aboard rather than ashore and are frequently on the move. By the same token, the requirement for a British skipper in charge of a UK registered pleasure boat flying the UK flag to carry a Certificate of Competence after their first 90 days in Spanish waters also appears to be waived. Many yachtsmen have reported cruising Spanish waters for extended periods with no documentation beyond that normally carried in the UK.

4. The RYA suggests the following technique to obtain an equivalent Spanish certificate:
   a. Obtain two photocopies of your passport
   b. Have them notarised by a Spanish notary
   c. Obtain a copy of the UK Certificate of Competence and send it to the Consular Department, The Foreign and Commonwealth Office, Clive House, Petty France, London SW1H 9DH, with a request that it be stamped with the Hague Stamp (this apparently validates the document). The FCO will probably charge a fee so it would be best to call the office first (☎ 0207 270 3000).
   d. Have the stamped copy notarized by a UK notary.
   e. Send the lot to the Spanish Merchant Marine for the issue of the Spanish equivalent.

It may be both quicker and easier to take the Spanish examination.

VI. VALUE ADDED TAX

The Spanish phrase for Value Added Tax (VAT) is *Impuesto sobre el valor añadido* (IVA), levied at 16% in 1996. Note that for VAT purposes the Canaries, Gibraltar, the Channel Islands and the Isle of Man are outside the EU fiscal area.

Subject to certain exceptions, vessels in EU waters are liable for VAT. One exception is a boat registered outside the EU fiscal area and owned by a non EU citizen which remains in EU waters for less than six months.

For a boat built within the EU fiscal area after 1985 the following documents taken together will show VAT status:
a. An invoice listing VAT or receipt if available
b. Registration Certificate
c. Bill of Sale
For a boat built prior to 1985 the following documentation is required:
e. Evidence of age and of ownership. The full Registration Certificate will serve but the Small Ship Registry Certificate will not.
f. Evidence that it was moored in EU fiscal waters at midnight on 31 December 1992 or, in the case of Austrian, Finnish and Swedish waters, 31 December 1994.

Any boat purchased outside the EU by an EU resident is liable for VAT on import to the EU.

EU owners of boats built within the EU, exported by them and which were outside EU fiscal waters at the cut-off date may be entitled to Returned Goods Relief. In the latter case, HM Customs and Excise may be able to issue a 'tax opinion letter'. The office has no public counter but may be approached by letter or fax. The address is: HM Customs and Excise, Dover Yacht Unit, Parcel Post Depot, Charlton Green, Dover, Kent CT16 1EH (☎ (01304) 224421, *Fax* (01304) 215786).

All the rules change when a yacht is used commercially – most commonly for chartering.

VII. CHARTER REGULATIONS

Any EU-flag yacht applying to charter in Spanish waters must be either VAT paid or exempt (the latter most commonly due to age). Non-EU flag vessels must have a valid Temporary Import Licence and may also have to conform to other regulations.

Applying for a charter licence can be a tortuous business. Firstly the *Director General de Transportes* at the *Conselleria d'Obres Publiques i Ordenacio del Territori* must be approached with a pre-authorisation application. This obtained, the application itself is sent to the *Capitanias Maritimas* together with ships' papers and proof of passenger insurance and registration as a commercial activity. A safety and seaworthiness inspection will be carried out. Finally a fiscal representative must be appointed and tax paid on revenue generated.

It will probably be found simpler to make the application through one of the companies specialising in this type of work.

VIII. OFFICIAL ADDRESSES

Spanish embassies and consulates

London (Embassy)
39 Chesham Place, London SW1X 8SB
☎ 020 7235 5555 *Fax* 020 7259 6392
Email embespuk@mail.mae.es

London (Consulate)
20 Draycott Place, London SW3 2RZ
☎ 020 7589 8989 *Fax* 020 7581 7888
Email conspalon@mail.mae.es

Manchester
Suite 1a Brook House, 70 Spring Gardens, Manchester M2 2BQ ☎ 0161 236 1262/33

Edinburgh
63 North Castle Street, Edinburgh EH2 3LJ
☎ 0131 220 1843 *Fax* 0131 226 4568

Washington
2375 Pennsylvania Ave DC 20037
☎ (202) 452 0100 *Fax* (202) 833 5670

New York
150 E 58th Street, New York, NY 10155
☎ 212 355 4080 *Fax* 212 644 3751

Spanish national tourist offices

London
22-23 Manchester Square, London W1M 5AP
☎ 0171 486 8077 *Fax* 0171 486 8034
www.tourspain.co.uk

New York
666 Fifth Avenue, New York, NY 10103
☎ 212 265 8822 *Fax* 212 265 8864

British and American embassies in Madrid

British Embassy
Calle de Fernando el Santo 16, 28010 Madrid
☎ (34) 91 700 8200 or 319 0200, *Fax* (34) 91 700 8210

American Embassy
Calle Serrano 75, 28006 Madrid. ☎ (34) 91 587 2200, *Fax* (34) 91 587 2303

British Consulates

Alicante
British Consulate, Plaza Calvo Sotelo 1-2, Apartado de Correas 564, 03001 Alicante
☎/*Fax* (34) 376 839 8440
Email uktiben@cyberbcn.com

Barcelona
British Consulate-General, Edificio Torre de Barcelona, Avenida Diagonal 477-13, 08036 Barcelona
☎ (34) 93 366 6200 Fax (34) 93 366 6221
E-mail bcon@cyberbcn.com

Málaga
British Consulate, Edificio Eurocom, Bloque Sur, Calle Mauricio Moro Pareto 2-2°, 29006 Málaga
☎ (34) 952 352 300 *Fax* (34) 952 359 211

IX. CONVERSION TABLES

1 inch = 2.54 centimetres (roughly 4in = 10cm)
1 centimetre = 0.394 inches
1 foot = 0.305 metres (roughly 3ft = 1m)
1 metre = 3.281 feet
1 pound = 0.454 kilograms (roughly 10lbs = 4.5kg)
1 kilogram = 2.205 pounds
1 mile = 1.609 kilometres (roughly 10 miles = 16km)
1 kilometre = 0.621 miles
1 nautical mile = 1.1515 miles
1 mile = 0.8684 nautical miles
1 acre = 0.405 hectares (roughly 10 acres = 4 hectares)
1 hectare = 2.471 acres
1 gallon = 4.546 litres (roughly 1 gallon = 4.5 litres)
1 litre = 0.220 gallons

Temperature scale

t°F to t°C is 5/9 (t°F -32) = t°C
t°C to t°F is 9/5 (t°C +32) = t°F
So:
70°F = 21.1°C   20°C = 68°F
80°F = 26.7°C   30°C = 86°F
90°F = 32.2°C   40°C = 104°F

Index

Index